THE MYSTERIES OF DEVELOPMENT

Studies Using Political Elasticity Theory

Herbert H. Werlin

University Press of America,® Inc.
Lanham • New York • Oxford

Copyright © 1998
University Press of America,® Inc.
4720 Boston Way
Lanham, Maryland 20706

12 Hid's Copse Rd.
Cummor Hill, Oxford OX2 9JJ

All rights reserved
Printed in the United States of America
British Library Cataloging in Publication Information Available

ISBN 0-7618-1178-8 (cloth: alk. ppr.)
ISBN 0-7618-1179-6 (pbk: alk. ppr.)

∞™ The paper used in this publication meet the minimum
requirements of American National Standard for information
Sciences—Permanence of Paper for Printed Library Materials,
ANSI Z39.48—1984

Contents

ABBREVIATIONS AND ACRONYMS   v

ACKNOWLEDGMENTS   vii

INTRODUCTION   1

CHAPTER 1   Understanding Development: Using Political Elasticity Theory   21

CHAPTER 2   Political Software: Understanding What Works   59

CHAPTER 3   Breaking Administrative Bottlenecks: With Truisms   83

CHAPTER 4   Linking Decentralization to Centralization   103

CHAPTER 5   The New Development Administration (NDA): A Disappointing Literature   127

CHAPTER 6   Partisanship Versus Statesmanship: Understanding Corruption   163

CHAPTER 7   Democracy and Development: The Case for a Linkage   201

CHAPTER 8   Politics Versus Culture: Which is Stronger?   243

CHAPTER 9   Ghana and South Korea: Explaining
             Development Disparities   269

CHAPTER 10   Conclusion: Treating Political Illness   305

REFERENCES AND CITATION INDEX   349

SUBJECT INDEX   405

Abbreviations and Acronyms

The following abbreviations and acronyms have been used on more than one page.

AKRSP	The Aga Khan Rural Support Program.
BIP	The Bustee Improvement Program (Calcutta's slum upgrading program).
BRAC	Bangladesh Rural Advancement Committee (a non-governmental organization).
CP	Comparative Politics.
CPF	Singapore's Central Provident Fund (a funding arrangement for housing).
EAC	East African Country.
ERP	Economic Reform Program (referring to Ghana).
FUNDASAL	An El Salvadorian low income housing program.
GDP	Gross Domestic Product.
GNP	Gross National Product.
HDB	The Housing Development Board of Singapore.
ICMA	International City Managers' Association.
IDA	International Development Association (the World Bank's subsidized funding program for impoverished countries).
IMF	The International Monetary Fund (the organization that attempts to protect national financial systems).
KIP	The Kampung Improvement Program (Indonesia's slum upgrading program).
KMT	The leading political party of Taiwan.
LAWMA	The Lagos Waste Management Authority.
LDCs	Less Developed Countries.

LSWDP	The Lagos State Waste Management Disposal Board.
M&E	Monitoring and Evaluation.
MDCs	More Developed Countries.
MEC	Middle Eastern Country.
NDA	New Development Administration (see Chapter 5).
NGOs	Non-Governmental Organizations.
NICs	Newly Industrialized Countries.
OECD	The Organization of Economic Cooperation and Development (consisting of the wealthy countries of the world).
OED	The World Bank's Evaluation Department.
PA	Public Administration.
PEs	Public Enterprises.
PE Theory	Political Elasticity Theory (see Introduction).
PS	Political Science.
PVOs	Private Voluntary Organizations.
SAC	South American Country.
SAP	Structural Adjustment Program (an internationally supported economic reform program).
SEAC	South East Asian Country.
SEWA	The Self Employed Women's Association of Ahmedabad, India.
SOEs	State Owned Enterprises.
SUM	The Saemaul Undong Movement (Korea's village development program).
T&V	Training and Visit (a type of agricultural extension service).
USAID	The United States Agency for International Development.

Acknowledgments

The origins of this book are explained in the INTRODUCTION. Particularly important were my professors at Berkeley: Carl Rosberg, Dwight Waldo, and Sheldon Wolin. I should also mention various friends from my Berkeley days (Aaron Segal, Timothy King, and Richard Stren) who have helped me over the years.

Aaron Segal (who unexpectedly died in April, 1997) put me touch with the Council for International Urban Liaison, leading to a six year job (1977–83) as editor of the World Bank publication, THE URBAN EDGE. This was facilitated, on the one hand, by John Garvey and George Wynne of the Council for International Urban Liaison (now the Academy for State and Local Government) and, on the other hand, by Kim Jaycox and Tony Churchill of the World Bank. Based upon my World Bank work, Richard Stren invited me in 1988 to lecture at the University of Toronto at a time when I desperately needed some encouragement to carry on with my writing.

Timothy King was responsible for my editing for the World Bank's Economic Development Institute a special issue (May/June, 1991) of PUBLIC ADMINISTRATION AND DEVELOPMENT (PAD). Several of my articles (which helped me develop my theory) appeared in this issue. I should mention in this regard Brian Smith, who served as PAD editor for many years, because he and Richard Batley (the assistant editor) were responsible for five of my articles which appeared from 1989 to 1992. Because so much of my recent work has been with foreign aid practitioners, I have been encouraged (particularly by Ladipo Adamolekun, John Redwood, and Bill Jones of the World Bank) to refine my theory to make it useful to them. As such, this book attempts to bridge academic and practitioner literature. The summer of 1994 was especially fruitful in this regard, working for Mike Stevens of the World

Bank's Operations Policy Department on problems of corruption in countries being assisted.

I have been able in recent years to try out my theory with students (including my daughter Rebecca, who graduated in 1996 from Oberlin and now lives and works in Portland, Oregon), using various drafts as they were prepared for or appeared as journal articles. Teaching courses on American and comparative urban problems for the University of Maryland (from which I retired at the beginning of 1993) has been very helpful in this regard, made possible by Sidney Brower, Marie Howland, Bill Hanna, and Charles Christian.

I have frequently taken advantage of the reaction of friends and colleagues, boring them perhaps in the process. I have also sometimes used or misused my position (since 1986) as head of the Development Administration Workgroup of the Washington, D.C. chapter of the Society for International Development for this purpose.

I am dedicating this book to my wife Louise (USAID desk officer until 1998 for Niger and Guinea, with previous responsibility for Mali and Cape Verde), who has put up with me since 1979. While inherited money has helped me, I could not have done it without her encouragement and assistance, even when she thought I ought to be doing more lucrative things.

I have used suggestions from Tim Shaw of Dalhousie University's Centre for Foreign Policy Studies to prepare the final draft of this book. I also appreciate the financial assistance of my brother Ernest, president of the New York investment firm of High View Capital. Joe Nogee of the University of Houston and sister Joella Werlin of Portland, Oregon provided useful information regarding publication and marketing. Lee Graham, a family friend and retired foreign service officer, kindly assisted with proofreading.

Some acquisition editors rejected the manuscript of this book, considering it too theoretical and heavily documented to be easy reading. Others objected to my effort to lighten (or enlighten) it by making it a little personal, polemical, iconoclastic, and, above all, provocative. So, I appreciate the willingness of Nancy Ulrich of the University Press of America to support it. We hope that the reception will be positive enough to warrant eventually a paperback edition. Herbert H. Werlin Independent Counsultant 5910 Westchester Park Dr. College Park, Maryland 20740–2802; Phone/Fax: 301-474-2764; E-mail: werlin@crosslink.net.

April, 1998

Introduction

OBJECTIVES

This book goes beyond what other books on political development have attempted. It introduces a unified theory of administration and politics. It is "unified" in two ways: (l) reconciling contradictory theories and (2) presenting a single direction for political development, regardless of culture or form of government. Without it, students of development, as well as practitioners, will remain haunted by the title of this book: "the mysteries of development." These mysteries refer to the strange combinations of characteristics found in both administrative and political success stories: leadership/followership, bureaucracy/democracy, centralization/decentralization, public choice/public control, regulation/deregulation, fraternity/authority, loose controls/tight controls, behavioral modification/cultural constraints, and private sector/public sector arrangements.

In the absence of a useful theoretical framework, the following questions (among others), which are examined in this book, cannot be answered: is corruption functional or dysfunctional for development?; are the impediments to development primarily cultural or political?; is democracy useful or harmful to rapid economic development?; how can centralization and decentralization be combined?; and why is technical and financial assistance so often useless?

This framework will also be used to deal with one of the basic questions of our lifetime: why is it that some countries seem to be developing (improving their standard of living) much more rapidly than others? Indeed, why is it that, while many of the countries of Africa have retrogressed since 1960, certain Asian countries (particularly, the so-called "little dragons," Hong Kong, Singapore, Taiwan, and South Korea) have moved from the "Less Developed Country" (LDC) to the "More Developed Country" (MDC) status?

I appreciate B. C. Smith's recent effort (1996) to analyze the prevailing theories used to understand Third World politics (particularly, functionalism), but I find these theories practically useless (for reasons perhaps best explained in Chapter 2). I write this with some embarrassment considering the years I spent as a graduate student trying to understand these theories and then, as a young assistant professor, imposing them upon innocent students.

Yet, my own theory takes us only so far. For example (see Chapter 1), it explains why the Japanese are MORE ABLE to successfully handle garbage than Nigerians, but it does not completely explain why they are MORE MOTIVATED to do so. In other words, I provide various levels of explanation for motivation without getting to the bottom of it. While I do not fully understand political motivation, I do suggest (in Chapter 10) ways to promote it.

In answering the questions examined in this book, most of the leading scholars have been economists. While economists certainly have made important contributions to the literature of development, their analysis is often misleading. For example, in regard to South Korea, World Bank economists attempted to dissuade the government from manufacturing ships, steel, and automobiles because of the supposed "lack of a comparative advantage." For reasons explained in this book (Chapter 9), South Koreans created their own "comparative advantage." In the urban development field, World Bank economists discourage public housing projects, new towns, and subways; but both Hong Kong and Singapore have successfully undertaken them.

The message of economists tends to be "limited government," with freedom of the marketplace, deregulation, and minimum interference emphasized. They view with great skepticism State Owned Enterprises (SOEs). Yet, many Western European and Asian countries have had great success with such enterprises. In an article on Taiwan's SOEs, Crane (1989, 40) summarizes the results of independent studies indicating that "the SOEs have been instrumental to Taiwan's becoming an industrialized country." One of them, China Steel, has been judged by Western industry experts as being the third most efficient steel producer in the world. Its South Korean rival (POSCO, which is also largely state-owned) may be even more efficient, as noted in Chapter 9. At the same time, privatization, which is preferred by economists, is often far more problematic than SOEs.

"Corporatism," the merging of private and public sectors, seems particularly difficult for economists to understand. Nevertheless, this is the approach used in many of the Asian countries (see my discussion of Japanese solid waste management in Chapter 1, for example). In Chapter 7, I present a number of other examples of corporatism in explaining such Asian success stories as Singapore's public housing program where the government has nurtured the private sector more effectively than has the American government in comparable programs.

I am especially interested in the underlying factors that account for the success and failure of development. Such factors are often missed by economists, judging, for example, by Michael Porter's excellent study, THE COMPETITIVE ADVANTAGE OF NATIONS (1990), which is concerned with the stimulating of rivalry among local firms, the formation of specialized suppliers and related industries, the development of advantageous productive assets, and the strategies used for aggressive international marketing. This is perhaps understandable insofar as economists are, much like sports reporters at the Olympics, interested primarily in who wins/who loses. What makes the Olympics possible, as I see it, are not so much good athletes, as consensus on rules and regulations, the hiring and training of respected referees, the existence of good stadiums and facilities, the availability of water and electricity, etc. So it is with economic development.

In LDCs, the underlying factors of production can obviously not be taken for granted. At various times in Ghana, for example (see Chapter 9), the national currency was so overvalued as to be useless; banks were untrustworthy; officials stole as much taxes as they collected; and to get anything from the government required a bribe. As we will see in this book, poverty is far more than lack of income. It has to do with the lack of an ability and willingness to generate income. This book is primarily about the implications of what has to happen for development to take place. In the final chapter, I will look closely at how practitioners of foreign aid can facilitate the development process.

In addition to the objectives of (1) facilitating a better understanding of development and (2) making useful suggestions for foreign assistance, this book attempts to link Public Administration (PA) to Comparative Politics (CP). Professor Robert Bates, the head of the CP Section of the American Political Science Association, recently (1996) summarized the contributions of CP literature to modernization theory. The importance of anthropology (the study of acculturation), economics (the capacity to accommodate economic forces), and statistics (analyzing large political data sets) is emphasized. While Bates recognizes that we need to go beyond these fields to understand political institutions, to explain political outcomes, and to account for cases that deviate from existing trends, he fails to include PA.

Bates's short summary of the literature would be unremarkable if I did not consider it indicative of a general neglect of PA literature by students of CP. Part of the reason has to do with Bates's emphasis on "cross-national statistical research," which I consider of limited usefulness in dealing with the "mysteries of development." This form of research, for example, cannot be used to explain why it it is that such a totalitarian country as the Soviet Union, with all its coercive power, lacked the capacity to provide the majority of its people with a high quality of life; or, why it is that, as it has become more democratic, Russia's economy and standard of living apparently have worsened (THE ECONOMIST, July 12, 1997). Indeed, the fact that a country is described as a certain type in a typical CP textbook (e.g., totalitarian, authoritarian, military, single-party, democratic, presidential, and parliamentary) gives us no indication of its capacity for development. This is where Political Elasticity (PE) theory attempts to be useful insofar as it links PA to CP.

I also believe that the confusion over the definition of politics is partly to blame. Bates's definition of politics, "the authoritative allocation of values," is often found in the political science literature. However, values cannot be IMPOSED. They emerge from a consensus-building process.

Using the 1960 book by Sheldon Wolin (combined with Oxford linguistic analysis), I suggest a different definition of politics: the relationship of leadership to followership for the purpose of governance. From this definition, we see a triangular relationship among the categories: leadership, followership, and governance. This definition may also clarify PE theory, as it is presented in this book.

My definition of politics is deeply rooted in the classical Greek meaning of the word—"polis," referring to community or, to some extent, community development. With Wolin (1960, ch. 2) as my guide to their political philosophy, I consider Plato and Aristotle primarily as community development experts. Being in a "writing is fighting" mood,

I assert that, insofar as definitions of politics deviate from this classical Greek foundation, they are less meaningful.

THE ORIGINS OF POLITICAL ELASTICITY THEORY

A book of this sort is obviously the product of the author's life. My interest in other countries began in travelling with my father (Joseph S. Werlin), a sociologist and historian at the University of Houston from 1934 until his 1964 death. My father conducted educational tours to Mexico, Guatemala, and Cuba in the 1940s and early 1950s and then to Europe during the 1950s and early 1960s.

At Oxford University (where I studied in the mid-1950s after my undergraduate degree from the University of Chicago), my interest in Africa was stimulated by the friends that I had at Exeter College from the British colonies. At Yale, where I received a M.A. degree in political science, I wrote a report on Northern Rhodesia (now Zambia); and my fascination with Africa, which emerged from this research, led me eventually to Berkeley.

I arrived in Berkeley in the summer of 1960 to study under Carl Rosberg (who died in October, 1996 to the dismay of his students), one of the leading experts on Africa, whom I had met in the process of gathering information on Northern Rhodesia. (Chapter 9 is dedicated to remembering him because I relied constantly on his kindness to complete my Ph.D.)

I had come from two years of teaching American government at Texas Technological College (now University). Here I had used the 1955 edition of Leonard White's INTRODUCTION TO THE STUDY OF PUBLIC ADMINISTRATION. It was this excellent textbook that brought me into Dwight Waldo's seminar on administrative theory in the fall of 1960.

While I was fascinated by Waldo's presentation of the administrative theory literature, I was quite doubtful that I could use any of this literature in doing African studies. Waldo showed clearly the weaknesses of the so-called "classical" writings of Luther Gulick (1937) and Henri Fayol (1949), among others. The new science of administration, based upon testable propositions, statistical and mathematical formulations, and elaborate scientific models, seemed interesting. But it conflicted with the "human relations" approach, stemming from

Elton Mayo (1933), emphasizing "followership," rather than leadership; motivation, not control; and development from below, instead of from above. So, imagine my shock upon reaching the final examination and finding only a single question: to reconcile (not just summarize, which is all any of us could do) the theories that we had studied, particularly scientific management and humanistic management.

As I understood (or misunderstood) the question, it was the equivalent of "Fermat's Last Theorem." Douglas McGregor (1960), with his presentation of Theory X and Theory Y, had clearly indicated the difficulty (perhaps impossibility) of reconciling scientific management, stressing strong leadership and bureaucratic control, and humanistic management, maximizing self-control and self-direction of employees.

Later, when I read Waldo's 1980 published lecture, in which he points out that the task of reconciling bureaucracy and democracy (the "two major forces shaping the twentieth century") was "an insoluble problem" (p. 82), I sadly concluded that he might have failed his own final exam. This is because, as Waldo suggests, bureaucracy is linked to the values of scientific management (including the Weberian characteristics of hierarchy, expertise, discipline, obedience, loyalty, control of communication, efficiency, legalistic and formalistic procedure, and impersonal relationships) and democracy to the opposite values of humanistic management (including equality, liberty, human rights, free expression, free association, widespread debate, enthusiastic participation, representation, and opportunity for opposition or dissent).

However, many of us in the academic world have had the queasy feeling that comes from asking examination questions that we ourselves cannot answer. And, insofar as education is a mutual learning experience, asking impossible questions may be the essence of wisdom.

At the Dwight Waldo Symposium at Syracuse University's Maxwell School, June 27–29, 1996, Waldo's friends and students were called back to the examination room to deal with the "relationship of bureaucracy and democracy," which Waldo continues to consider "the core of my own interests." I believe that this is so because he recognizes that his bureaucracy/democracy dichotomy is related to the other mysterious dichotomies mentioned earlier. Yet, to overcome these dichotomies requires a unified theory of administration—one that is easy to understand, commonsensical, and highly explanatory. For me, the search for such a theory has been a challenge lasting more than thirty years.

When my wife complained that this preoccupation (or incurable obsession) was undermining my efforts to find or keep a proper occupation, I sometimes exclaimed: "BLAME DWIGHT WALDO!" So, I appreciate Waldo for his encouragement to me personally and his inspiration to all of us.

Political Elasticity (PE) theory is put forward here as my way of, not only dealing with Waldo's challenge, but also, reducing some of the confusion in the literature. I have in mind particularly foreign aid practitioners for whom I have worked and written for many years. These practitioners suffer from the fact that, we lack "a science of comparative public administration" (Heady 1991, 452), and also "nothing approaching a paradigm for the study of public administration..." (Peters 1988, 1).

In addition to Waldo's seminar, I should mention the following experiences with led to PE theory:

1. MY STUDY OF THE NAIROBI CITY COUNCIL. For my Ph.D. dissertation under Rosberg (completed in 1966 and published in 1974), I did a study of the Nairobi City Council as it shifted from British colonial rule to African control. What I found was that organizational relationships were breaking down. Officials no longer trusted one-another, with the result that they were uncertain what they were supposed to be doing and reluctant or incapable of carrying out their duties. Authority within the bureaucracy and between the central government and the City Council could no longer be delegated with any expectation of implementation.

I described this situation as "inelasticity of control." In other words, the "rubber band" characteristics of political power, which we take for granted in an ordinary bureaucracy, were no longer functioning in any effective way. Political power could be exercised for purposes of repression or corruption but not for providing public services or carrying out development.

Theory is a dangerous thing, Barbara Tuchman pointed out (1981, 23), because it tends to distort observation, causing authors to select and analyze facts according to their conceptual framework. My theory, however, emerged AFTER my observations in Kenya, not BEFORE them.

"Elasticity of control," as I initially called my theory, had some defects which I did not completely overcome in reformulating it during the 1980s as "political elasticity theory" (see Werlin 1988). Yet, it served the purpose of helping me understand and explain why Less Developed Countries (LDCs) could appear to be "highly authoritarian and repressive" and, at the same time, "soft" and very weak. None of the theories that we had studied under Waldo seemed to me useful in this regard. Indeed, I agreed with Warren Ilchmen (1968, 228), who argued that "most of what the intellectual has to say is useless to the statesman."

2. MY ANALYSIS OF CONTINGENCY THEORY. From 1977 to almost 1984, I edited a newsletter (THE URBAN EDGE) for the World Bank. When this job ended, I went back to the academic world and to my work on administrative theory. Perhaps recognizing the defects of my "elasticity of control" theory, Waldo suggested during the mid-1980s that I take a look at "contingency theory," which I did in a 1989 article.

Contingency theory suggests that there is "no best way" and that "what works, works." "If organization matters," James Q. Wilson points out (1989, 25), "it is also the case that there is no one best way of organizing." This conclusion causes public administration to be seen as "atheoretical" (Rhodes 1991, 540) and leaves us with "a huge cookbook from which readers can compare recipes and select those that best suit their circumstances" but without any justification (Caiden 1982, 222).

I eventually decided that we needed a theory of leadership which could account for the fact that, for every success story in public administration, there seems to be an equal and opposite failure story, and that different evaluations of the same approach (be it public housing or housing vouchers or whatever) are irreconcilable. I therefore came to the conclusion that governance (the capacity "to guide or steer" in its original Latin meaning) should be analyzed on the basis of two dimensions: "political hardware" (referring to rules, procedures, technology, organizational arrangements, methods, etc.) and "political software" (referring to the quality of relationships between leaders and followers essential for the effectiveness of political hardware).

Whereas political hardware can be written down or promulgated (takes an objective form, in other words), political software is SUBJECTIVE (within the minds or spirit of participants), manifesting itself in productive or counterproductive attitudes, prejudices, emotions, teamwork, and morale. I concluded that there are "iron laws of bureaucracy;" but these depend, not on particular Weberian requirements (hierarchy, rules, procedures, rights, contractual duties, specialized positions or roles, etc.), but on the commonsensical steps required for political software development: establishing acceptable goals, hiring qualified personnel, encouraging training, delegating responsibility, stimulating motivation and competition, paying attention to morale, expanding two-way flows of communication, promoting legitimacy, maintaining supervision, cultivating contractors, protecting independent spheres of authority, and developing conflict-resolution procedures. Inasmuch as any of these steps (with appropriate variations) are neglected or mismanaged, all reform efforts in both micro- and macro-administration are going to be difficult, if not impossible.

3. MY REREADING OF WOLIN'S POLITICS AND VISION. In 1960–61, while studying under Waldo, I was also studying under Sheldon Wolin. If Waldo can be considered America's leading administrative theorist, Wolin can be considered America's leading political theorist. Wolin, in the final chapter of POLITICS AND VISION (1960), points out that organizational theorists had "sublimated politics" in trying to make the science of administration value-free: "where the symbol of community was fraternity, the symbol of organization was power" (p. 364). In attacking politics, these theorists were forgetting what political theory was all about (p. 434): "that form of knowledge which deals with what is general and integrative to men, a life of common involvements."

Emerging from my rereading of Wolin during the 1980s, I noticed the basic definition of politics mentioned earlier: the relationship between leadership and followership for the purpose of governance. In addition, I found two other definitions of politics (considered by me as subordinate definitions): the struggle for competitive advantage (partisanship, in other words) and the struggle for consensus (essentially, statesmanship).

While partisanship is dangerous for organizational effectiveness (though also important for motivation), statesmanship is essential, if political software is to be effectively developed. Using these two subordinate definitions of politics, I came up with a distinction between primary and secondary corruption (see Chapter 6) and between primary and secondary democracy (see Chapter 7). Earlier presentations of these chapters can be found in two 1994 articles (Werlin 1994 and Werlin 1994c).

Whereas primary democracy refers to elections, majority rule, empowerment, confrontation, conflict, and dissent, secondary democracy refers to continuous discussion, persuasion, consensus-building, reconciliation, and the "reaching out" of leaders for popular approval. My emphasis on secondary democracy suggests that successful bureaucracy need not be as undemocratic as Weberian theory would indicate. This is because of Weber's simplistic conception of legitimacy as resting on its "lawfulness" (with a definite and fixed quality), rather than on its persuasiveness. Consequently, for Weber and the later "scientific management" theorists, politics seems of little interest inasmuch as "obedience to commands is expected to be prompt, automatic, and unquestioning" (Thompson 1961, 11).

4. THE OXFORD SCHOOL OF LINGUISTIC ANALYSIS. In rethinking the origins of PE theory, I now recognize that I was influenced by the "ordinary language school of analysis" taught at Oxford University during the 1950s. At Oxford, I considered the approach, associated now with Wittgenstein and J. L. Austin (Pears 1966), to be tedious; but, in retrospect, I benefited from it. This approach searches for the linguistic origins of confusion and controversy: how are words being used?; why does their usage cause problems?; how can they be used more effectively?

Wolin, as I remember, understood this school of analysis but did not himself use it, being more concerned with a meaningful presentation of Western political thought. I hope, therefore, that I have not done injustice to Wolin's book in deriving from it (in ways that he did not) the three definitions of politics used for PE theory.

The steps that I have taken to lessen confusion in political and administrative linguistic usage (particularly, decentralization, corruption, and democracy) somewhat conform to those suggested by the Oxford school of analysis: (1) examining ordinary usage; (2) comparing various ways in which scholars or experts have used controversial words; (3) examining the etymology or origins of these words; (4) suggesting new classifications of confusing terminology; and (5) introducing, where necessary, new terminology (Wollheim 1966).

The philosophers I remember being within this movement include: A. J. Ayer, Gilbert Ryle, G. E. Moore, P. H. Nowell-Smith, S. E. Toulmin, and T. D. Welden. I found most useful Welden's 1953 analysis of political vocabulary noted in Chapter 2. Not being primarily a political theorist, I do not know how much use is now being made of their work. Since I do not find references to it in general political science literature, I assume it is neglected. Hopefully, my own use of linguistic analysis for PE theory will revive an interest in it.

PE theory, as I have now formulated it, based upon these experiences, contains the following propositions:

1. The more governments or those in authority can integrate and alternate soft forms of political power (linking incentives to persuasion)

with hard forms of power (including disincentives and coercion), the more effective they will be.

2. As leaders integrate and alternate soft and hard forms of power, their political power takes on "rubber band" and "balloon" characteristics, allowing them (a) to decentralize or delegate power in various ways without losing control and (b) to expand their influence, reliably and predictably affecting the behavior of wider circles of citizens, participants, and subordinates.

3. Political elasticity depends partly on the selection of appropriate political hardware (including "objective" forms of organization, regulation, procedure, and technology) but mostly on political software (which, as mentioned earlier, has to do with the "subjective" quality of relationships between leaders and followers).

4. Political software can be made more effective in the commonsensical ways suggested by the steps earlier referred to as "good governance."

5. The enhancement of political software requires a balancing of Wolin's two meanings of political power: the struggle for competitive advantage and the struggle for consensus. These two meanings of politics (i.e., partisanship and statesmanship) can be considered as subdivisions (primary and secondary politics) of my overarching definition of politics (which, as indicated earlier, is also derived from Wolin's 1960 book): the relationship of leadership to followership for the purpose of governance.

PE theory enables us to defend Waldo's assertion (1980, 1) that civilization always has been and still is "intricately and intimately joined" to administration. The attack on bureaucracy has come from several directions in recent years. On the right, we have conservative, antigovernment economists, "with an abiding faith in, rather than scientific demonstration of, the superiority of market outcomes over all types of government controls" (Amsden 1994, 96). On the left, we find the New Development Administration which seems to reflect three interrelated viewpoints: (a) a benevolent view of communities; (b) a hostile view of bureaucracies; and (c) a favorable view of participatory and humanistic management, as against scientific and coercive administration (see Chapter 5).

Somehow, we need to find room for legality, authority, hierarchy, accountability, control, responsibility, expertise, and judicial neutrality to give credibility to decentralization, empowerment, choice, participation, community development, and the other concepts favored by the proponents of what Peters (1994) calls "the hollow state:" the shifting of responsibility for public services away from the central government to local governments, communities, and the private sector. This is why, as indicated in Chapter 5, I have trouble with the New Development Administration, despite my sympathy for this literature.

THE USE OF PE THEORY

The reader will find a certain amount of repetition, as my theory is used as an exploratory instrument on a number of difficult journeys. I also anticipate readers skipping about, thereby missing the theoretical thrust of this book, unless I periodically remind them of it. Moreover, while I have tried to integrate the chapters, linking them in various ways, this book does not completely escape the fact that it consists of revisions of published articles.* My excuse is that I needed the reaction of reviewers. Moreover, as I wrote the articles, I developed my own thinking in my effort to overcome confusion in the literature of development and comparative administration and politics.

Chapter 1 starts out examining the question, what is development? It will suggest the importance of, not simply promoting economic growth, but also of improving the quality of life. This requires an "enabling environment." It then expands upon the political elasticity (PE) propositions here mentioned. Two aspects of development are examined, using PE theory: financial development and environmental protection. A comparison of Lagos and Tokyo in regard to solid waste management is made to illustrate PE theory. At the conclusion, I compare Nigeria to Indonesia in trying to understand the factors that have promoted or inhibited development.

Chapter 2 develops the concept of "poltical software," suggesting that "what works" has to do more with "subjective" factors (noted earlier) than "objective" ones. In other words, politics (focusing on political software) is more powerful than administration (focusing on political hardware). My purpose is to regain confidence in the validity of public

---

*Since about 1990, all of my publications have had more or less the following notation to readers: "What is presented here is intended in a revised form to be used for a forthcoming book." Editors, of course, have accepted these articles on this basis, seeing them perhaps as similar to "previews to movies." My older articles have been so drastically revised that they bear only slight resemblances to the chapters here.

administration (including both political software and political hardware), particularly as it affects urban areas. Unless we can understand "what works" in the U.S. and other MDCs, it is no use giving advice to LDCs.

To illustrate the importance of political software, I begin with some American urban literature before turning to LDC urban studies. By focusing on political software, I try to show that it is possible to overcome the contradictory conclusions of the experimental design methodology and similar efforts to reach blanket conclusions about "what works." Examples drawn from the World Bank's Operations Evaluation Department (OED) literature are presented to emphasize the importance of political software. I conclude by noting that, when political software is taken into account, two World Bank approaches that have become controversial (sites and services and subsidized credit) may be seen as quite useful and worthy of possible support.

Chapter 3 is primarily concerned with showing how PE theory provides a simple theoretical framework that practitioners can actually use. I challenge the reader to work as a consultant for the World Bank on a Training and Visit (T&V) project and, in doing so, to overcome the contradictory evaluations of this approach: "good idea," "bad idea," and "mixed bag." In making a case for my theory, I have to show that it is, not only easy to understand, but also that it "will do for all projects" and that "it is appropriate for all cultures." In doing so, I suggest that, if the political software steps here advocated are taken, we need not worry too much about the particular "political hardware" used because its defects will eventually be eliminated or made less harmful. So it is with T&V.

Chapter 4 attempts to link decentralization to centralization by examining the assertion: "you cannot have decentralization without centralization, and vice-versa." In doing so, I require the reader to shift attention from LDCs to MDCs, much as one would watching a tennis match, from one side of the net to the other. My objective is to overcome the confusion associated with the concept of federalism, the division of responsibility, and the measurement of decentralization.

Using PE theory, I attempt to illustrate the following propositions: (1) under political elasticity, forms of decentralization can be expanded without reducing centralization; (2) under political inelasticity, leaders fear decentralization, thereby weakening their implementation capacity; (3) under political elasticity, various forms of decentralization and centralization merge; and (4) under political inelasticity, forms of centralization and decentralization tend to be so ineffective as to be meaningless. Finally, the implications of my analysis for international efforts to promote decentralization are presented.

In Chapter 5, I criticize the New Development Administration (NDA) literature, reflecting a hostility toward centralization and bureaucracy and enthusiasm for decentralization and a "bottom up" learning process. I explain that my criticism stems from several experiences during the 1980s, particularly my analysis of humanistic administrative theory and of slum upgrading theory. In revisiting the NDA literature, I conclude that, while I remain an enthusiastic supporter of public choice, public participation, and privatization, I insist that they be undertaken within an enabling environment conducive to their success. In this regard, I end with examples of programs that successfully link an "enabling" to a "controlling" environment.

In Chapter 6, I superimpose a new definition of corruption, "partisanship that threatens statesmanship," on others that are currently being used. It is put forward: (1) to be realistic as well as moralistic about corruption; (2) to understand why corruption has a more devastating impact upon LDCs than MDCs and (3) to explain why corruption, even when it is "standard operating procedure," must be a great cause for concern. The origins of this definition go back to Wolin's two sides of politics (partisanship and statesmanship) within an overarching definition of politics: the relationship of leadership to followership for the purpose of governance. It is from this tension between partisanship and statesmanship that corruption emerges.

Under primary corruption (as in Japan, the United States, and Italy), governance (referring to political software) is strong enough to mitigate the worse aspects of corruption; under secondary corruption, it is not. Therefore, secondary corruption takes the form of a basketball game in which the referees are corrupt so that fouling becomes essential rather than merely a "part of the game," as under primary corruption. At the conclusion of this chapter, I ask the following questions: (1) how important is it to do a cost-benefit analysis of corruption?; (2) is rent-seeking a form of corruption?; and (3) should those in MDCs criticize the corruption of LDCs? I end with a suggestion (followed up in Chapter 10) that we have to consider secondary corruption as "a political illness," rather than simply "a political problem" as in MDCs.

In Chapter 7, I look at the linkage between democracy and development, beginning with the question, "what is the relationship between democracy and development?" I point out that development in Western countries did not take place under democracy and that few of the LDCs that have democratized in recent years have shown much economic development. Because of my special sensitivity to Africa, I pay particular attention to the debate among Africanists as to the desirability of democracy.

To reduce confusion, I introduce a primary/secondary democracy distinction, again using Wolin's two sides of politics (noted earlier): partisanship and statesmanship. I show that in the Asian Newly Industrialized Countries of South Korea, Taiwan, and Singapore, secondary democracy has been strong enough to allow development to take place. In regard to the usefulness of foreign assistance for the purpose of promoting democratization, I reach three conclusions: (1) when governments have reached a modicum of development (indicating a high level of secondary democracy), primary or liberal democracy should be encouraged; (2) while an effective bureaucracy can prevent or destroy primary democracy, it is essential for it and, as such, should be encouraged; and (3) in many LDCs, it is better to promote secondary democracy than primary democracy.

In Chapter 8, I dig into the widespread belief that cultural factors, more than anything else, explain the rapid economic progress of Asian countries in recent years, as against the slow progress (and even retrogression) of African countries. While acknowledging the relationship of cultural factors to development, I conclude that they are less important than political factors.

In making this case, I examine the meaning of culture, the relationship of acculturation to Westernization, and the importance of leadership. Using PE theory, I give a number of examples of the capacity of leaders (in Singapore, Indonesia, and Botswana) to significantly change culture. I end by questioning the extent to which African culture (in its contemporary form) is conducive to African development, as it affects African women and rural productivity, and, therefore, by suggesting experiments to modify or reform African culture.

In Chapter 9, I compare Ghana and South Korea, examining (to begin with) the argument that colonialism is responsible for Africa's political and economic problems. I also criticize the argument that authoritarianism and corruption are primarily responsible for Africa's problems (insofar as Ghana and South Korea share certain similarities in this regard). Using PE theory, I present a number of case studies, showing political elasticity in South Korea and political inelasticity in Ghana.

I conclude by indicating that, if politics is properly understood (which it seldom is), it may be, not only more powerful than administration (referring only to political hardware) and culture, but also more powerful than economics. Since I believe that Ghana's lackadaisical approach (in contrast to South Korea's determination), is responsible for her slow progress, I suggest that the World Bank and the donor community are going to have to directly confront this apathy (even though the roots of it remain an enigma).

In Chapter 10, I examine the question, what can be done about political illness (defined as secondary corruption or greed unchecked by governance)? Using the concept of political illness, I concentrate on perhaps the most perplexing "mystery of development" examined in this book: what can be done to help those countries (comprising about two-thirds of the world's population) that suffer from it?

Based upon PE theory, I assert that ANYTHING WHICH IMPROVES GOVERNANCE IS A STEP IN THE RIGHT DIRECTION. However, I recognize the following political constraints discouraging an improvement in governance: a sufficating public sector, crony statism, a weak private sector, decentralization impediments, dangerous social or ethnic diversity, and democratization pressures. With the World Bank in mind, I also recognize the limitations of foreign assistance.

Despite the difficulties of treating political illness, I explore small "windows of opportunity," using PE theory. Among these possibilities are: requiring prior reform, intensifying pressure, promoting competition, combining decentralization and centralization, and using benchmarks. However, unlocking doors to reform also requires extensive social science research. Finally, I propose "an Olympics of Economic Reform," using debt reduction as a "prize to be worked for," rather than a "gift to be waited for," inducing countries to compete for the amounts available.

SOURCES OF INFORMATION

In developing PE theory, I have had the advantages and disadvantages of being in and out of the academic world. During a post-dissertation decade (1965–75) of teaching, first at the State University of New York/Stony Brook and later (six years) at the University of Maryland/College Park and an additional year at Hofstra University, I had a chance to do useful field work in Kenya (preparing my 1974 book on Nairobi) and in

Ghana. I also spent an interesting year (1967–68) as an Adlai Stevenson fellow at the United Nations Institute for Training and Research.

A declining interest in Africa and developing countries in the 1970s forced me to leave the academic world, going first into the health field (doing research on both domestic and international problems) and later into international development work. When my World Bank job (1977–83) editing THE URBAN EDGE ended, I combined teaching at various universities in the Washington, D.C. area with editing/writing/research work for international organizations, particularly the World Bank.

At various times in my career, I tried to become a tenured faculty member (rather than simply adjunct) and a civil servant or a permanent World Bank employee (rather than a consultant or contractor). If this had happened, this book might not have been possible.

By moving frequently from academic to practitioner worlds, back and forth, I have been able to take advantage of both to an unusual extent, including experiences as well as contacts. While I have sometimes suffered financially and psychologically as a result of this insecurity, I have also needed an appalling amount of unemployed or underemployed time, made possible to some extent by inherited income and a forbearing wife (with the financial security of a civil service position). Our trips in 1990 (to Taiwan, Hong Kong, Thailand, Indonesia, and Singapore) and in 1994 to Japan were especially useful, giving me a chance to see what I was reading about, the wonderful transformation of this part of the world.

My work for the World Bank and my position for many years as a voluntary chairperson of the Urban Workgroup and, later, the Development Administration Workgroup of the Society for International Development have given me access to World Bank materials. However, my use or misuse of this literature (while essential for this book) requires some justification.

When I wrote and/or edited (1977–83) the World Bank publication, THE URBAN EDGE, I sometimes found staff "up-tight" about their writing. I remember getting into trouble about using a solid waste management report because it was not "a final version" and had not been "officially cleared" by whoever did that sort of thing. This seemed to me, to use the Swahili phrase, "takataka mingi sana" (much garbage). In truth, there is no such thing as "a final draft." There is nothing so good that it cannot be revised.

With the end of the Cold War, the Bank has become far more open, making available to the public most of its materials, including even some of its evaluation (OED) reports. Consequently, I am inconsistent about identifying countries in using OED reports—not doing so in Chapter 2 (originally written in the 1980s) but less inhibited in other chapters. While many documents have on them, "not to be quoted or used without permission," I would not know how to get such permission for documents more than a few years old inasmuch as staff change their positions very frequently.

Moreover, I take seriously the demand of the new Bank president Wolfensohn for a "more effective, results-oriented institution" (Chandler 1996, C8). This, as I see it, means that the Bank is going to have to be "open" or "transparent" about its work. Consequently, if anything in this book is considered by Bank staff to be "indiscrete," so be it. I apologize, but (considering those at the Bank who are fearful or oblivious of politics, as noted in Chapter 10), not really. After all, what we should be concerned about is the potential impact of this book ON development inasmuch as it is ABOUT development.

A FINAL NOTE

When my political elasticity theory (in its primitive form) was presented in my Ph.D. oral examination in 1964, some Berkeley professors (though, fortunately, not those I most respected—Rosberg, Waldo, and Wolin) objected that it was not "scientific" inasmuch as it was not "formal theory." There was no effort to quantify political words, separate independent from dependent variables, isolate variables, develop testable hypotheses, and make predictions that could be verified.

After studying the philosophy of theory, I came to the conclusion (also see Behn, 1992) that a useful theory may be only a conception of reality. Such a limited view of theory is particularly appropriate in the social sciences. However, even in physics and biology, much theory is actually "conceptual," rather than "formal." Thus, my terminology is no less scientific than that of physicists with their mathematical models (really, vague approximations) of the biggest things (e.g., origins of the universe) and the littlest things (e.g., arrangements of atomic particles).

No conceptual theory, mine included, can altogether escape the tautological trap, particularly the circular argument. While I may appear to be overanxious to equate success with political elasticity, I try to look for multidimensional evidence. Yet, the pitfalls of formal theory seem to me far more dangerous.

To ask for a social science theory that permits political terminology to be quantified and conditions to be rigorously or definitely predicted is as futile as asking for a perpetual motion machine. To pretend otherwise is to be either fraudulent or foolish (I am uncertain which), as do too many contemporary social scientists. (See Chapter 1 in regard to predictability and Chapter 2 in regard to the quantification of political words.) Instead, what I have tried to do is QUALIFY or explicate such political words as decentralization, corruption, and democracy.

There are strong assertions in this book which are linked to QUALIFIED predictions and supported, as best I can, by many documented examples and case studies. However, there are no RIGOROUS predictions in it (Heaven forbid!). So, when I describe my political software requisites as the "iron laws of bureaucracy," I am being facetious as well as serious.

The justification for PE theory is a simple one—if it helps you, the reader, in your own conceptualization process, that is good enough. If so, THANK DWIGHT WALDO!

CHAPTER 1

Understanding Development
Using Political Elasticity Theory

WHAT IS DEVELOPMENT?

Since this is a book about the "mysteries of development," we need to begin with the question: "why is development mysterious?" To deal with this question, I believe it is important to reduce some of the confusion associated with this word by emphasizing the following points:

1. Development is more than the production of goods and services. Lindenberg (1993, 15) points out that after World War II, when national income accounts began to be collected, economists tended to equate development with unadjusted per capita Gross National Product (GNP). This was soon seen as unsatisfactory for many reasons: (a) it did not take into account income distribution, environmental considerations, quality of life, or political and civil liberties; (b) it failed to measure purchasing power as it is affected by real exchange rates or inflation; and (c) it overemphasized the temporary economic benefits that might come from the high price of certain minerals or agricultural exports.

A 1966 Northwestern University study of Liberia (Clower ET AL.) showed clearly how unsatisfactory GNP per capita figures are. While Liberia's per capita GNP in 1965 (US $642) put it within the category of a "mid-level" country by World Bank estimates, 75 percent of the population remained illiterate and 75 percent of the national income went to foreign households, business firms, and the political elite. Thus, this study concluded that much of the growth that occurred during the post World War II years had not led to meaningful development.

Indeed, by 1987 (even before disintegrating into civil war), Liberia was considered one of the world's forty economically poorest nations and among the thirty countries with the lowest physical quality of life and human development index scores (Lindenberg 1993, 11). A similar conclusion has been reached by students of Soviet development, noting that the "low quality" of goods and services produced obscured statistics showing above median world growth prior to 1990 (Easterly and Fischer 1994).

In recent years there has been an effort to make GNP per capita more sophisticated, including the World Bank's "atlas method" (accounting for reporting procedures, real exchange rates, and annual rates of inflation), Morris Morris's Physical Quality of Life Index, and the United Nations Human Development Index. Nevertheless, we find distinguished economists jumping too quickly to conclusions about development based upon dubious concepts of economic growth.

For example, Mancur Olson starts his 1982 book, THE RISE AND DECLINE OF NATIONS, trying to explain the reasons for the slow economic growth of Britain, as against the rapid economic growth of Japan, without considering whether the ordinary resident of London really lives any worse than the ordinary resident of Tokyo. While Japan may be more "productive" than Britain, it is far weaker in regard to urban planning (also see Chapter 6 on the impact of Japanese corruption). This may explain why a 1980 survey found only a minority of Japanese (44 percent) expressing happiness with their housing conditions, whereas 80 percent of Singapore's population did so. As of 1982, only 30 percent of Japanese houses were connected to a sewer system, as against 72 percent in the United States and over 90 percent in Western Europe (Calder 1988, 409).

2. Development is not Westernization. Barkan (1994a, 89) points out that those writing about political modernization in the 1950s often equated it with the replication of Western democratic systems. While scholars in later decades attempted to search for non-Westerncentric models of political development, they could not altogether escape Western democratic models of government and Weberian models of administration.

The success of many of the Asian countries, not only in significantly achieving economic growth, but also improving standards of living, despite authoritarianism and even corruption, will be examined later in this book. What I will attempt to do in this chapter is to put forward political elasticity theory as a way of explaining several aspects of development while avoiding the "trap" of favoring a particular Western approach.

Much of the confusion about development, as I see it, has to do with the failure to distinguish "political hardware" (including forms of organization, technology, procedures, and rules of conduct) from "political software" (emotions, prejudices, beliefs, values, aspirations, and all else hidden in the mind). The implications of political software will be examined in the next chapter. Here I will simply emphasize that it is not enough to conceive development as "the successful transformation of the structure of an economy" (Hollis Chenery, quoted in Riddell 1993, 216) or complying with the Weberian definition of a modern state—"a hierarchical system of authority relations ultimately maintained by a monopoly of legitimate coercion" (Sandbrook 1985, 35).

Without denying the importance of political hardware, I see development primarily in terms of improving political software, particularly the relationship between leaders and followers. In Africa, political software tends to be extremely weak. That is why the African state (exemplified by Nigeria in this chapter) appears to many observers so confusing, characterized simultaneously as "overdeveloped" and "underdeveloped" or "soft" and also "authoritarian" (Callaghy 1994, 200, 202). In contrast, the Japanese system of government (also examined in this chapter), while equally confusing to many scholars, operates successfully because of a high quality of political software.

3. Development is more than policy reform. "Policy reform," according to Elliot Berg (1988, 1) "is the central theme" in recent development economics. Thus, policy-based lending has become the prevailing form of economic assistance carried out by the International Financial Institutions (IFIs) and bilateral donors.

The result has been, Callaghy (1994, 186) points out, confusion about the role of the state: "In the early 1980s the strategy was to get the state out of the economy; by the late 1980s external actors were emphasizing contextual factors, including political liberalization or 'democratization' which was now claimed to be a necessary and positively reinforcing correlate." While Lofchie (1994, 179) agrees with the World Bank's criticism of African governments, particularly their protectionism, reliance on state-owned enterprises, mismanagement of exchange rates, mistrust of markets, and discrimination against agriculture, he considers simplistic the "notion that governments should leave markets alone and confine their role to the correction of market failure."

One cannot simply blame economists for an "anti-governmental bias." The functional-structural analysis put forward in 1960 by the political scientists Almond and Coleman failed to adequately explain what has to happen for development to take place (Apter and Rosberg 1994, 24). Government seemed a mysterious "black box" to transform "inputs" into "outputs" in "an almost reified fashion. . . ." (Hyden 1992, 20).

While the concept of political development remains an important topic for political scientists, it also continues to be an elusive one. For example, Bratton and Rothchild (1992, 284) point out that while "a stronger state may paradoxically be necessary to achieve economic and social development," it also must be a "responsive state." How can it be both?

The point is sometimes made that "China has made more economic progress than India because it is more coercive." Such a statement would indicate that development can be "forced." Can it be? I believe that such a question indicates misunderstanding about development. Let us see why this is so.

POLITICAL ELASTICITY THEORY

Our discussion so far of development suggests the following points: (1) what is more important than economic growth is THE POLITICAL CAPACITY for promoting economic growth; (2) while economic growth is essential for development, it also must include AN IMPROVEMENT IN QUALITY OF LIFE; and (3) the ability of government to promote development requires an "enabling environment," which can be FOSTERED but not DICTATED.

These points raise the question suggested by Lofchie (1994, 178), which has not been satisfactorily resolved in the economic and political literature: how can a state at the same time be assertive enough to push economic growth while being permissive enough to allow entrepreneurialism? In searching for an answer to this question, we will have to meet Ruttan's 1991 challenge, that scholars must introduce a conception of an expanding polity to match their conception of an expanding economy.

Political Elasticity (PE) theory, as summarized in the Introduction, is here put forward as a way of explaining what has to happen for a government to promote development, conceived, first of all, as expanding financial power, and, secondly, as environmental protection. A broad comparison of More Developed Countries (MDCs) and Less Developed Countries (LDCs), in regard to financial management, will be followed by a comparison of Japan and Nigeria in solid waste management. This will hopefully prepare the way for other aspects of development to be examined in later chapters.

At the conclusion of this chapter (with a brief comparison of Nigeria and Indonesia), I will suggest the limits of my theory. It can explain the REQUISITES for productivity but not the REASONS for counterproductivity. Why governments may be UNINTERESTED in development will thus remain an unresolved mystery. In other words, as pointed out in the Introduction, I suggest a variety of answers without reaching an ultimate one. Yet, I am confident enough in my theory to suggest in Chapter 10 ways of using it to stimulate some motivation for development.

It should be clear from my presentation of PE theory that I depart from Weberian theory, partly because of Weber's mechanistic conception of hierarchy, qualifications, responsibilities, and privileges, but more because of his "idealization" of impersonal rationality, with expertise and rules, rather than humans, being in control (Chung, Shepard, and Dollinger 1989). For me, politics is essential for administration, whereas, for Weber, depoliticizing administration is essential.

The difference stems from the fact that I have a "multidimensional" conception of politics, linking politics to consensus-building, rather than limiting its meaning to the maximization of personal or partisan advantage. Consequently, I insist that political relationships must be developed to improve administration, whereas Weber (except in his ambiguous use of the word, "legitimacy") would consider such relationships dangerous and, thus, to be suppressed.

Weberian theory, as I understand it, fails to explain why the so-called "predatory regimes," while powerful enough to be highly repressive, are not powerful enough to promote development. In any case, I believe that the reader will find my description of them as "inelastic" more useful than such alternative descriptions as "soft," "authoritarian," or "statist."

DEVELOPMENT AS EXPANDING FINANCIAL POWER

While there is much dispute among economists as to the usefulness of aggressively promoting economic growth, rather than simply liberalizing the market system, there is no disagreement on the importance of carefully and systematically releasing funds to the country's productive sectors. Ideally, a country's financial system can be seen as similar to a well-functioning irrigation system, in which the treasury is used to expand or restrict funds in accord with changing needs and circumstances (indicating "political elasticity" in my terminology).

What is essential is an appropriate legal, regulatory, and prudential framework allowing needed funds to flow efficiently into banks, bond and equity markets, and other financial institutions (Popiel 1994). In the process, currency is made more valuable. A unit of money, in other words, has to be equivalent to a quantity of goods and services to be meaningful. The enhancement of the value of money is, in my view, a political process—an indication of political elasticity.

However complex the financial infrastructure of a country might be, its management depends on such political software considerations as the legal and regulatory powers of the central bank, its information system, the skills of its staff, its political independence, and the ability to enforce its directives. Assuming a powerful central bank, governments can undertake the following measures, among others, to expand bank lending (Sheng 1991, 240–266):

1. Liberalizing lending powers, as was done in the U.S. during the 1980s by providing more opportunity to Savings and Loan institutions.

2. Allowing universal banking, particularly permitting banks to go into corporation and capital market fields (as done in the U.S. and Canada).

3. Reducing accounting requirements and supervisory controls (in the U.S. and a number of other countries during the 1980s).

4. Interest rate liberalization (in Chile, for example) or variable rate lending (in the U.S.).

5. Allowing speculation in shares and real estate (in Thailand, among other countries).

6. The injection of soft loans (in Malaysia, for example) or expanding liquidity loans (in the U.K.).

7. Introducing deposit guarantee funds (Colombia in 1986) or expanding the deposit insurance safety net (in the U.S.), thereby encouraging more risk exposure.

8. Allowing more interstate or national banking (in the U.S., for example) or more mergers and acquisitions to reduce risk concentrations.

9. Reduction of capital requirements.

10. Developing a secondary market where investment or loan portfolios can be sold or traded.

This expansionary stage can, of course, lead to tremendous losses. During the 1980s, the American financial system suffered a loss of more than $500 billion; and there have been huge insolvencies reported in recent years by British, German, Australian, and Japanese banks (THE ECONOMIST, April 10, 1993, 3–4). Fortunately, MDCs are able to tighten their control of the banking system in various ways (Sheng 1991, 240–256), including:

1. The taking over and disposing of failed thrift assets and the placing of troubled thrifts in the hands of professionals and then merging or selling them to other banks (the U.S. example).

2. Improving bank supervision with more timely and realistic on-site examinations. Demanding better accounting and auditing, using a combination of internal auditors, external auditors, and supervisors (the Canadian example).

3. Requiring more adequate capital and more carefully determining asset quality and solvency.

4. Forcing owners and managers to risk more of their own capital and more carefully controlling their risk exposure.

5. Giving the central bank more legal authority to supervise and control all deposit-taking institutions, particularly the so-called "fringe banks" (U.K. example).

6. Developing an early warning system to alert the government to solvency problems (in Colombia, for example). In the U.S. such a system has been developed by regulators, ranking each bank against its peers, based upon CAMEL (Capital, Assets, Management, Earnings, and Liquidity) reporting requirements.

7. Punishing politicians for interfering with regulatory controls (the U.S.) or more severely punishing managerial theft of assets and fraud.

8. Preventing lending to "connected" borrowers and excessive borrowing (the Philippines).

9. Preventing concentration of or excessive risk.

10. Encouraging more competition and reducing financial distortions.

Dimitri Vittas (1992, 14), a World Bank financial specialist, points out the persistent debate going on among advocates of deregulation (the "free banking" approach), regulation (control of risk-taking), and "permissible failure" (allowing banks within limits to fail and requiring depositors and investors, rather than the general public, to pay for mistakes and risk taking). The pendulum naturally swings among these positions.

Yet, as I see it, what distinguishes MDCs from LDCs is their greater ability and willingness to evaluate the impact of their regulatory system and then to make the necessary adjustments. This means using a variety of direct and indirect controls to affect the behavior, not only of bankers, but also of dealers, brokers, savers, and investors.

Turning to LDCs, to use the irrigation analogy again, the components of a typical MDC banking system (consisting of a powerful central bank as a "lender of last resort," a deposit insurance arrangement, and a network of central government regulators or supervisors) often fail to work for the following reasons:

HYPERINFLATION. In countries, such as Zaire, Brazil, and Russia, where the rate of inflation has been horrendous (amounting to four digits in Zaire), it is almost impossible to operate a useful banking system. The average rate of inflation in LDCs reached 51 percent during 1983–87 (Long 1991, 162). The number of countries with above 20 percent inflation rates rose from 4 to 27 between 1965 and 1987. Such high inflation rates inevitably lead to uncertainty and fear of saving and financial investment, capital flight, or an excessive shift of funds into real or physical assets, despite policies designed to protect the value of currency holdings.

Because of a distorted interest rate policy in many countries, high inflation reduces the real value of financial holdings (Popiel 1994, 9). In Vietnam, for example, banks during the early 1990s offered interest rates of just 1.2 percent, which were not attractive to most people (Larimer 1994, A21). Even in Tunisia, where inflation rates were relatively modest, the real value of bank deposits declined about 37 percent during 1980–1985.

Foreign investment is of course discouraged in the process. For example, the U.S. Housing Guarantee loan of $42.3 million to Peru suffered a 79 percent erosion between 1975 and 1982, causing USAID experts to avoid lending in inflationary economies (Von Pischke 1991, 274).

MISUSE OF BANKS. In a number of LDCs, the banks are used, not for economic development, but as a easy source of revenue, forcing them to undertake politically motivated lending or to purchase low-yielding government securities (Roe 1991, 12). In Cameroon, for example, the banks have been required to put massive amounts of funding into poorly performing public enterprises (Thillarajah 1993, Volume II). A similar situation in Niger meant during the 1980s that banks could recover only half of the assets that they were required to lend to public or semi-public enterprises (Bendavid-Val and Downing 1991, 72, 74).

In Tanzania government activities are financed by banks, with practically no prospect of repayment. This has undermined their capacity to act as commercial entities. "By mid-1991, it was estimated that 35 percent of Tanzania's money supply was circulating outside the official banking system, primarily in the hands of illegal moneylenders" (Chege 1994, 272).

This situation has persisted. A 1996 World Bank report on Tanzania (Eastern Africa Department, iv) noted that bad debtors, including parastatals and cooperatives, caused the dominant state-owned National Bank of Commerce losses of over US $180 million in FY 94, reducing by 1.2 percent in FY 95 the private sector's access to credit.

DISREGARD OF DEBT. When banks are forced to disregard normal creditworthiness criteria, they cannot expect to recover debt. In Morocco, for example, arrears in government payments to domestic creditors has led to illiquidity in the banking system and an increasing proportion of defaults (Lopes 1988, 14). In Kenya, the Local Government Loan Authority, set up during the 1970s, became moribund during the 1980s because of the failure of the Central Government to pay for properties used or leased from local governments (Stringer 1991, 6).

The failure of the Kenyan government to meet its financial obligations, to pay for property owned, and to enforce tax collections caused the city of Nairobi, as of 1990, to be four years in arrearage on debt service to Kenya's National Social Security Trust Fund. Thus, this city, which prior to 1963, could borrow on international markets, was no longer creditworthy.

WEAK MANAGEMENT. Lending institutions are often so poorly managed that it is impossible to keep track of accounts. This mismanagement takes four forms, according to de Juan (1991, 45): technical, cosmetic, desperate, and corrupt. All of these are intensified by unqualified staff, poor accounting systems, and inadequate supervision.

In Africa, "banks are generally able to hide their insolvency through various accounting manipulations, such as delaying the classification of nonperforming loans, capitalizing interest on these loans, and overvaluing dubious loan securities and guarantees" (Popiel 1994, 57). Because risk assessments are hardly ever made, problems remain unindentified until losses become so high that it becomes necessary to seek assistance from foreign donors.

ILLEGITIMACY. In many countries, land ownership records are so unclear as to prevent lending institutions from insisting on security of land for advancing loans. This forces low-income farmers to depend upon unreliable and expensive forms of informal financial arrangements (using moneylenders, pawnbrokers, savings groups, landlords, and relatives or friends).

Moreover, the entire legal framework protecting both debtors and creditors is generally outmoded or weakly enforced. Consequently, loans are often regarded as "gifts," with little effort made to even recover the interest due. In Bangladesh, for example, the default rate became so high during the 1980s that the government periodically declared moritoriums on past loan repayments (Thillairajah 1993, Vol. II).

POLITICAL TIMIDITY. Supervisors often lack legal authority to declare banks insolvent, close banks, and transfer ownership to the government or new investors. "Foreclosing on collateral is a lengthy and complicated adventure that may take over five years in many cases" (de Juan 1991, 47).

However, political fear and corruption, more than anything else, causes "zombie banks" to emerge. "Because banks are undercapitalized, management is often forced into hiding losses that would make insolvency apparent" (Polizatto 1991, 177). Thus, in the process of rolling over bad loans to keep their problems hidden, "the results in the books and those in reality may become merely coincidental" (de Juan 1991, 44).

CONSEQUENCES. Whereas almost all farmers in MDCs have access to formal credit markets, only 15 percent of agricultural producers in Latin America and about 5 percent in Africa received institutional credit during the 1980s (Lieberson 1985, 14). In Latin America, an estimated 80 percent of total credit went to about 3 percent of all agricultural producers (Ray 1984, 204).

So difficult is it to profitably lend to African farmers that some experts suggest that "credit may not be the best form of assistance. . ." (Lieberson 1985, 10). A World Bank review of 167 African agricultural credit projects in the late 1980s found a 100 percent failure rate, despite nearly US $400 million of World Bank commitments (Thillairajah 1993, 53, 58). When farmers are undermined by the many problems they face (e.g., commodity and input price controls, inappropriate or inadequate technology and marketing facilities, and poor infrastructure), they obviously cannot use credit profitably (Bendavid-Val and Downing 1991, 17).

Turning to MDC urban development, the variety of financial techniques used to reverse the decline of inner cities include, among others, grants, loans, debt guarantees, tax concessions, equity investments, special contracts, and subsidies (OECD 1987b, 51). Hamburg, Rotterdam, and Dortmund have been among the most sucessful European cities in using these techniques to develop new or expanded shopping centers, cultural facilities, port and industrial sectors, technology parks, and housing programs (Parkinson 1991).

In many LDCs, on the other hand, people have such fear of banks and other formal financial institutions that they keep their money "under their mattresses." At the same time, so much housing is illegally built on land for which there is no clear title, financial institutions have no security against default. (As explained in Chapter 5, this makes slum upgrading extremely difficult.)

In Africa and other impoverished areas, Adams (1991, 39) suggests that it may be best to forget about banks altogether and return to forms of "informal finance" mentioned earlier: "Giving three cheers for the informal lender is far more in order than driving him out of business." Yet, the cost of "parallel markets" can be very high. In Tanzania, for example, borrowers in 1991 "were paying a 120 percent interest for loans in the illegal banks, as opposed to the official 30 percent in the cash-starved state bank" (Chege 1994, 272). However, until confidence in the banking system is restored, African governments will never be able to differentiate between "legitimate profit-making" and rent-seeking, bribery, and other forms of illicit profiteering (Lofchie 1994, 178).

Since the purpose of this first chapter is to introduce PE theory in the process of analyzing the concept of development, I might ask the reader to turn to the beginning of the third section of Chapter 9, comparing South Korean and Ghanaian program implementation. Here I point out that in South Korea, unlike Ghana, leaders have been able to use the banking system to promote all aspects of development. Whereas South Korean leaders have been able to manipulate many different market-sustaining incentives and disincentives, Ghanaian leaders can only "urge" private businesses to undertake more investment.

The more impoverished a country is, the more useless its banking system is likely to be. According to THE ECONOMIST (November 30, 1996, 17), more than 100 poor countries have suffered one or more banking crises since 1980, with losses amounting to more than $250 billion. A typical poor country would have to spend over a tenth of its annual GDP on nursing sick banks back to health or on closing them down. The truth is, however, that, because of political inelasticity, such a country is unlikely to be willing or able to improve its banking system. (This point should also be apparent in the next section, as I turn from generalizations regarding financial management to a comparative case study having to do with solid waste management.)

DEVELOPMENT AS ENVIRONMENTAL PROTECTION

According to a study of garbage management in Japan (Hershkowitz and Salerni 1987), the Japanese could strongly compete for the gold medal if the Olympics included it as a sport. While in most MDCs about 50 percent of their waste stream continues to go to landfills (after reduction, reuse, recycling, and recovery efforts), in Japan only about 10 to 15 percent of it goes to landfills, with the rest either burned or recycled (Macdonald and Vopni 1994; Bartone 1990; Tanaka 1992; Sullivan 1997).

As of 1994, only half of American states had recycling rates above 25 percent (Rabasco 1994). Therefore, American officials reading a 1987 letter to THE NEW YORK TIMES (Hummert 1987) about Japanese solid waste management could not help but be impressed, assuming that they realized how comparatively primitive was American solid waste management. This letter noted that in many parts of Japan, a different type of trash is picked up each day of the week (wood and paper, glass, metals, plastics, and compostable garbage), most of it intended for recycling or conversion into energy. Every Japanese citizen and industry participates in some way, including the handicapped, who are employed to use compost to make botanical arrangements for sale to help support their activities.

Because so much garbage is separated into categories and recycled before collection, the Japanese can keep their waste-to-energy incinerators relatively small, inexpensive, and harmless. Moreover, the volume of ash residue is much less than found in American incinerators and it is safer to use for cementing and asphalting. The metric tons of carbon emitted for each million dollars of GDP is about 50 percent less than in the U.S. However, overreliance on waste incineration in some towns, such as Atsugi (a U.S. naval base near Tokyo), has caused dangerous air pollution and medical problems (Sullivan 1997, A18).

Tokyo, with its population in excess of 25 million, still has a long way to go to cope with solid waste management problems (Linden 1993; MEIP 1994). Despite excellent recycling and incineration programs, the city relies on landfills for about one-third of total waste, amounting to 22,000 tons each day. As it runs out of dump sites, it must create artificial islands in Tokyo Bay to hold garbage, thereby endangering fishing and shipping industries.

Yet, what has been achieved by officials in Tokyo must be considered wonderful by their Metropolitan Lagos counterparts responsible for the waste of more than 8 million people. Let us turn therefore to the dismal situation in Lagos:

THE PROBLEMS OF LAGOS. It was estimated during the early 1980s that only one-half of Lagos's domestic refuse generated daily was being collected (Bartone, Bernstein, and Wright 1990, 60). Large areas within the city, containing an estimated one-third of the population, received no refuse collection service. Even in areas where service was available, many households dumped their garbage illegally on the roadside near their dwellings, thus impeding vehicular flow and endangering health (Luger 1989, 16).

The garbage bags that were supposed to be used proved to be too expensive and delicate for Lagos conditions. Only about 18 percent of the industrial and commercial premises were being served. And there were an estimated 15,000 abandoned vehicles on vacant land, footpaths, road shoulders, and medians.

Because the Lagos State Waste Disposal Board (LSWDB) could not afford adequate supplies of ash, lime, and topsoil to cover dumped refuse, many dumps were, not only dangerously unsanitary, but also hazardous (burning uncontrollably) and noisome. Considering also the practices described by Aina, Etta, and Obi (1994, 209) of direct dumping of faecal matter, oil spills from boats, and discharge of untreated industrial wastes, the listing of Lagos in the 1983 GUINNESS BOOK OF RECORDS as "the dirtiest city in the world" (Peil 1991, 188) may be justified.

In trying to explain the difference between the Japanese success in solid waste management and the corresponding Nigerian failure, the tendency is to look at the availability of funds, equipment, and expert personnel. "Send in the computers," is often the reaction of foreign aid agencies to administrative problems. The 1986 US $164.3 million World Bank Lagos Solid Waste Management and Stormdrainage Project provided extensive funds for equipment, maintenance, training, improved financial management and revenue generation, and the establishment of a research and development group.

While the 1994 World Bank (Western Africa Department) LAGOS SOLID WASTE AND STORMDRAINAGE PROJECT COMPLETION REPORT noted some success during the late 1980s, it concluded that this project had failed inasmuch as only one-third of the city's daily refuse output could be collected, as of July 1993. Among the problems reported were the following: (1) an inability to keep operational about 40 percent of the equipment supplied to the Lagos Waste Management Authority (LAWMA); (2) the reassignment of a number of senior managers trained under the project; (3) the failure to collect enough revenue to meet LAWMA's budget for payroll, purchase of spare parts, and maintainence of equipment; (4) the refusal of Federal and State governmental organizations to pay what they owed to LAWMA; (5) the uselessness of the postal system for bill delivery and collection; (6) the inadequacy of management systems to control use of equipment, spare parts, etc.; (7) unsatisfactory accounting and financial control systems; (8) inadequate salaries to attract enough experienced and competent staff; and (9) civil service restrictions preventing dismissal of unnecessary or incompetent staff. The financial problems of Lagos, perhaps more than anything else, undermined this project. Because of the high concentration of industrial and commercial activities in Lagos, state and local government jurisdictions have been more financially independent than their counterparts elsewhere. Between 1970 and 1990, Lagos State received less than 40 percent of its revenue on average from federal sources. During this period Lagos's two primary local governments (Island and Mainland) generated up of 50 percent of their total revenues, as against only 4 to 5 percent in local governments as a whole.

Yet, serious problems were evident (Olowu 1992): property valuation lists were scandalously incorrect and inadequate (not having been updated since 1963, thus keeping off the tax rolls many industries); rates were increasingly uncollected and in arrears; revenue courts were useless; rate clerks and collectors were inefficient and corrupt; and the handling of documents and information, cumbersome and uncomputerized. Above all, the State Valuation Office was insufficiently funded to retain enough competent staff and logistical support to undertake property taxation.

Complicating this situation was tension between state and local governments in Lagos. In addition to the need to comply with a stream of directives from the state government, local governments had to endure a slow and laborious budget approval process, with final approval usually coming late in the financial year. As was true of Nigerian local governments generally, those in Lagos were not empowered to raise loans from commercial sources, the capital market, or from special government banks without state government approval. The difficulty of getting approval for any form of contractual obligation with other corporate entities discouraged joint venture activities among the 15 local councils currently existing in Lagos.

The World Bank hoped to improve operations by providing more funding and operational freedom, but that was not enough to resolve the problems of the LAWMA, according to Cointreau-Levine (1992). Its staff lacked the ability and/or willingness to keep operable vehicles and other equipment. Much time was lost for meals and snacks, performing special services for tips, and sorting out recyclable materials for private gain. Vehicles frequently required 3 to 6 days for minor repairs and from 3 to 6 months for major repairs. Moreover, unmotivated staff may be responsible for selecting a composting plant and incinerators that have proven technically inappropriate and/or too energy-intensive.

The inefficiency of the public sector made privatization here an attractive option. Private haulers were generally more efficient in repairing and maintaining equipment than their public sector counterparts. In Lagos, there were nearly 100 private contractors during the 1980s, though only ten of them had more than five vehicles. Most commercial and industrial firms used private refuse collectors (Carroll ET AL. 1995, 44). And in newly developed areas not served by public waste collection, residents typically depended on private refuse collection firms for service twice a week.

Unfortunately, the privatization of solid waste management in Lagos also proved problematic. In 1985, the LSWDB divided the city into zones and gave contracts to selected contractors to collect wastes from large firms. It collected user charges from these firms, which it divided with contractors, reserving 40 percent of the funds for administration, residential collection, and service to small businesses and government agencies.

Using corrupt methods, these contractors were often able to avoid carrying out agreed-upon services, steal spare parts from the LSWDB inventory for repairs, and dump their refuse carelessly or covertly. As a result, the LSWDB revoked the licenses of private refuse haulers in 1991 (Western Africa Department 1994, 11). Lacking licenses, private collectors were unable to obtain credit and to form responsible associations. Moreover, they remained unsupervised.

The World Bank's hope that privatization would improve Lagos's solid waste management performance rested on an excessive faith in political hardware. For it to work, Nigeria's political software had to be significantly improved.

This consideration gets us back to PE theory, which we will use here to find deeper answers than so far presented to explain the greater ability of officials in Toyko than in Lagos to collect solid waste. In doing so, we will have to widen our viewpoint to see why it is that political elasticity is far more prevalent in Japan than in Nigeria.

THE DEVELOPMENT OF MUTUAL RESPECT

If the book by B. Guy Peters (1988) is any indication, comparative public administration has been diverted into such topics as the social background of civil servants, the structures of bureaucracies, the measurement of behavior and power, and the duration of organizations. None of these topics, we will here argue, is of much use in explaining the effectiveness of Japanese solid waste management, in contrast to the Nigerian situation. Particularly irrelevant is their form of organization - their arrangement of official positions and subunit responsibilities (i.e., the political hardware). "Organizational charts in the United States often contain the names of each official," Wilson (1989, 307) points out, adding: "in Japan, many of the boxes have no names in them."

Instead of organizational charts, the Japanese are primarily concerned with the avoidance of conflict and hostility among individuals and groups. This accounts for the "RINGI" system that is typically used in Japanese organizations, under which planning is the responsibility of lower-level officials, together with job rotation and the formation of quality circles. Workers in incineration plants commonly exercise together before work, regardless of hierarchy, and clean windows and floors as a team effort, Hershkowitz and Salerni note, adding (p. 89): "The Japanese view workers involved in solid waste management as ambassadors who are often in a good position to help generate local cooperation. . . ."

Training is also taken very seriously in Japan. Incinerator workers have to undertake extensive and continuous training, including "three feet of textbooks" prepared by the Japan Environmental Sanitary Association. Those with control room responsibilities must have a college degree in engineering, in addition to special training.

Training, however, does not preclude the application or threat of harder forms of power. For example, many weigh-in stations broadcast recorded messages to truck drivers about dumping regulations, including penalities for violation. Operators of solid waste incinerators are subject to fines for emissions violations, with the proceeds going to certified victims of environmental pollution; and they may have to cease operations.

This description of the operation of Japanese incineration plants points to the appearance of a very different "ideal type" than presented by Max Weber. According to Kenney and Florida (1993), the Japanese model has a number of aspects: careful selection of workers, self-managing work teams, job rotation, overlapping functions, flexible and limited job classification and specialization, employment commitment and job security, close alignment between work and home life, social control rather than control from above, social reinforcement of norms and practices, use of persuasion rather than commands, good community relations, white collar/blue collar overlap, welfare corporatism, single cafeterias, labor-managment cooperation, quality circles, innovation from below, perpetual innovation, and continual training.

As with any model, one can see many variations and violations in actual Japanese practice. Nevertheless, despite Japanese corruption noted in Chapter 6, many scholars writing about Japan are impressed by the extent to which leaders at all levels of society take seriously the engendering of mutual respect, which lies at the heart of the Japanese model. The meritocratic nature of the Japanese bureaucracy is obviously an important explanatory factor. While Japan's public sector is relatively small, (4.4 employees per 100 inhabitants, which, as of 1980, was one-third the figure for Great Britain and just over half for the U.S.A. and Germany), it attracts the best educated. In 1982, there were more than 40 applicants for each position; and in 1988, only 6.3% of those taking the higher civil service examinations passed (Pempel 1982, 269; Koh 1989, 80).

It should also be noted that most of these applicants come from Japan's top universities which are notoriously difficult to get into. The elitism of the Japanese bureaucracy (its small size compared with most other nations and its stringent processes of selection) has aroused public animosity as well as admiration. Nevertheless, "bureaucratic rationality, the bureaucratic style, and no doubt bureaucratic self-interest as well, have been unusually influential in Japan" (Campbell 1989, 135.)

Respect for Japan's central government bureaucracy is essential in explaining the success of its solid waste management program because antipollution initiatives are primarily developed by the Japan Environment Agency in consultation with the Ministry of International Trade and Industry (MITI) and other competent authorities (MEIP 1994, 43). Eventually these initiatives must be approved by the Central Pollution Control Council, which consists of representatives from academia, industry, public interest groups, and local government, prior to submission to the Diet. MITI plays a central role in all this, using its Industrial Technology Institute to facilitate negotiations over standards, financing mechanisms, and technology development.

NIGERIA. In contrast to Japan, there has been an intensification of mistrust within the Nigerian political system since independence. According to Williams (1992, 114), "much of the acrimony among elites is attributable to intemporate personality conflicts and quarrels dating back to the First Republic." Positions in public administration are seen primarily as opportunities for private enrichment (Koehn 1990, 274). Thus, politics is nothing more than a way of distributing public patronage in appointments and expenditures (Forrest 1993, 7).

How this affects public administration has been summarized by Phillips (1991a in an article which I edited), including the following deep-rooted political and administrative weaknesses:

1. LACK OF MEASURABLE OBJECTIVES. Because most Nigerian agencies lack clear, measurable objectives, administrators must work within an environment of "consistent instability." Long term planning therefore becomes impossible.

2. INADEQUATE EVALUATIONS. Nigeria operates a political culture which places no premium on performance or achievement. Since access to governmental power has come through the barrel of a gun or through rigged elections, those in power are not motivated to provide good public services and are unable to compel the civil service to do so. Although annual performance evaluation forms were introduced in 1975, little use is made of them, with across-the-board automatic annual salary increments defeating the purpose of rewarding achievement.

3. MISMANAGEMENT OF TIME. The emphasis of the Nigerian civil service is largely on form, strict hierarchy, and subservient obedience to superiors; not on time-management. With numerous links in the bureaucratic chain and excessive caution in the processing of decisions, the public can expect long delays even on trivial matters. To speed up the process, the public is encouraged to make illegal payments.

4. DISORGANIZATION. The internal structure of most ministries is confusing. Consequently, there is little control over what goes on and much conflict between professional and administrative personnel and between career and political appointees. What has contributed to the confusion is the conflict among the Ministry of Finance, the Central Bank, and the Ministry of National Planning, resulting in serious deficiencies in data collection, information management, coordination of agencies, and decision-making.

5. PERSONNEL MISMANAGEMENT. Because the Federal Civil Service Commission consists of nearly illiterate political cronies of the president, members lack the knowledge, experience, and reputation to command the respect of civil servants. Staff is wasted, with too few qualified personnel hired and retained at the top levels and excessive reliance on underpaid and untrained clerical cadres for routine operations and contact with the public. Little formal training exists, and it tends to be sporadic, poorly funded, and at the whim of departmental heads or permanent secretaries. Those who are trained have no guarantee that their training will be respected or used, particulary inasmuch as they are frequently shifted among ministries.

SOFT FORMS OF POWER COMBINED WITH HARD FORMS. In both American political science and public administration literature, Max Weber's concept of bureaucracy as a "system of social domination," continues to be emphasized (Harmon and Mayer 1987, 310). David Easton's statement that "politics is the authoritative allocation of values," is often quoted in textbooks (Coulter 1987, 23). This seems to suggest (as noted in the Introduction) that values can be "imposed," overlooking the importance of alternating and blending persuasive and coercive forms of power, as the Japanese effectively do in their solid waste management effort.

Municipalities are expected to undertake extensive public education regarding safe and clean solid waste disposal. Children are required to take classes on the subject, frequently going to garbage-burning plants for this purpose. Since housewives generally take out the garbage, special attention is paid to their needs and preferences, using female interviewers in selecting appropriate waste collection technology and procedures.

Ben-Ari (1990, 474) describes the publicity campaign carried out by officials in the city of Otsu in the Osaka-Kyoto region. Using a combination of newspapers, radio, the school system, and neighborhood and women's associations, 300 municipal officials and 100 volunteers held public meetings in every neighborhood in 1982 prior to implementing a more extensive recycling program. To facilitate the communication process, special moisture-resistant bags were designed with, not only promotional material, but also detailed directives regarding the handling of trash and its removal.

Because so much attention is paid to public education and generating commitment, most Japanese self-police their waste sorting, even tying different categories of garbage in special ways or using different types of bags to identify the contents. But harder forms of power can be used, with names having to be on garbage bags so that out-of-compliance bags can be traced to the embarrassment of the family. Improperly filled bags of garbage are sometimes purposely left, also to embarrass a family or neighborhood.

While this cooperation results partly from effective governmental monitoring and on-site inspections, together with judicial penalties, it may be caused more by concern about social disapproval of misbehavior. The fact that pressure to recycle and maintain the cleanliness of public areas comes from neighborhood organizations in Japan makes it more effective than coming only from sanitation enforcement officers, as in New York. Ben-Ari (1990, 487), however, points out that the community he studied insisted on having an input into the process. The original effort to require families to put their names on garbage bags was withdrawn following a series of protest efforts. Nevertheless, as a gesture of support for recycling, an estimated 80 percent of households throughout this community continued to record their names on the bags.

The extent and form of social pressure put on families to cooperate seems to vary from neighborhood to neighborhood in Japanese urban areas. In one Tokyo neighborhood during the early 1980s, reported on by Bestor (1989, 146), members of the women's auxiliary inspected the refuse at collection points on garbage pick-up days, carefully removing cans, bottles, and bundles of newspapers. However, this practice was then considered so unusual as to be a bit shocking. In addition to social pressure, people responded to the opportunity to get toilet tissue, household items, or cash from scrap dealers for bundled magazines, newspapers, cardboard boxes, and other discarded materials.

About 20 percent of municipalities now charge households for solid waste collection, usually by selling certain types of plastic bags (or stickers for bags) to householders at a predetermined price (MEIP 1994, 29–30). Only authorized bags are collected by the municipality. Industrial establishments have to pay for the collection and disposal of solid waste, based upon the volume or weight of such wastes. So far, the system of charging for solid waste collection has led to a reduction in solid waste generation by up to 50 percent without causing illegal dumping. Because this system of charging for solid waste management collection appears to be successful, it is becoming more widespread, with the impetus coming largely from the Japan Municipal Mayors' Association, rather than the central government.

The Japanese administration is sometimes presented as "overbearing," with corruption and favoritism, arbitrary and secretive authority, suppression of individuality and conflict, excessive promotion of obedience and passivity, intimidation of minorities and women, and disregard of the public (see, for example, van Wolferen 1989). The evidence present by Hershkowitz and Salerni suggests, instead, that Japanese officials are just as concerned about public opinion as those in other MDCs and perhaps go to greater lengths to satisfy the public. After all, there were, as of 1991, an estimated 20,000 environment-related Japanese groups, and these have found various ways of trying to "maintain a vigilant watch over politicians, bureaucrats and companies" (Crump 1996, 121).

Because of the concern of the Japanese about accidents, garbage truck traffic, air pollution, and lowering of property values, many communities oppose incinerators. In Tokyo, officials had to learn the hard way during the early 1970s to respect public opinion in the handling of solid waste (MacDougall 1989, 140). During this "garbage war," housewives and other concerned citizens sat down in front of garbage trucks and bulldozers until officials responded constructively to their protests. This opposition was responsible for the fact that Tokyo (as of about 1990) needed, according to some of these officials, twice as many incinerators as then existed here.

To mollify neighborhoods willing to accept incinerators, they are often equipped with heated swimming pools, recreation facilities, greenhouses, workshops, and other amenities desired by the public. Some also provide energy to sewage treatment plants, homes for the aged, schools, public buildings, and car wash or snow melting machinery. Tokyo's new city hall and a number of other public buildings are now heated from its Urban Garbage Heat System (Linden 1993, 38).

All plants and equipment, including garbage trucks, are kept spotless and in top shape. Plant interiors are beautifully designed, and the surrounding areas, attractively landscaped. To alleviate citizens' concerns about emissions, data recorded by the plants are displayed on outside billboards. Thus, despite citizen opposition during the 1980s, there were 13 incinerators operating in Tokyo, as against only two in New York where there was far more justifiable concern about air pollution (TRANS-ATLANTIC PERSPECTIVES/Autumn 1987). (In parts of the United States during the 1980s, incinerator emissions ran at a hundred times aceptable levels.)

NIGERIA. Nigerian officials rely far more on coercion than their Japanese counterparts. For example, the military government in 1984 declared a "War Against Indiscipline," requiring civil servants to spend Saturdays cleaning the streets and citizens, the last Saturday morning of each month, to clean up their environment (Peil 1991, 133-189). Mobile courts were set up to enforce the regulations emerging from this "War Against Filth."

While this program had temporary and limited success in Lagos, it proved unsustainable. The Waste Disposal Board seldom supplied garbage bins or emptied the "refuse houses" that were constructed. It could not maintain its vehicles and other equipment. While sanitary inspectors were supposed to educate people about cleanliness and punish the uncooperative, their reputation as bribetakers undermined their authority.

Since industrial firms continued to dump their wastes wherever it was convenient, ordinary citizens were uninclined to take environmental cleanliness very seriously. Thus, by the early 1990s, Aina, Etta, and Obi (1994, 208) could write: "The disposal of refuse is hardly ever done correctly, with garbage being dumped in valleys or swamps, and untreated industrial liquid being pumped into public drains and surface water bodies."

The lack of public cooperation in Nigeria also stems from the lack of services provided by local government. According to Lee and Anas 1992, III-3), "the capacity, regularity, and quality of infrastructure vary from bad to worse within and across Nigerian cities." Only about half of

Nigeria's urban population have access to piped water in or around their houses (Carroll ET AL. 1995, 20). Poor public telephone and postal services require the use of messengers on motorcycles or radio transmitters. Because of the lack of spare parts and maintanence capacity for repair equipment, roads are often in bad condition.

The unreliability of electricity supplied by the Nigerian Electric Power Authority, for example, means that firms with more than 20 employees, must invest an average of US $130,000 for stand-by generators, making the cost of power to them about nine times higher than is observed in MDCs. For small-scale entrepreneurs, the cost of doing business resulting from inadequate public services is estimated to be 25 percent higher than it otherwise might be (Carroll ET AL. 1995, 20).

For the reasons indicated, we find in Nigeria, on the one hand, the use of force as "a prevalent method of governance" (Agbese 1990, 244) and, on the other hand, the unenforceability of laws. Policemen and soldiers often set up illegal toll booths on highways to extort bribes, ransack markets to loot goods, steal the proceeds of sporting events, and in other ways maximize their income. Those who resist are arrested and/or beaten.

Aina, Etta, and Obi (1994, 214) point out that "the urban poor, who are the main victims of weak and ineffective environmental planning and management, are made the scapegoats of environmental policies and laws." For example, following the enactment of the 1984 War Against Indiscipline, members of the Sanitation Task Force in Benue State used a vague law that was then enacted, disallowing coughing, spitting, or improper nose blowing, to harass numerous people, particularly those unable to come up with adequate bribes. However, such sanctions can hardly lead to sustainable development.

THE INTEGRATION OF CENTRALIZATION AND DECENTRALIZATION. While the Japanese system is often described as a "vertical control model," it is, according to Muramatsu (1986, 321), "a convoluted marble cake," in which intergovernmental political connections and coalitions encourage innovation. The relationship is cooperative, allowing a variety of approaches to be used to attain flexible goals, based upon local needs and conditions. "Over the years," MacDougall (1989, 162) points out, "local authorities in Japan have become more independent in determining the particular mix of programs appropriate to their communities and have adjusted them to fit local needs."

In Japan, nearly 75 percent of total government expenditures are made by local governments, including 47 prefectural governments and 3,255 municipalities (Muramatsu 1986, 326). However, respect for these local governments results not simply from their financial capability. "In fact, the Japanese believe that allowing municipalities the greatest authority regarding waste management generates the most locally appropriate mix of waste management options" (Hershkowitz and Solerni 1987, 17). Because there is diversity of processing methods used, the relative amounts of reduction by incineration differ from one city to another, with some recording more than 80 percent; others, less than 50 percent (Tanaka 1992, 459).

While in Japanese law and practice environmental quality standards are continually being changed by the national government in response to new scientific knowledge, the approach used can vary considerably among municipalities, with many imposing more stringent environmental regulations than required by the national government. The actual implementation of pollution control, including establishment of local standards and enforcement, are entrusted to local government. The national government establishes systems for monitoring, measuring, and inspecting pollution control measures. This, in turn, requires municipalities to record and maintain data concerning domestic waste managment. Consequently, an increasing number of waste incinerators have machines for truck drivers to insert a computerized card indicating the area from which the garbage has come to provide precise data about how much garbage each area is generating.

Under Japan's Waste Disposal Law, the national government subsidizes one-quarter to half of the expenses for waste incinerators, and the rest is covered by municipal loans guaranteed by the national government (Bonomo and Higginson 1988, 140). In 1991, the central government provided about 50 percent of the funds for investment in solid waste management, of which 30 percent consisted of loans and 20 percent, of grant subsidies (MEIP 1994, 78).

What makes the Japanese system of solid waste management work so well is the great respect that exists for local government officials. "Indeed, while formal mechanisms suggest that the national government takes the lead in the development of strategic policies, local governments have historically been in the vanguard of environmental policy reform in Japan" (MEIP 1994, 116).

However, the Ministry of Health and Welfare exercises influence, not only through subsidies and loans, but also provision of information, education, and training. Japanese prefectures, Muramatsu (1986, 324) points out, develop their programs through intensive communication with central ministries, relying on the latter's technical expertise. In this regard, Japanese experts insist that their technology and know-how "compare favorably in waste management ability with countries leading the world in this field" (Tanaka 1992, 459).

NIGERIA. During the 1950s, prior to independence, Nigerian state and local governments were responsible for about half of the nation's public expenditures (Olowu 1990). Currently, their net expenditure levels have declined to about one-third of the total, with local governments spending less than seven percent of public expenditures. With access to taxes on petroleum exports and foreign exchange earnings, the Federal Government manages to collect over 90 percent of tax revenues.

In anticipation of the inflow of funds from the central government, most state governments during the 1970s or early 1980s abolished or suspended such major local government revenue sources as poll and cattle taxes (which formed about 80 percent of local taxes before 1976 in most states). The state governments have since the 1970s depended upon the federal government for between 70 and 90 percent of their annual recurrent expenditure (Phillips 1991, 106). By 1993, internally generated revenues accounted for only 17% of total state revenues (Carroll ET AL., 1995, 29).

As Nigerian states became more dependent upon federal revenues, they found themselves increasingly in financial trouble with changes in the international price of oil, particularly with the falling price of oil during the 1980s. In the early 1990s, oil revenue had dropped to about one-third the $25 billion received in 1980 (Maier 1992, 46). While a stabilization arrangement does exist, it has not yet been institutionalized, causing payments to fluctuate significantly from month to month, as well as from year to year. Intensifying uncertainty is the central government's practice of arbitrarily diverting funds from the state and local share of the Stabilization Account to cover its debt-service requirements (World Bank 1994b, 28).

What worsened the situation for local governments was the failure of state governments to pass on to them federal funds intended for local services. The slowness of states to approve the budgets of local governments added to these difficulties. As a result of complaints about undue state interference with local governments, the central government changed its Revenue Allocation System in 1990 so that 15 percent of federal revenues go directly to local governments.

Between 1987 and 1995, the World Bank and the African Development Bank loaned Nigeria about US $1.7 billion for urban infrastructure projects, with the understanding that local governments were to pay for much of the recurrent costs. However, until there is a matching grant system to adequately measure and stimulate local government efforts, not much progress towards administrative efficiency and effectiveness is possible (Phillips 1991).

Because of inadequate salaries and working conditions, few local govenments can hire and retain qualified personnel. More than 80 percent of the workforce are lower level employees without training, clear assignments, or the means to carry out what they are supposed to do. Moreover, staff performance is poor due to low salaries and insufficient equipment (Carroll ET AL. 1995, 3l). Efforts to hire more qualified personnel are often undermined at the state level by long delays in processing applications for hiring, deploying, training, and disciplining local staff. Since morale is low, staff seldom stay more than four years in any position.

Without trained staff, the preparing of budgets and the handling of accounts cannot be properly done, even when there is an honest effort to do so. Revenue estimates tend to be unreliable and unrelated to priorities. There is seldom any significant financial planning, and no meaningful accounting for sums expended. Because the reporting systems for both revenue and expenditure are so unsatisfactory, it is impossible to ascertain the financial status of a local government at any given time. Even when local governments employ large numbers of tax collectors, their success remains meagre (Dillinger 1991a). Ibadan, for example, had 158 revenue collectors and only two technical officers in 1990. Since the cost of enforcement generally outweighed the modest revenue received, payment was seldom rigorously pursued. In Onitsha, officials threatened to cut off water service to those failing to pay property taxes. However, since services were unreliable, taxpayers considered the threat meaningless (Dillinger 1991a, 28). Moreover, much of what was collected was lost by poorly kept receipt books and deficiencies in the supervision of the collection service. This situation accounts for the apathy of the public in July, 1989, when the president dissolved all 543 local governments in the country by administrative fiat, claiming that their performance was not conducive to public welfare (Gboyega 1991,

53). "Today LGs are little more than caretakers, unable to carry out their assigned functions" (Carroll ET AL. 1995, 12).

PRIVATE SECTOR/PUBLIC SECTOR COOPERATION. In its study of urban services in More Developed Countries (MDCs), the Organization for Economic Co-operation and Development (OECD 1987, 72) notes that "Governments are increasingly involving the private sector in the provision of urban services. . . ." In the U.S., as in other MDCs, private and public sectors are so intertwined that Bozeman (1987) views all organizations as public. Inasmuch as all organizational activities are affected by the government, "neocapitalism" becomes linked to "neosocialism."

I noted in the Introduction that "corporatism" (the merging of public and private sectors) seems difficult for economists to understand and accept. Yet, a completely "free enterprise system" is a problem for American public administration specialists, according to White (1989, 525), because there "is a bias within the public administration literature for centrism and control and a wariness about diffused authority." (This is where PE theory can be useful, as suggested in Chapter 4.)

The Japanese, in undertaking solid waste management, see privatization arrangements, not as undermining but as contributing to public administration. It is simply another form of decentralization, with the public sector using the private sector without being dominated by it. For example, while all incinerators are municipally owned, one-third have contracts with private companies for operation. These plants, whether private or public, have telemetering systems connected to the prefectural environment agency on air quality so that they can be instructed to take emissions reduction measures upon indications of deterioration. They also use full color television monitors to continuously display the inside of the furnace and the stack exit.

While most Japanese local governments continue to rely upon private individuals and firms for solid waste management, they increasingly use their own employees for some aspects of it, operate waste disposal sites or incinerators, and ensure that the contractors operate efficiently (MEIP 1994, 29). The complex private sector-public sector linkage is illustrated by the situation in Tokyo where waste collection is done by city employees, using collection vehicles and drivers supplied by private contractors.

Resource recovery dealers are generally responsible for supplying recycled materials to industry, but they have to be properly registered by municipal governments. Most municipalities operate their own recycling programs as well as licensing voluntary groups or private companies to do so. Municipal governments usually subsidize the recycling efforts of the handicapped, youth, women's or neighborhood associations, making up the difference if the prices of specific commodities drop below an established floor price.

However, an increasing percentage of waste (about 50 percent, as of 1988) is collected by licensed private contractors. These contractors often work directly with businesses, cooperating with them and with various levels of government to reduce problems caused by products and containers that are difficult or expensive to recycle. Retailers also play a role inasmuch as they are responsible for retrieving large home electric appliances, automobiles, glass bottles, and batteries (Tanaka 1992, 455).

Bestor (1989, 146) describes the impact of scrap dealers on the life of the Toyko neighborhood that he studied in 1979–1981: "Throughout the month scrap dealers slowly crawl through the neighborhood in small trucks piled high with bundled magazines, newspapers, and flattened cardboard boxes." They collect the material from the curbside collection spots and from a small "collection hut" near the neighborhood headquarters. Based on the weight of the materials collected, scrap dealers pay a fee to the community. Because of the success of their business, "recycling is a widespread and highly visible part of everyday life. . . ."

NIGERIA. As in many LDCs, the private sector is described by the World Bank as "vibrant, entrepreneurial, and rent-seeking," but at the same time, is undermined by prohibitions, high rates of duties, poor infrastructure, and unpredictability of trade barriers and transaction costs (World Bank 1994b, 2, 13). While business development has been made easier in recent years, the private sector has never been treated with the same respect and encouragement as is common in Asia. Despite improvements in the import-export system introduced in 1986 under the Structural Adjustment Program, businesses suffer from arbitrary and unexpected shifts in prohibitions, controls, fees, and tariffs (World Bank 1994b, 13).

The difficulties of Nigeria's private sector have undermined privatization efforts affecting solid waste management. For example, Ibadan experimented during the 1980s with a system under which firms were selected to collect refuse in high income areas based upon availability of equipment, payment of license fees, and business credentials (Cointreau-

Levine 1993, 38). While significant improvement in city cleanliness temporarily resulted, the drastic devaluation of the local currency during the 1980s caused an increasing number of customers of private haulers to discontinue paying for this service. Consequently, Bammeke and Shrikhar (1989, 115) noted, in regard to the 43 organized markets that cater to the city's two million population, "there is no organized system for the collection, transport, and hygienic disposal of solid wastes which are continually being generated."

Under the World Bank-supported Infrastructure Development Fund (IDF), begun during the late 1980s, merchant banks were to finance 10% of urban infrastructure projects with their own funds. Because of inflation, the breakdown of Nigeria's capital market, and lack of confidence in the public sector, the banks refused to cooperate. Moreover, by the end of 1992, the banking system had nearly collapsed with about two-thirds of all loans estimated to be non-performing and more than one-third of all deposits in "distressed banks" (World Bank 1994b, 47).

The reasons for this situation bring us back to the previous section—the inability or unwillingness of the government to effectively regulate the financial sector. However, with high inflation and uncertainty about exchange rates, even well-managed banks had difficulty surviving (see Carroll ET AL. 1995, 35).

IMPROVEMENT AND CORRECTIONAL POTENTIAL. Japanese incinerators are constantly being retrofitted or improved, as new problems are identified and technology developed. The results of research, including the sponsorship of international conferences, are taken seriously. In regard to persistent air pollution from dioxin, this research led to a reduction in the mercury content of batteries and to a greater effort to recycle forms of plastic. While in December, 1997, Japan finally introduced a legal standard for dioxin emission, it was found that in Atsugi (the U.S. naval base mentioned earlier in this chapter) dioxin emissions were 3,000 times higher than in an average American city (Sullivan 1997, A18). Yet, according to a World Bank study (MEIP 1994), Japan has transformed itself over the last 25 years from one of the industrial world's most polluted countries into one of its least polluted and most energy-conscious, proud enough to host in December, 1997, the Climate Change Conference.

As part of this devotion to "perpetual innovation," the Ministries of Health, Welfare, and Construction are experimenting with pneumatic transportation systems for solid waste, instead of relying on vehicles (Bonomo and Higgenson 1988, 134). As a result of the 1991 Revised Waste Disposal Law, a number of Japanese cities are undertaking new programs to reduce and recycle wastes at all stages of its circulation: production, consumption, and final disposal (Tanaka 1992, 454). The next step in Japan's solid waste management program is to move toward the new "producer responsibility" system of requiring those responsible for wastes to accept responsibility for their products (Wilson 1996, 393–4). The country's powerful Ministry of Trade and Industry has resisted the Health Ministry's effort to impose such a law (THE ECONOMIST, October 5, 1991, 13). But as 2005 approaches, when Japan is expected to run out of landfill space, the government will probably shift from voluntary to mandated recycling targets. There also must be stricter enforcement of waste reduction legislation and harsher punishment of violators.

Japan's capacity for reform, as against Nigeria's, has to do, in my terminology, with the political elasticity of its administrative system, including both political hardware and political software. Experts on Japan describe Japanese political software in various ways. MacDougall writes about a "Japanese-style democracy—one . . . that emphasizes equality in human welfare as well as in participation" (1989, 155). Keehn (1990, 1034) notes an informal exchange mechanism within the bureaucracy that "is intended to balance institutional interests and maintain avenues of information exchange, negotiation, and compromise between powerful ministerial actors and clients." Koh (1989, 256) refers to the consensus-building devices of RINGISHO and NEMAWASHI, by which the administrative elite undertake "a painstaking process of touching bases with all important persons who probably will impinge upon a decision. . . ."

This is not to deny the Japanese ability to use coercion and sanction. However, as Haley (1991, 191) points out: penalization "must be recognized as fair," adding: "For all the conflict, inefficiency, and dysfunction manifested in so many aspects of postwar Japanese social, political and economic life, Japan maintains a remarkably just as well as stable social order." Official poverty in Japan is estimated at only 1%, as against 15% in America and Western Europe; and homelessness in Toyko is less than 10% of the figure for New York City (THE ECONOMIST, December 21, 1996, 46).

Turning back to Nigeria, we see that what Haley (1991, 191), referring to Japan, calls, "the social glue that holds the system together," is absent for all the reasons mentioned. Whereas the Japanese administrative system is sometimes presented as "mysterious," I believe that the Japenese are doing nothing more than taking the commonsensical steps noted in the Introduction.

I have been criticized by reviewers of submitted journal articles for referring to these steps as "the iron laws of bureaucracy" ("as valid as the laws of physics"). While I do not want to equate "soft" social science assertions with "hard" physical science ones (and thereby being as "pretentious" as those I criticize in the Introduction), I do not think I am saying anything that would not appear in typical management textbooks. When the Japanese themselves disregard these steps, they generate the same manifestations of corruption, mismanagement, exploitation, and resistance encountered in other countries.

Caiden (1991, 235), in his comprehensive study of administrative reform, points out that Japan has encountered many of the same barriers as Nigeria in undertaking reform of its public sector: "large government deficits, growing government indebtedness and large interest repayments, imbedded corruption at the highest levels of government, and bureaucratic dominance of public policy-making." The fact that these problems are universal suggests to me that, by shifting our emphasis to political software (as we will do in the next few chapters), we can look for the essential elements that make Japan's administration work without insisting upon the organizational forms and practices involved.

CONCLUSION: DEVELOPMENT AS INCREASING MOTIVATION

Before going on to the other chapters of this book, we should briefly stop to address the fundamental question raised by this introduction to political elasticity theory: is the Japanese management approach relevant to Nigeria? After all, whereas Japan is a relatively homogeneous country, Nigeria includes about 250 ethnic groups, a large number of languages, and a dangerous Christian/Muslim division (along with a sizable number of traditional religions).

Because of the disparity in education and income between Nigeria's largely "Christian South" and its "Muslim North," an increasingly meritocratic administration in Nigeria might be seen as "discriminatory." If such an administration could lead to another civil war in Nigeria, the price would indeed be too high. However, Nigerian leaders, in bringing "religion into the political arena," have seriously damaged the political system (Adamolekun 1991, 9).

In any case, the social divisions that profoundly affect Nigeria's administrative capacity are irrelevant to Japan. Even preparing a reliable census in Nigeria has been undermined by political considerations in a way that would be inconceivable in Japan.

While I believe that a comparison of solid waste management in Tokyo and Lagos illustrates the difference between political elasticity and inelasticity that I have been anxious to explain in this first chapter, I recognize that the "cultural gap" between these two countries (see the dicussion of political culture in Chapter 8) might be considered too wide for this long-winded explanation of Japan's greater garbage-collecting capacity to be considered a "mystery of development." But what about a comparison of Nigeria and Indonesia?

Indonesia, it can be argued, with its many islands and ethnic groups, its problem with ethnic Chinese economic domination, and its village-oriented system of authority, came into independence in 1949 with even less of a concept of national power and national administration than did Nigeria in 1960 (Pye 1985, 112). Whereas Indonesia's per capita GDP was below that of Nigeria in 1965, it was three times that of Nigeria in 1990 (World Bank 1994b, 17). Because Nigeria's per capita GNP fell by 75 percent in the 1980s, Indonesia's per capita GNP, which has sustained 4.4 percent growth since 1965, ended the 1980s twice that of Nigeria (Lewis 1994, 10). Indonesia's per capita income is estimated to have climbed from $100 in 1970 to about $900 (THE ECONOMIST, August 3, 1996, 21).

Between 1970 and 1990, the percentage of the Indonesian population in absolute poverty has declined from 60 percent to 15 percent, thereby achieving "one of the fastest reductions in poverty and improvements in key social indicators among all developing countries" (Bhattacharya and Pangestu 1993, 43). Meanwhile, Nigeria has declined from a country of relative affluence (about $1,000 per-capita annual income) in 1980 to poverty (less than $300 annual per-capita income).

Between 1960 and 1980, Nigeria's gross domestic income grew at the extraordinary annual rate of 8.1 percent, propelled by export earnings from petroleum up by more than 1,500 percent during these years (Olayiwola 1987, 1, 108). By 1985, this wealth had largely vanished, leaving the country increasingly in foreign debt, amounting to over $32 billion by 1992 (Maier 1992, 44). In the early 1990s, an estimated $2.1

billion in petroleum receipts disappeared into extra-budgetary accounts, largely for the benefit of regime loyalists (Lewis 1994a, 330).

Despite recent improvements in Nigerian agricultural productivity (see Chapter 3), Indonesian agriculture has grown roughly three times faster than Nigerian output. Indonesian farmers have far greater access than those in Nigeria to subsidized inputs and credit, together with relatively stable prices (Thorbecke and van der Pluijm 1993, 280). Likewise, in manufacturing, Indonesia was able to sustain a 12 percent annual growth during the 1980s, while Nigeria's production remained almost stagnant. Thus, Indonesian manufacturing comprised 20 percent of its GDP in 1990, as against about 8 percent of Nigeria's GDP.

Development in Indonesia is not simply a matter of increasing per capita GDP. The quality of life has also clearly improved, despite my awareness of the inadequacy of community or urban development, noted in Chapter 5. With a tripling of the annual production of general practitioners in Indonesia between the 1960s and the 1990s, there has been great progress in access to health services. Life expectancy has gone up during these years from 41 to 63 and infant morality per 1,000 live births has declined from 139 to 56.

Meanwhile, there has been retrogression in Nigeria. In terms of such social indicators as infant mortality, life expectancy, per capita calorie intake, and access to safe water, Nigeria is considered among the poorest countries of sub-Saharan Africa (World Bank 1994b, 1).

Whereas in 1971 70% of the Indonesian workforce had less than a primary school education, only one-third were similarly uneducated by 1994 (East Asia and Pacific Region 1996, 72). During the 1980s, the number of teachers nearly doubled and there was a 50% reduction in class sizes.

The fact that females now constitute 48 percent of primary school enrollment and 45 percent of secondary school enrollment in Indonesia partly explains the greater success of family planning here (see Chapter 8) than Nigeria. Another important factor in this regard is that female employment in manufacturing and in the formal sector has been growing faster than for males since the mid-1980s (East Asia and Pacific Region 1996, 66).

There is a natural tendency to blame Africa's troubles on the wealthy countries of the world. "The poor are poor," my students at Howard University in 1990 would tell me because "the rich are rich." They believed in what might be called an "ICRC theory"—International, Capitalist, Racist Conspiracy.

Some Nigerian scholars partly agree with this. Oil importing countries, according to Olayiwola (1987, 175) had deliberately used strategies to cause excess supply and depressed prices and to discourage industrialization. Yet, a comparison of Nigeria and Indonesia suggests a very different answer: that Nigerian leaders are far less serious about development than their Indonesian counterparts. In other words, the MOTIVATION FOR DEVELOPMENT has been far greater in Indonesia than Nigeria. Let us summarize some of the evidence for this conclusion:

BETTER ECONOMIC POLICIES. Following the decline of oil prices during the 1980s, Indonesia deliberately decreased dependence on oil income (from 45 percent in the early 1970s to 38 percent in the 1990s), whereas Nigeria increased its dependence from about two-thirds of income in the early 1970s to more than 90 percent (Lewis 1994, ll). A number of useful steps were taken to open up the economy: decreasing protection of the industrial and agricultural sectors; reducing non-tariff barriers; improving the incentive system for the private sector; keeping inflation and government related debt relatively limited; and supporting essential infrastructure and agricultural services.

President Suharto has taken a personal interest in certain industries, such as textiles, overcoming existing problems and barriers (Macintre 1991). Also he has used and protected Chinese business groups, encouraging a productive alliance of Chinese business interests and retired military officers. Under this arrangement, as explained by Campos and Root (1996, 131), "the Chinese provide the bulk of the capital investment and the organizational and management expertise, while their military partners facilitate the granting of licenses and contracts and provide protection from harassment by regulatory bodies." While the President is himself untrained in economics, he has used and protected a highly respected group of U.S.-trained economists and technical experts for purposes of economic development (Lewis 1994, 17; Bhattacharya and Pangestu 1993). There is evidence that, whenever there is an economic crisis or indications of serious mismanagment, President Suharto has dismissed his associates considered responsible and turned to respected technocrats and distinguished citizens (Campos and Root 1996, 140).

The most recent World Bank study of Indonesia (East Asia and Pacific Region 1996, 1, 118) points out that "Indonesia has a well-deserved reputation for sound macroeconomic management," with strict oversight of national budget expenditures. Inflation has been carefully controlled under a balanced budget constitutional provision introduced in 1967. What makes this provision effective is the determination of President Suharto to make the balanced budget a foundation for the legitimacy of his government, thereby keeping "the Indonesian technocrats one step removed from the political demands of legislators and other parties" (Campos and Root 1996, 159). If so, the Indonesian economy may recover quite quickly from its downfall at the end of 1997. According to THE ECONOMIST (March 7, 1998, 5), GDP per head is expected to rise by 2.9% in 1999, after a 5.2% fall in 1998.

BETTER GOVERNANCE. While Indonesia remains a highly authoritarian regime, there is indication of a growing willingness to tolerate the participation of parliamentarians, the press, industry groups, community-based non-governmental organizations, and foreign investors and experts (including those from the World Bank). It should also be noted that the employment of university graduates in the civil service rose by 48 percent between 1988 and 1992, suggesting the slow shift to a meritocratic administration.

In the last few years, there has been considerable political violence in Indonesia, indicating dangerous uncertainty about the future, with the ruler reaching the age of 75 in 1996. Moreover, the situation in East Timor remains volatile. However, considering the remarkable socio-economic progress in Indonesia, there is less likelihood of sustained political chaos in Indonesia than in Nigeria. Consequently, using the terminology introduced in Chapter 7, we can suggest that, insofar as there is greater secondary democracy in Indonesia than in Nigeria, there is also more possibility here of eventual primary democracy. In Nigeria, politics continues to be seen "as a competition between ruling-class factions over access to state resources" (Forrest 1993, 4). Where this is the case, I refer to it as "political illness" in Chapters 6 and 10.

Corruption (see Chapter 5) has clearly had a serious impact on the quality of Indonesian life: industrial pollution is extensive; the urban poor continue to depend on polluted or expensive private water sources; human and solid waste disposal and drainage are badly neglected; and funds that could go for better living conditions are wasted on general administration and office buildings. This corruption, according to various sources (Mehmet 1993; World Bank 1991, 1994a; Devas 1989), is intensified by low salaries, an emphasis on seniority and loyalty rather than competence, an inadequate legal system, and unreliable taxation and cost-recovery efforts. However, Lewis (1994, 15) considers Indonesian corruption as "productive accumulation," as against Nigeria's "primitive accumulation." Consequently, the proceeds from Indonesian corruption have been reinvested in the country, whereas, in Nigeria, they have been sent abroad.

During the 1960s, the Nigerian federal civil service was relatively well respected, in accord with the British Westminster-Whitehall model (Metz 1992, 239). Since then, it has become "reputedly the most bureaupathologic in the area" (Caiden 1991, 257). The deterioration of the civil service is acknowledged by a leading Nigerian business organization (the Organized Private Sector Group): "corruption has become institutionalized at all levels of government affecting industrial and business operations" (Maier 1992, 44).

The undermining of governance in Nigeria can be seen as a deliberate process. "The ruling class has shown remarkably little capacity or inclination to restrain itself" (Koehn 1990, 283). According to a World Bank report (1994b, 22-23), "Nigeria has not published audited, final budgetary accounts since 1982," and extrabudgetary spending has increased from 22 percent of total spending in 1986 to 65 percent in 1992. (Also see Chapter 6.)

Much of the military equipment sold to Nigeria is intended for payoff purposes, not for real use (Coll and Shiner 1994). This is also true of a large number of industrial projects, such as the Ajaokua Steel Complex (World Bank 1994b, 25). Meanwhile, neglect of operation and maintenance expenditures and supervision has undermined the country's entire infrastructure system. Likewise, the government's capacity to deliver health and education services has been seriously reduced.

WHY THE DIFFERENCE? In trying to explain why African ruling classes seem so much more counterproductive than their Asian counterparts, the most compelling argument is that nationalism has failed to develop in Africa, as against ethnic, religious, or other traditional ties. While nationalism has taken various important forms in Africa (as anticolonialism, pride in African culture, and justification for authoritarian rule), it has not yet led to a real sense of patriotism. "As the expectations created by the promises of of militant nationalism gave way to disappointment, disillusionment, and—by 1990 in much of Africa—despair, state-based nationalism had a hollow ring" (Young 1994, 69).

While I respect this argument, that nationalism is less well-developed in Africa than in Asia, I have my doubts about it. Likewise, for reasons explained in later chapters, I am dubious about other explanations that are given for the more rapid development of Asia than Africa: the longer period of colonial rule in Asia than Africa, Confucian beliefs, the precolonial domination of particular individuals or groups, greater external threats, and the influence of Japan (Perkins and Roemer 1993).Moreover, I remain uncertain why political illness seems so much more pervasive in some countries or parts of the world than in others. Looking at more or less neighboring countries, we find development more apparent in Botswana than in Zambia, in Tunisia than in Algeria, in Costa Rica than in Nicaragua, in Thailand than in Burma, in Chile than in Bolivia, in Hungary than in Romania, and so forth.

The answers found in the literature point to different historical circumstances, socio-economic factors, and choice of policies. Yet, I hestitate to buy these answers. Just as with alcoholism, we remain uncertain why it affects certain societies, families, and individuals more than others. So it is with political illness. Ultimately, it seems to me a matter of leadership. The persistence of irresponsible leadership is a mystery that I cannot provide an answer for.

My uncertainty about the causes of political illness leaves room for optimism. There is, after all, free will. Once leaders decide that development is important, I see nothing to prevent it. For example, Peru, which was considered a "bomb-scarred basket case" during the 1980s, recorded the world's highest growth rate in 1994 (Brooke 1995, Dl). While President Fujimori has been properly criticized for failing to address the country's terrible living conditions and poverty (particularly, following the terrorist hostage seizure at the Japanese ambassador's home in December, 1996), he seems to have shown more enthusiasm for development than his predecessors. Under a 1989 property registration reform program, nearly 300,000 benefited by 1996 from lower transaction costs and faster implementation (World Bank 1997, 101). Peru's tax collecting improvements, stemming from better governance, are noted in Chapter 10.

According to THE ECONOMIST (November 16, 1996, 33–34), the Philippines made remarkable progress under President Fidel Ramos in 1996, with a 7% growth rate, low inflation, and an overall surplus balance of payments: "At last, the Philippines looks ready to emulate the sustained rapid growth enjoyed by much of the rest of the region." Yet, without contradicting this assertion, one has to be skeptical, based upon persistent public administration weaknesses noted in later chapters.

In the spirit of cautious optimism, we can also find indications that a new generation of Nigerian leaders is becoming more interested in development. Indeed, recent news coming from Nigeria (THE ECONOMIST, November 9, 1996, 46) suggests that General Abacha, who seized power in 1993, is fighting corruption and inflation. The budget was in balance in 1995; GDP growth was 2.2%; and privatization of major industries (telecommunications, electronics, oil and gas) was being implemented.

It is, of course, too early to be seeing much progress in Nigeria considering that, as of 1995, Nigeria's financial sector was "in a state of virtual collapse," according to a 1997 article by Lewis and Stein (p. 17). These authors suggest that corruption remains so pervasive in Nigeria as to belie reports of successful reform programs and economic progress. More than half of total federal expenditures is covered by extrabudgetary funds, indicating the continued uselessness of financial accounts and audits (World Bank 1997, 83).

In any case, until leaders (wherever they be) are clearly committed to development, donors of assistance can provide charity, nothing more. But, as pointed out in Chapter 10, we must not mistake charity for effective foreign aid.

CHAPTER 2

Political Software
Understanding What Works

INTRODUCTION

Dennis Rondinelli, a leading expert on foreign aid, pointed out in his 1987 book (p. 23) that, during the 1950s and 1960s, there was great optimism "that successful methods, techniques, and ways of solving problems and delivering services in the United States or other economically advanced countries would prove equally successful in developing countries." Institutes of public administration (PA) offering courses in accounting, budgeting, statistics, office management, and other technical subjects were set up in many countries, and more than 7,000 students from developing countries were brought to the United States to study PA under the auspices of international funding agencies.

By the early 1970s, confidence in the transferability of U.S. administrative technology had largely disappeared. The Ford Foundation, in its evaluations of expensive PA programs in countries, such as Nigeria and Zaire, doubted the usefulness of this expenditure. And Congressional critics of U.S. Agency for International Development (USAID) programs in Vietnam and Latin America considered PA programs to be useless, if not counterproductive (Rondinelli 1987 52–53). At the same time, funding for the work of the Comparative Administration Group (CAG) of the American Society of Public Administration significantly declined.

This malaise affecting comparative administration seems to me to go deeper than simply the failure of US-sponsored PA programs. It arises from the loss of confidence in the scientific validity of PA, as noted in the Introduction. Kettl (1990, 411–412) points out that the intellectual challenge to PA has come from three directions in the decades after World War Two: from those critical of weak PA implementation; from those seeking practical guidance; and from those denying PA's "claim to prescriptions for effective management." Wamsley (1990, 20) concludes: "The landscape of public administration theory has thus been markedly bleak."

In this chapter, I will be looking at the weakness of PA from my own vantage point, as a student of comparative urban studies. (In Chapter 3, I will return to this topic, focusing on rural development.)

For every success story in the American urban literature, there seems to be an equal and opposite failure story. Thus, there is much cynicism and pessimism regarding possibilities of improving living conditions in the inner city. "It has recently been fashionable to deny that we can do much about these conditions through deliberate social policy," Currie (1985, 225) points out. He goes on to cite evaluations of different approaches to handling troubled youth in New York, indicating that, without "a fundamental change in opportunities and intergroup relations," none appear successful. James Q. Wilson (1994, A10) reaches a similar conclusion regarding welfare reform programs to strengthen troubled families, noting that "we must now face the fact that we don't know what to do about the problem."

On the basis of "nothing works," a number of effective rehabilitation efforts were discontinued in American prisons during the 1970s, disregarding the factors undermining the less successful programs (Kerr 1993). Likewise, American governmental programs in support of enterprise zones, urban rehabilitation, child care, job training, and youth employment efforts, among others, have been curtailed or terminated because of simplistic evaluations. The contradictory evaluations of the Urban Development Action Grant has led some critics to consider them more ideological than meaningful (Barnekov and Hart 1993).

However, unless we can understand what works in the U.S. and other More Developed Countries (MDCs), it is no use trying to give advice to Less Developed Countries (LDCs). To overcome this problem, I believe that we need to take a closer look at administrative theory.

Comparative urban studies have been adversely affected by the fads (as well as the confusion) encountered in PA. For example, the "entrepreneurial" approach to government, put forward by Osborne and Gaebler (1993), is being tried by an increasing number of cities. How do we account for the mixed results? The inner-city poor have not really benefited in most American cities from the Osborne-Gaebler approach, according to Robin Hambleton (1993, 256), a British scholar. The fact that private sector interests have come to prevail "has had adverse consequences, not only for the quality of city government, but also for the quality of life of large numbers of US citizens." On the other hand, entrepreneurial government, particularly public-private partnerships, has worked well in many European cities (OECD 1987).

POLITICAL ELASTICITY THEORY

As noted in the Introduction, PA has been accused of being "atheoretical" (Rhodes 1991, 540). If we accept theory to mean nothing more than "a conception of reality," such an assertion is nonsensical. Even a child, after his first day of school, has a "conception" of how that school operates. As that child grows up to earn a Ph.D. in educational administration, his conception will, of course, change as he recognizes the complexity of reality. It is more appropriate to suggest that PA is multitheoretical, with the theory of what is best (e.g., scientific management or humanistic management) so conflicting as to cause utter confusion.

My understanding of theory as "a conception of reality" seems to be supported by a 1995 article in ADMINISTRATIVE SCIENCE QUARTERLY by Paul DiMaggio, in which he presents three theories about administration: that it describes the world as we see (or measure it); that it is a device for enlightenment; and that it attempts to account for "how the actions of real humans could produce the associations predicted or observed" (pp. 391–2). The objective of political elasticity theory, as mentioned in the Introduction, is to facilitate the conceptualization process by linking meaningful metaphors in ways that are easy to understand, commonsensical, and explanatory.

According to Weimer (1992, 238), politics is broadly defined "as the processes by which people make and execute collective choices." This seems to me about as meaningful as to conceive of biology as "the processes of organic survival" or physics as "the processes of inorganic motion." Surely, politics is more than this.

For reasons presented in the Introduction, I define politics as "the relationship between leadership and followership for the purpose of governance." Yet, even if we include within our conception of politics, the making and executing of collective choices, we must also include the reasons for these choices and their effectiveness (especially, how people respond to them). Weimer's inadequate definition of politics leads him to the confusing question: "What can political science contribute to the improvement of practitioner skill, taking institutional arrangements as given?" and then, to the answer, "not much" (p. 241). To see how astonishing this conclusion is, imagine asking a medical doctor: "Since you cannot cure AIDS, why do you bother to study biology?"

While I agree with Weimar that "the standard approaches of political science . . . offer little to the study of public management" (p. 244), I insist that political theory (as here presented) has a greater potential than economic theory to explain PA success and failure. Indeed, substantiating this assertion is one of the purposes of this book.

Institutional arrangements (as noted in the Introduction) are comparable to the physical parts of a computer and, as such, might be referred to as "political hardware." Yet, it is obvious that even the best computer is useless unless it is properly programmed or instructed and skillfully handled so that the physical parts do what we want them to do. I have therefore introduced the concept of "political software" to refer to the quality of relationships between leaders and followers essential for the components of political hardware (rules, procedures, technology, organizational arrangements, authorizations, etc.) to be respected.

In looking at Caiden's list of administrative malpractices (1991a, 492), including such bureaucratic pathologies as abuse of authority, bias, inaction, indifference, and carelessness, I see weaknesses in political software more at fault than political hardware deficiencies. Political software refers to nothing more than the psychological predispositions which organization theorists have long been aware of and concerned about (Harmon and Mayer 1986). Yet, perhaps out of the growing demand for scientifically justified conclusions in PA, the subjective side of the discipline has come to be deemphasized and even ignored.

According to Wamsley (1990, 19), "public administration theory has been trapped in an intellectual cul-de-sac created by behavioralism. . . ." Yet, the appeal of behavioralism lingers on in PA, assuming that we agree with the criticism of Whicker, Strickland and Olshfski (1993, 532) that PA has "remained largely unquantitative and unscientific." This conclusion is supported by Van Wart and Cayer (1990, 245), in regard to comparative PA, suggesting that there "are not enough theory-testing articles," based upon quantification.

Those who demand "testable hypotheses" in PA are misleading and possibly disingenuous, if we accept the argument of the English linquistic analyst Weldon (1953) that political words are imprecise, subjective, and appraisive (ascriptive as well as descriptive). Compare, for example, the technical word "tall," with the political word, "trustworthy" in the following two sentences: "President Clinton is tall" and "President Clinton is trustworthy."

While an assertion about Clinton's tallness (if we mean only much above average height) is likely to be noncontroversial, describing him as trustworthy without further explanation would be baffling. We need to know, not only how the word "trustworthy," is being used, but also the political and moralistic orientation of the person making this value judgment.

However, one does not have to be a political scientist to use political language meaningfully. If historians or journalists clarify their use of the word, "trustworthy," and present evidence from many points of view about Clinton's trustworthiness, they can possibly reach a "multidimensional" conclusion, instead of the confusion emerging from quantification efforts using a typical public opinion poll.

I have no trouble with the quantification of political words, if it is recognized as a vague approximation of reality. Unfortunately, by attempting to narrowly define political words, avoid value judgments, and develop standardized measures and variables for describing reality, behavioralists often end up reaching such dubious conclusions as the following: "Chief executives who reward departments for professional accomplishments do not have as much influence as those executives who reward departments for their personal and political support" (Abney and Lauth 1982, 139); "Early-career public administrators and those from smaller jurisdictions are more likely to experience the need for the science of administration, while those later in their careers and in larger jurisdictions are more likely to see the art of administration as the dominant skill" (Crewson and Fisher 1997, 380). These conclusions result from survey sample techniques that trivialize political reality in favor of computerized data spinning (Whyte 1991, 10).

Often we find in the ADMINISTRATIVE SCIENCE QUARTERLY the development of typologies using so-called "scientific methods." Typically, these break down, with the authors admitting that there are too many exceptions or variants. For example, Earley (1994) suggests that organizations in Hong Kong and the People's Republic of China are more "collectivistic" than those in the United States; but he concludes

(p. 115) that this approach "blurs the unique differences among individuals within a given culture." Wageman's 1995 typology (interdependent, independent, and hybrid), suggesting that hybrid groups are the least effective, is undermined by her conclusion that "favorable outcomes or unfavorable outcomes may depend a great deal on the motivational properties of the tasks and the characteristics of the people who perform them."

The classical "iron laws of bureaucracy," as developed by Gulick (1937) and Fayol (1949), refer largely to political hardware: hierarchical or scalar principle, span of control, specialization, unity of command, unity of direction, etc. As earlier noted, I believe there are "iron laws of bureaucracy;" but these depend, not on particular Weberian requirements (hierarchy, rules, procedures, rights, contractual duties, specialized positions or roles, etc.), but on the steps required for political software development: establishing acceptable goals, hiring qualified personnel, encouraging training, delegating responsibility, stimulating motivation and competition, paying attention to morale, expanding two-way flows of communication, promoting legitimacy, maintaining supervision, cultivating contractors, protecting independent spheres of authority, and developing conflict-resolution procedures.

Inasmuch as any of these steps are neglected or mismanaged, we encounter manifestations of political inelasticity. Moreover, (even if I cannot quantify or exactly predict this relationship), I assert that, without political software development, all reform efforts in both micro- and macro-administration are going to be difficult, if not impossible.

My comparison of solid waste management in Japan and Nigeria in the previous chapter was intended to illustrate the difference between political elasticity and inelasticity. Another example can be found in an article by Sanger (1992a, A3), pointing out that, in the Philippines, electricity is unreliable, preventing businesses from operating efficiently. However, people will not pay taxes to repair or improve the generators because they neither respect nor fear the responsible bureaucracies. Even when harsh forms of political power are used to raise taxes, they have no effect because officials can easily be bribed to falsify payments. Average collection rates by the early 1990s dropped below 50 percent. Since the central government then prohibited inflation from being taken into account, cost recovery was doubtful even when collection efforts were more successful.

By paying attention to political software, political elasticity may be effective even in one of the "impossible jobs in public management" (Hargrove and Glidewell 1990): maintaining humanitarian homeless shelters. Philadelphia seems to have had some success in its program for the homeless with a well-managed incentive-disincentive system (Culhane 1992).

Those in shelters had an opportunity for subsidized permanent housing or specialty shelters ("clean and sober" ones) if they avoided violation of rules for 60 consecutive days. These rules included using 60 percent of their income for a savings account, paying 15 percent of their income for shelter, cooperating with random urine drug tests, and participating in addiction treatment or mental health programs. While more funding was needed to deal with the underlying causes of homelessness, officials here believed that they were effectively responding to the homeless, rather than simply being overwhelmed by them.

The linkages between political software and political hardware within PA are so interconnected that, as with a computer, it is sometimes difficult to determine the source of a particular problem. For example, in Jakarta, only about 60 percent of the population has access to the treated water supply system despite World Bank-supported slum-upgrading (KIP) efforts here since 1974 (Clarke, Hadiwinoto and Leitmann 1991; also see Chapter 5). While part of this failure apparently results from corruption reported by Lovei and Whittington (1991), it may also stem from the lack of career opportunities within KIP units and from discrimination against ethnic Chinese contractors with the most experience and expertise. Likewise, in New York, it is difficult to determine the relationship of rent control to PA in accounting for the poor maintenance of low-income apartment buildings.

Despite the problems of analyzing political software, the failure to do so inevitably undermines the conclusions of PA literature. To illustrate the importance of political software, I will begin with some American urban literature before turning to LDC urban studies. The objective, as noted earlier, is to better understand what works in MDCs in order to provide better guidance to LDCs.

AMERICAN URBAN STUDIES

Gueron and Pauly's FROM WELFARE TO WORK (1991), which is described in the blurb as "the definitive book on welfare-to-work programs," is a product of the Manpower Demonstration Research Corporation (MDRC), with extensive funding from the Ford Foundation, the Department of Health and Human Services, and the Russell Sage Foundation. It reviewed 45 completed and in-progress studies relevant to the 1988 Family Support Act, which provided federal matching funds for state welfare-to-work intiatives under the Job Opportunities and Basic Skills Training (JOBS) Program. These studies used primarily an "experimental design" methodology, under which the performance over time of an experimental group (targeted for the welfare-to-work program) was compared to a control group (those of similar background not eligible for the services of the program).

Manski and Garfinkel (1992, 1) note that the widespread use of this methodology is relatively recent, going back to the 1960s when attempts were made to evaluate programs established under President Johnson's War on Poverty. The MDRC, primarily supported by the Ford Foundation, was highly successful in establishing the legitimacy of its experimental design methodology (Oliker 1994, 205). This methodology has now become a "growth industry," with Congress even demanding in 1988 its use in connection with the JOBS Program.

Some of the findings of Gueron and Pauly—that welfare-to-work programs generally lead to sustainable earnings gains and that public investments in such programs are more than returned in increased taxes and reductions in transfer payments—seem well-supported by the evidence presented. While their methodology can be useful in reaching certain broad generalizations, we can challenge their attempt to use it for their primary objectives: (1) evaluating the usefulness of various options and strategies; (2) determining which services are more effective than others; and (3) structuring JOBS initiatives "so that the most appropriate services are targeted to groups in the caseload who can benefit from them most" (p. 240).

Their constant pleas for "more research support" notwithstanding, it is IMPOSSIBLE to answer the question they pose—"What works best for whom?" (p. 211)—without taking into account political software considerations. The reasons for skepticism include the following:

PROBLEMS OF COMPARABILITY. Imagine using an experimental design methodology to evaluate Harvard University, comparing the success of graduates with those of similar background and qualifications. We would be laughed at if we tried. After all, how do we measure success? The truth is that those from affluent families who are successful in high school generally end up doing fairly well in life, regardless of where they go to college. Fortunately, Harvard graduates, unlike the less advantaged, can avoid being treated as flora and fauna, subject to controlled experimentation.

Turning to welfare-to-work programs, we find problems of comparability equally difficult. The programs differ from one-another in so many respects (e.g., costs, services provided, extent of targeting, requirements, penalties, and benefits) that generalizations become almost impossible. Even how the programs are publicized (for example, emphasizing obligations rather than benefits) may affect comparability measurements.

In many cases, the services and benefits available to non-participants are almost as great as those given to participants. The favorability of the job market cannot be easily separated from other factors. Thus, it is hard to know what to make of a recent Labor Department-sponsored evaluation of the Job Training Partnership Act, which found that, whereas those under age 22 did not seem to benefit financially from the job-training and educational programs provided, older participants advanced educationally and had significantly higher earnings than comparable control groups (Rich 1992, A11). One explanation suggested by Levitan (1990, 55) for women on AFDC rolls is simply that they have an easier time escaping welfare as their children become older and require less of their attention.

CONTRADICTIONS. The programs that do best carefully screen applicants, providing higher cost services to those most qualified. This finding by Gueron and Pauly (p. 178) contradicts one earlier presented, criticizing the practice of "creaming," i.e., serving only those with the highest potential for success (p. 157). (Indeed, the creaming process, which makes for a successful program, is precluded by the methodological requisite for a randomized selection of participants.)

While one study found larger impacts for groups facing fewer employment barriers (particularly women over 30 years of age), another found employment gains greater for women with children under age 3 and still another, no relationship between potential for employment and usefulness of the program (p. 213). Although some programs found an education component useful (p. 28), the research literature, according to Gueron and Pauley (p. 219), provides "little solid evidence that education programs for adult welfare recipients can improve their educational attainment or achievement." As we encounter these and other contradictory conclusions, we emerge more confused than the proverbial blind men describing an elephant.

OVERSIMPLIFICATION. My criticism of the experimental design methodology is supported by a number of social scientists who have studied it. Manski and Garfinkel (1992, 20) are especially critical of the tendency to ignore the complex social processes that make programs work over a long-term period, treating them as "black boxes" that do not fit into "assembly-line evaluations." Oliker (1994, 199) adds that the enthusiasm of policymakers for quick answers about what works in the short run, which the methodology seems to provide, has dimmed their curiosity about "how programs create effects." This requires the sort of sociological studies, linking work, welfare, and private life, which, while complicating efforts to deal with the question, "does workfare work?," makes emerging answers more meaningful.

A 1995 update (Friedlander and Burtless, 204) of the Gueron and Pauly study notes "severe problems . . . when the studies to be compared are carried out under differing local labor market and AFDC conditions, with samples having different characteristics, and with difference research methodologies." Friedlander and Burtless, therefore, suggest modifications of this approach; but, in the absence of political software considerations, I do not see how more field experiments will get us the answers to the high priority questions on the impact of welfare reform that all of us are looking for. I therefore agree with Mead (1997, 115) that this method "reveals surprisingly little about how results are achieved."

For an understanding of the relevance of political software considerations, we have to turn to case studies. Looking at a program in Baltimore (the Lafayette Family Development Center), which attempted to consolidate a variety of federal, state, and private resources into one large public agency, Pines (1991, 93) points out that the "fragmentation of these human investment programs remains one of the major unmet challenges to domestic policy in America." While this center has been somewhat successful, according to Pines, collaboration among disparate agencies has not been easy (p. 99).

Whereas, for example, some child welfare specialists discourage mothers of young children from working, many programs pressure these mothers to work. Yet, based upon the enactment of the 1996 welfare reform bill, the implications of doing so have not really been addressed. "What is needed," Pines concludes, "is a vision of what needs to happen and then sustained leadership that builds an effective partnership framework for policy, planning, and implementation at every level of government, and in every targeted community" (p. 100). Unfortunately, we still lack such a vision.

By focusing on political software, it may be possible to overcome the problems of the experimental design methodology and similar efforts to reach blanket conclusions about "what works." Some of these conclusions have been, not only misleading, but also counterproductive in undermining or threatening such potentially useful programs as the following:

PUBLIC HOUSING. American public housing, which has become a repository for poor, minority, single-parent families, exemplifies the consequences of neglecting political software considerations. The deterioration of Chicago's Robert Taylor Homes, as described by Lemann (1991), shows what can happen when commonsensical bureaucratic requirements are violated.

From this experience with public housing, the conclusion that it should be avoided is understandable. According to Massey and Kanaiaupuni (1993, 120), public housing "represents a federally funded, physically permanent institution for the isolation of black families by race and class, and it must be considered an important structural cause of concentrated poverty in U.S. cities." Lauber (1991, 68) adds that mixed communities "should also do their best to persuade public housing authorities not to build additional public housing. . . ."

Yet, public housing is common in most MDCs, including a wide variety of governmental subsidies and arrangements for construction, maintenance, and management. In France, for example, 13.5 percent of all housing (as against only 1.6 percent in the U.S.) is within this category (Schwartz 1991, 188). To prevent the stigmatization of public housing, French projects include a diversity of socio-economic categories. This was also true of earlier American public housing programs, such as Chicago's Wentworth Gardens.

Looking back at the 1937–1950 period, residents of American public housing were selected on the basis of strict criteria, with preference given to two-parent families with a good credit rating and control over their children (Brown 1990). However, by starving public housing of funds for maintenance and security and discouraging anyone but the very poor from using it, the government made it no longer politically viable (Atlas and Drier 1993). During the 1980s, only 150,000 public housing units were constructed, despite long waiting lists and the general satisfaction of tenants in smaller cities and low-rise projects (NAHRO 1990).

In an article comparing New York's public housing with Newark's, DePalma (1989, E23) points out that New York has been far more successful because it has more carefully selected tenants, integrated different races and income levels, nurtured a core of professional managers, and developed good relations with tenants. Newark's troubled experience with public housing has caused it (along with many other cities) to promote private non-profit housing sponsored by community organizations, churches, unions, and tenant groups; but this also requires good political software to be successful.

Newark's New Community Corporation is an example of what is needed. It places a heavy emphasis on security, creating an economic mix of tenants, screening prospective tenants, and ousting those who commit crimes or otherwise break the rules (Lemann 1994).

HEAD START. Barnett (1992) summarizes more than 100 studies on the effects of compensatory preschool education on disadvantaged children. While these "meta-analyses" generally find that the effects of American preschool programs, measured by Intelligence (IQ) tests, disappear within three or four years, they seldom take into account the typical problems of these preschools: poor funding, low salaries, excessive numbers of children, poor physical conditions, etc.

A recent study of the Child Care Action Campaign, based upon evaluations in four states, concluded that only one in seven child day centers could be considered really good (Chira 1995, A12). In regard to Head Start, Zigler, Styfco, and Gilman (1993, 31) point out that per-child funding significantly declined during the 1980s, reaching a level of only half that considered desirable. Teachers tend to be poorly trained and paid. Although the programs expanded in number and enrollment during the 1980s, only one in five of them was monitored in 1988.

Focussing, however, on a superior program (the Perry Preschool Project in Ypsilanti, Michigan), where there were experienced and qualified teachers in addition to adequate direction, planning, discussion, inservice training, and other requirements, Barnett (1992, 299–300) found much more positive results. At age 19, those who had attended this Head Start program, in comparison to a control group, achieved, not only better academic results, but also greater economic success and social adjustment (including less teen pregnancy and need for welfare assistance).

What is necessary, Barnett (1992, 306–307) concludes, is, instead of a simplistic concentration upon IQ tests, taking into account "the effects of program characteristics, population characteristics, and the environment (e.g., peer pressures, later educational quality and practices) on program outcomes." This conclusion is supported by Zigler, Styfco, and Gilman (1993, 24), who point out that, until the quality of Head Start programs is carefully assessed, "expansion will proceed without specific information about which program features work best and for whom."

THE JOB CORPS. Since its establishment in 1964, the Job Corps has received mixed reviews, some concluding that those enrolled in it were not signficantly more successful in finding employment or increasing earnings than comparable control groups. With the costs amounting (as of fiscal 1991) to more than $15,000 per student for a combination of vocational, academic, and social components, cost-benefit analyses showing only modest improvement in the basic skills of Job Corps graduates are quite discouraging. There have also been reports of violence, gang activity, and drug abuse at some of the centers (Anderson and Binstein 1995, B23).

Levitan and Johnston (1975, 99–100) are critical of these cost-benefit analyses, noting the following problems: estimating benefits, setting program costs, treating foregone earnings and the value of work projects, and finding a truly random control group. Nevertheless, they conclude that enrollees who remained for the duration of Job Corps programs did considerably better in the labor market than non-participants. However, in reaching this conclusion Levitan and Johnston go beyond typical pseudo-scientific evaluations.

Not all the Job Corps Centers were successful, Levitan and Johnson point out, adding: "Staff morale and administrative quality were crucial to the success of centers" (p. 31). What is essential is an enthusiastic staff, hard work, an orderly atmosphere, and an environment conducive to education and training. While linkage to unions and careful screening and placement proved to be useful, "the key factors influencing the quality of individual programs seem to have been the direction given them by their management . . ." (p. 105). This assertion underscores the argument here presented, that unless political software aspects are taken into account, we cannot effectively evaluate public administration programs.

A similar conclusion is reached by Levin and Ferman (1985) in their evaluation of nine programs established under the 1977 Youth Employment and Demonstration Project. They emphasize the importance of a talented executive, experienced staff, incrementalism, and the ability to detect and correct errors. Among their conclusions (p. 104) is that "the role of the schools' staffs, as shaped by the program executive . . . , is much more important in achieving improved academic performance and improved behavior than educational innovations . . . and new facilities."

LDC URBAN STUDIES

Let us assume that our ideal of what we want to achieve in public administration conforms to the "reinvented government" described by Osborne and Gaebler (1993): community-owned, results-oriented, enterprising, decentralized, and market-oriented. For this to work requires the high quality of political software that is absent in much of the world, particularly in LDCs. Yet, those sent out to improve public administration in LDCs often ignore this fact, introducing new training, technology, organization, and operational procedures that do not get to the fundamental problems in these countries. The truth is, as noted in Chapter 10, it is easier and faster to send in better computers or suggest technical improvements and training than to get at the underlying political software weaknesses.

To illustrate the importance of political software, I will turn to reports of the World Bank's Operations Evaluation Department (OED), which I worked for on several occasions during the 1980s. Because OED reports are confidential, I will refer to them by geographical area, rather than particular city or country. (For reasons indicated in the Introduction, I am less inhibited in my use of OED reports in later chapters.) However, since these OED reports may be available by request (or in newsletter summaries), I have indicated their report numbers and publication year.

LACK OF COMMITMENT. In a South American Country (SAC), the country's Minister of Planning agreed to a World Bank loan for slum upgrading and self-help construction ("sites and services") that was not fully supported by top officials of the National Housing Bank, which was primarily responsible for these projects (Report No. 7581, 1989). Because these officials were busy with their own projects, they considered the World Bank loan too small to justify the required changes in their operational procedures.

Some of these officials also felt that the World Bank's refusal to provide more than infrastructure to sites and services beneficiaries was impractical inasmuch as it forced poor families to pay simultaneously for their current accommodation, their project lot, and the cost of building a house on this lot. Thus, World Bank-supported programs were not adequately promoted until there was a change in administration in SAC and a willingness of the part of the World Bank to amend its loan criteria.

In an East African Country (EAC), top officials agreed to a World Bank urban development project because of their need for financial assistance rather than their agreement with the objectives of the project: low-cost shelter for impoverished residents, administrative decentralization, and cost recovery (Report No. 9730, 1991). While top officials paid lip-service to affordable housing, they were more interested in "dignified housing," particularly rental units for middle class families. Instead of slum upgrading, provided for by the project, officials continued to promote slum demolitions, resulting in 50,000 homeless in less than a month.

Under colonial rule and for some years thereafter, municipalities in EAC had relied on a progressive personal tax. Because Central Government officials here distrusted municipal officials, they disallowed this tax, with the promise of grants instead. However, as these grants were phased out, they were never replaced by anything else, leaving the municipalities bankrupt and demoralized. The World Bank therefore insisted on a revaluation and an increase of property tax rates to enable municipalities to pay for the project. The opposition initially of property owners and then by the cabinet to higher taxes caused the project to be drastically scaled down. Thus, the situation persisted of central government being indebted to municipalities and vice-versa. In the process, the project's objectives were increasingly lost sight of.

In a South East Asian Country (SEAC), the Prime Minister wanted a World Bank loan to reduce traffic congestion in the capital city, but his interest was not shared by the Minister of Interior, who was in charge of project implementation, and the leading executing agencies (Report No.

7068, 1988). Because of their ignorance of the situation, World Bank staff failed to realize that they could not "take the word of the Prime Minister and assume that an expression by him of special concern about a problem was equivalent to a willingness to adopt radical measures towards its solution."

The success of this project required strict enforcement of traffic regulations and coordination of about 15 agencies responsible for different aspects of urban transport. Better enforcement of regulations and interagency coordination proved extremely difficult to achieve, particularly when there was also strong popular opposition. Yet, World Bank staff and their host country counterparts continued to treat these problems as "technical," rather than "political and managerial with dimensions large enough to induce inaction."

LOW MORALE. In a Middle Eastern Country (MEC), recuitment and retention of competent staff were difficult because of low salaries paid by the public sector (Report No. 6561, 1987). The salaries of beginning engineers, for example, were at least twice as high in the private sector as in the public sector; and the disparity increased tremendously for experienced professionals. In EAC, the lack of adequate salaries caused 40 percent of professionals in a city council to be vacant.

In EAC, a special department was set up to handle a housing project in the capital city, but this led to conflict between it and the regular city department responsible for housing. The resulting splintering of the city's engineering department undermined the morale of this department. Since funding for urban projects was dependent upon the central government, local governments in this country were unwilling to take responsibility for these projects. In one city, the treasurer was completely unable to pay contractors and could only pay municipal workers by "borrowing" from the Water Supply Department's accounts.

Low pay and poor supervision undoubtedly intensified mismanagement. In EAC, plot allocation in a sites and services project (providing infrastructure and foundations for self-help housing construction) was affected by major political interference. A number of senior officials were arrested for corruption, and several of the city councils were dissolved. Eventually, most of the regular senior staff running the project were either encouraged or forced to go on leave. Personnel changes, however, could not prevent the project from gentrification—i.e., being taken over by a much wealthier clientele than originally intended—because of building requirements and market forces, as well as corruption and policy disputes.

COMMUNICATION BREAKDOWN. In SAC, the first phase of a project was delayed because federal funding was withheld as a reprisal for the State Governor's support of the opposition candidate for president (Report No. 9490, 1991). In a Latin American Country (LAC), the executing agency had difficulty monitoring local activities because its headquarters was in the capital, 800 kilometers away from where the project was being implemented (Report No. 7007, 1987). In MEC, extensive reorganization following administrative decentralization meant that policy making and technical teams that prepared the project were broken up, with the personnel generally confused about their role.

In EAC, many problems emerged when World Bank staff failed to explain adequately to government officials the importance of linking the elements required for low-cost housing: reduced standards, building credits, secure land tenure, cost recovery, and, above all, community involvement. Of course, such communication is difficult when there is a contradiction between the need for cost-recovery and the desire to target shelter to the lowest income groups. The poorest are inevitable excluded when the costs of construction and land are included. In MEC, however, problems emerged simply because few of the World Bank staff spoke Arabic, and few of the local staff were fluent in English.

Politicians have a tendency everywhere to promise a great many benefits, without pointing to the costs and requirements involved. Thus, in EAC, politicians were unwilling to evict recipients of housing loans. This caused a situation in which 30 percent of borrowers were in arrears of six months or more. In SAC, the same situation led to agencies providing subsidized grants to a selected few rather than implementing cost recovery policies to help the majority of the population.

When, however, in one sites and services project, 66 families who had not made the required downpayment were forced to give up their plots to others, the performance of the project improved considerably (Report No. 7032, 1987). In SAC, as municipalities were given more local responsibility, local leaders were more willing to dicuss cost recovery and improved financial management (Report No. 9490, 1991).

There is a also a natural tendency to ignore difficult problems to "get on" with a project. Consequently, World Bank staff proved too receptive of EAC government assurances that tribal trust properties could be easily and cheaply purchased. Although these properties were eventually expropriated, the former owners returned to squat or reclaim their land, claiming that they had been "illegally" forced off their land and inadequately compensated.

When two-way flows of communication were used, it was sometimes possible to get good results. In one EAC city, local authorities were involved in project preparation to a much larger extent than was usually the case. Consequently, the family planning and nutrition programs here appeared to be unusually successful.

In studying the reasons for the World Bank's neglect of political software considerations, Michael Cernea's point (1991, 45–46) about the prevailing influence of technical experts needs to be recognized, together with his assertion that they "lack understanding of what social science and social engineering could bring to their own efforts." Because these experts "are often being trained today as though people did not matter for the solution of technical issues," they use social scientists as an "after thought" or on a "pro-forma" basis, dismissing their advice as irrelevant. (This point is also emphasized in Chapters 8 and 10.)

CONCLUSIONS

In considering the implications of our political software analysis, two conclusions would be INAPPROPRIATE: (1) that political hardware (e.g., rules, organization, and procedures) are unimportant and (2) that quantitative forms of evaluation are unnecessary. The problem-solving capacity of bureaucracies in MDCs depends upon careful monitoring and evaluation, including cost-benefit studies.

In the Netherlands, for example, extensive research is continuously undertaken on facilitating public understanding of tax obligations. Based on this, a fleet of "tax buses" was introduced, allowing public servants to help clients free of charge with their tax problems, using the motto: "We will help you to pay no more than you have to pay" (OECD 1987a, 104). In LDCs, on the other hand, officials neglect and even oppose monitoring and evaluation, with the result that useful reform is accidental and rare (Ahmed and Bamberger, 1991).

If I have made my point about the importance of political software, PA may be able to escape its overemphasis upon political hardware. Two articles in PUBLIC ADMINISTRATION REVIEW (Poister and Streib

1995 and Berman and West 1995), surveying American municipal managers about their use of Management by Objectives (MBO) and Total Quality Management (TQM), underscore this point.

Both MBO and TQM were found to be useful only if and when they included such political software factors as: top management commitment and participation; two-way flows of communication; monitoring worker satisfaction; employee empowerment; recognizing and rewarding achievement; and appropriate training and information-gathering. Both approaches could easily be undermined by the failure to address emerging problems, fears, criticisms, and forms of resistance.

In regard to LDCs (as earlier mentioned about American urban studies) there has also been a tendency to jump to conclusions about "what works." Yet, as the following examples show, when the political software is good, these conclusions often turn out to be bad:

SITES AND SERVICES PROJECTS. The World Bank seems to have become discouraged by the problems of doing urban development noted in the previous section. Consequently, according to Baken and van der Linden (1993, 3), the Bank has mistakenly shifted to emphasizing market efficiency, a reduced role for the government, and "some sort of trickling down mechanism." In other words, Bank loans are to go less for governmental urban projects and more for reducing constraints on urban productivity and for better access to infrastructure, credit, and social services.

The Bank has been particularly unhappy with its experience doing sites and services projects, failing to recognize that its problems result primarily, not from defective political hardware (the approach itself), as from political software weaknesses. This is clear from a review of El Salvador's FUNDASAL, which may be considered the Bank's most outstanding urban "success story" during the period (1977–83) that I edited the Bank's newsletter, THE URBAN EDGE. (I visited this project in 1978 to see for myself the reasons for its success.) It was also one of its first attempts to finance low-cost housing projects on a large scale (Deneke and Silva 1982).

The FUNDASAL program goes back to 1968 when Padre Ibanez, together with a group of concerned citizens, relocated 69 families left homeless after a flood in the eastern section of San Salvador. Its mode of operation was to organize poor people into mutual help groups to build the infrastructure and lay the foundations for low-income housing. After contributing about 30 weekends of labor, each family gained tenure and services and then the opportunity to expand its own house over time. Using this method, FUNDASAL's units of housing were from one-half to one-third the cost of government-built public housing. Thus, its early projects provided the only housing accessible to the poorest 50 percent of the population.

Because FUNDASAL's "site and service" approach was in accord with the policies then advocated by the World Bank, it received Bank funding in 1974. By the late 1970s, FUNDASAL's production of housing units represented almost half of the total annual number of new formal housing units in El Salvador's urban areas (Schmidt 1993). All FUNDASAL communities had by then completed construction of community centers, schools, cooperatives, parks or gardens, and pedestrian pathways, and taken over responsibility for garbage collection and other services.

A number of factors contributed to FUNDASAL's high quality of political software, enabling it to provide 1,000 housing units annually during the worst years (the 1980s) of El Salvador's civil war. It was managed by a twelve-member Board of Directors, consisting of eminent Salvadoreans from a broad range of occupations. Members of the Board were elected by a General Assembly of participating households. This assembly, which met annually, was also responsible for approving the Board's budget.

FUNDASAL's staff (numbering about 200, as of 1980) was highly respected, developing innovative methods to enhance the attractiveness of the layout and to reduce infrastructure costs. Participating families were carefully selected, based on income, capacity to pay mortgages and service charges, residency, and commitment; and, after selection, were required to attend orientation and training sessions. They also had to assist with the preparation of infrastructure and foundations. Particular attention was paid to FUNDASAL's social goals, enabling the development of viable community organizations, assisted by teams of social promoters (one for every 25 families).

The high quality of FUNDASAL's political software meant that it could integrate soft and hard forms of power in "politically elastic" ways. For example, the Delinquency Section of its Finance Division seldom needed to obtain from the courts judicial sanctions against those failing to meet mortgage payments. First of all, it attempted to get beneficiaries to recognize the importance of punctual mortgage payments. Secondly, when families got behind in their payments by more than a month, it did an investigation.

Based on mutual respect, FUNDASAL attempted to reach an agreement with delinquent families on some sort of repayment program or schedule. These families were then periodically revisited by social workers until the problem was resolved. Finally, to encourage punctual payments, some of the risk reserve (amounting to a five percent surcharge) was returned to those who maintained their payments up-to-date via a lottery, which also boosted morale.

FUNDASAL also earmarked donations for very needy families who could not meet mortgage payments. Consequently, to an extent unusual in World Bank projects, FUNDASAL was highly successful in recovering costs from beneficiaries, using accumulated surpluses to finance additional housing programs.

SUBSIDIZED CREDIT PROGRAMS. In considering the question, should credit programs for low-income beneficiaries be subsidized, we also find the literature distorted because of a failure to consider the relevance of political software. Von Pischke (1991), writing for the World Bank, pointed out the many problematic consequences of subsidized credit, including: (1) distorting the supply or allocation of credit; (2) generating excessive borrowing and debt; (3) discouraging savings and efficient use of funds; (4) undermining the linkage between saving and credit; (5) excessively subsidizing large borrowers; (6) eroding the capital of lending institutions; (7) increasing transaction costs and inefficiency; (8) promoting inflation; (9) encouraging reckless investments and expenditure; and (10) intensifying corruption and mismanagement.

Yet, Bangladesh's Grameen Bank, which Von Pischke (1991, 232–245) wrote enthusiastically about, operates a successful subsidized credit program, using a group-lending model. Under this model, individuals wishing a loan must join a small group, with the group as a whole responsible for repayment when members cannot manage their debts. By 1994, this Bank had reached nearly half of the country's villages, providing more than US $160 million annually to about two million members.

From 1981 to 1993, Grameen Bank received more than U.S. $150 million in funds (mostly grants) from foreign donors for the expansion of its efforts to help impoverished rural women (Hubbard 1994, 6–7). With this assistance, it was able to keep the effective cost to its borrowers at about 25 percent less than other financial institutions would have had to charge, assuming a desire to compete for this risky business (Thillairajah 1993, 68–69). However, its high administrative costs could not be covered by its 20 percent interest rate on loans.

The Grameen Bank's 97 percent repayment rate (as against the country's commercial bank recovery rate of between 15 and 45 percent) would not be possible without an intensive client-oriented approach to program delivery, a committed and highly motivated bank staff, decentralization of operations, careful monitoring and supervision, rapid response to problems, experimentation and learning by doing, quick detection and punishment of malfeasance, accessibility of senior staff, and an informal but highly developed communication system (Holcombe 1993; Hubbard 1994).

The Bank prides itself on employing highly qualified staff (terminating about a fourth of trainees lacking adequate skills or commitment), and then training employees to fully understand the problems of women borrowers. It also prides itself on the transparency and efficiency of its operations.

As a result of its high quality of political software, borrowers, as well as staff, see the Grameen Bank, not simply as a source of credit but as a "poverty alleviation organization" (Holcombe 1993, 11). Thus, all work together to deal with common problems (e.g., animal diseases, agricultural marketing, and theft by husbands) and to pressure local leaders and bureaucrats for a positive response to community development needs. (Considering Bangladesh's weak governance, noted in Chapter 10, official cooperation cannot be taken for granted.)

My emphasis on political software also suggests that what works comes from the capacity to "fine-tune" whatever political hardware is selected. In the case of Sweden's child care centers, Kahn and Kamerman (1975, 44–45) point out that there is constant debate and discussion as to every aspect of the program, with persistent testing of new arrangements. In regard to France's publicly supported housing associations, this process takes the form of changing programs to make funds from major financial institutions more or less available on shifting terms (Schwartz 1991, 228–229). Without such a process, perverse consequences can rapidly emerge, so that, as happened in the case of American federal government education loans, a potentially useful policy eventually promoted a number of useless or fraudulent schools or colleges.

A FINAL NOTE

In emphasizing political software, I see the study of political science (PS) as essential for an understanding of PA, and vice-versa. Indeed, my definition of politics presented in the Introduction (the relationship of leadership to followership for the purpose of governance) prevents PA from being excluded from the study of PS. This is because PA should be defined as "the exercise of governance."

As it is, political scientists too often see PA as a dull technical subject; and PA specialists want to keep politics out of the subject altogether. In many universities, the departments are completely separated. The tendency of both is to misunderstand the relationship between the two fields. In the concept of political software, as here presented, I hope we can find that fundamental linkage. In other words, the art and science of governance (which is another way of defining PA) requires the felicitous linking of political software to political hardware.

A recent article in THE AMERICAN POLITICAL SCIENCE REVIEW (Schneider ET AL. 1997), having to do with expanding choice in public education, may illustrate the deleterious consequences of disconnecting PA from PS. Based upon a statistical study of telephone interviews with parents of school-age children in Montclair, New Jersey (where I happen to have relatives), the authors conclude that public choice policies can "enhance the social fabric necessary for building and maintaining effective democracy" (p. 83). Such an article, which is typical of so much published in the leading PS journals, seems to me indicative of a declining quality of this literature.

What is ignored is the unusual socio-economic nature of Montclair, being affluent and highly educated as well as progressive in outlook (Young and Clinchy 1992, 106). Also ignored are political software considerations. While the superintendent is powerful enough to transfer teachers and principals within the school system, there is effective use of collaborative planning with the input of administrators, teachers, and parents. Where financial problems have been greater and public administration weaker (as in Richmond, California), public school choice has been largely eliminated and considered a failure (Young and Clinchy 1992, 58).

CHAPTER 3

Breaking Administrative Bottlenecks
With Truisms

INTRODUCTION

Caiden (1991, 15) notes that much contemporary theory in Public Administration (PA) is devoid of any practical application or guidelines. The challenge of this book, as pointed out in the Introduction, is to fill this gap, providing a simple theoretical framework that practitioners can actually use. Whereas in Chapter 2, I concentrated on urban development, here I turn to rural development.

The administrative bottlenecks already presented in this book are so obvious that the reader may feel no PA theory is necessary. A quick look at the development administration literature reveals a continual reappearance of the following: inadequacies of staffing and budget; lack of cooperation among agencies; neglect of supervision; mismanagement of time and resources; overcentralization; slow and confusing decision-making; legal disarray; corruption; etc. Yet, if these bottlenecks to development are so obvious, why is it that administrative theory remains "a fascinating mess" (Siffin 1991, 12).

In making another case for my theory, let me challenge the reader to work as a consultant for the World Bank on a Training and Visit (T&V) project. T&V is a system of reaching farmers through Village Extension Workers (VEWs). Based upon their visits, VEWs bring back problems to researchers and administrators who then develop solutions useful for increased agricultural production. Since introduced by the Israeli expert Daniel Benor in the 1960s, the World Bank has invested more than US $5 billion in more than 600 projects (as of 1992). Yet, it remains controversial.

In assisting the introduction of T&V, you may find yourself hopelessly perplexed, particularly in the absence of a useful theory, by such contradictory reactions to it as the following:

GOOD IDEA: Arturo Israel (1987, 186), a leading World Bank administrative expert, argues that T&V is successful because of "the continuous dialogue between farmers, extension workers, and researchers."

BAD IDEA: Professor George H. Axinn (1988, 6–7) of Michigan State University's Department of Resource Development refers to T&V as "Tragic and Vain." This is because it tends to be a "top-down, straight line ministry approach," in which the voice of farmers and professional agriculturalists is ignored.

MIXED BAG: Jerald Hage and Kurt Finsterbusch (1987, 109) of the University of Maryland's Sociology Department suggest that T&V "works best when the same technology package can be delivered to many farmers over a wide area." Thus, it is not suitable when delivery systems require flexibility, adaptation, and innovation.

Within the World Bank, Charles Ameur (1994, 1) points out that extension continues to be "a topic that generates prolixity, controversy, and passion." Whereas Robert Picciotto (1992, 16), the head of the Bank's Operations Evaluation Department, describes T&V as an "important development innovation," Antholt (1994, 15), a senior Bank agriculturalist, argues that "T&V needs to be put behind and attention turned to developing extension efforts . . . that are relevant, responsive and cost-effective. . . ." Yet, despite persistent criticisms of T&V, "it is by no means clear whether higher rates of return could have been achieved through a private sector-based system" (Umali-Deininger 1996, 2).

If you had received this assignment in the early 1950s, you might have been able to turn to a coherent body of administrative theory, including the so-called "classical" writings of, among others, Woodrow Wilson, Luther Gulick, Frederick Taylor, Henri Fayol, and Max Weber (well summarized in Harmon and Mayer 1986). As noted in the Introduction, these classical theories have been undermined, particularly by the "human relations" approach, stemming from the work of Elton Mayo

(1933), emphasizing "followership" rather than leadership; motivation, not control; and development from below instead of from above.

More recent theorists attempted to introduce a new science of administration based upon testable propositions, statistical and mathematical formulations, and elaborate scientific models. Still others, such as Fred Riggs (1964), emphasized the cultural dimensions that need to be taken into account. By the end of the 1980s, the practitioner could choose among a great variety of approaches summarized by Louise White (1987): bureaucratic, institutional, social, political, and "anarchistic" (taking advantage of unanticipated opportunities).

In the quest for fresh approaches, Argyriades (1991, 573) notes the appeal of systems theory. This is the "generic framework" used by the U.S. Agency for International Development-supported International Development Management Center of the University of Maryland to analyze T&V projects (Gustafson 1991). According to this theory, an organization must produce outputs of sufficient value to attract enough inputs to continue functioning.

When an organization reaches sustainability, it becomes an "institution," matching tasks, products, resources, and strategies to its external environment. If an institution cannot adapt to changing demands for its goods and services and to variations of support provided by stakeholders, it will no longer be viable.

Systems theory, it seems to me, raises more questions that it answers: How does an organization motivate its members to produce valuable outputs? How does it influence outsiders to supply needed inputs? What is the relationship of leadership to followership in matching tasks, products, resources, and strategies? In other words, as pointed out in previous chapters, I am searching for the political dimension which is absent in systems theory.

Coralie Bryant (1991, 2) notes that, inasmuch as systems theory correlates institutionalization with sustainability, it frustrates the hopes of people in most parts of the world. These people "are less interested in sustainability than they are in a different and better future, for themselves and their children."

In doing a T&V project, we ideally aim, not for sustainability, but for usefulness. Statements regarding the adaptability of an institution to its environment appear meaningless to me. What is meaningful is the political context: are farmers being given useful assistance by VEWs? Are they responding to this assistance? If not, why not?

A COMMON SENSE APPROACH

Political elasticity theory, as so far presented, suggests that you, as a manager, cannot take for granted what Weberian and scientific management theorists tend to do, that followers automatically or unquestioningly respond to directions. As emphasized in previous chapters, political power generally takes three forms: persuasive (derived from consensus), manipulative (building upon the desire for advantage or reward), and coercive (inculcating fear). Insofar as leaders rely upon a mixture of persuasion and inducement, their power expands and becomes more reliable. However, to be effective, leaders also need the ability to harden forms of power (using combinations of disincentives and punishment). As they say in international relations, "diplomacy without force is farce."

The ability to link soft and hard forms of power and to move back and forth, from one to the other, is the essence of political elasticity. Partly this capacity is derived from "political hardware" - what Siffin (1991, 10) refers to as "organized arrangements that work to serve auspicious aims." But, as emphasized in previous chapters, I am more concerned with developing "political software:" the relationships essential for the effective functioning of organizations.

The institutionalization sought by systems theory depends, not so much on organizational structures, procedures, rules, and technology, as on the quality of political software, including emotions, values, prejudices, and the other psychological or cultural baggage that all of us carry. Without an appropriate quality of political software, a leader loses or fails to develop political elasticity, with the capacity to integrate and alternate soft and hard forms of power.

In making a case for my theory, I need to show that it is easy to understand. In doing so, I will come up against the argument that "no standard implementation strategy will do for all projects" (Kottack 1991, 452) or that "a management technique or philosophy that is appropriate in one national culture is not necessarily appropriate in another" (Jreisat 1991, 667). However, let us assume that you approach your T&V project (or, indeed, any agricultural extension system) as a serious, enlightened, and experienced businessperson. Using only common sense (consisting perhaps of truisms), I believe that you will recommend to officials undertaking the T&V project (regardless of their culture or form of government) the following steps essential for political software development:

ESTABLISH COMMITMENT. Many projects fail simply because there is no commitment to them. This is especially true of foreign aid projects which are acceptable only because they bring with them foreign exchange and generate employment. This point is brought out in the wonderfully cynical remark of a West African agricultural official quoted by Siffin (1991, 10): "If the World Bank sends a livestock man, we shall have a livestock project. If the Bank sends a cotton specialist, we shall have a cotton project." Siffin goes on to point out that this country eventually got Bank funding for both livestock and cotton projects.

How serious governments are about T&V can be seen by their willingness to provide operational funds for their extension systems. While, ordinarily, there should be a ratio of one-third to two-thirds for operational funds to salaries, this ratio is seldom reached (Antholt 1994, 9). In Tamil Nadu, for example, 88 percent of its 1990/91 US $10 million extension budget went for salaries (Antholt 1992, 3). In Kenya, two thirds of extension workers complained about delays in reimbursements of claims and half about lack of transport (Bindlish and Evenson 1993, 9).

In Bangladesh's T&V project during the 1980s local councils that were given funds for agricultural extension work diverted these funds into non-agricultural activities (Ahsan ET AL. 1991). Because these councils were not interested in agriculture, the agricultural staff hired for this project seldom had adequate transport, accommodation, and other support services and facilities needed for their work. These councils, however, may have been somewhat justified in their reluctance to support agricultural extension work, according to a World Bank summary of the defects of the Bangladeshi extension service: "top-down recommendations, demonstrations with limited relevance, poor quality in subject matter specialists, lack of attention to economics and farming constraints, poor use of mass media and poor results with the contact farmer concept" (Purcell 1994, 20).

HIRE QUALIFIED EMPLOYEES. All the good bureaucracies, you can suggest, are meritocracies. Debates persist regarding recruitment systems (favoring specialists or generalists; closed or open entry); but all include a combination of rigorous entrance examinations, educational criteria, appropriate experience, and "intense socialization to internalize core civil service values" (Nunberg 1992, 21).

In the World Bank's review of 31 agricultural extension projects, staff quality was a major constraint in nearly all of them, particularly those that required large numbers of personnel (Purcell 1994, 32). Unqualified workers were most likely to be found in African T&V programs. In many cases, according to Cleaver (1993, 61–62), they "know little more than the farmers know." Their technical messages tend to be inapplicable and contradictory. As such, their advice becomes "noise" and is "often wisely ignored by farmers." However, when competent personnel are used for extension work, as in Kenya and Zimbabwe, an increasing number of farmers have benefited in expanding hybrid corn and crop husbandry.

ENCOURAGE TRAINING. More training is often the answer given by foreign donors to problems of administration; but it is frequently useless because of mismanagement, corruption, and mistaken policies. In Liberia, USAID and other donors funded for many years extensive training programs. Most of this effort was wasted because of the persistent patrimonial system. In Somalia, USAID staff discovered that civil servants were being paid so little that they had no incentive to take training seriously. In Mauritania, the Civil Service Ministry distributed scholarships to high school students for study abroad, based upon personal or patronage considerations, rather than the real technical needs of administration (Boyle 1986, 82).

In Ecuador, bureaucrats trained for rural development work had no desire to spend their lives in rural areas (Perlman 1989, 688). Thus they ended up in urban areas where they were least needed. Even when qualified staff stay in rural areas, the social distance between them and ordinary farmers may seriously reduce their authority and ability to provide assistance (Freeman and Lowdermilk 1991, 128).

In his review of the World Bank's experience with agricultural extension projects, Purcell (1994, 18, 32–33) notes that staff often were so deficient in basic education that training did not help them very much. Consequently, training programs were unable to ensure that front-line extension staff had sufficient knowledge of production systems and of relevant technology to be useful to farmers. Particularly in regard to subject matter specialists, the training "was often overly theoretical or too general" (Purcell 1994, 32–33). What was most needed was better training in communication theory and techniques.

Yet, training can eventually lead to progress. Phillips (1991a) noted, in regard to Nigeria, that training is poorly funded and unsystematic and that, those with training have no guarantee that their training will be respected or used. However, a more recent report on Nigeria's extension service (Cleaver 1993, 15) shows that, in combination with policy reform and other measures, those trained for this work can have a positive long-term impact on agricultural growth (with a 4–5 percent annual growth rate, 1986–1991). This indicates a great improvement over the Nigerian situation prior to 1980 when, according to Koehn (1991, 243), "most farmers had never met an agricultural extension worker."

HIRE ONLY ESSENTIAL EMPLOYEES. After independence, African bureaucracies became bloated. Nigeria, with its oil wealth, may be the most extreme example (as noted in Chapter 1), with the growth of the public sector from 200,000 in 1969 to two million in 1980 (Baker 1991, 356). However, much poorer states, such as The Gambia, doubled the size of its civil service between 1974 and 1982, and Ghana, increased its civil service by 14% each year between 1974 and 1984 (World Bank 1989, 57).

In regard to extension work, the overall numbers of personnel need to be reduced by over 50 percent, according to Antholt (1992, 18), based upon his study of this subject in many countries. For example, India's Secretary of Agriculture in 1989 listed over-manning as one of the principal issues facing India's agricultural research system (Antholt 1994, 9). Consequently, few Indian scientists that year even had as much as US $400 to carry out research.

Kenya successfully introduced T&V into 30 districts during the mid-1980s with World Bank financial assistance (Purcell, 1994, 24–25). However, it undermined this program by its policy of employing all agricultural school graduates. This increased the salary load in the service, causing difficulty in funding the recurrent costs of the program and providing adequate operational support. The lesson emerging from both the Indian and Kenyan experience is that agricultural research services should be kept "small, but smart" (Antholt 1994, 25).

INCREASE EFFICIENCY. The easiest way of facilitating agricultural extension work is to rely more heavily on modern communication technology. In Pakistan in 1988, the cost of reaching each farm family was estimated to be US $0.02 per radio message (Antholt 1992, 12). Kenya's extension services rely heavily upon radio programs (Bindlish and Evenson 1993, 14). According to surveys, about one-third of farmers listen to extension programs on the radio, and two-thirds of these listeners rated them to be highly useful. India has successfully used satellite television to reach wide audiences in remote areas. And where there is high enough literacy among rural people, radio and television can be combined with illustrated booklets, comics, and other print media.

Borrowing appropriate technology from foreign countries is another way to save money. Antholt (1994, 25) points out that Chile's success in the export of table grapes was largely built on technology from California. The linkage of agricultural research among scientists across national boundaries that went on during the colonial period (before nationalism discouraged this cooperation) might again be facilitated for this purpose. While there is indeed much international agricultural cooperation, supported by the World Bank, the United Nations, and MDCs, LDCs could do much more to encourage this process.

PAY ATTENTION TO MORALE. T&V agencies have clearly not escaped the typical problems of LDC bureaucracies. Ameur (1994, 5) writes that it is not uncommon "to find countries ending up with oversized, ill-equipped, cash-strapped, and inefficient extension services." Because scientists and front line agents spend much of their time "looking over their shoulders at headquarters, as well as depending on seniority for transfers and promotions, it is unrealistic to expect their their first loyalty will rest with their clients, particularly the small, marginal farmers" (Antholt 1994, 17).

Extension services have so far largely failed to help small farmers in LDCs and, particularly, agricultural women. In Africa, outside of a few countries, the majority of the rural poor earn less than $1 per person per day (Cleaver and Donavan 1995, 1). For example, in Malawi, where 70 percent of full-time farmers are women, "the undernutrition and poor health of women in rural areas is of particular significance" (Donavan 1994, 32). And in India, where 70 percent of the farm work is done by women, there is not much evidence that new agricultural knowledge is being effectively transferred to them (Antholt 1992, 15).

"Your employees are avaricious human beings," you can point out: "They want more pay and promotion. So, pay and promotion need to be tied to performance." In More Developed Countries (MDCs), farmers are increasingly expected to pay for extension services (Ameur 1994, 18–19). In Denmark, for example, farmers are charged by the hour for each visit to their household. This has meant that government funding of extension services has decreased from 37 percent in 1972 to 14 percent by 1991, with further cuts contemplated. In the Netherlands, the average share of extension services farmers are expected to pay will reach 50 percent by 2003, based upon the size of the farm, direct contributions for services, and taxes and levies on farm produce.

Turning to LDCs, there are a number of possibilities of tying pay to performance. The Kenya Tea Development Authority pays factory managers and staff partly on the basis of a cost-benefit analysis and published prices obtained in the London tea auctions (Salmen 1991). In Taiwan (see Chapter 7), local staff serving farmers are motivated simply because they are employed by the farmers (Freeman and Lowdermilk 1991, 128).

Based upon experience in the highlands of Ecuador, Ameur (1994, 16) suggests that "extension agents be allowed to share in the profits of joint farming enterprises established with groups of farmers." In China, where agricultural extension goes back 3–4,000 years, Farmer Technicians are typically compensated, based upon 20 percent of the value of the crop above the agreed target, with their pay and bonuses subject to being docked as a result of poor technical recommendations or nonsupply of timely inputs. In Tunisia an increasing number of extension agents and veterinarians are establishing private practices. In Brazil, as of 1988, there were over 2,000 private consulting firms largely catering to the commercialized livestock sector (Umali-Deininger 1996, 8).

In Costa Rica, farmers are being given vouchers for individual and group technical assistance to be delivered by private extensionists. Under a Nicaraguan pilot project, beneficiaries receive 15 vouchers per year, 40 percent of which are to be used for group visits and the remaining 60 percent for individual visits (Umali-Deininger 1996, 13). The providers of technical assistance can either be a single individual or a legally established organization (including non-profit NGOs and private-for-profit firms).

Because African livestock owners are willing to pay for veterinary services if these services are useful, Cleaver (1993, 68) suggests that extension services, relying upon the private sector, be encouraged wherever possible. However, this is easier to do to the extent that farmers and ranchers are educated and organized, the infrastructure and economy are good, and there is access to capital. Unfortunately, the public sector is often too weak to support a strong private sector. In many countries, Umali-Deininger (1996, 14) points out, "private sector capacity has been continuously suppressed."

In Africa, foreign donors have often had difficulty maintaining cooperatives and other rural organizations that were well-established during the colonial period. Consequently, African farmers are seldom well enough organized to pay for, motivate, and control an independent agricultural extension service. In Uganda, for example, more than half of the nation's cooperative societies ceased functioning during the 1970s because of poor financial health, unavailable spare parts, excessive governmental interference, and dangerous travel conditions. In Ghana by 1989, less than 10 percent of the registered cooperatives existing in the early 1960s were in operation (Porvali 1993, 2) In Kenya, outside of the coffee-growing areas, cooperative unions were practically defunct by the end of 1989 (Lindberg 1993, 16). The most recent evidence indicates that "there is a resurgence of interest in cooperatives in Cameroon, Tanzania, and Uganda, but not elsewhere" (Cleaver and Donavan 1995, 15).

In any case, motivation requires more than simply higher pay or promotion. There must be an increased dedication to public service, combining an appeal to self-interest with one to mutual interest (going back to the multi-diminsional conception of politics presented in the Introduction). Otherwise, incentive systems can easily fail. For example, in Malawi, T&V services tend to go primarily to the less-than-thirty percent of farmers affiliated to creditworthy groups (Purcell 1994, 59). Consequently, the objective of providing services to the majority of smallholders has not been met.

To motivate the delivery of agricultural services to impoverished farmers, it may be necessary to turn from private-for-profit arrangements to the private non-profit sector, including NGOs, universities, commodity boards, foundations, and other non-commercial associations. The Mexican government has attempted to make good use of both sectors by maintaining public sector extension services for small farmers, while shifting larger-scale farmers to fee-for service extension (Umali-Deininger 1996, 12).

ENCOURAGE COMPETITION. Larry Salmen (1991) gives useful examples of governments stimulating competition between public and private sector organizations. In Chile, for example, a voucher system allowed private institutions to compete effectively with municipal schools. These vouchers were targeted to low income households and could be transferred to both public and private schools willing to provide free education on the basis of payments per student enrolled. Largely as a result of this system, enrollment for private schools more than doubled between 1980 and 1986. It also enhanced competition among private and public schools, thereby increasing the quality of education available to the poor.

An increasing number of countries, including the United States, offer vouchers for such services as education, housing, transportation, and health care, previously provided exclusively by the public sector. Where citizens possess adequate market information, competing suppliers exist, and proper standards are set and enforced, this approach tends to work well (OECD 1987, 55). Some of the advantages of encouraging public sector/private sector competition include decreased administrative costs and greater responsiveness to consumer concerns. "Our public sector can learn to compete, or it can stagnate and shrink, until the only customers who use public services are those who cannot afford an alternative" (Osborne and Gaebler 1992, 107).

Cleaver (1993, 60) strongly advocates giving contracts in Africa to private agricultural research institutions and PVOs, encouraging them to compete with public agencies. In Zimbabwe, most fruit, vegetable, sugar, poultry, and livestock research is carried out by private companies; and Zambia is now moving in this direction.

A primary result of this approach is to treat farmers as "partners," rather than merely beneficiaries. Consequently, "private traders have succeeded in providing a market for farmers in accessible localities, improving food supplies, and stabilizing food prices in urban areas" (Cleaver and Donavan 1995, 11). Based upon the experience of Chile with the use of private consulting firms or NGOs for the provision of extension services, Antholt (1992, 18) writes: "The exact form is not so important, but the bottom line must put farmers in the driver's seat as far as the extension services provided to them is concerned."

Yet, some caution regarding privatization is also appropriate. Ameur (1994, 14) points out that setting up sufficient private entities to cover a large number of users has often been difficult and time-consuming. Insofar as the private sector is essentially driven by profit, it may be uninterested in certain categories of users. Indeed in Africa, private traders have avoided areas where the costs of marketing are excessively high. While private organizations may provide highly professional, economically efficient, and effective extension services, Purcell (1994, 38–39) concludes "that some public services for the private good of smallholder families are likely to be needed and justified in the foreseeable future on economic and poverty alleviation grounds."

Where there is a high percentage of small and subsistence farmers, full privatization of extension services may be neither practical nor desirable. Even in Chile, which has gone further than most other Latin American countries toward privatization of extension services, there has been disappointment with the result (Umali-Deininger 1996, 14). Consequently, the government has had to return to the public sector to target extension services to the small and marginal farmers.

DELEGATE RESPONSIBILITY. In the public sector, as in the private sector, employees are useful only insofar as they are given responsibility to do their work. The more responsibility you can give them, the more useful they are. Old fashioned scientific management viewed workers as "pieces of machinery," with limited and strictly defined functions. Common sense, together with more sophisticated literature, suggests allowing and encouraging employees (and administrative units) to do as much as they are capable of doing.

Unfortunately, as noted in the next chapter, LDC leaders are reluctant to delegate responsibility. In Senegal, for example, very little is allowed to happen until approved by the Office of the Presidency: "The President of the Republic, as head of state in Senegal's parliamentary system, is responsible not only for policy guidance and direction, but also for myriad administrative details such as the approval, appointment, promotion, reclassification and retirement of all civil servants down to the level of department director" (Rondinelli and Minis 1990, 451). Regarding Guatemala, J. L Weaver observed in 1973: "Everything rises to the top; the top does not delegate and thus cannot fix responsibility, adding: "compliance, not performance, is the standard for evaluation" (Quoted in Hopkins 1991, 701). Similar observations continue to be made in most LDCs.

While Management by Objectives (MBO) is quite new in a number of MDCs, it has been practiced in Sweden for centuries, using semi-autonomous agencies (Nunberg 1992, 13). The managers of these agencies are held responsible for efficient use of inputs and the achievement of performance targets. At the same time, the ministers to whom they report remain ultimately responsible for performance outcomes.

A similar approach is now used in New Zealand in regard to personnel management (Nunberg 1992, 17). Here a central agency is assigned only a quality control and oversight role, allowing government departments to handle most aspects of personnel recruitment, training, classification, and control.

In regard to T&V, Antholt (1992, 17–18) suggests that the central administration take a supportive, rather than a directive role. Under this arrangement, extension departments could be encouraged to develop cooperative and/or contractual agreements with local groups or NGOs, allowing these groups to hire and support extension agents but sharing in the costs of salaries, training, pensions, and other expenses. As extension services are increasingly provided by the private sector, the government's role is "to provide the appropriate regulatory framework to ensure fair competition and maintain quality standards" (Umali-Deininger 1996, 3).

MAINTAIN SUPERVISION. As you delegate responsibility, you must improve your supervisory capacity. A good example of successful supervision is South Korea's performance evaluation system described in Chapter 9. New Zealand has introduced a participative system to evaluate all employee levels, using performance agreements between departments and ministers (Nunberg 1992, 37). This is considered responsible for strengthening accountability throughout the administration.

In regard to agricultural extension work, Cleaver (1993, 63) points out that, unless higher level managers frequently visit farmers' fields, there is no guarantee that extension agents will even interact with farmers, much less really help them. Without appropriate supervision, deficiencies cannot be identified and remedied. On the other hand, supervision can be done so inefficiently as to be counterproductive. In Guinea during the 1980s, the Ministry of Agriculture required its field units to go through nineteen steps (often needing as much as six months) to purchase a tool for rural development (White 1988, 20).

To be effective, contractors must be as carefully supervised as employees. As noted earlier, Chile has shifted in recent years towards the commercial delivery of extension programs. However, problems resulting from high costs, deteriorating service quality, and poor feedback mechanisms have undermined these programs (Umali-Deininger 1996, 12, 14). Consequently, the government is now intensifying its efforts to require firms seeking contracts to meet technical and professional staffing criteria and to be effectively monitored by a designated public agency. Based upon the Chilean experience, the Nicaraguan government, in its new World Bank-supported voucher program, "includes accreditation of technical assistance providers, the establishment of a selection criteria, and monitoring and evaluation of the program" (Umali-Deininger 1996, 13).

While the importance of supervision is increasingly recognized, LDCs continue to neglect it. In his review of World Bank extension projects, Purcell (1994, 33) concludes that monitoring was weakly developed. While some effort was made to monitor the mechanics of extension operations affecting credit, investment, or input delivery, there was inadequate attention paid to the actual adoption of recommended technologies. Moreover, there was very little use made of the results of adoption surveys.

PROMOTE LEGITIMACY. In irrigation projects, Freeman and Lowdermilk (1991, 124) point out, "Farmers require and respect solid, enforceable agreements which provide the basis for trust and genuine cooperation. . . ." Unfortunately, the legitimacy of rules for allocating water and maintaining infrastructure are often undermined by official favoritism, volatile local disputes, inadequate staffing, uncertain service, uncollected revenues, and failure to enforce agreements. However, community-based irrigation systems tend to work better in arid areas where water is desperately needed, suggesting that, when communities develop a consensus on what must be done and on enforcement arrangements, they will respond to requirements for irrigation maintenance, water sharing, and cost recovery (Cernea 1991b, 369).

The engendering of legitimacy is clearly an evolutionary process under which an activity is recognized as valuable enough to cause participants to promote and protect it. A soil conservation project in the Dodoma region of Tanzania (the "Kondoa Eroded Area") supports a combination of popular participation, training, development of acceptable practices, and a long-term educational campaign (Blackwell, Goodwillie, and Webb 1991). Based upon this approach, the government has been able to temporarily clear cattle from the highland area and encourage widespread tree planting. Its actions have thus become enforceable.

In Uganda, where field staff in extension work were paid during much of the 1980s practically nothing (U.S. $2.50–5.00 a month), the government was successful in using respected local farmers for purposes of agricultural innovation and leadership. This practice was responsible for the success story reported on by Tukahirwa and Veit (1992). Farmers in the Nyarumembo Subparish of soutwestern Uganda, who cultivate steep hillslopes, now follow "some of the best soil-conservation practices in sub-Saharan Africa" (IBID., 1).

While terracing has been carried out for many years, beginning with colonial pressure during the 1930s, it was disrupted by Uganda's political and economic turmoil. The soil was overcropped, livestock were allowed to cause damage, terracing was neglected, conflicts arose, pests became more of a problem, harvests were poor, and famine emerged.

What seems to have turned around the situation was the government's willingness to support a highly regarded community elder as the agricultural officer. While there was nothing charismatic about this local leader (as Weberian theory suggests might be needed), he was clearly respected because of his expertise, access to external assistance, and, above all, diplomacy: "The officer's skills include listening, negotiating, mediating, and strategic planning" (IBID., 24).

The agricultural officer used his skills to persuade the local chief to close Nyarumembi Hill to all agricultural and livestock activity for five years (1984–89). Those allowed to reuse the hill had to conform to strict terracing and other soil-conservation requirements and be willing to accept fines and imprisonment for violations. However, farmers became so cooperative that few had to be punished.

While new central government initiatives to toughen soil-conservation by-laws and strengthen local administration were useful, the recognition of the importance of soil-conservation gave legitimacy to the implementation efforts of local authorities. "This internalization, coupled with the appropriateness and effectiveness of terracing, suggests that these soil conservation practices are sustainable and that they will continue" (IBID., 22).

EXPAND TWO-WAY FLOWS OF COMMUNICATION. "Public management, to some degree, has become a popular catchword for many different approaches to administration" (Kettl 1990, 413). Inasmuch as this is a recognition of the importance of leadership in administration, this is appropriate. Yet, as Salmen (1991) points out, the success stories in development administration depend upon LISTENING—to subordinates and also to the people.

A good example of the importance of what Salmen calls "qualitative research" was a World Bank agricultural project in central Zaire, using respected Non-Governmental Organizations (NGOs). These NGOs discovered that the major concern of farmers was the poor condition of roads, rather than the improved seeds or fertilizer provided by the project. This concern stemmed from the dependence of farmers on owners of powerful vehicles needed for these roads, giving these owners most of the profits. Farmers were thus discouraged from growing more food by transportation problems - a finding that probably would have escaped bureaucrats who were primarily interested in narrowly conceived project objectives.

A T&V project can never be successful unless the needs and concerns of farmers are fully taken into account. While farmers tend to appreciate on-farm technology demonstrations, they are seldom involved in problem definition, problem solving, and extension planning, Purcell (1994, 32) points out, adding: "In the rare cases where participation was emphasized, results were very positive." Because of poor linkages between researchers, extension staff, and farmers, research institutions often fail to develop or adapt technology which is appropriate to the constraints and potentials of farm households. Consequently, the World Bank is increasingly encouraging extension agencies to offer "menus" of options to farmers, allowing them to decide what is in their best interest.

Cleaver (1993, 64) suggests, in regard to African extension work, that much more attention will have to be paid to women's needs because a growing percentage of farm household heads (e.g., 70% in the Congo) are women, as men leave for urban and industrial work. Thus, the World Bank and other donor organizations are encouraging T&V agencies to use more women as extension agents and contact points, amounting in some cases to half of personnel, according to Antholt (1992, 18). Kenya has responded by progressively incorporating women into its extension service. The effort of these female agents to work with women's groups has had a substantial positive impact (Purcell 1994, 25).

DEVELOP CONFLICT-RESOLUTION PROCEDURES. Every organization needs procedures for overcoming conflict and reconciling diverse interests. As we move from microadministration (referring to a single business or agency) to macroadministration (affecting an entire nation or sector), acceptable arrangements for facilitating coordination and dealing with conflict become even more essential. Time and again, we see bottlenecks to development stemming from an absence of such arrangements.

This was clearly illustrated in the case of the Bangladesh T&V program (Ahsan ET AL. 1991). Because of a conflict between the Ministry of Finance and the Department of Agricultural Extension, regarding an acceptable method of paying custom duties on needed imports, the World Bank had to temporarily suspend project funding.

In reporting on the success and failure of African integrated rural development projects, Montgomery (1991, 516) points out that "when different agencies were expected to share the operating costs of integrated operations, public-sector managers were rarely able to do so effectively." This seemed particularly the case when there were no coordinating mechanisms in place or when international donors dropped out or changed roles. Confused mission assignments and inadequate program design always intensified organizational rivalries. Managers from private companies or parastatal organizations, on the other hand, usually could cooperate when there was an economic incentive to do so and widespread commitment to implementing agricultural development programs.

CONCLUSIONS

The literature of public administration, B. Guy Peters (1991, 396) points out, "provides a much better catalog of why things do not work than of how they can be made to work." However, following his suggestion that "the simplest ideas are often the most successful" (1991, 397), I believe that, in your role as a World Bank consultant, you can at least advocate these commonsensical or "platitudinous" steps in regard to a T&V project.

These steps lead, not to some ideal-type "formal organization" that certain administrative theorists continue to look for (Jreisat 1991a, 18), but to a high quality of political software that I see as more essential. If you agree, we can say to those debating the usefulness of T&V that their evaluations ("Good Idea," "Bad Idea," or "Mixed Bag") are meaningless in the absence of these political software considerations.

Antholt (1994, 15) makes this same point, without my terminology, noting that it is the persistent problems of T&V, ("lack of relevant technology, poorly trained and motivated staff, insufficient operational resources, etc.") rather than the principles of T&V, that underlie the continued disappointment with T&V and other extension systems. Purcell (1994, 36) adds that many of the principles of the T&V management system have become widely accepted as useful extension practices. Unfortunately, because of the various weaknesses noted, particularly "an established research culture which was not accustomed to being responsive to farmers' needs in planning research programs," these principles are seldom adequately implemented.

Returning to our political elasticity theory, we should be able to see how the steps normally taken by enlightened businessmen/women can be linked to both the "rubber band" and the "balloon" metaphors put forward in the Introduction. As leaders become (a) more influential and (b) more willing to delegate responsibility, they also become (c) more capable of monitoring progress and correcting problems without undermining morale. At the same time, followers become more loyal, cooperative, and creative.

In the process of improving the quality of political software, an organization gains a problem-solving capacity, allowing it to become self-correcting. Thus, we need not worry too much about the particular "political hardware" (methods, procedures, structures, etc.) used because its defects will eventually be eliminated or made less harmful.

Readers may object that the steps I advocate, even if recognized as commonsensical, may be too idealistic for the realities of most LDCs. While I agree that the attainment of political elasticity must be gradual, I believe that the process begins with acknowledging the importance of political software. For an amusing example of political software in action, the Easy Toilet Society of Bihar, India was reported to be successful, partly because of its appropriate technology (simply designed water-sealed latrines), partly because of government support, but mostly because it is a society built upon mutual obligation, responsibility, and respect (Calibrone 1985).

Agricultural development has gone much farther in Asia than in Africa. Indonesia and Bangladesh more than doubled their production of rice between 1960 and 1990; and India and China more or less tripled grain production during this period (Antholt 1994, 3). While agricultural extension services are not entirely responsible for this, they have clearly made an important contribution. "Although methodological problems have clouded the measurement of the benefits from agricultural extension, the debate has centered more on the magnitude of returns generated rather than its positive contribution" (Umali-Deininger 1996, 1).

William and Charlotte Wiser (1971, 250–252) described the impact of the agricultural extension process in Karimpur, an ordinary village of North India. Here, remarkable agricultural progress was made when members of the cooperative society were assisted by a trusted Village

Level Worker, using new seeds developed by a nearby agricultural university, combined with better irrigation and fertilizer.

World Bank evaluations reveal that half of completed rural development projects in Africa fail to show an adequate economic rate of return (World Bank 1989, 27; Cleaver 1993, 25–26). While all sorts of reasons can be found for this failure (infertile soils, erratic rainfall, poor roads, mistaken policies, price distortions, macroeconomic instability, dysfunctional legal services, lack of clear title to land, inadequate storage and processing facilities, etc.), they can usually be linked to lack of governmental seriousness about development.

In regard to T&V in Africa, Cleaver (1993, 59) emphasizes: "that no agricultural research system in Africa is up to present Asian standards, and that only nine systems meet minimum acceptable standards, despite large annual expenditures." For example, in a project in Benin, "the food crop extension suffered from poor research back-up, insufficient technology and lack of attention to production economics" (Purcell 1994, 58). The unwillingness of African governments to invest enough effort to produce national agricultural master plans or enough funds for operations and training indicates lack of commitment. Cleaver (1993, 110), therefore, concludes that "creation of commitment with borrowing countries" is the World Bank's top priority in agricultural development and that it "should not go forward with major sector programs without this commitment." This means that you, as a practitioner, will also have to take into consideration the suggestions presented in Chapter 10.

Moreover, T&V, even at its best, will not improve rural living conditions unless the factors earlier mentioned facilitate its performance. In the Central African Republic, for example, the T&V extension was effectively provided by a parastatal to increase cotton production; but this was undermined by the collapse of cotton prices (Purcell, 1994, 58). What was really needed was a program devoted to crop diversification. Unfortunately, the country's leaders were not sophisticated or interested enough to recognize and deal with this problem.

In Malawi, where nearly two-thirds of the rural population are below the poverty line, half of rural households are at least two kilometers away from a water source. Moreover, there is virtually no supply of electricity to rural areas (whereas more than 80 percent of India's villages are reached with electricity). The impact of such inadequate infrastructure on women's time, energy, and health is particularly severe, considering that 70 percent of Malawi's full-time farmers are women (Donavan 1994, 31). Consequently, even a good T&V system is likely to be ineffective under these circumstances.

We can, however, end this chapter on a positive note. Harvey (1987, 1) points out that, when these countries (e.g. Botswana and Malawi) get serious about their problems, they can improve agricultural productivity while taking various painful measures, including: "an increase of several hundred percent in the official cost of foreign exchange, major cuts in public services such as health and education, large cuts in real wages, and the loss of large numbers of private- and public-sector jobs."

Miller and Yeager (1993, 137) write about the many problems facing small farmers in Kenya's rural areas, resulting in the fact that: "economic conditions in the rural areas have not advanced from the early 1980s, when subsistence farmers received less than 3 percent of the income gained by commercial producers." Yet, they also point out (p. 131) that, "on a per hectare basis, smaller farms tend to be more productive than large ones in arable locations. . . ."

T&V may be partly responsible for this productivity, according to a detailed evaluation of its performance in Kenya. While there is much to criticize here, "the present T&V-based system in Kenya is contributing to production, at least in the short run" (Bindlish and Evenson 1993, 30). If T&V can work in a country where 41 percent of the rural population are estimated to be below the poverty line, you, as a practitioner, can at least hope that it can work elsewhere.

Alas, even this cautious conclusion may be misleading. According to an informant, declining funding for Kenya's T&V, as of 1995, (particularly for vehicles and fuel) prevented staff from reaching farmers. More effective assistance, including advice, credit, seeds, and other needed inputs, was then being provided by those in the horticulture export business. Yet, this too depended on a high quality of political software. As a result, horticultural exports grew in 1995 by 89%, full-time employment, by 30%, and temporary employment, by 58% (Development Alternatives 1996).

CHAPTER 4

Linking Decentralization to Centralization

INTRODUCTION

All of us who have been in the academic world want the freedom to teach our classes as we feel they should be taught—selecting textbooks, preparing syllabi, and conducting classes as we have been trained to do. But our autonomy as teachers is dependent upon an "enabling environment" within which we can operate, including appropriate offices, classrooms, schedules, compensation, libraries, bookstores, record keeping, etc. As such, we work within a web of relationships, each strand of which can be manipulated in various, often subtle ways. We beg for assistance as much as we beg for freedom, and this need for assistance controls our sphere of independence. Yet, the system is ultimately "elastic," as explained in earlier chapters.

If we taught within a typical Francophone African university, as described by Assie-Lumumba (1993), we might have some degree of independence as teachers, but such classroom freedom is likely to be useless. Buildings are in poor condition and are overcrowded; libraries, bookstores, laboratories, and student facilities (such as dormitories and cafeterias) are practically useless; records are mismanaged; there is no meaningful academic credit system; salaries are poor and uncertain; students have no say in what they study and are often on strike; exams are difficult to give because registration is vague and degrees are not respected.

The situation presented in the 1993 Assie-Lumumba World Bank report is so dismal that one wonders why teachers even bother to teach under these conditions and students, to come to class. The answer can be found in a 1996 article by Nelson. In a typical African university, every aspect is dominated by patronage considerations: hiring, promotion, assignments, salaries, perquisites, etc. Students attend and staff members teach, not for the purpose of education, but to participate in the patronage system (despite its meagre and uncertain nature), funded to a large extent by foreign aid.

The patronage system, as explained in the Nelson article, is a highly inelastic one. While students and faculty are powerfully controlled by patronage opportunities and the threat of being denied them, the system is incapable of promoting education. Students can hardly pretend to be learning anything beyond the fact that this is simply another step in the patronage ladder, with the next step hopefully being a bureaucratic job, within which they can perpetuate the system.

In asserting that decentralization and centralization are intertwined, I seem to be saying something that, on the one hand, is commonsensical, and on the other, is contrary to ordinary language. Our linguistic inability to break the "centralization-decentralization dichotomy" was suggested many years ago by Fesler (1965, 537) in noting that "we have neither a term that embraces the full continuum between the two poles, nor a term that embraces the middle range where centralizing and decentralizing tendencies are substantially in balance." The objective of this chapter is to overcome this dichotomy, using political elasticity theory.

The gap in organization theory emphasized by McGregor (1960) between Theory X, stressing strong management and bureaucratic control (i.e., scientific management), and Theory Y, maximizing self-control and self-direction of employees (advocated by humanistic management) remains unresolved (as noted in the Introduction). Yet, those writing about microadministration (referring to organizations or businesses) tend to more readily accept the relationship of centralization to decentralization than those concerned with macroadministration (particularly within large national or federal systems). "The excellent companies are both centralized and decentralized," Peters and Waterman (1982, 14) assert, adding: "For the most part . . . they have pushed autonomy down to the shop floor or product development team. On the other hand, they are fanatically centralized around the few core values they hold dear."

Using the Peters-Waterman analysis, Harold Williams (1986, 19) points out that in American public administration, there is too often a "tight-loose" culture: "Federal employees are given little opportunity to exercise initiative, but there is a great tolerance of ineptitude." Instead, what we need to strive for is a framework within which employees are given enough freedom to do outstanding work and at the same time, enough control to prevent misuse of this freedom. Inasmuch as such a framework exists in practice, rather than theory, there is an analytical problem to be solved, which is, of course, an objective of this book.

SOURCES OF CONFUSION

Because this chapter is primarily concerned with macroadministration, we need to look at the confusion engendered by the unwillingness of scholars to understand the assertion here presented, that "you cannot have decentralization without centralization, and vice-versa." In doing so, we will require the reader to shift attention from More Developed Countries (MDCs) to Less Developed Countries (LDCs), much as one would in watching a tennis match, from one side of the net to the other. Examples of this confusion in the macroadministrative literature include the following:

THE CONCEPT OF FEDERALISM. Having studied under three leading experts on federalism (Herman Finer at the University of Chicago, K.C. Wheare at Oxford, and William Livingston at Yale), I assumed, when I eventually received my Ph.D. during the 1960s, that there was more decentralization under federal than unitary systems. However, teaching of comparative urban studies led me to agree with Rufus Davis (1978) that, knowing that a country is "federal," give us no indication about the actual independence or vitality of state and local governments. In other words, the term has no operational meaning, even though it may have symbolic or emotional significance for those, such as the Canadian scholar LaSelva (1993), who insist that federalism is "a way of life."

Those who have done comparative case studies having to do with the implementation of policies (affecting, for example, health care, housing, urban planning, or community development) do not find that the techniques used in MDCs are any different or more effective in unitary, as against federal systems (see, for example Heidenheimer, Heclo, and Adams 1990). In health services, each of the OECD countries has evolved various mixtures of private incentives, public subsidies, insurance systems, tax rebates, block funding, and cost containment policies (Gray 1987). "All regulators," Day (1988, 49) points out, "are constantly juggling to achieve the right balance between coercion and enlisting co-operation, between seeking to establish a bargaining relationship with the regulated while yet avoiding regulatory capture."

In comparing British and German governmental action to stimulate urban economic development and to cushion the effect of declining industries, Bennett and Krebs (1991, 65) find the same packages of tax incentives, labor subsidies, grants and loans employed. While there are different types and sources of incentives and disincentives used, these seem, not so much affected by the nature of the decentralization system, as by the need to take into account a variety of factors, including personal preferences, business considerations, population size, financial resources, and economic problems.

I do not want to disregard the importance of the American federal system of government, particularly the Tenth Amendment. Certainly the American Secretary of Housing and Urban Development might look with envy at the power of the Dutch Minister of Housing, Physical Planning and Environmental Planning who can, not only supervise public sector and private sector use of land, but also control local zoning boards; force neighboring jurisdictions to cooperate; change boundaries to facilitate planning and equalize taxation; or prevent businesses and wealthy individuals from playing off one jurisdiction against another (Hamnett 1985).

Without denying the American governmental barriers to effective urban planning, we can argue that they stem more from prevailing American political thought than from the Constitution. Such manifestations, as excessive devotion to uncontrolled market forces, hostility to powerful government, racial and ethnic prejudices, disregard for land and the environment, and enthusiasm for the automobile, could fade in time.

In Chapter 6, I attribute part of the blame for the American urban malaise to systemic corruption. Nevertheless, an older generation of Americans can point to the "can do" spirit of the New Deal, responsible for the Greenbelt Towns (still affordable and desirable places to live), and the Tennessee Valley Authority, which raised per-capita income in the region from half of the national average to parity (Leiserson 1983, 150). There is thus nothing to prevent the Federal Government from returning to its responsibility for impoverished communities.

While the American federal government may be currently weak in regard to urban planning, "on balance the restrictions the United States has placed on corporate conduct affecting public health, safety, and amenity are at least as strict as and in many cases stricter than those adopted by other capitalist nations" (Vogel 1986, 267). Moreover, American urban officials seeking financial assistance for public housing, highway construction, and disadvantaged youth can feel just as frustrated or tightly constrained by central government policies and requirements as, let us say, their British counterparts (see Rapp and Patitucci 1977).

L. J. Sharpe (1979, 9) points out that, until recently, the vast majority of social scientists in Western democracies assumed "that society and the state were becoming more centralized, more homogenized, more metropolitanized, and more integrated." This would naturally follow from the emergence of the welfare state. Insofar as federalism is incompatible with socialism and the welfare state, it would have to disappear, according to Harold Laski (1939). Gunlicks (1986, 188), writing about the German federal system, and LaSelva (1993, 220), writing about Canadian federalism, see the welfare state as undermining decentralization.

Simeon (1986, 460), however, suggests that the traditional centralist-decentralist dichotomy is no longer relevant to such federal systems as Canada insofar as administration is increasingly both decentralized and centralized. For example, one or more levels of government have established special-purpose corporations to undertake land-use planning in every major Canadian city (Kierman 1990, 70). They operate within an urban intergovernmental web, affected by a coordinated system of federal, provincial, and local funds and controls.

As such, Canadian urban planners might reject even the terminology of "sovereignty versus autonomy under federalism" presented by Lakoff (1994). By avoiding the confusion engendered by such legalistic terminology, we recognize decentralization as simply "intergovernmental relations," including various shared power models (Agranoff 1994). In many respects, local and regional governments have become more important in unitary as well as federal systems without reducing central control. In Sweden, for example, only about 44 percent of public sector employees worked for municipal and regional governments in 1927; by 1987, nearly 80 percent did so (Wallin 1991, 99). This leads Wallin (1991, 119) to conclude that "the Swedish experience clearly shows that the economic problems of the nation as a whole cannot be tackled without paying close attention to local government in the decisions that must be made."

How decentralization works in practice in Sweden in regard to child care is described by Gormley and Peters (1992). To receive national grants, providers must conform to agreed-upon community plans, but the planning process and the supervision are done in a cooperative environment. "To enter the world of Swedish politics and policy," Heclo and Madsen (1987, 21) write, "is to enter a small, ingrown realm of group decisionmaking, in which a professional class of politicians, administrators, and interest group functionaries must constantly expect to keep dealing with one-another." This same situation prevails in the federal systems of Canada and Australia.

Turning to LDCs, we also find no operational differences between federal and unitary systems, but the reasons for this have to do with the fact that centralizing tendencies are simultaneously too powerful and too weak. On the one hand, national leaders frequently see decentralization as a source of disunity and disloyalty. On the other hand, by so doing, they prevent development from taking place at local and regional levels. In Latin America, for example, as explained by Borja (1992, 133): "the low level and fragmented nature of socio-economic development and the shallow penetration of the state into society are at one and the same time the cause and consequence of the weakness of local government."

While many LDCs have constitutionally established federal systems, few allow their states or provinces much authority to raise financial resources or to exercise decision-making power. "Thus, in federal countries as disparate as Mexico and Nigeria, central governments clearly dominate allocation decisions at the state-level" (Silverman 1992, 23). In India, for example, the constitution is increasingly seen as nothing more than a useless "piece of parchment," with the federal form as envisaged given short shrift (Tummala 1992, 553). Generalizing about LDCs, Bahl and Linn (1992, 402) find no evidence that subnational governments are given more fiscal powers under federal than under unitary systems.

Because there is so little real decentralization in LDCs, the so-called "four D's" of decentralization (deconcentration, delegation, devolution, and debureaucratization), pointed out by Hasan (1992, 802), have hardly any meaning. In many countries, governors and mayors are appointed, rather than elected. But even when they are elected, it is often within a one-party system. In Francophone Africa, for example, municipal elections are so controlled by monopolistic political parties that "the people do not really choose their representative, they simply ratify the choices made by political authorities" (Attahi 1997, 174). Consequently, they do not identify with those they elect.

Under single party control, the public is seldom able to make a distinction among national, regional, and local officials. Since at the same time the salaries and decision-making authority of officials also stem largely from the central government, it is difficult to see any difference between what is derived from above (as delegated authority) and what emerges from below (referring to devolution). As explained by Attahi (1997, 175), in regard to Francophone Africa, local administration has adapted to the demands of a centralized "patrimonial system," under which political survival takes priority over effective government.

In many countries, one can hardly speak about "debureaucratization" when there is no effective bureaucracy insofar as officials at all levels are poorly paid, trained, and supervised. In the case of Tanzania, for example, Kulaba (1989, 228) writes about the country being "over-governed," with higher administrative officials duplicating the actions of regional and district officers, but also "lawless," when these same officials abrogate local by-laws and regulations. (The Nigerian case study presented in Chapter 1 illustrates this situation.)

THE DIVISION OF RESPONSIBILITY. If the reader agrees with the assertion here presented, linking decentralization to centralization, it follows that many of the questions frequently raised in the literature as to the proper level at which a function should be discharged and paid for are meaningless. In saying this, I include such questions as the following: "What should be the powers and capabilities of local government in modern states?" (Page and Goldsmith 1987, 1); "What patterns of shared and separated governmental roles are appropriate?" (Stenberg 1984, 86); Is a single-tier system of unitary all-purpose authorities more decentralized than a complex (or multi-tiered) system of authorities with coordinate jurisdictions? (Smith 1985, 90); and "Do central grants increase or decrease local autonomy?" (Boyne 1993, 94). I also consider such value-judgment questions as the following to be nonsensical: "Is centralization or decentralization the best for developing countries?" (Huque 1986, 80).

The "marble cake" analogy used by Elazar (1965) and Grodzins (1966) to describe American cooperative federalism is also used by scholars writing about France, Japan, and many other MDCs. Despite a general recognition that each function of government entails a linkage of government from every level, Ashford (1980, 22) notes that local governments in the welfare state are embedded in a much more complex network of political and economic relationships than most analysts realize. Consequently, Keating (1991, 56), in his book on comparative urban politics, suggests that it is "necessary to speak of an intergovernmental system of greater or lesser complexity," rather than simply "center and locality" in understanding the handling of any problem. "The finely meshed institutional network and the multitude of paths of communication that characterize the modern welfare state guarantee this interconnection" (Wallin 1991, 118).

Central government grants can, of course, be coercive. In Norway, for example, Kjellberg (1981, 154) refers collectively to the nearly 100 different grants of various types as "the golden whip." Yet, these grants are also looked upon as providing opportunity as well as control. Above all, they facilitate a constant reshaping of tasks here among levels of government.

Local government officials and organizations, in an effort to improve the programs they care about, frequently appeal to central government politicians and administrators for, not only financial assistance, but also technical assistance and supervision. Power (1987), for example, in writing about the problems of British public housing, complained that, unless the central government provides better inspections and more enforceable standards of housing management, council housing will continue to deteriorate. A similar situation exists in Sweden. Although Swedes are committed to local government, they are less concerned with "who governs" than the quality of government (Jones 1993, 129).

In MDCs, there is a constant process of delegating authority (even mandating responsibility), not only to various levels of government, but also to non-governmental organizations (NGOs), interest groups, professional associations, non-profit organizations, state owned or controlled enterprises (called in Britain, "quangos" or quasi-autonomous non-governmental organizations), special purpose corporations, businesses, neighborhood or grass-roots organizations, etc. While European governments may appear highly centralized, their central governments decreasingly carry out public services, preferring them to remain the responsibility of subordinate subdivisions and units. This explains the upward trend in the proportion of local expenditure to total public expenditure in most MDCs (Sharpe 1979, 31–32).

In Britain, the central government is entirely dependent on local governments for housing, health, education, police, etc. (Goldsmith and Norton 1983). However, much of the work is actually carried out by the private sector or publicly supported interest groups, such as the building societies which account for 80 percent of home purchases (Boddy 1981).

The fact that the implementation of British national programs is done in a decentralized way is a cause of confusion in the literature. For example, if one read only THE ECONOMIST, one might assume that decentralization has almost disappeared here. The May 4, 1996 issue (p. 60) contains the following statement: "Since the Tories came to power in 1979, they have done their damnedest to exterminate local councils." In the August 2nd, 1997 issue (p. 43), it was noted: "So long as nearly 90% of councils' revenues come from central government, local government will be something of a sham whoever is in charge."

It is certainly true that the British central government has been heavyhanded, imposing an uncollectable and unpopular poll tax under Prime Minister Thatcher, which eventually had to be withdrawn (see Ashford 1989 and Carmichael 1994). The fact that the Greater London Council was eliminated in 1986 (to be restored under Prime Minister Blair) undermined efforts to develop a comprehensive approach to metropolitan problems. According to Drohan (1996, A8), "the tangled planning shows up in more congestion, more pollution, shorter tempers and a bewildered population unsure of whom to complain to when things go wrong."

Yet, a deeper look at British decentralization suggests that local interest groups, the local media, and "community influentials" continue to exercise a powerful decentralization force (Carmichael 1994, 243). Local councils can always rely upon their legitimacy as elected bodies, their highly respected bureaucracies, and their social and political ties to the mandarins of Westminster and Whitehall. Consequently, the "co-operation of local authorities is not always forthcoming and cannot be guaranteed" (Stoker 1995, 108).

What seems to be happening in Britain, as in other countries, is a greater complexity of decentralization arrangements, with the rise of non-elected forms of local and regional government, such as Development Corporations, housing associations, Training and Enterprise Councils, Commissions for New Towns, and Economic Partnerships (see Charlesworth and Cochrane 1994). While these new public-private partnerships sometimes attempt to bypass traditional elected governments, they more often cooperate to formulate an economic strategy, to attract new investment, and to diversify the employment base.

The message of the most recent studies of British intergovernmental relations, according to Carmichael (1994, 246), "appears to be that the old assumptions of centralization and autonomy (especially in respect of finance) no longer apply." Thus, those opposed to local government policies may seek central government support for their opposition without wanting centralization.

Whereas many forms of decentralization are encouraged in MDCs, they are discouraged in most LDCs. This discouragement partly accounts for the fact that, while nearly 60 percent of all government jobs in MDCs are classified as "local," the African proportion is only 6 percent, compared with 21 percent in Latin America and 37 percent in Asia (Garnett, Merrill, and Miller 1988). However, it manifests itself more directly in a general disabling environment. Consequently, the questions here raised as to the appropriate division of responsibility are useless in regard to LDCs, not because there is so much sharing of responsibility, but so little.

In Zambia, for example, the Local Government Act of 1980 devolved significant authority to district councils. In fact, according to a 1991 study by Silverman and Yang, these councils needed permission to act from the Prime Minister's Office, and such permission was seldom given. As a result, they lacked the authority, as well as capacity, to efficiently and effectively collect property taxes. Instead, they irresponsibly borrowed from banks to pay their wage bills, accumulating arrears because of non-payment of loans.

In Kenya, the central government, ignoring its own plans and the recommendations of national and international experts, has persistently undermined local government performance (Smoke 1993, 902). While the government mandated in the 1970s increased personnel salaries and free drugs, it abolished local school fees and transferred the Graduated Personal Tax to central government without providing the necessary funds to replace these revenue sources. Consequently in Kenya, as in Zambia, local councils often borrow from many sources, despite their inability to repay these loans, forcing the Treasury to retire their debts from general revenue.

As we turn to local governments in LDCs outside of Africa, we find the same weakening process is evident. In Mexico, for example, local governments were not allowed to take into account inflation in their budget preparation (Dillinger 1993, 19). In Egypt, the central government did not allow Cairo's government to raise the fares of its bus services during a 30 year period (Davey 1993, 22). In Bangladesh, urban councils were not allowed to collect higher fees than rural councils, regardless of greater needs and the capacity of citizens to pay (Hasan 1992, 805). And we could go on with many other examples of this "disabling environment."

Because local governments perform so poorly in LDCs, there is an inclination to ignore them altogether. Huque (1986, 91), for example, suggests, in regard to Bangladesh, that "it might be wise to abandon efforts directed at complete decentralization . . ., and concentrate on limited decentralization." Many LDC leaders would sympathize with Jawaharlal Nehru's comment that "A village, normally speaking, is backward intellectually and culturally, and no progress can be made from a backward environment" (quoted, Tummala 1992, 545). These leaders, however, generally discover that centralized administration is seldom very successful.

Nellis (1983, 159–160), writing about field administration in Tunisia, could just as well be describing the situation in any LDC: "Each ministry is divided into many competing, overlapping, ill-coordinated sections, most of which are managed as nonaccountable fiefdoms by powerful directors." Central governments tend to suffer from the same problems as local governments: lack of trained personnel and adequate resources; limited ability to collect taxes and gain popular cooperation; extensive corruption; etc. Consequently, the "yo-yo process of delegation and withdrawal of delegation," described by Harris (1983, 192), going on in Latin America, can be found throughout the developing world.

The suggested alternative to relying upon local governments is to turn to NGOs. NGOs are often more successful than local governments in providing needed services. An estimated 60 million people in Asia, 25 million in Latin America, and 12 million in Africa are affiliated with them (Fisher 1994, 130). In Latin America, they form a constantly changing maze of organizations, providing many types of assistance to the poor (Annis 1987). While formal local government institutions in Bangladesh have been largely unsuccessful, NGOs, such as the Bangladesh Rural Advancement Committee (BRAC) and the Grameen Bank (see Chapter 2), are internationally respected for their work in education, public health, and community development, particularly among women and the landless poor (Ingham and Kalam 1992).

Yet, to be effective, NGOs need judicial frameworks, credit systems, training programs, and various forms of supervision (a point to be emphasized in the next chapter). While LDC officials often rely upon and even coopt NGOs, they also distrust and undermine them, thereby engendering mutual hostility. In the Gambia, for example, donor-supported NGOs provide their staff with much higher salaries, fringe benefits, and working conditions than received by field officers of line ministries (Davis, Hulme, and Woodhouse 1994). This causes tension and mistrust between the two sectors, with no concern for planning, coordination, or guidelines.

In Uganda, NGOs provide a series of unconnected services, so that interventions may work against one-another and basic needs become ignored (Kapoor 1993, 124). The government, not only has little control over what is going on, but also little knowledge and little interest, often leaving responsibility entirely in the hands of foreign donors, who must bribe officials to implement projects. While a vision of poverty alleviation through a facilitation model, using NGOs, businesses, and small farmers has been articulated by Ugandan leaders, it is not yet widely understood and shared within the government. Consequently, services provided by NGOs are viewed as "gifts under a Christmas tree."

THE MEASUREMENT OF DECENTRALIZATION. B. C. Smith (1985, 84) argues that "it is necessary to be able to measure decentralization if we want to know whether changes have in fact occurred and what the consequences of these changes are." However, he goes on to point out that it is extremely difficult to do so because of the need to hold the various determinants of local autonomy constant, particularly in doing cross-national comparisons.

The easiest variables to quantify are obviously economic ones: the percentage of local government budgets collected by local government officials and the percent of total government spending channelled through elected regional and local government (Bullmann, Goldsmith, and Page 1994). The most problematic have to do with legal structure, personnel quality, popular participation, and commitment (Vengroff and Ben Salem 1992).

If local governments are highly dependent upon central governments for their revenue, it would appear that they have limited scope for independent action. Keating (1991, 66), however, points out that dependence on grants does not necessarily reduce the autonomy of local government because it may free them from the constraints of market competition for tax revenue. One can argue in this regard that the mayors of impoverished American cities often have less real power to deal with urban problems than Scandinavian burgomasters or board chairmen who have the benefit of equalizing grants, thereby somewhat offsetting per-capita income differences.

While in MDCs, there does not appear to be a relationship between financial dependence on central government grants and the power of local government, in many LDCs there is such a relationship. This is because in LDCs central government grants tend to have a far more dysfunctional impact than in MDCs. Grant allocations are often given for partisan reasons, rather than for real needs; are uncertain and unreliable; and are indifferent to local tax collecting efforts and improvements in operational efficiency (Bahl and Linn 1992, 428–429).

This situation is exemplified in the Ivory Coast where local governments are so heavily dependent on central government grants that people assume that the central government has an obligation to provide services without any effort on their part to pay for them (Garnier, Noel, Schwabe and Thomson 1992). In South Korea, in contrast (also see Chapter 9), urban officials have been able to exercise considerable initiative despite limited authority over revenue sources (Bahl and Linn 1992, 46). Decentralization here seems to have increased with development, but it has taken a cooperative form, which defies measurement.

Based upon a comparison of MDCs and LDCs, we can conclude that it is not so much the QUANTITY of decentralization that is of importance, but the QUALITY (referring to political software). This means, as we will show in the next section, that we need to use political elasticity theory to understand how to maximize simultaneously centralization and decentralization.

THE THEORY OF POLITICAL ELASTICITY

Our difficulty in linking decentralization to centralization stems from the fact that our political vocabulary consists of words (such as power, authority, and control) that are considered as "finite," rather than "elastic." Consequently, we see politics as a "win-lose" situation, with each source of revenue or jurisdictional responsibility lost to the local government thereby gravitating to the central government, and vice-versa. This fits in with the popular unidimensional view of politics ascribed to Harold

Lasswell's 1936 book, POLITICS: WHO GETS WHAT, WHEN, HOW (Crick 1960).

To see politics in this way (as noted in the Introduction) is as misleading as to see the Olympics as nothing more than competing individuals and teams, neglecting the organizational arrangements and consensus on rules, guidelines, judging, and participation essential for what takes place. An elastic conception of politics enables us to avoid Ruttan's criticism (1991, 277–278) that political scientists lack as clear a conception as economists of the meaning of development. PE theory, in other words, enables us to understand what an expanding polity really is and why it is essential for an expanding economy. It also enables us to understand why the simultaneous arguments for more and less state control need not be contradictory (Frischtak 1994, 7).

I assume that, based upon the previous chapters, the reader understands my use of soft and hard forms of power and political hardware and political software. In using the language of computers, I am reminded of the point made by Simeon (1986, 445), that each generation has pursued the themes of centralization and decentralization within the context of current preoccupations and political beliefs. Whereas the authors of THE FEDERALIST PAPERS may have thought about clocks and other mechanical devices in suggesting "checks and balances" and "separation of powers" (see Wolin 1989, 115–19), I have in mind "political software" to emphasize the importance of the "subjective" aspects (emotions, ideologies, cultural predispositions, etc.) that make the functioning of "objective" forms of institutions possible.

Allow me here to reiterate that, improving political software entails, not such Weberian requirements as hierarchy, rules, procedures, rights, contractual duties, specialized positions, or rules, but, rather, the commonsensical steps advocated in typical business administration and public administration textbooks: establishing acceptable goals, hiring qualified personnel, delegating responsibility, stimulating motivation and competition, encouraging training, paying attention to morale, expanding two-way flows of communication, promoting legitimacy, maintaining supervision, cultivating contractors, protecting independent spheres of authority, and developing conflict-resolution procedures. When leaders neglect or mismanage these steps, they are likely to rely upon coercive and corrupt forms of political power, causing "inelasticity," and hostility towards every type of decentralization.

The propositions associated with political elasticity overcome the centralization/decentralization dichotomy by suggesting: (1) under political elasticity, forms of decentralization can be expanded without reducing centralization; (2) under political inelasticity, leaders fear decentralization, thereby weakening their implementation capacity; (3) under political elasticity, various forms of decentralization and centralization merge; (4) under political inelasticity, forms of decentralization and centralization tend to be so ineffective as to be meaningless. In illustrating these assertions with the following case studies (together with those in Chapters 1 and 9), we can perhaps cut through the confusion presented in the previous section.

EXAMPLES OF POLITICAL ELASTICITY

THE UNITED STATES. While many American federal programs, such as President Johnson's War on Poverty, were eventually undermined by alternative national priorities and policies, others (e.g. the national highway program, clean air, and the safety of food and drugs) have remained largely effective. The fact that American inner-city life (in comparison, let us say, to that of Canada) remains so dismal suggests to me that political inelasticity may be evident, even though the political system as a whole may be highly elastic. In other words, political elasticity is affected by political motivation (which gets us back to political software).

Peterson, Rabe, and Wong (1986) explain the factors having to do with the success of legislation relating to the handicapped enacted during the 1970s: (1) a widespread sharing of goals; (2) the desire of politicians at all levels to promote programs from which they can gain politically; (3) the willingness of all concerned to work out differences and clarify guidelines; (4) the emergence of a core of professionals, tied by common training, expertise, values, and orientation; (5) the adequacy of federal grants-in-aid to promote the legislation; (6) the development of good statistics and computers to permit meaningful evaluation programs; (7) the existence of powerful interest groups with the capacity and willingness to make the political system work for them; (8) the undertaking of careful inspections and audits; (9) the ability of federal officials and other supporters to use the courts in requiring local action mandated by federal requirements; and (10) the ability and willingness of federal officials to threaten the loss of funding in gaining cooperation and better performance. Thus, over time, officials at all levels work together with professionals and parents to develop a common framework for implementation.

The powerful role of the federal courts is explained by Augustus Jones (1995), noting that between February 1993 and March 1995, the federal appellate and district courts, in more than two-thirds of the Americans with Disabilities Act (ADA) cases reaching them, rejected claims of "undue burden." These ADA decisions are expected to cost county governments alone more than $3 billion between 1994 and 1998.

Because the American governmental system is so politically elastic, interest groups often seek centralization and decentralization at the same time. Lee (1996), for example, points out that chemical industries wanting deregulation and less supervision also want clear Federal Government regulations, preventing states from imposing food safety codes more stringent than federal rules.

HOLLAND. The Netherlands would appear to be one of the world's most planned and controlled countries, with building regulations covering, not only location within a plot, use, and relation to surroundings, but also the color of the paintwork and choice of materials (Davies 1988, 211). It would also appear to be a highly centralized country, with specific and general grants amounting to about 90 percent of local government revenue and with Crown-appointed Burgomasters and Governors (Netherlands Scientific Council 1990, 197).

Yet, the Netherlands is also "a decentralized state in which the municipalities have considerable autonomy" (Davies 1988, 220). Within limits set by central and provincial officials, each municipality prepares its own plans and regulations, following extensive discussions, negotiations, and opportunities for objection. The effort of the central government is to give guidance without excessive interference and coercion (Hamnett 1985, 27).

Because of the democratic nature of the Dutch system, national agencies seek the support of local governments to increase their budgets, as well as vice-versa (Toonen 1987, 124). While Dutch provinces and municipalities guard their autonomy jealously, urban planners here realize that, without national direction and legislation, "plans are just so much paper" (Morris 1985, 65). Consequently, inter-governmental relations in the Netherlands require "specific provisions for co-ordination, negotiation, conflict resolution, consensus and coalition-building to enable parties to deal with their diverse and sometimes conflicting interests and relationships (Toonen 1987, 126).

The responsibility for Dutch housing, education, and social services has been largely in the hands of four segments or pillars (Catholic, Protestant, Liberal and Socialist); but this pillarization system is affected by various regulations, subsidies, grants, financial and fiscal policies (Flynn 1986). Central government officials have increasingly used a system of block grants to municipal and provincial governments to enable them to exercise greater control over this system. Consequently, "decentralization now provides a means for extending and indeed strengthening central, national control over local housing corporations, but in indirect ways which do not appear to jeopardize their long-established ideological, legal and political independence" (Flynn 1986, 618). Also active in this regard are professional organizations, the business sector, the Association of Dutch Municipalities, and journalists and experts with access to the media.

The Dutch intergovernmental system is in a constant state of reconsideration and reform, according to a 1996 article by Toonen. Pillarised institutions have been crumbling since the 1960s, but this has placed more responsibility on local and regional levels of government. While various reform proposals have been made or attempted (elected mayors and provincial governors, new forms of urban regional government, etc.), the central government continues to be responsible for appropriate democratic guidance and control. Yet, "ample opportunities exist to challenge, modify and even redefine and renegotiate national decisions at various levels of government" (Toonen 1996, 619).

EXAMPLES OF POLITICAL INELASTICITY

THE PHILIPPINES. Ostrom, Schroeder, and Wynne (1990, 36–48) summarize the effort of the United States Agency for International Development (USAID) to sponsor decentralization in the Philippines from 1968 to 1981. Much of the effort proved unsuccessful. Until 1991, "national-local relations were characterized by strong centralism" (Tapales 1996, 211).

Excessive centralization is considered to be one of the causes of rural poverty, affecting more than 50 percent of the population outside of Metropolitan Manila, according to 1990 census data (Tapales 1996, 202). In regard to the National Irrigation Administration (NIA), for example, farmers seldom participated in anything but a passive way. Farmers did not even bother to join Irrigation Associations (IAs) because the benefits received were not worth the costs of joining. Because farmers were not required to invest funds or labor in constructing or maintaining irrigation facilities, IAs proved to be weak, without the capacity to prevent misuse and deterioration of the system. Likewise, in villages, people were allowed to illegally tap into public faucets, undermining efforts to meet demand, recover costs, and pay for maintenance and better service (Fox 1994, 14).

Under the Local Government Code of 1991, the Philippines was supposed to become Asia's most decentralized country (Tapales 1996, 215). Local governments are now expected to finance many services previously provided by the national government. Unfortunately, most seem to be mismanaged, without expertise, and under the control of corrupt leaders. Property taxes are extremely low and based on uncertain market value. Collection performance is poor in regard to all forms of taxes and fees.

To improve the quality of local government, the National Government has offered to devolve a high percentage of its personnel. Yet, many local governments have refused to accept devolved personnel because their salaries are "too expensive for them to assume, and would cause demoralization among the locally hired personnel" (Tapales 1996, 212). Consequently, such services as police and fire protection and infrastructure provision and maintenance continue to remain largely national responsibilities and, at the same time, badly implemented. While National Government grants have increased, they fail to take into account income levels, the needs of the population, and the quality of administration.

In the absence of effective national oversight and control, decentralization here has become counterproductive, according to a recent World Bank report (East Asia and Pacific Region 1995). A more positive evaluation of the 1991 local government code is presented by Tapales (1996, 218), a professor of public administration at the University of the Philippines; but it recognizes the need for "more technically competent local administrators, and more politically committed local politicians together with the continued participation of the people."

EGYPT. In 1982, President Sadat abolished the Ministry of Local Government, shifting responsibility to 26 appointed provincial governors, giving them power over provincial and local administrators (Palmer,

Leila, and Yassin 1988, 21–23). However, the basic administrative problems of Egypt remained: unwieldy organizational structure, excessive red tape and inefficiency, overstaffing, low salary levels, poor working conditions, employee apathy and indifference, low skill levels, lack of coordination and communication among and within agencies, and corruption. Consequently, the "centuries-old tradition of autocratic rule" remained, with the government more than ever fearful of "political opposition in general and Islamist groups in particular" (Al Sayyid 1993, 241). The failure of Sadat and Mubarak to improve administration largely accounts for Egypt's economic retrogression during the 1980s, declining from the World Bank's group of lower middle-income countries to its group of lower-income countries.

Autocratic rule may have intensified under the Mubarak regime, with the termination in 1994 of the century-old practice of villages electing their own mayors and deputy mayors because of the government's fear of rural political instability (Cassandra 1995, 16). This caused USAID to terminate its successful Basic Village Service Project, under which villages received grants for successfully undertaking and funding agreed-upon projects (Chetwynd and Samaan 1984). This grant-in-aid program was part of the most expensive decentralization project that USAID had ever undertaken.

In Egypt, we see clearly how political inelasticity has reduced the capacity of the government to deal with serious environmental problems affecting the megacities of Cairo and Alexandria where about one-third of the country's 70 million people live (Cooperative Housing Foundation 1992). Most urban residents live in unauthorized settlements where land ownership and value remain unrecorded or uncertain. An estimated one-fourth of Cairo's housing lack water supply; one-fifth, lack public sewerage services; and 40 percent, lack electricity. What is available is often unreliable, so much so that the political survival of the Mubarak government was threatened during the early 1980s when Cairo's wastewater system failed.

Egyptian urban problems, however, do not entirely stem from lack of resources, particularly foreign assistance, of which USAID gave more than $20 billion in Economic Support Funding from 1973 to 1993 (Zimmerman 1994). Instead, it is largely derived from the failure of the government to fund the operation and maintenance of infrastructure provided by foreign donors.

Municipal authorities are empowered to levy a betterment charge on properties benefiting from public works, but efforts to do so encounter endless disputes over questions of title, responsibility, and equity. Since local governments are weak, they are dependent on taxes administered by the Ministry of Finance. This Ministry attempts to impose land, building, and vehicle taxes, but is unwilling to enforce payment, particularly from affluent landowners. Inasmuch as the affluent escape taxes, the more impoverished communities insist that municipal services should be extended free of charge. Consequently, many USAID officials increasingly believe that American financial assistance for Egypt's infrastructure has become counterproductive, discouraging its government from escaping dependence on foreign donors both for new construction and for maintenance.

During the 1970s, the Egyptian government invested heavily in New Towns, which were expected to absorb about half of the five million added to the urban population between 1976 and 1986 (Feiler 1992). So far, however, despite significant assistance from foreign donors, particularly USAID, the New Towns have been able to absorb only about 20 percent of population growth.

The history of the New Towns indicates the great potential of the private sector to respond to financial opportunities (based upon my own research for the Cooperative Housing Foundation), particularly if rent control and land registration can be somewhat reformed. Yet, this potential was largely undermined by the lack of urban planning and co-ordination among government agencies. Here was another "lost opportunity."

CONCLUSION: PROMOTING DECENTRALIZATION

USAID has been disappointed with many of its efforts to promote decentralization, as indicated in the previous section by its experience in the Philippines and Egypt. It continues, therefore, to search for a better approach to decentralization. Thus, the primary objective of the 1988 $16.6 million Decentralized Finance and Management for Development (DFMD) project was to provide advice to USAID missions on "what kinds of institutional and fiscal structures will most encourage effective initiation, management and recurrent cost financing of specified local development functions" (Thomson, Connerley, and Wunsch 1986).

Much of the DFMD project was directed toward the Francophone African countries. While some achievements were reported and numerous interesting studies were carried out, there is no indication of more substantial results in any of the countries involved. For example, despite many forms of international assistance, municipal tax collection "suffers from a lack of professionalism, political pressures, and corrupt practices" (Attahi 1997, 182). Consequently, the collection rate is low and there is little cooperation between taxpayers and responsible government agencies.

The primary weakness of the DFMD approach seems to me to be a neglect of political software considerations which, as here explained, have to do with the quality of political relationships essential for effective decentralization. This criticism can be extended to Uphoff's 1986 effort to draw conclusions from 80 case studies of rural development projects and Perlman's Megacity Project (1990), which attempts to identify, document, and disseminate innovations having to do with urban problems. By using political elasticity theory, we can go beyond case studies and examples of successful innovations into the underlying requisites for both rural and urban development.

The policy implications of earlier chapters (to be further developed in Chapter 10) are that anything which improves political software automatically improves governance, thereby making political elasticity more possible. In the MDC literature, certain factors stand out more clearly than others in regard to particular countries. In France, Ambler (1991, 21) mentions "pride in the quality of its central administration;" in Sweden, Heclo and Madsen (1987, 6–7) note the concern for transparency and legality; in the Netherlands, Williams and Colijn (1980, 196) stress mutual respect among experts across levels of government. However, I believe all the aspects previously mentioned are important and interrelated.

The International City/County Management Association (ICMA), under its 1990 contract with USAID, appears to emphasize political software factors in its "Making Cities Work" approach (ICMA 1994). Thus, it has not imposed its "city manager" system of local government propagated in the United States, perhaps recognizing that this is not inherently more effective than the mayoralty form.

According to a 1994 description of its Municipal Development Project (MDP) in Honduras, ICMA has persuaded mayors of the importance of hiring professional city administrators and engineers, improving working conditions to motivate employees, installing reliable computerized accounting systems, modifying internal audit procedures to make them easier to comprehend, holding open town meetings to increase transparency of local government administration, publishing newsletters to keep citizens informed, and developing a trustworthy competitive bidding process for contracts and then properly monitoring them.

As a result of this MDP, five Honduran municipalities have secured outside funding for needed infrastructure projects. The Inter-American Development Bank continues (as of 1997) to support the MDP, particularly its Foundation for Municipal Development. More important, the Honduran government is increasingly willing to implement its 1990 Municipal Law providing for meaningful decentralization along with needed financial and technical assistance. In so doing, existing fears (that local governments would undermine the authority of the central government; that professionals would challenge mayoral control; and that additional tax revenue would be wasted) have gradually decreased.

In linking decentralization to centralization in politically elastic ways, foreign aid agencies might consider a number of additional possibilities. One of them is the sponsoring of highly respected urban institutes, such as the Brazilian Institute of Administration (IBAM), which received from USAID about $10 million between 1962 and 1980 to construct new headquarters, upgrade its staff, and expand its technical assistance and training activities to local governments. This has now become a model for national technical assistance programs in many countries (Bartone ET AL. 1994, 51).

A second possibility is to sponsor grant-in-aid programs, such as the successful USAID-supported Basic Village Service Project in Egypt (Chetwynd and Samaan 1984). While, as indicated earlier, this particular project was unsustainable, good grant-in-aid programs are essential for effective decentralization (note the Swiss example in the next chapter).

A third useful possibility (presenting a menu of well-researched options) has been demonstrated by the Tennessee Valley Authority under a USAID-supported Managing Energy and Resource Efficient Cities (MEREC) project (Hobgood 1992). MEREC was particularly successful in Portugal where it helped local administrators, politicians, and groups of citizens prioritize projects, determine costs, and select appropriate technology. It thereby encouraged the central government to double national subsidies and grants, while reducing its excessive involvement in a range of local operations.

Finally, it should be noted that the concept of "reinventing government" is increasingly accepted in LDCs. The French government has helped establish successful examples of public-private partnerships in West Africa (McCoy-Thompson 1993). The Water Supply Corporation of the Ivory Coast and the Togolese Refuse Collection Company now provide such good services that they have recovered costs from consumers. However, these partnerships have often been unsustainable, according to Attahi (1997, 207), without a qualified public sector staff for supervision, legal machinery for the management of conflicts, and arrangements to advise and support community organizations regarding contractual relationships with companies.

Politically elastic forms of decentralization, as emphasized in the next chapter, require a CONTROLLING as well as an ENABLING administrative environment. As this is effectively established, decentralization will take on a more fluid and benign meaning—a "delegation," rather than a "transfer" of authority—and, as such, it will be recognized as a "gain," rather than a "loss," of power for both central and local governments.

CHAPTER 5

The New Development Administration (NDA)
A Disappointing Literature

INTRODUCTION

In a 1989 article in PUBLIC ADMINISTRATION AND DEVELOPMENT (Werlin 1989a), I felt the need to criticize the "development from below" literature, as had been attractively presented in the articles and edited books of David Korten (Korten and Alfonso 1983; Korten 1986). This literature seemed to me to reflect three interrelated viewpoints: (1) a benevolent view of communities: (2) a hostile view of bureaucracies; and (3) a favorable view of participatory and humanistic management, as against scientific and coercive administration. The following assertions (including supporting quotations) illustrate the orientation of this literature:

(1) The people know best. "All the lessons we are learning stem from this basic concept of responsiveness, this conviction that the people whose lives will be directly affected by development efforts know best what they need and want and how to do it" (Ickis 1983, 57).

(2) Social learning is self taught. "Social learning cannot be mandated by the pre-emptive action of central political authority. Nor can it be programmed by bureaucratic procedures. It is a product of people, acting individually and in voluntary association with others, guided by their individual critical consciousness and recognizing no organizational boundaries" (Korten 1986b, 325).

(3) The community is best able to mobilize local resources. "When people at the local level are committed to an idea, they can often mobi-

lize an astonishing variety of resources to realize it—from underutilized land and buildings, to skills, communication channels, and money" (Korten 1986a, 4).

(4) State interventions have been largely counterproductive. "Too often they have simply undermined existing local capacities, created burdens on the national treasury, and exacerbated inequities by transferring resources and power from local to national elites while doing little to increase productivity" (Korten 1986a, 4).

(5) Central governments tend to be inefficient. "Central bureaucracies, which function according to standardized rules, have little capacity to respond to the special needs and preferences through which such adaptation might be achieved" (Korten 1986a, 4).

(6) Public bureaucracies reinforce dependency and powerlessness. "Ultimately only the poor can define their own aspirations and negotiate their adjustment to the possible" (Soedjamoko 1986, 23).

(7) Motivation is more important than control. "Cooperation must be gained through desire rather than command" (Tanco 1983, 57).

(8) Development is a "bottom up" learning process. "The top-down approach to development has been thoroughly discredited by hard experience" (Soedjamoko 1986, 22).

Based upon the previous chapters of this book, the reader can understand my skeptical reaction to this literature. While I do not disagree with any of the assertions of the "development from below" literature, I believe that these assertions, to be meaningful, must be compatible with the Political Elasticity (PE) propositions presented in the Introduction.

In the conclusion of my 1989 article, I asked how can we reconcile Soedjamoko's suggestion (1986, 23) "that the bureaucratic approach to the poor will have to be replaced by . . . self-organized activity" with Waldo's assertion (1980, 1) that civilization (including its derivative, community development) always has been and still is "intricately and intimately joined" to administration? My answer went back to PE theory, which I used to deal with the conflicting theories of popular participation pointed out by Louise White (1987, 177): one seeing local groups as clients; the other, as masters of the bureaucracy.

Using PE theory, the public may be seen as both master and client of the bureaucracy, as the source of ultimate authority and also subject to its authority. In the same way, we are both the boss of our doctor, inasmuch as we employ and pay him, as well as his patient. Insofar as we respect his expertise, we give him the authority to treat us—to guide us so that we will recover from our illness. If we challenge or undermine him, we reduce his capacity to treat us and damage our relationship with him. Yet the doctor must also treat us with respect because we can refuse to pay him, change doctors, sue him, or ignore his advice. Similarly, mutual respect (i.e., a high quality of political software) is essential for a proper relationship between the community and its bureaucracy.

During the 1980s, several of my intellectual endeavors (criticizing humanistic administrative theory and slum upgrading theory) reinforced my skepticism regarding the "development from below" literature. Indeed, my analysis (Werlin 1988) of what Dubnick (1994) calls "the debureaucratization movement" and of World Bank efforts to improve the conditions of the urban poor (Werlin 1987) led me to question attacks on public administration coming from both the political left (particularly the plea for "local empowerment") and the political right ("let the market rule"). Because these endeavors are relevant to my analysis of the "mysteries of development" presented in this chapter, I will briefly discuss them here.

HUMANISTIC ADMINISTRATIVE THEORY

In the Introduction, I noted the conflict between scientific administrative theory and humanistic administrative theory. As I then pointed out, this conflict persists. Textbooks covering business administration or organizational management (reviewed in my 1988 article), therefore. often left readers with mixed messages. "The successful organization," noted Hersey and Blanchard (1977, 83), "has one major attribute that sets it apart from unsuccessful organizations: dynamic and effective leadership." At the same time, these authors emphasized the need for an employee-centered or democratic leadership style, without explaining the relationship between these two requirements. Likewise, Brown (1982) never reconciled his assertion (p. 214) that "many an executive has learned that the best supervision is often the least even if unwilling to admit it" with his earlier observation (p. 89) that there is "an awakening of concern with oversight and accountability. It underlines the importance of the setting of objectives at all levels and the use of monitoring and auditing techniques to see that they are achieved."

While "bureaucracy" increasingly became a "dirty word" in the literature of administration, those insisting upon "debureaucratization" generated more confusion than the exponents of scientific management. Bennis (1966) became so critical of bureaucracy that he proclaimed its coming death only to realize as president of the University of Buffalo that the failure to develop a strong bureaucracy undermined the structure, security, and controls required for his proposed objectives (Drucker 1974, 233–234). Heirs and Pehrson (1982, 59) emphasized "the deadening effects of bureaucratic controls" while also pointing out (p. 120) that the success of the Polaris missile program depended on management providing "the correct procedures and the necessary incentives for its proper functioning."

Those writing for World Bank practitioners were (and still are) similarly ambivalent about bureaucracy. Kubr and Wallace (1983, ii), in a World Bank staff working paper, argued that "the basic problem in improving the management of public enterprises is not managerial and business-like behavior, but administrative and bureaucratic." Since the approaches advocated in this paper were "administrative and bureaucratic," the reader must have been perplexed.

In my 1988 article, I indicated a need for a bureaucracy manifesting both authoritarian and democratic decision-making but failed to indicate, using PE theory, my conception of such a bureaucracy. As indicated in the Introduction, it was not until I began to use the concept of political software in the 1990s that I was able to explain how a bureaucracy can develop the capacity to integrate and alternate soft and hard forms of power.

Despite the weakness of my 1988 article, I emerged convinced that the debureaucratization literature was, not only confusing, but also misleading. For example, Brown (1982, 83) argued that, in the United States, "the large organization is taking on increasingly the characteristics of an association or confederation with large pockets of group and individual autonomy within it."

Such an organization would be a disaster, I argued (1988, 55), unless leaders had the capacity to supervise what goes on and, if necessary, tighten control. It would resemble the picture Iacocca (1984) presents of the Chrysler Corporation when he took it over: "There were thirty-five vice presidents, each with his own turf. There was no real committee setup, no cement in the organizational chart, no system of meetings to get people talking to each other." He had to purge the corporation of 33 vice presidents, replace them with people he trusted, and set up a new system of financial controls before he could introduce participatory management.

I concluded in my 1988 article that, under political elasticity, Weber's ideal-type bureaucracy, with its rigid hierarchy of positions, qualifications, responsibilities, and privileges, can be relaxed, allowing for informal or unauthorized influential relationships and for conflict and dissent, without undermining its integrity. In reference to modern progressive organizations, I quoted Crozier (1964, 185): "Direct coercion is still in reserve as a last resort, but it is very rarely used, and people apparently no longer have to see it operate to retain it in their calculations." In such organizations, the virtues of Weber's ideal type of bureaucracy can be respected without stifling creativity and innovation, impeding the flow of communication, diminishing the cooperation of subordinates, and undermining the fulfillment of goals.

SLUM-UPGRADING THEORY

As mentioned in the Introduction, I wrote and/or edited (1977–83) THE URBAN EDGE, a newsletter for the World Bank's Urban Projects Department. During these years, the first generation of Bank urban projects emerged. The most exciting and expensive of these projects had to do with slum-upgrading, intended to improve the lives of millions of people.

The Bank's sites and services projects (see Chapter 2), as well as its slum upgrading projects, were primarily influenced by the theoretical writing of John F. C. Turner, particularly by his 1972 book, FREEDOM TO BUILD, edited with R. Fichter (Pugh 1990, 57; van der Linden 1986, 20). Because of the problem of finding relatively unoccupied land suitable for self-help building, the Bank's sites and services projects generally affected far fewer people than its slum upgrading projects. Consequently, those concerned with these efforts followed carefully what was happening, particularly in Asian megacities where slum conditions were most appalling.

The Turner theory was very much in tune with the "development from below" literature presented at the beginning of this chapter. Based upon his observations in Peru, Turner argued that the solution to slums is not to demolish the housing but to improve the environment: if governments can rid existing slums of unsanitary human waste disposal, inadequate or polluted water supplies, and litter and filth from muddy unlit lanes, they need not worry about shanty dwellings. Because squatters often showed great organizational skill in their land management, they could be trusted to maintain the infrastructure that was provided.

This theory also suggests that, as the environment improves, most residents will gradually better their homes and living conditions, especially when encouraged by security of tenure and access to credit. The role of government, according to Turner, should be a minimal one, simply to provide the essentials necessary to expand human aspirations. Otherwise, he was opposed to whatever large, central, and hierarchical organizations attempted to do (van der Linden 1986, 24).

Based upon my study of Nairobi (Werlin 1974), I sympathized with Turner's ideas. I had seen soldiers and police play a cynical and counterproductive "cat and mouse" game with squatters. In November, 1970, for example, the Nairobi City Council authorized the destruction of 49 illegal settlements, containing perhaps 40,000 people. This resulted in a swelling of housing demand, a decreasing housing supply, and greater exploitation of tenants in the remaining unauthorized settlements where an estimated third of the population lived.

Because slum clearance was so widespread during the 1970s, United Nations officials estimated that governments were destroying annually more low-income housing than they were building. These officials also estimated that there had been almost a 50 percent rise in the LDC urban population during the 1970s (Hauser ET AL. 1982). Consequently, governments were decreasingly able to meet the housing needs of their impoverished urban residents.

Slum upgrading seemed to be the least expensive approach to dealing with the urban poor. Churchill (1980) estimated the costs of World Bank upgrading projects to average US $38 per household, as against $1,000–2,000 for a core housing unit in a site-service project and more than $10,000 for a low-cost public house or apartment. With this approach, the unserved LDC urban residents—one-fourth of the LDC population—could be taken care of in an affordable way, requiring only 0.2–0.5 percent of GDP annually over a fifteen year period (Kessides 1997, 28).

The slum upgrading approach could also be justified for other reasons: (1) the potentially violent or politically troublesome reaction of slum dwellers; (2) the economic costs of removing slum dwellers from sources of employment; and (3) the disruption of social or ethnic support systems. While governmental subsidies might be necessary, they could be kept "within a predictable limit while ensuring that the poorest households and communities will be able to obtain at least minimal services" (Kessides 1997, 28).

Since leaving the World Bank's Urban Projects Department, I have paid attention to evaluations of three of the Bank's largest and most expensive slum upgrading efforts—in Calcutta, Jakarta, and Manila. While these projects included more than slum upgrading, the magnitude of these efforts is indicated by the costs (in millions of U.S. dollars) of the projects approved affecting these cities during 1972-92: Calcutta—US $428.4; Jakarta—US $353.7; and Manila—US $280 (OED 1994). Early evaluations of these projects indicated, not only remarkable success, but also the validity of Turner's theory.

By 1986, Calcutta's Bustee Improvement Program (BIP) had improved nearly two-thirds of the Central City's slums, affecting some three million people (Pugh 1990, 211). During the 1970s, reported deaths from waterborne diseases in Calcutta fell by nearly a half, and deaths from cholera showed an even steeper decline.

By 1979, Jakarta's Kampung Improvement Program (KIP) had benefited about 3.3 million residents, representing over 70 percent of the city's estimated slum population, at a cost of only about US $118 per capita in 1993 dollars (Kessides 1997, A2; Viloria 1991, 643). Within fourteen years, practically all of the eligible kampungs (i.e., impoverished neighborhoods) had benefited from the program.

KIP residents, according to evaluations, invested twice as much in home improvement, as compared with those in similar non-KIP areas (Schubeler 1996, 42). It also had a positive impact upon home industries and workshops. In 1983, the Indonesian government was given the Aga Khan Foundation international award for its KIP approach in Jakarta.

Manila's efforts, beginning in 1975, were more expensive than Jakarta's (US $83 per capita, as against US $60 in 1975 dollars) and primarily concentrated on the Tondo Foreshore area reclaimed from the sea in the 1940s, occupied by about 200,000 squatters. According to Keare and Paris (1983), the area had undergone "fantastic improvement" by 1981, with, not only better housing and environmental conditions, but also increased business opportunities, more recreational, transportation, and health facilities, and greater family stability and community cohesion.

Yet, by the end of the 1980s, the benefits of these slum upgrading efforts appeared ephemeral, giving rise in my mind to doubts about Turner's ideas, despite my continuing admiration for Turner personally (having worked with him in 1984 at an international conference on urban problems in the Hague). This was not simply my opinion. The term "slum upgrading," according to Kessides (1997, 8), "has rarely appeared in Bank projects since the late 1980s." Especially worrisome were persistent environmental problems.

K. J. Nath, a professor of environmenal sanitation in Calcutta, reported (1992, 5) that bacterial contamination remained a very serious problem caused by a leaky sewerage system and an intermittent water system. Many of the 8,000 standposts provided by the Calcutta Municipal Corporation had become useless because 25–35% of the water supplied was wasted through leakages in the worn out pipes, public taps, and standposts. And in the non-municipal urban areas, there was no organized public water supply system whatsoever. The collection and disposal of human excreta, solid waste, and cow dung and cattle shed wastes continued to be problematic.

According to Bannerjee and Chakravorty (1994, 79–80), public apathy after forty years of post-colonial organizational development remained disturbing and puzzling regarding Calcutta's poor or nonexistent services such as street cleaning or garbage pickup, electricity, and transportation. Consequently, they concluded: "In short, planning in Calcutta is back to square one."

Thomas (1997, 88) suggests that, while the BIP improved conditions for a large number of people, "it has not effectively dealt with the housing problem." Because only a small percentage of BIP beneficiaries are paying for the services they receive, the government seems unable or unwilling to address the problems of the expanding squatter settlements. Discouraged by this situation, World Bank officials almost discontinued funding the BIP in the 1990s.

In Jakarta, as of June 1991, less than 20 percent of households had in-house water connections (Crane 1994, 73–74). According to a 1989 survey, about 40% of Jakarta's population depended on groundwater, but 93% of the city's shallow wells presented signs of fecal contamination (World Bank 1994a, 129–133). "Most rivers and canals in metropolitan areas are polluted, affecting not only the water supply but also dense kampung areas" (OED 1994a, xvii).

The health costs of Jakarta's waterborne infectious and parasitic diseases are indicated by the fact that the mortality associated with diarrhea alone is estimated to cost around $200 million a year. To escape these diseases, one-third of the city's population must depend upon water vendors, or to go to great energy expense (amounting to more than $50 million, one percent of the city's GDP) to boil water (Bartone ET AL. 1994, 42).

While each of the kampungs affected by the KIP had been provided with communal toilet and washing blocks, a 1990 World Bank report (OED 1990, 24) noted that a high percentage of them were ineffective because of poor maintenance, unreliable water supply, and poor location, suggesting that they were becoming "a wasted investment." Consequently, users abandoned them.

Because community commitment to maintenance was low, many kampungs needed to be "re-KIPped" (Kessides 1997, A3). The kampungs that most benefited were those transformed by upscale commercial investment; but this was not the purpose of the KIP. Indeed, so dissatisfied were World Bank officials with the KIP approach that they reduced the proportion of urban lending for it from about 70 percent in the 1970s to less than 10 percent in the 1990s (Kessides 1997, A2).

There was also extensive industrial pollution in Jakarta, contributing to the metropolitan area's high cost of air pollution, amounting to an estimated $200–$500 million per year. According to the 1990 OED report, an estimated 30 percent of Jakarta's solid waste went uncollected, with a much higher percentage going uncollected in the more densely populated and impoverished kampungs. Much of what was collected was dumped in the open or in uncontrolled landfills, leading to the spread of diseases and contamination of groundwater.

Turning to the Metropolitan Manila Region (MMR), we find the same dismal situation as in Calcutta and Jakarta. Of the 41 public sanitation facilities constructed during the 1980s with World Bank assistance, only seven seemed to be in good condition in 1992, requiring only minor repairs (Luna, Ferrer and Ignacio 1994, 1–2). Water losses from leaks and unauthorized connections amounted to more than one-third of supply, causing low water pressure, service breakdowns, and extensive flooding.

According to a World Bank report (Bartone ET AL. 1994, 92–94), all MMR surface water was contaminated with human, solid and industrial wastes to varying degrees. Much of the pollution was caused by inadequate solid waste management, with 1,000 tons going uncollected every day. Also threatening human health was the fact that the MMR has some of the worst urban air pollution in the world.

What these evaluations indicated to me was, not so much that the slum upgrading approach is wrong, but that it required a very powerful as well as humanistic bureaucracy to successfully carry it out. While such a bureaucracy is rare in LDCs, that the "minimal state," advocated by Turner, can deal with the following problems typically encountered in slum upgrading was a dangerous illusion:

LAND ACQUISITION. Slums are often located in precarious areas (ravines, hills, beaches, or floodplains), making them difficult or expensive to upgrade. For example, two-thirds of Rio de Janeiro's slum dwellers occupy the steep slopes surrounding the city, which are subject to flooding and landslides (Bartone ET AL. 1994, 10). In 1988, the city had to spend nearly a billion dollars to deal with those affected by that year's heavy rains. The challenge of upgrading a Rio FAVELA can be overwhelming, according to a World Bank official (Mejia 1994, 8): "Houses appear to sit on top of one another, and often actually do. Population density is extremely high. There is neither rhyme nor reason to the layout. Virtually every bit of space is in use by someone, somehow. The laying of pipes, even undergound, most always intrudes on someone's sense of ownership. Adjudicating disputes from the outside is next to impossible."

Slum upgrading inevitably requires the government to purchase land for upgrading and resettlement purposes. To do so may not only be excessively expensive but also benefit an already wealthy group of large landholders. Land banking is one possibility, even though it can be costly and administratively difficult. Consequently, the World Bank has discouraged its use (Pugh 1990, 113). Yet, the municipal government of Curitiba, Brazil has used this strategy to provide housing for 17,000 lower-income families near new public transportation facilities (Rabinovitch and Leitmann 1993, 18).

Another approach is simply to improve tax mapping (identifying untaxed properties), assessments, and collections. If this were done in Manila, according to Strassmann and Blunt (1994), land for residential purposes would become far less costly and much more available. However, administrative corruption in Manila would have to be reduced.

This corruption undermined a 1979 Presidential Proclamation declaring the entire Metro Manila as an Urban Land Reform Zone, freezing the prices of land designated for upgrading at current market values. Because these areas continued to be sold at inflated prices during the 1980s, the government could do little to improve Manila's slums. On the other hand, Singapore has been able to freeze land values (as set forth in revised gazette notifications) to acquire the land that it needs for its public housing program (Lee, Yuan, and Poh 1993, 97).

TENURE. The ownership of slum land tends to be very complex. Seldom do residents own both their houses and the land on which they live. While many residents may simply be casual squatters, illegally occupying vacant land, they are sometimes part of highly planned invasions or informal arrangements worked out with landowners (Amaral 1994, 85). In any case, they may own dwellings or rooms and manage various subletting arrangements which have been negotiated with or even facilitated by landowners without the approval of local authorities.

Because the ownership of slum land may be unclear, there may be extensive violence between groups of squatters for control over this land and the right to profit from the sale or rent of lodgings (Amaral 1994, 85). In Brazilian cities, this violence has often been associated with efforts to control illegal drug trafficking and other gangster activity.

Problems of undertaking land registration cause World Bank officials to want to delink it from infrastructure improvements, "with titling to follow as demand permits" (Kessides 1997, 29). However, until land ownership is clear, it is difficult to get residents to pay for public services that are provided and to improve their dwellings.

Unless officials can threaten residents with loss of property or expulsion from the community, they lack leverage with which to bargain with residents. In Tunisia, for example, repayment contracts with households were unenforceable so long as there was a lag in the granting of land titles (Kessides 1997, 27). The absence of land tenure has also made slum upgrading problematic in Brazil because eviction is almost impossible. Consequently, based on the experience of slum upgrading in Rio's favelas, "bills aren't paid, illegal connections blossom, and care and maintenance are the exception rather than the rule" (Mejia 1994, 7).

The problems of Indonesia's KIP would be far less, Struyk, Hoffman, and Katsura (1990, 372–373) suggest, if the formal land titling process were less expensive and time consuming. A private developer of land is required to go through 34 steps, requiring 6–12 months and various "dirty means of land acquisition" (Server 1996, 26–7). Because only some 37% of land owners actually have a land ownership title, few home purchasers in Indonesia, compared with their counterparts in such countries as the Philippines, Malaysia, Thailand, and Jordan, can use their land as collateral for a loan to develop income-earning property, thereby providing the government with greater cost recovery opportunities.

Governmental corruption in Indonesia is clearly to blame for, on the one hand, slowness to use expensive World Bank-funded photomaps for land titling and property tax collections, and, on the other hand, for "the preferential treatment given to civil servants and military personnel in obtaining loans" (Struyk, Hoffman, and Katsura 1990, 292). Server (1996, 28) writes that corrupt practices, including land banditry, have become rampant, and this corruption "has resulted in severe losses to the resources available for urban development."

MAINTENANCE. To keep slum-upgrading costs down, development agencies often propose low standards of infrastructure. Contractors therefore tend to deemphasize quality of construction, particularly when contractual arrangements are corrupt and supervision is inadequate. Consequently, facilities rapidly deteriorate. Primarily because of problems of maintenance, only a minority (47 percent) of the World Bank's urban projects are considered by its Operations Evaluation Department to be "sustainable" (OED 1994, 19).

While there are many reasons for lack of maintenance in slum upgrading projects, the problems of how to pay for it seem most daunting. Almost everywhere politicians are more eager to promise cheap or free public services than to emphasize adequate cost recovery. It is, after all, much easier for officials to find external financing for expanding urban water and sewer systems than to confront the political and administrative problems of increasing necessary revenues for maintenance (Israel 1992, 87).

In the Indonesian KIP program, "direct cost recovery from beneficiaries was avoided based on the view that the poor should not pay for urban services which had already been provided virtually free to the middle and upper classes" (Viloria 1991, 641). Only about half of the estimated value of Jakarta's property taxes, 8% of sanitation fees, and 1% of parking fees are collected (Server 1996).

Inasmuch as the wealthy avoid paying for services, how can the poor be required to do so? This means, on the one hand, that investments in KIP cannot be sustained and replicated and, on the other hand, that these investments "may have provided windfall gains to high income real estate dealers in Indonesian cities" (OED 1994a, xix). With corruption so extensive (causing an estimated $US 100 million to be stolen by Jakarta's mayor between 1988 and 1993), efforts to increase cost-recovery and local income are frustrated (Server 1996, 35).

It is often argued that the more the government attempts to enforce cost-recovery in slum-upgrading projects, the greater the likelihood of gentrification. However, gentrification may be more the result of other factors than cost recovery efforts. As land is improved, it will almost certainly go up in value.

A 1981 study of Calcutta's BIP indicated that rents in improved bustees had risen by an average of 43 percent (despite official rent control), as against 16 percent in unimproved bustees (Gupta 1985, 102–106). Whereas an estimated 10 percent of Calcutta's bustee residents were estimated to have been displaced by the BIP, an estimated 50 percent of Delhi's squatters who were forced to resettle on suburban land "illegally sold their rights of occupancy to higher-income households" (Pugh 1990, 182).

While some cross-subsidization of the costs of maintenance in slum-upgrading projects may be appropriate, governments cannot escape the need to build in the principle of "no pay, no project." This will work to the extent that there is beneficiary accountability, beneficiary representation in rule making, a graduated system of penalties, and an easy process for conflict resolution (Watson and Jagannathan 1995, 18).

Ultimately, the government must enforce cost recovery. For example, in a Madras sites and services project, cost recovery stood at over 96 per cent in 1986 when evictions were pursued in cases of serious arrears of payment (Pugh 1990, 244). On the other hand, in Indian cities where slum residents were legislatively protected from eviction, cost recovery proved to be impossible. Because slum residents tend to be impoverished, governments may find it necessary to expand income earning possibilities to encourage cost recovery for maintenance of services. The governments of Singapore, Hong Kong, and Malaysia, among others, have shown great ability to facilitate the income-earning opportunities of hawkers and others who are considered "within the informal sector" (see McGee and Yeung 1977).

Facilitating income-earning is clearly easier to do in sites and services projects, where land can be set aside for residents to build extra rooms for rent or for small-scale enterprises, than in slums where huts (typically 4 x 6 sq. ft. in Manila) tend to be extremely small. The development of rental housing in Malawi's sites and services schemes has contributed to the success of its housing policy (van der Linden 1986, 76–77).

More densely populated countries generally lack enough land for this cost-recovery approach. However, based upon my participation in a 1978 World Bank mission to San Salvador, I am convinced that governments can do much to mobilize the entrepreneurial potential of squatters for sustainable slum upgrading projects.

In many countries, the cost of slum upgrading can readily be recovered from beneficiaries if governments will make the effort. In Morocco and Tunisia, for example, households benefiting from World Bank slum-upgrading projects were willing and able to pay for the services provided inasmuch as real estate values in the project areas expanded by up to 400 percent. Unfortunately, because the local governments failed to undertake adequate property tax collection, these projects were evaluated as "unsustainable" (Kessides 1997, A4). Instead of dealing with this situation, the Moroccan government decided to discontinue slum upgrading as a national policy.

COMMUNITY PARTICIPATION. Without substantial community support and initiative, slum upgrading is difficult, if not impossible. Community cooperation is particularly important to resolve questions of tenure, mutual help, relocation, compensation, type or quality of services, charges, tax or fee collection, and enforcement of requirements.

However, there are often deep-rooted social and economic divisions preventing effective community participation. Lack of education among slum dwellers complicates these divisions, and political unrest and economic hardship intensify them. Politicians often prefer to exploit or ignore slum conditions rather than ameliorating the social tension preventing community cooperation.

While the World Bank has come to recognize the importance of community participation in its slum upgrading projects, it has also learned the difficulties involved. In its third Calcutta project (Calcutta III), beginning in 1983, the Bank introduced a fiscal-linkage mechanism by which municipalities gained funds for investments based on their ability to raise funds for operation and maintenance of previous government-sponsored investments. Unfortunately, political divisions within West Bengal, combined with declining regional economic growth and with political hostility to decentralization, undermined this project (Bannerjee and Chakrovorty 1994, 79). Calcutta III had to be discontinued when loans to municipalities were not repaid. Overall, this project was evaluated as unsatisfactory and unsustainable.

In Jakarta special KIP units were set up to help manage project implementation. However, because these special units were never fully recognized by governmental agencies, they largely ceased to exist upon project completion. Consequently, they never developed any administrative capacity to sustain the slum upgrading efforts (OED 1994a, 32).

The importance of community participation was evident in Manila in regard to Public Sanitation Facilities (PSFs) provided by the government with World Bank assistance (Luna, Ferrer and Ignacio 1994). While officials often allowed people to use the PSFs without payment or proof of residency because of public health considerations, they apparently could not prevent them from wasting the water and destroying or stealing equipment. Transients were often blamed for this. Yet, without some form of identification, there seemed no way of distinguishing transients from qualified residents or controlling their actions. In any case, the legal process was too disorganized to allow the Manila Water Supply authority to expel illegal or irresponsible users (Israel 1992, 57).

In their report to the World Bank, Luna, Ferrer and Ignacio (1994, 97-98) advocate putting PSFs clearly under the authority of users, giving them power to elect a management team but subjecting officers to by-laws, supervision, and financial auditing by the city government. However, these authors acknowledge that the water and sanitation situation will not be resolved until residents have their own carefully metered private sanitary facilities. This solution, of course, requires security of tenure, economic development, and community participation.

The importance of community acceptance was also revealed in a World Bank urban development project in India—the Madya Pradesh project (Kessides 1997, 21). The sanitation facilities provided suffered low acceptance by users because they were below the level of service demanded. Consequently, the agencies responsible took little interest in them. More effective implementation of this component occurred only when communities or NGOs were heavily involved in decision-making.

There are a variety of ways to encourage community participation in slum upgrading, assuming adequate government support. Yet, the approaches that work are generally "tough-minded" ones, as well as being sensitive to public opinion.

The experience of the Old Naledi estate in Gaberone, Botswana has been that residents will pay reasonable cost-recovery charges for trustworthy metered connections if they are given security of tenure (Potts 1994, 218). At the same time, to get security of tenure, all plots must have enough room for the type of pit latrine considered acceptable by sanitation experts.

In a World Bank project in Rio de Janeiro, the Water Company provides water to groups of households (called "condominiums") only if and when these groups commit to Operation and Maintenance (O&M)

of the service (Mejia 1994, 10). Another approach attempted in Lusaka and other cities is a block-metering system, under which water is supplied to groups of interested households with the understanding that, after a given level of default, supply will be cut off for the entire group (van der Linden 1986, 130). In Uganda, communities are selected for a water and sanitation project based upon their willingness to contribute up-front the equivalent of one-year's O&M costs and to organize Water User Groups (Kessides 1997, A21).

RESURRECTING A GOVERNMENT ROLE. I do not want to leave this section without emphasizing my sympathy with Turner's distrust of governmental activity. An article in THE ECONOMIST (May 6, 1995, 35–36) points out the extent to which Bombay's high property prices (with a square foot of commercial property costing about three times more than in New York City) and miserable slums are largely the government's fault, including legislation excessively limiting the size of urban land ownership, controlling rents, and disallowing the closing of bankrupt factories.

Yet, I am more in agreement with the writing of Hernando de Soto (1989), who emphasizes how counterproductive the Peruvian government was, prior to the 1990s, in regard to Lima's squatters and small-scale entrepreneurs. His message, however, is that what is needed is not, "less government," but, "better government"—one really concerned about and capable of dealing with Lima's terrible living conditions.

De Soto's emphasis on the importance of responsible and effective government leaves us with a quite different message from the one found in much recent urban development literature, such as the following: "the appropriate role of government would seem to be to minimize direct intervention, allowing the urban poor to find solutions that they can afford in their traditional way" (Choguill 1994, 944). Even if we agree with van der Linden (1994, 225) that "illegal systems have in the past achieved far more than any official initiative," the three alteratives that that he presents (the "muddling through" approach; "the public extra-legal model;" and "an imitation of the illegal system") can never substitute for good urban planning and public administration. Slum upgrading remains a worthy objective; but to suggest that it is going to happen by "formalizing the informal system," without overcoming the problems emanating from such a system, is certainly a myth.

This conclusion was underscored in the summer of 1995 when I officially reviewed for the World Bank a slum-upgrading project in Colombo, Sri Lanka. This project was intended to improve the living conditions of about 100,000 people in 185 low-income settlements by providing them with basic services and income-earning opportunities.

As I saw it, this project contained the following contradictory objectives: (1) There was to be "minimum disturbance and dislocation" but also "full cost recovery," with beneficiaries required to cover 100% of operation and maintenance costs. (2) While "lease hold rights or clear title" were to be provided, there was no clear insistence that only those willing and able to pay for tenure would be included.

Based upon my knowledge of similar World Bank slum upgrading projects, I argued that those responsible for this project needed to be very clear about the procedures and penalties for handling cost-recovery, together with enforcement arrangements. If public sanitation units were to be used (and this was uncertain), they must be under the authority of users, giving them power to decide location and quality of service and to elect a management team but subjecting officers to by-laws, supervision, and financial auditing. (Here I had in mind the suggestions of Luna, Ferrer and Ignacio regarding the Manila project earlier mentioned.)

Unfortunately, it is rare that World Bank officials take the trouble to anticipate the problems that are likely to be encountered in a project of this sort and then to work out in advance possible solutions. For reasons explained in Chapter 10, Bank staff are under pressure to sweep difficult problems under the rug so as not to delay the lending process and the beginning of new projects.

As is here indicated, I believe that slum upgrading must include land ownership arrangements, together with the enforcement of cost recovery. Despite the difficulties that must be anticipated, the following suggests what might be possible in this regard based upon the experience of several countries:

BRAZIL. THE ECONOMIST (October 14, 1995, 56) describes a project in Sao Paulo (the Cingapura project), under which 500,000 slum dwellers ("favelados") have been reinstalled in new homes, to be paid for with low-interest 20 year mortgages: "In public projects, tenants who pay for their property will tend to take care of it." This is also the approach in Curitiba, Brazil, with the understanding that people will be allowed to add rooms which they can rent out.

Brazilian officials have sometimes recognized that a certain amount of slum clearance is essential for slum upgrading. In Belo Horazonte, those in difficult areas, such as steep hills, have been removed (with adequate compensation) to safer areas and to places with better infrastructure with the financial assistance of the governments of Italy and Germany. This approach has been used to provide more than 90% of favela dwellers with electricity and water and 50% with access to a sewerage system (Fernandes 1995, 123).

Brazil has learned the hard way (as noted later in this chapter) that, without disincentives, incentives cannot work. In the Parana Market Towns Improvement Project begun in the 1990s, the state development bank provided loans to municipalities for slum upgrading efforts (Kessides 1997, 27). However, these communities were expected to repay these loans by taking advantage of the potential fiscal gains from increased land values, using "betterment levies." Those that failed to do so were threatened with the denial of grants-in-aid from the central government. As a result, 200 out of 287 municipalities were using betterment levies as a source of revenue within two years into the project.

MALAYSIA. Slum upgrading need not be the only solution to urban misery. In Penang Island, Malaysia, the government has seldom undertaken slum upgrading or sites-and-services options, despite a high percentage (31 percent) of low-quality "indigenous" housing and the need for about 30,000 housing units (Ruland 1992). Because of the high quality of its administration, Penang Island has been able to maintain a central sewerage system, serving about 45 percent of the population, leaving about 20 percent dependent upon a bucket system. Moreover, since most houses have piped water and electricity, there has been a significant decline in the infant mortality rate since the early 1970s, from 38 per 1,000 to 14 per thousand.

While officials in Penang would agree with Turner's hostility toward high-priced condominiums and subdivision units, they would have trouble with his hostility toward state-based and market-based housing solutions (Turner 1996, 339). In other words, simply by strong administration (the sort opposed by Turner), these officials have been able to combine humanistic and authoritarian approaches to slum conditions.

Indeed, Singapore (see Chapter 7) has entirely eliminated slums in an approach that might be called, "development from above." Its success in doing so supports my criticism, not simply of Turner's slum upgrading theory, but also, the NDA literature as a whole.

REVISITING THE NDA LITERATURE

My critique of the "development from below" literature in my 1989 article generated a heated response from Korten (1989), as I hoped it would because of my faith in academic debate. I therefore followed it with a 1992 article, in which I took a broader look at the "New Development Administration" (NDA) literature, as presented by Milton Esman (1988). The remaining sections of this chapter present a revision of that article (Werlin 1992), building upon the previous chapters.

While the NDA school of thought incorporates the "development from below" viewpoints mentioned at the beginning of this chapter, it goes beyond them in searching for ways to make administration more vigorous, effective, efficient, trustworthy, and even democratic. It has emerged from disillusion with the optimistic, scientific management, faith in government, and Western orientation of the 1960s. It also builds upon a greater willingess of Less Developed Country (LDC) leaders to rethink their earlier commitment to socialism and large-scale government and their hostility to democracy, capitalism, and decentralization.

With the collapse of Eastern European regimes and the success of the East Asian Newly Industrialized Countries, Gorbachev's proclamation of "glasnost" and "perestroika," combined with the end of the Cold War, were exciting as well as disturbing to LDC intellectuals. Yet, these intellectuals remain confused and hesitant in seeking reform. And for reasons here indicated, the NDA does not provide them with the guidance they need.

SOURCES OF DISAPPOINTMENT

Everywhere we turn in LDCs, we see evidence of what I call "political inelasticity." This is clearest in Africa under the "predatory rule" described by Fatton (1992, 28) where authoritarianism coexists "with a definite lack of authority." As we turn more broadly to the literature having to do with the least developed parts of the world, we find "the declining relevance of formal state structures which results partly from economic incapacity" (Garvey 1991, 591).

Because people have decreasing faith in government, they have to turn to non-governmental organizations (NGOs) and unauthorized or "informal" self-help and mutual-help initiatives. Instead of facilitating these forms of popular participation, "system elites will try to oppose, squash, preempt, and manipulate new development initiatives" (Gran 1983, 148). Thus, according to Migdal (1987, 391), we have a clashing image of a state being simultaneously strong enough to knead society "into new forms and shapes" and yet "nearly hapless in the swirl of dizzying social changes that have overtaken these societies."

As I see it, we are caught in a terrible dilemma. The NDA is basically a reaction to the weaknesses of public administration everywhere, but particularly in LDCs. To overcome these weaknesses, NDA supporters emphasize the importance of debureaucratization, decentralization, deregulation, privatization, public choice, and community control. However, these alternatives often lead to disappointing results. To be more successful, a much stronger public administration is necessary—just the sort that is so rare in LDCs. So, we are back to where we started from.

The point that I am making is also made by Arturo Israel (1990), though without the theoretical context suggested here. On the one hand, he points out that (p. 1) a "worldwide concensus has emerged about the limits of what can be achieved by public sectors" and, on the other hand (p. 11) that a larger role for the private sector requires "a greatly modernized and higher quality public sector."

The primary objective of this chapter is to explore what "reinventing government" might mean, using political elasticity theory, concentrating upon aspects not covered in the previous chapters. The need to do so is explained by Dubnick (1994, 260), who suggests that "the reinventors offer little theoretical underpinning, relying on anecdotal evidence and theory borrowed from others." Consequently, they do not offer a realistic alternative to the bureaucratic model for providing public services.

PUBLIC CHOICE

Public choice theory has been greatly influenced by Albert Hirschman's 1970 book, EXIT, VOICE AND LOYALTY, in which he makes a distinction between "exit" (economic response opportunities) and "voice" (political response opportunities). Paul (1994, 48) has built upon this work for the benefit of World Bank staff, suggesting possibilities for enhancing "exit" (using vouchers and grants, contracting out, privatization, etc.) and "voice" (using referenda, public hearings, panels, public surveys, etc.). Based upon a case study of Indonesian water user associations, he gives examples of effective exit and voice mechanisms.

Paul (1994, 36–37) is quite realistic in recognizing the limitations of public choice theory. Exit alternatives, for example, can be easily undermined by inadequate legal requirements and information, weak enforcement of regulations, and corruption. Voice mechanisms, without appropriate arrangements for decentralization, legislative and judicial independence, and bureaucratic resources, are likely to be useless. "Failure to take these steps which encourage the public to use voice may result in increased public frustration" (Paul 1994, 37).

In the United States, public choice theory has been linked to the writing of Osborne and Gaebler (1992), who have become America's most influential advocates of "entrepreneurial government"—decentralized, problem-solving, innovative, and mission-driven. Yet, this form of government is common in Europe, emphasizing the importance of two-way flows of communication. In Norway, for example, the public is frequently asked to present its experiences with the public service and its proposals for increasing administrative responsiveness (OECD 1987, 102). The member states of the Council of Europe have even granted resident non-nationals the right to vote in local elections and, in the case of Luxembourg, required consultative committees to represent their interests.

While housing vouchers for low income tenants remain relative uncommon in the United States, the majority of households in Sweden receive them, allowing them to choose among the housing alternatives available on the open market. In Germany, since 1970, all families are able to apply for assistance to cover the difference between "actual rent" and "tolerable" or affordable rents. Butler and Kondratas (1987), among others, advocate giving vouchers to American students, with bigger vouchers available for schools accepting difficult students. Vermont has had a voucher system since the 19th Century, under which local school districts can either designate a local private school as eligible for students to go to with public funds or provide vouchers to students to attend any approved nonsectarian school.

The World Bank has increasingly come to accept public choice theory in its development of projects, including an expanded role for the private sector in the delivery of public services and for competition and increased opportunity for clients, users, or beneficiaries, to influence the planning and operation of these services (Israel 1992, 1–2). How this has affected Bank-funded agricultural extension projects, together with the problems involved, was presented in Chapter 3. As I then indicated, I have no trouble with public choice theory, so long as we understand the political software requirements essential to its success.

In the United States, public choice expanded during the 1980s in many sectors without leading to better public service, according to articles in Kamerman and Kahn (1989). While competition grew between for-profit and nonprofit day-care centers, this competition "led to lower staff/child ratios, larger groups, larger centers, less equipment, and lower caregiver salaries" (Kamerman and Kahn 1989, 254). Since for-profit centers could exclude more impoverished and difficult youngsters, poor families became decreasingly able to find high quality service.

The same thing happened in Wisconsin in regard to nursing homes, accounting for greater complaints against for-profit nursing homes than against their non-profit and government counterparts (Bendick 1989, 113–114). Inasmuch as the public sector neglected its regulatory, monitoring, and enforcement functions, the public (especially the poor) ended up worse off.

In LDCs, public choice theory has encouraged many cities (e.g., Buenos Aires, Cairo, and Calcutta) to allow associations or unions of privately owned taxis and minibuses to compete with forms of public transportation (Roth and Wynne 1982). When governments have been able to negotiate with these associations agreements on rules and regulations and then enforce them, the public has greatly benefited from the diversity of service provided.

In the case of Nairobi, however, the opposition of the Kenya Bus Service, together with the weakness of paratransit ("matatu") cooperatives, undermined the World Bank's effort during the 1980s to develop a safe and reliable paratransit system here (Lee-Smith 1989). This failure indicates that, without the government's ability to integrate and alternate incentives and disincentives (as required by political elasticity theory), matatu drivers and owners will continue to ignore parking or traffic regulations, insurance requirements, and safety conditions.

POPULAR PARTICIPATION

Many NDA supporters argue that the topic of decentralization, as presented in the previous chapter, should be primarily concerned with expanding opportunities for Non-Governmental Organizations (NGOs) to "help people help themselves." Bureaucracies, whether originating at the central or local levels, have a tendency to stifle local participation. Thus, in the words of Gran (1983, 169): "development cannot and should not be externally managed."

While few writers on development go so far as to deny a useful role that government can play in development, many emphasize the danger of hurting NGOs in the process of helping them. In rural development, Uphoff (1991, 467) points out, people should not be seen as "target groups" but, rather, as "intended beneficiaries": "Putting people first in development projects comes down to tailoring the design and implementation of projects to the needs and capabilities of people who are suposed to benefit from them." Hardoy and Satterthwaite (1989, 300) make a similar point in regard to urban development, that "most governments' legal and regulatory systems for planning and managing urban areas inhibit and repress the effort of their citizens to meet their own basic needs with their own resources and organizations."

In arguing for popular participation, the point is often made that there are some traditional organizations and methods that work well without outside assistance. A good example is the "njangis" or "tontines" in Cameroon (Nchari 1990). Several types exist: rotational and non-rotational. In the rotational ones, members make fixed contributions of money periodically with the amount contributed by the entire group assigned to each of the members in rotation. The second type functions as a bank, with loans granted to needy members from the deposits made and repaid at an agreed-upon interest rate. The njangis are democratically run, with members selecting their management committee, which is responsible for holding meetings, registering decisions, keeping accounts, and imposing discipline.

About 50 percent of Cameroon's population participate in these njangis. Unlike the regular banks, the njangis charge high enough interest rates to accommodate the high rate of inflation which Cameroon has been exposed to. For this reason, civil servants, who constitute the majority of the country's formal sector employees, prefer njangis to the banks.

The njangi system does have its weaknesses. Since the njangis are not legally constituted bodies, they cannot take legal action against members in default. The vast majority of them remain small and scattered throughout the country, with assets seldom amounting (during the 1980s) to more than US $40,000. In the absence of promotional services and governmental support, they are severely limited in what they can do. At the same time, they undermine the capacity of the banks to fund large investments. Yet, efforts to link the njangis to some governmentally supported superstructure (such as credit unions or cooperatives) have so far failed.

There are many examples of local governments, as well as community organizations, persuading citizens to voluntarily contribute for such projects as buildings for secondary schools, town halls, community centers, and health clinics (Adamolekun, 1991a). In addition to voluntary contributions in cash, contributions can take the form of the donation of services.

In Malawi, village leaders formed project committees and work teams, led by Project Assistants, to complete nearly 50 gravity-fed water supply systems during the 1970s and 1980s (Ostrom, Schroeder, and Wynne 1990, 24–25). While the government assumes much of the costs of maintaining these systems, ordinary villages have provided the skills and labor for construction and maintenance. By using appropriate technology and local knowledge of terrain and water use patterns, costs have been kept relatively low. Repair teams can generally replace broken pipes within two days.

In Kenya, on the other hand, excessive centralization has undermined cooperatives, which are active in food production and marketing of cash crops, and "harambee" (community) schools undertaken by self-help committees (Adamolekun 1991a). At the same time, the harambee system has been somewhat discredited by the practice used by some officials of coercing the local population into contributing to government-sponsored activities. The controversy over "coercive voluntarism" in Kenya is summarized by Hill (1991). While harsh and undemocratic measures have been clearly used in Kenya to enforce harambee payments, the results in the areas that Hill studied seem to be more positive than negative. In particular, "Harambee schools appear to have increased proportionally the number of secondary school places for girls" (Hill 1991, 292).

The success of Kenya's harambee schools has encouraged World Bank officials to examine this approach in their effort to increase the percentage (estimated to be less than 10 percent) of African education policies and projects that are successfully implemented (Colletta and Perkins 1995, 12). However, efforts in Ghana and Uganda to get community participation in school construction and maintenance met with mixed success. Lack of consensus among community groups, donors, NGOs, government departments, and professional interest groups makes such efforts extremely difficult, Colletta and Perkins (1995, 12–13) point out, adding: "Even when consensus is achieved, decisions reached by the participants may be contrary to the donor's or government's perception of the national interest."

The report by Colletta and Perkins (1995, 19–21) notes the success of primary schools run by the Bangladesh Rural Advancement Committee (BRAC). In comparison with government schools, the 6,000 BRAC schools have, not only proven to be more efficient and cost-effective in reaching children (particularly girls) of low-income families, but also in maintaining much lower drop-out and repeater rates.

BRAC is a good example of how popular participation can be mobilized by a NGO which has a reputation for being "an honest, accountable organization" (Lovell 1992, 70). Whereas the Bangladeshi government is characterized by the poor political software mentioned in previous chapters, the BRAC bureaucracy is well trained, qualified, and supervised. As such, it "operates in a learning atmosphere in which a spiral of program design, implementation, change, new implementation, and expansion is the norm" (Lovell 1992, 175). Its sustainability strategy relies on its ability to empower the poor by maximizing their savings and self-reliance, thereby reducing their dependence on outside agencies, including BRAC itself (Lovell 1992, 186).

The concept of the "informal sector" emerged from International Labor Organization research during the 1970s to describe the efforts of the urban poor to survive economically in the face of official opposition and other difficulties: zoning regulations, expensive fees, unobtainable licenses, price controls, restrictions on what can be sold, and other forms of official harassment. Consequently, slum dwellers tend to work in areas without good roads, water, electricity, police protection, or other basic services. And because they are usually working in these places without permission, their businesses remain marginal and tenuous. To survive at all often requires extensive systems of grassroots organizations, noted in the previous chapter.

Within the informal sector, hawkers are often seen by officials as problematic because they interfere with traffic, contribute to crime, undermine health and environmental conditions, annoy citizens and tourists, and unfairly compete with tax-paying shopkeepers. Yet, McGee and Yeung (1977) take a positive view of hawkers, seeing them, not only as providing essential employment opportunities, but also as facilitating the economic functioning of LDC cities. What is essential are policies and practices that maximize the usefulness of hawkers while reducing the problems associated with their activities.

Despite these strong NDA arguments for popular participation, there is much disillusionment with the concept. While few experts in this field would go so far as to agree with Jones and Wiggle (1987, 107) that "most international organizations and national governments have written off community development as a lost cause," many would agree with Annis's conclusion (1987, 133) that "state policy is crucially important in determining the character and capacities of grassroots growth." "It may well be that wildflowers grow by themselves," he points out: "But grassroots organizations do not."

Michael Cernea, the World Bank's senior sociologist, is an enthusiastic supporter of popular participation, having edited several editions of the well-known publication, PUTTING PEOPLE FIRST (1985, 1991). Yet, he notes (1992, 2) that "there is a wide agreement that popular participation in public programs is insufficient." While many donor-assisted projects emphasize community participation, "evaluation report after evaluation report usually show that these projects were as short on accomplishments as they were long on intentions and promises" (Cernea 1992, 1). Cernea's conclusion is supported by Montgomery (1988, 43), who notes that participation has degenerated into "formalism," inasmuch as "development and lending agencies are urging public bureaucracies to design and manage local programs to maximize popular participation, even where there is little direct evidence that better results will thereby accrue."

PRIVATIZATION

Privatization, in all its many forms (divestment of state-owed enterprises, contracting out of services, leasing of public facilities or assets, etc.) is often combined with public choice and popular participation or community control in NDA literature. During the 1980s, more than 50 countries attempted to sell their state-owned enterprises (SOEs) and in other ways, to roll back the boundaries of the public sector (Aharoni 1991, 73–74). Using contractors and mobilizing the private sector have been part of this process.

Silverman (1990, 54), points out that roads financed by World Bank loans and credits during the 1960s and 1970s are deteriorating at a rate which will make many of them unusable long before the loans for their construction have been repaid. Yet, in Tanzania, which has a notoriously weak public sector, local governments managed during the 1980s to find an estimated US $9 million per year to hire private contractors to undertake road construction and maintenance. At the same time, highway authorities at the central level were unaware of such activities and the capability of private contractors.

In Bangladesh, sugar mill owners have used a portion of the sale price of their sugar for road development and maintenance (Ostrom, Schroeder and Wynne, 1990, p. 22). Tea producers in Bangladesh also impose a cess on marketed tea to help develop and maintain the roads serving the producers. They even supplement these funds with their own to carry out some road work to reduce the damage done to their transport vehicles.

However, privatization has encountered much the same skepticism as public choice and popular participation. "Privatization alone, without the introduction of competition, may simply transform a public monopoly into a private monopoly," Aharoni (1991, 75) points out, adding: "a change of ownership without a change in market structure may not improve efficiency." Privatized firms, if provided with inappropriate subsidies, tax advantages, or forms of protection, may end up benefiting a small number of wealthy people or managers without concern for the quality and cost of their products or services (Bounin and Michalet, 1991).

The effectiveness of privatization depends (as suggested earlier with regard to public choice and popular participation) on the ability of the state "to define, set up and control macroeconomic and sectoral policies" (Bounin and Michalet 1991, 226). In other words, the public sector must establish the economic, legal, financial, and political environment under which the private sector can develop. Otherwise, the market economy will become a "free-for-all jungle," in which corruption prevails, contracts are ignored, and the public is cheated.

PROBLEMS WITH THE NDA

While, as here indicated, I have much sympathy for many of the NDA propositions, I also (somewhat reluctantly) take issue with them. At an earlier time, I might have been accused of having a "Western bias." But with the success of the Asian Newly Industrialized Countries (NICs) in adopting the approaches of More Developed Countries (MDCs), we need not be so apologetic about using their experience to analyze the problems of LDCs.

I continue to find many NDA supporters with a "mythical image of the benign, united, knowledgeable community." Even if I have misperceived their position, as Korten (1989, 569) suggested, I maintain the following points:

- Impoverished communities generally require leadership to develop. The concept of "development from below" is a naive one. Korten (1989, 572–573) took umbrage at my insistence that the Self Employed Women's Association (SEWA) of Ahmedabad, India is an example of "top-down" development. However, I was merely reiterating the paradox suggested by Esman and Uphoff (1984, 258) that it is often necessary to use "top-down initiative to get bottom-up development."

I argued in my 1989 article that SEWA emerged in 1974 from the charismatic leadership of Ela Bhatt, who was then associated with the Women's Section of the Textile Labor Association (TLA) of the State of Gujarat (Sebstad 1982). It was organized to help self-employed women obtain small bank loans, handle savings and funds, and undertake new business opportunities.

Gradually, SEWA became an independent economic and political pressure group. Because of the failure of the banks to understand and relate to low-income clients, SEWA began in 1976 to lend directly to members. When the TLA (consisting largely of factory employees) became too fearful of competition from self-employed women, SEWA ended its affiliation with the TLA. SEWA then persuaded the State of Gujarat's Labor Ministry to improve the wages and working conditions of laborers in Ahmedabad's cloth market. Eventually, SEWA expanded into running training courses, overcoming production problems, upgrading the skills of members, helping women enter such nontraditional occupations as plumbing and carpentry, and providing members with life insurance and maternity benefits.

While SEWA seems to me to be the product of the sort of charismatic leadership emphasized by Max Weber, strong organization was certainly essential for its success. In other words, SEWA's authority was based on the control exercised by its organization as well as on the loyalty engendered by its political and economic activities.

Loan applicants were carefully scrutinized with regard to their reputation in the community, their personal background, their business skills, and their capacity to repay. New applicants were frequently visited by a field worker, often unannounced, to determine the accuracy of answers given and any problems which might affect their ability to repay loans. In cases of serious delays in repayment, field workers helped borrowers identify their problems and overcome them. They were trained to deal with family and personal problems as well as with problems of production, storage, and marketing. Yet, if necessary, they could expel women from SEWA membership and deprive them of benefits. Consequently, SEWA remains one of India's most successful NGOs, according to a 1992 book (Rose).

Charlick (1984) provides another example of community development emerging from strong leadership in his analysis of the "Animation Rurale" approach used in Haiti and Francophone Africa. The most extreme proponents of this approach, the liberationists, shared a vision of society in which people were encouraged to organize on a voluntary basis in small-scale collective units and to operate on the principle of self-reliance.

However, in reality, "animation tends to promote a top-down style of communication and training" (Charlick 1984, 97). Without effective information dissemination and training, villagers could not check abuses of power. Thus, in a program in Niger, small producers had to be taught how to defend themselves against the potentially dishonest practices of cooperative peanut market officials.

- The development process requires strong bureaucracies. Those associated with the NDA, according to Wunsch (1991, 10), agree with the following conclusion: "the centrally directed, hierarchical bureaucracy has been ineffective in undertaking the complex, uncertain and resource-strapped task of Third World rural development." While I also criticize the rigid apolitical Weberian conception of hierarchy, rules, procedures, rights, contractual duties, and specialized positions or roles, I consider them essential for the successful functioning of organizations. What is necessary, as I pointed out in previous chapters, is a high quality of political software for these bureaucratic requisites to be effective.

This point is underscored by Charlick (1984, 126), in reviewing efforts to help rural communities in a number of French-speaking countries, suggesting that local people did not necessarily benefit more from private sector than public sector assistance. Factors which Charlick (1984, 135) finds important in determining the success of community development (Animation Rurale) efforts include: methods of gaining popular involvement, the extent and quality of training offered to participants, the style of communication maintained between participants and supervisory staff, and the level of commitment required of participants at the outset. Not so important, according to Charlick, were the nature of the staff (professionals or volunteers), links between local and international groups, social homogeneity of the community, and origins of the staff (from outside or inside the community).

- Development requires the cooperation of beneficiaries. Development, in other words, is not charity. The organizations that work best to facilitate development insist that communities really want the assistance being offered and are capable of contributing to it.

  Successful community development organizations described by Finin, Uphoff, and Wallen (1984, 65–76) are usually insistent upon "local commitment." For example, the Kottar Social Service Society of India, affiliated with the Catholic Church, charges fees to cover all recurrent costs, requires compulsory savings, and insist on attendance and quality work in infrastructure projects. The Penny Foundation of Guatemala focuses on producer groups "with shared responsibility for loan repayments and self-reliance through social learning." Likewise, Save the Children Federation (SCF) in Indonesia will continue funding only those communities that have successfully carried out previous SCF projects.

- Successful development agencies must have the ability to shift from soft to hard forms of power. Such hard forms of power may be nothing more than a threat to withhold or discontinue financial assistance.

  Korten (1989, 572) criticized my effort to point out this fact as "Machiavellian." As a political scientist, I respect Machiavelli. Leadership involves manipulation, just as it also involves consensus-building. More to the point is the bargaining process at work in any successful decentralization effort.

  In the health care field, the bargaining process can take many forms, according to an article in THE ECONOMIST (May 25, 1991, 64). An increasing number of OECD countries are requiring purchasers to choose among providers; forcing providers to compete for business; encouraging people to shop around among insurers; obliging hospitals to publish details of their costs; cancelling contracts with inefficient hospitals; shifting resources from hospitals to primary care; encouraging more competition among providers; financing providers according to the number of patients they can attract; etc. Such bargaining would be meaningless without an enforcement capacity.

Turning to LDCs, we also see, in cases of effective development efforts, a bargaining process being employed, with agencies using persuasion and inducement but, when necessary, hardening forms of power. Even the Inter-American Foundation, an American government-funded organization devoted to "development from below," will suspend its funding of projects if it is not satisfied with an organization's implementation or accounting procedures. Its success in doing so encouraged Congress during the 1980s to use the same approach for Africa.

CONCLUSION: COMBINING AN ENABLING WITH A CONTROLLING ENVIRONMENT

While I remain an enthusiastic supporter of public choice, popular participation, and privatization, I insist that they be undertaken within an enabling environment conducive to their success. Such an environment, according to my theory of political elasticity, suggests a relationship between central or sponsoring agencies and communities or local organizations, under which leaders are willing and able to use their power in acceptable ways to increase cooperation and to decrease opposition.

The enabling environment I have in mind incorporates the political relationships stressed by Lijphart (1968) in describing the business of politics in the Netherlands as "the politics of accommodation." Thus, without the political software considerations emphasized here, we cannot deal with the question raised by Bryant and White (1982, 75): "What kinds of structures and processes are best able to facilitate development?"

In the view of Bryant and White (1982, 75), the basic problem in development administration is "one of organizational design." However, the closer we look at the problems of LDCs, the more we see that their problems stem, not so much from administrative organization, as from administrative orientation.

In Mali, for example, the morale of the civil service was low during the 1980s because salaries had not kept up with inflation and were not paid on time and because officials lacked materials with which to work (Geilar 1985, 29). Here, as elsewhere, rules and regulations were not seen as a way of guiding public behavior but as opportunities to impose a "taxe sauvage" on the general public. So long as this is the situation, leaders can endlessly reorganize the civil service without improving its functioning.

I also find the "institutional analysis" suggested by Wunsch (1991, 18) unsatisfactory. What he is searching for are "conceptual arrangements to help analyze and link goods, tasks, incentive systems, and rules." In other words, there must be a match between what people want (roads, let us say) and the institutional arrangements (rules, charges, tasks, etc.) for cost-recovery and maintenance. However, unless these institutional arrangements are RESPECTED, they will be useless. This point is illustrated in Nellis's study (1989) of Contract Plans (CPs), as used in France and Senegal, to stimulate the performance of public enterprises.

In France, the government has used the CP process to guide and evaluate the performance of most major public enterprises. It has given firms more authority to set prices, reduce the workforce, and terminate unprofitable product lines or factories. At the same time it has facilitated the use of quantified performance indicators to publicize and evaluate results and to reward management. While CPs have seldom caused public enterprises to dramatically improve performance, they have enhanced "the clarity of goals, the transparency of operations and achievements, and the ease of evaluation" (Nellis 1989, 26).

In Senegal, on the other hand, CPs have become almost meaningless. They are often drawn up by foreign consultants without taking into account the extent to which goals are realistic and funds available for their achievement. Officials then approve these CPs without taking seriously their implications. Consequently, they seldom pay for services rendered by public enterprises, thereby forcing these enterprises into high indebtedness and encouraging mismanagement. While the government periodically promises to reform the CP process, there continues to be "a steady stream of delays, missed deadlines, disagreements, and misunderstandings in the creation and implementation of CPs" (Nellis 1989, 54).

In looking at the sad history of Senegal's CPs, I end agreeing with Korten and Uphoff (1981) on the need for "bureaucratic reorientation," including reform of rewards, supervision, personnel procedures, training, and so forth. However, Korten's call (1989, 571) for a bureaucracy "that works more in an enabling than a controlling mode" shows a misunderstanding of administrative requisites for development. My theory suggests that "enabling" and "controlling" go together. You cannot have one without the other.

To show the linkage between the enabling and controlling modes, we might briefly compare the functioning of administration in Brazil and Switzerland. While both countries are attempting to help their more impoverished regions, Brazil's central government has been far less effective than that of Switzerland in distributing funds in a useful and equitable manner.

Brazil's failure to promote the development of its less affluent states largely stems from the fact that its federal government does not exercise enough control over municipal fiscal capacity in its distribution formula (Shah 1991). Consequently, the availability of generous federal funds has allowed some municipalities to underutilize property taxes and user charges. Moreover, the inadequate project review and approval process has meant that inter-governmental transfers have served "not as means of safeguarding any federal objectives, but more as a vehicle for pork-barrel politics . . ." (Shah 1991, 75). In other words, because grants are not made conditional on achieving certain objectively verifiable criteria relating to minimum standards and access, they promote administrative inefficiencies without helping the poorer segments of the population.

In Switzerland, aid to less affluent (mountain) regions and to regions facing economic difficulties is not automatic (OECD 1991). Communes must put forward projects which offer a strong probability of maintaining or creating jobs and diversifying the economy. A three-stage screening process includes: banks, using normal profitability criteria; the surrounding canton, based upon an evaluation of the project's chances and its importance for the local economy; and the Federal Department of the Political Economy, which currently emphasizes such non-economic factors as socio-cultural diversity and protection of the environment.

In Switzerland, as in other countries, there continues to be conflict between the objectives of equity and efficiency. Nevertheless, federal and cantonal policies combined to promote during the 1980s (for the first time in almost thirty years) a more rapid increase in the population in mountain regions than the national average, a diversification of jobs in electronics and microtechnology, and the development of the services sector. While the Confederation, in dealing with regions and cantons, "plays the role of parents vis-a-vis their children," it does so in a consensual and constructive way to strengthen their competence and political economy (OECD 1991, 52–53).

Turning to LDCs, we can seldom find governments mobilizing local development, as exemplified by Switzerland. In their study of local government in Pakistan in the 1960s, Nicholson and Khan (1974) concluded that such local institutions as Basic Democracies and cooperatives organized by the government could claim little success in facilitating economic activities, infrastructure, and health or educational services. While under the Zia regime during the 1980s, elected local and district councils were given significant powers to impose taxes and mobilize resources for local development, "routinized corruption" continued to undermine the delivery of governmental services (Islam 1989).

The Aga Khan Rural Support Program (AKRSP), in contrast, was able to benefit about 54 percent of the population in the Northern Areas of Pakistan during the 1980s, according to the World Bank's Operations Evaluation Department (OED 1990a). Among its accomplishments have been: improved roads and water supply; the planting of trees; better seeds and planting material; and expansion of training programs. Nearly 40 percent of identified projects were completed from 1983 to 1989, with most of the others under construction. Village organizations were able to accumulate US $3 million, and women's organizations, nearly $300,000.

By virtue of its careful assembling and testing of new technologies, the AKRSP was able to persuade farmers to try them. What also helped was its effort to train about 2,500 people in agriculture, livestock, and marketing. Particular attention has been paid to getting villagers to recognize the need to preserve the area's unique fauna and flora, thereby opening up tourism possibilities which would bring prosperity to the area without threatening natural ecosystems.

The most recent OED study of the AKRSP (1996) suggested that it was largely responsible for a doubling in real terms of household incomes in the Northern Region since 1983. While weaknesses and difficulties remain, "AKRSP must be considered a successful program" (1996, 9).

The AKRSP, using a model based upon experiences with rural cooperatives in 19th century Europe and villages in Taiwan and Korea after World War II, together with more recent work in Bangladesh, Pakistan, and Sri Lanka, requires each village participating in its program to establish a Village Organization (VO) and enter into a contract (OED

1990, 88–89). The VO must meet as a general body on a regular basis to identify projects to be undertaken by the villagers for the benefit of the village as a whole and to review progress made.

All members must make savings deposits at their regular meetings, which are recorded in an individual pass book and are banked collectively. Only when the AKRSP and the VO are in agreement on the projects to be implemented, the group savings arrangement, and implementation plans does the AKRSP make the first installment of a grant (averaging US $9,100) for the work to be undertaken.

As the work progresses, additional installments are made; but the total grant covers less than half of the imputed cost of the agreed-upon projects, when taking account of the VO's labor contribution. The AKRSP makes only one grant to a village. All subsequent activities, including maintenance of the initial project, have to be financed by the VO or through credit.

The relationship between the AKRSP and the villages emerges from a series of diagnostic dialogues, with the General Manager (GM) initiating the first one. Thereafter, the organizational and institutional development of the VO is the responsibility of the AKRSP's Social Organizers (SOs), together with its technical specialists. An effort is made to keep the dialogues democratic and open to the general public to prevent powerful minorities from unduly appropriating the benefits. An effort is also made to develop local technical and managerial skills to enable the VOs to become less dependent upon the AKRSP.

The AKRSP's success is dependent upon its effective bureaucracy. All senior staff are well-qualified professionals, with many of them having had extensive international experience. Those working in the villages, not only have advanced degrees, but also speak the local languages of the Northern Areas. While management structure is relatively flat (egalitarian), the GM remains in close daily contact with staff activities and with all major issues that arise. Staff members are given great responsibility in dealing with the problems of more than 500 villages in the program; but delegation of responsibility is made possible by a system of regular senior staff meetings, a very high level of documentation of routine business, and attention to detail.

This summary of AKRSP's approach to community development is presented to show how "development from below" has to be linked to "development from above." Without institutional arrangements that can push and pull community development, the best that one can hope for, in regard to urban areas, is what Hardoy and Satterthwaite (1988, 99–100) refer to as "benign tolerance": "an acceptance of segregated urban societies ruled from above in ways which can only limit the potential of their citizens and undermine their dynamic and fruitful interactions." And in regard to the poorest and most disadvantaged segments of the population as a whole, any hope for sustainable, self-reliant development "is a vain hope" without effective governmental, international, and nongovernmental assistance (Lovell 1992, 188–189).

When development gurus (as noted in Goulet 1989, 165) urge "deprofessionalization in all domains of life," I sympathize with their respect for popular wisdom, but, consider their viewpoint to be counterproductive. For example, according to Mathur (1985, 25), the reasons for the decline of Panchayati Raj institutions in India "are related to the fact that the local levels lacked expertise which was needed to cope with the growing complexities of development." Indeed, there is so little evidence of real professionalization in LDCs that advocacy of "deprofessionalization" in these countries might be greeted with amusement, to say the least.

CHAPTER 6

Partisanship Versus Statesmanship
Understanding Corruption

INTRODUCTION

This chapter is a follow-up to several of my articles (Werlin 1972, 1973) on corruption in Ghana. In the 1972 one I purposely avoided trying to come up with a definition; and in the 1973 one, I defined it (with the assistance of Victor LeVine, whose useful book on Ghanaian corruption appeared in 1975) as "the diversion of public resources to nonpublic purposes."

Both approaches (avoiding a definition and using the one that I did) indicate my perplexity in confronting problems in the comparative corruption literature. I was also personally disturbed by the question (as presented to my students): was I corrupt in avoiding unrealistic exchange rates by using the blackmarket when I did my research in Ghana with a small stipend in the early 1970s?

In revisiting the topic of political and administrative corruption, I will, on the one hand, suggest why it is, to quote Gould and Amaro-Reyes (1983, 2) "that no single commonly accepted definition of corruption exists," and, on the other hand, why it is essential to have one to avoid the "difficulties traceable in large measure to the inability of scholars to agree on a definition of the term that would embrace all corrupt acts and yet anticipate distinctions among them" (Atkinson and Mancuso 1980, 463). The definition that I suggest for political and administrative corruption—partisanship that threatens statesmanship—is not intended to supplant the many currently in use, but to supplement, clarify, and integrate them.

The definition that I have in mind is put forward: (1) to be realistic as well as moralistic about corruption; (2) to understand why corruption has a more devastating impact on Less Developed Countries (LDCs) than More Developed Countries (MDCs); and (3) to explain why corruption, even when it is "standard operating procedure," must be considered a cause for concern.

The mysteries of development that will be looked at in this chapter have to do with the following questions: (1) Why should we worry about corruption in LDCs when there is so much of it in MDCs without preventing their economic development?; (2) Why should we condemn corruption when it may be legal, functional, socially acceptable, necessary, and unblameworthy?; and (3) Is it useful, meaningful, and fair for those in MDCs (ignoring their own corruption) to criticize the corruption in LDCs?

Because the definition used here may appear to the reader bewildering, its origins in political theory should be explained before we go further. In doing so, I will return to the two subdivisions of politics (partisanship and statesmanship) noted in the Introduction. This double meaning of politics will also be used in the next chapter in clarifying the relationship of democracy to development.

Introductory political science textbooks tend to use such meanings of politics as "the authoritative allocation of values" and "the pursuit of power" without indicating the relationship between these concepts (Nordquest 1991, 504). Actually, both of these meanings are misleading, as pointed out in previous chapters. Values cannot simply be IMPOSED (behavior, yes; values, no); and power cannot be PURSUED within an empty framework. The process of inculcating values requires a strong relationship between leaders and followers. Such a relationship cannot develop unless the struggle for power is carried out within an acceptable regulatory arrangement.

As explained in the Introduction, I have used Wolin's 1960 book on Western political thought to derive an overarching definition of politics (keeping as close as possible to the original Greek meaning of the word: "the relationship between leadership and followership for the purpose of governance"). Within this overarching definition, we can find two subordinate definitions of politics: the struggle for competitive advantage (partisanship) and the struggle for consensus (statesmanship). It is from this tension between partisanship and statesmanship (the two sides of politics) that corruption emerges.

According to Wolin's presentation of Plato (1960, 42), the essence of political philosophy or science has to do with "the right management of the public affairs of the community." However, Plato also conceived politics to be "the struggle for competitive advantage." Consequently, Plato and philosophers after him could not escape a paradox in their analysis of politics: "A science that is at odds with its own subject matter." I believe this paradox to be relevant to corruption.

To see the usefulness of superimposing my definition of corruption on others, we might begin by going back to the original meaning of corruption as something impure, debased, or defective—improper (corrosive) behavior, in other words (Caiden 1988, 7). The trouble with this basic conception of corruption is that it depends upon one's viewpoint. As Peters and Welch note (1978, 974): "What may be 'corrupt' to one citizen, scholar, or public official is 'just politics' to another, or 'indiscretion' to a third."

Even when people agree that an action is corrupt, they are likely to disagree about its seriousness. In this regard, Heidenheimer's classification of forms of corruption as "black, gray, or white" (1970, 26–27), based upon the seriousness with which both elite and mass opinion would consider them to be and the extent of ambiguity about them, is useful. However, this classification is also subject to an underlying system of values, which can easily be shaken, as the following illustration may indicate:

Imagine watching two basketball games. In each of them, we recognize what "fouling" is—physical contact with a ballhandler, for example. In Game A, a National Basketball Association professional game, fouling has a detailed and legalistic meaning and is enforced by carefully selected and trained referees. Distinctions between accidental, flagrant, intentional, technical, and other forms of fouling can therefore be made. A losing team may deliberately foul to "catch-up," hoping for a missed free throw, and would thus be infuriated if the foul were not called.

In Game B, on the other hand, where the referees are known to be easily bribed and partial to the team paying them the most, fouling becomes amorphous (done with indifference towards the rules or in contempt for them) because teams must, not only foul to win, but pay the referees to facilitate their fouling. The distinctions between types of fouling made in Game A become almost meaningless in Game B. Moreover, under these conditions, players cannot be "blamed" for fouling. They no longer know what they can legitimately do or not do. Fouling therefore becomes destigmatized or "standard operating procedure." After watching these two games of basketball, one might reach three conclusions:

(1) Fouling is a necessary part of the game. After all, in each type of game, we expect fouling to take place. If it does not, our reaction is likely to be: "they are not trying very hard," and "it's a dull game." Keeping fouling out of basketball is, as I see it, as impossible as keeping politics out of administration or economics. The competitive process is one in which political and business entrepreneurs (assuming that they are properly motivated) will seek the limits of what is legally allowable and, thereby, inevitably cross permissible boundaries.

(2) The significance of fouling cannot be separated from the systemic characteristics encountered. As we shift our attention from Game A to Game B, our normative conception of fouling becomes undermined. We can no longer be certain that fouling should even be punished, much less what the number of free throws should be.

(3) Destigmatized fouling is still fouling. Destigmatized fouling may be considered the most dysfunctional form of fouling inasmuch as it indicates lack of respect, not only for the officials, but also for the sport itself. While coaching and practicing may go on under Game B conditions, they are unlikely to be taken seriously. The outstanding teamwork and athletic feats that we associate with top-level basketball will certainly disappear. The sport is thus imperiled. Why play it? Why work to improve performance? Why pay to see it?

Our basketball analogy brings us to a distinction between primary and secondary corruption. Primary corruption (such as fouling in Game A) refers to excessive partisan behavior (amounting to greed) that is subject to official punishment or popular condemnation, as manifested in the existing governmental system. There is, in most cases, fear and shame associated with it. Secondary corruption (fouling in Game B) is partisan behavior that is carried out in the absence of viable statesmanship or governance. There is little fear of punishment or concern about dishonor or disgrace.

This concept of corruption suggests a balance between greed and governance. The weaker the governance, the more dangerous and dysfunctional the manifestations of greed. While under primary corruption, greed is somewhat controlled; under secondary corruption, it becomes more or less uncontrolled and even uncontrollable. However, as will be pointed out in later sections, primary corruption includes systemic as well as personalistic manifestations.

While primary corruption does not necessarily prevent development, secondary corruption has a corrosive effect on the requirements for development. This proposition follows from political elasticity theory. Under this theory (as presented in previous chapters), the effectiveness of leadership depends upon the ability to integrate and alternate soft and hard forms of power and requires a high quality of political software. Secondary corruption stems from as well as contributes to weak political software. In so doing, it causes or intensifies political inelasticity. This point will be later elaborated upon.

Since I consider secondary corruption to be a form of "political illness" (similar to alcoholism or drug addiction), whereas primary corruption to be merely a "political problem," why don't I reverse my nomenclature? My answer is that I have been influenced by medical terminology.

While a primary or first-degree burn may be painful, a secondary or second-degree burn penetrates deeper into the flesh and is harder to treat. So it is with corruption: because secondary corruption undermines an already weak governmental system, it requires fundamental political reform before punitive measures can be effective. However, our analogy also suggests that corruption is a natural consequence of primary politics (i.e., the struggle for competitive advantage), much as burning is of physics and chemistry.

THE NEED TO REDEFINE CORRUPTION

Heidenheimer, Johnston, and LeVine (1989, 8) classify definitions of corruption into three often overlapping categories: (1) misuse of money or favors for private gain; (2) inappropriate exchanges of money or favors for undue influence or power; and (3) violations of public interest or norms of behavior for special advantages or self-serving purposes.

Nye's 1967 (p. 419) definition of corruption, "behavior which deviates from the formal duties of a public role because of private-regarding . . . pecuniary or status gains or . . . private-regarding influence" is perhaps a useful effort to combine these categories. It distinguishes overt crime (i.e., robbing a bank or embezzling funds from a bank) from the covert actions that we associate with corruption (i.e., bribing a bank official to loan or divert funds for illegal purposes or unapproved policies). As such, it indicates where legitimate profiteering becomes unacceptable greed.

Where these conventional definitions of corruption fall down is in neglecting the systemic nature of corruption—the extent to which greed is an outcome of weak or defective governance. An article in THE WASHINGTON POST (July 5, 1995, A7), having to do with the practice of universities under federal contract billing the government for the tuition of the relatives and domestic partners of faculty working on these contracts, may illustrate this point.

Whereas the executive director of the National Coalition for Universities in the Public Interest suggested that this practice was corrupt, "subsidizing the college educations of the children of these highly paid researchers," it is not obviously so. After all, who is it here that is really "corrupt:" the faculty member who is exercising an established right; the university that is taking advantage of a possible defect in the federal guidelines; or government officials who knowingly allow this dubious practice to go on?

Inasmuch as the universities named in this article (the Massachusetts Institutue of Technology, the University of Chicago, Stanford University, and Johns Hopkins University) are highly respected ones, the public may not be unduly upset by this perk. However, many universities receive federal contracts and grants, not because of their qualifications, but because of the ability of Congressmen to use or misuse the legislative "porkbarrel-logrolling" system. Examples of this can be found in Brian Kelly's ADVENTURES IN PORKLAND (1993), of which the most notorious may be a $10 million unrequested and unwanted grant to Marywood College in Scranton, Pennsylvania to study stress in military families.

Kelly (1993, 229) estimates that about 10 percent of the federal government's operating budget goes for "pork," accounting in 1992 for between 10 and 15 percent of the $400 billion deficit. Yet, none of this waste can be considered "corruption," as conventionally defined. insofar as it does not appear to include illegality, bribery, or other unacceptable forms of behavior. After all, as Congressman (later Majority Leader) Richard Armey pointed out: "Pork is power, both the ability to distribute it and the ability to deny it" (quoted in Kelly 1993, 163).

Thompson (1993, 374) warns us in this regard against the danger of enervating political life in the process of confusing ordinary partisan politics with conventional corruption. However, to refer to this sort of "deal making" as "mediated corruption," as Thompson does, intensifies our confusion. I would, therefore, prefer to call it "systemic corruption."

Two articles in the June 9, 1994 WASHINGTON POST also indicate the weakness of the conventional definitions of corruption. One of the articles showed pictures of items found in the Chicago apartment building owned by Representative Rostenkowki, which he is alleged to have improperly purchased from the House Stationery Store with government funds. Because this allegation led in 1996 to his imprisonment, it is a clear example of the personalistic corruption identified in the conventional definitions of corruption.

The second article had to do with Representative Martin Lancaster of North Carolina who used his position on the House Armed Services Committee to prevent the construction of a fuel pipeline to Air Force bases in his district to save port, railroad, and trucking jobs. While this action is estimated to cost the taxpayers annually $4.1 million (far more than stolen by Rostenkowski), it can be considered simply an example of a Congressman doing nothing more than his job, practicing politics and protecting the interests of his constituents. Yet, it is also an example of systemic corruption, resulting not so much from bad behavior as from a weakness in the political process.

Inasmuch as corruption is "systemic," the value judgments that are necessary in the standard definitions to determine "misuse" or "inappropriate exchanges" of money or favors and other "violations" become undermined. Consequently, such definitions fail to answer the questions raised at the beginning of this chapter, particularly the following: how can we criticize behavior as "corrupt" if it is not illegal or disreputable, even if it harms the public interest? These standard definitions also have, it seems to me, the following defects:

A SIMPLISTIC CONCEPTION OF MORALITY. Corruption, as Caiden (1988, 5–6) points out, is everywhere, deeply rooted, and persistent. Is it also evil?

This question is, of course, difficult to answer because it covers behavior from the illegal or unethical to the simply opportunistic (what the economists call "rent-seeking"). The larger the gap between social norms or personal preferences and legal stipulations, the more likely corruption is to flourish, DeLeon (1989, 201) points out, noting the failure to eradicate prostitution, gambling, and hard drug trafficking.

Indeed, as Rose-Ackerman (1978, 9) emphasizes, "One does not condemn a Jew in Nazi Germany for bribing his way out of a concentration camp." While pressuring businesses to disobey laws may be corrupt as well as criminal behavior, Martin Luther King Jr. was internationally acclaimed for doing so in opposition to American segregation laws. If, as I have been arguing, we have to see corruption in a systematic way, we also have to be realistic as well as moralistic in conceptualizing it. Corruption may simply be part of the competitive process or the price for doing useful things. For example, Robert Moses, who was responsible for much of the infrastructure in and around New York City from the 1930s until the 1970s, is presented by Newfield and Dubrul (1977, 111) as a "distributor of bipartisan legal graft." Sayre and Kaufman (1965, 341–342), however, found him to be "brilliant, articulate, imaginative, energetic, honest, and confident." Similarly, in his book on Japan, Chalmers Johnson (1995, 191, 209) describes Tanaka Kakuei as being responsible for many important developments, such as science city, the tunnel to Hokkaido, the massive bridges to Shikoku and the new Tokyo airport, and also for much of the "structural corruption" that pervaded the Japanese government "which ultimately led, in 1993, to the LDP's loss of power."

Rent control, unless relatively lenient and/or combined with adequate subsidies, can be considered an unpersuasive form of power (perhaps "tyranny by the majority"). Whenever it has been rigidly enforced, it has discouraged private-sector investment in low-cost housing and in maintenance and repair; proven difficult to administer efficiently and fairly; undermined relations between landlords and tenants; and eroded the tax base (Bremmer and Franklin 1977). Rent control is most resented by landlords when it is accompanied by "unrealistic regulation"—attempting to compel owners to renovate their property for building codes or other requirements without allowing rent increases to cover their costs (Economic Commission for Europe 1996, 19).

Consequently, rent control has often been undermined by various forms of corruption (e.g., tacitly permitting some landlords in England to escape rent control when imposed by designating their property as "vacation housing") with positive results. Likewise, careless forms of zoning—e.g., disallowing subdivisions of single-family houses or small-sector commercial establishments within residential areas—is unlikely to be enforced (perhaps rightly so) in low-income communities.

In both New York City and Tokyo, the police are often bribed to allow illegal parking by delivery trucks. Until policies are changed to be more realistic about parking problems (allowing, for example, special hours for delivery and parking), corruption of this sort cannot be easily diminished.

A MISTAKEN PRIVATE SECTOR/PUBLIC SECTOR DICHOTOMY. Bozeman (1987) shows that all organizations are public because of their dependence upon government. This means that all of us are "civil servants," even when we are not officials. But if all of us are civil servants, we are also businesspeople. And as we go about our business, we inevitably divert resources from the public sector to our own use.

As I write this book, I remember that, as an independent consultant, I tax deduct my home office. If I could afford to rent an office, I would have no trouble with the Internal Revenue Service. But the rules for tax deducting a home office are necessarily complex and restrictive to prevent easy misuse. Consequently, I am never sure how much I am allowed. If I underdeduct, I feel stupid; if I overdeduct, I feel corrupt (using Nye's definition), shifting resources from the government to my own use. The difference between "being stupid" and "being corrupt" is a fine line which all of us (including, of course, officials) have to constantly walk.

Rose-Ackerman (1989) has pointed out the quickness with which businesses will take advantage of weak policies, legal loopholes, or inadequate enforcement. These businesses need not be governmental contractors. In California, for example, the consumer affairs department's chief in 1992 accused Sears auto repair shops statewide of so overcharging customers as to be a "systematic looting of the public" (Applegate 1992).

In America, health care providers frequently take advantage of the "fee-for-service" system because neither private insurance companies nor the government (under Medicare) can control exaggerated services and excessive charges and, as such, they generally escape punitive action. The fact that America spends a much higher percentage of its GDP on health care than any other industrialized country stems, according to many experts, not simply from overcharging by physicians, but also by unnecessary operations, excessive use of technology, and unnecessary efforts to prolong life—all of which can be considered as forms of systemic corruption.

A UNIDIMENSIONAL VIEW OF POLITICS. The tendency to see corruption as excessive partisanship stems, I think (as also pointed out in Chapter 4), from the use by writers on corruption of Lasswell's definition of politics as "who gets what, when (and) how" (see, for example, Johnston 1982, 18). Seeing politics in this way causes those concerned with public administration to want to diminish political manifestations.

An article by Moe (1991, 303), for example, emphasizes how the U.S. Housing and Urban Development Department (HUD) "became a dumping ground for the flotsam of the political community." The presupposition of this article is that, if the government could have kept politics out of administration, it could also have kept out corruption.

Conventional definitions of corruption assume that, if administrators can resist the temptation to allow their self-serving (i.e., partisan) tendencies to undermine their official duties, they will be free of corruption. This, I believe, is impossible for the following reasons:

1. Administrators are inevitably guided by politicians who, however altruistic they may be, are motivated by the need to seek for themselves and their supporters special advantages. Such advantages directly or indirectly divert public resources to private gain.

As Caiden points out (1988, 4), with Machiavelli in mind: "Why should anyone take on the burdens and responsibilities of public leadership if there were no personal advantages, no compensating reward?" An administrator who seeks to escape such political pressure may be, quite correctly, seen as insubordinate and untrustworthy. Administrators, after all, have a duty to be responsive to their political leaders inasmuch as administrators are supposed to have no political mandate.

2. Administrators are themselves politicians, struggling for higher salaries and promotion. If administrators cease to compete among themselves within their agencies and with colleagues of other agencies, they are likely to become listless and useless. To motivate civil servants, we must stimulate their "self-serving" tendencies. Much of the recent movement towards the privatization of public services is to encourage better performance by dangling the profit motive in front of administrators' eyes.

Administrators find many ways of exercising their avaricious tendencies. In Japan and France, as well as in the United States, a "revolving door" system has emerged, under which many senior administrators retire early to work in companies for which they have had regulatory responsibility (Campbell 1989; Rohn 1991). In the U.S., because of so many scandals having to do with defense contracts, we are especially sensitive to the misuse of this practice. However, as Rohn (1991, 287) points out, in regard to France, the "pantouflage" system does have the effect of "cross-fertilizing" the private and public sectors, thereby "moderating the all-too-familiar excesses of institutions driven by the profit motive," while reducing the insularity of governmental bureaucracies.

3. Administrators are responsible for economic development. Insofar as economic development necessitates motivating entrepreneurs, it also means allowing profiteering, which can take various forms of corruption. Newfield and Dubrul (1977, 109) emphasize this fact in their study of corruption in New York: "Politics is business. And legal graft is the currency of the permanent government." This takes the form of bond sale commissions, real estate leases, mortgage closings, and legal fees. In the process of attracting businesses, it is common to allow them to escape certain taxes and charges and to give them certain competitive advantages in contracting—all of which can blur the line between appropriate economic assistance and corrupt favoritism.

In seeing corruption as a never-ending contest between partisanship and statesmanship, I will be looking in the next two sections at offsetting and intensifying factors which tilt the balance in one way or another. To use a different analogy, one can see corruption as a form of fever affecting the political system. In MDCs, there are various forms of antibodies available to control the fever.

In LDCs, these antibodies are extremely inadequate or ineffective, so that the political system remains too weak to undertake development. But I do not consider the fever itself to be at fault. Fever, like corruption, is a functional reaction of the body to an invasion of bacteria or a viral infection. Without the capacity for fever, we would be dead! Yet, not to do anything about fever can also cause death. In other words, we cannot afford to be blase about corruption, as some analysts suggest. It is unlikely to be self-correcting.

OFFSETTING FACTORS

In this section, we will examine three countries (the United States, Japan, and Italy) which have experienced high levels of economic growth despite extensive patterns of corruption. At the end of 1993, THE ECONOMIST (December 25. 1993–January 7, 1994, 39–42) listed the United States as the top country in its tables of economic, social, cultural, and political indicators. Chalmers Johnson, who is otherwise highly critical of Japan, points out (1995, 202) that Japan is not only "one of the fastest growing industrial economies ever known," but also "characterized by an unusually equitable distribution of income." According to Spotts and Wiser (1986, 194), "Italian economic development in the postwar era has been proverbial, excelled only by that of Germany and Japan." THE ECONOMIST (June 26, 1993, 13) describes Italy as "the European equivalent of Taiwan and Hong Kong rolled into one."

Each of these countries has benefited from a number of merging historical developments: nationalism, imperialism, militarism, capitalism, urbanization, industrialization, and democratization (see Theobald 1990). What occurred in Great Britain, write Wraith and Simpkins (1963, 208), in explaining the gradual decline of corruption, was the spread of education to enlighten public opinion regarding malpractices, the growth of commerce and industry to encourage a middle class opposed to corruption, the rise of professional groups anxious to raise their status, and the improvement of auditing and other supervisory procedures. Emerging from these developments (and contributing to them) was the nonpartisan, professional, and meritocratic civil service.

Towards the end of the Nineteenth Century, Searle (1987) points out, the integrity of the British Stock Exchange was threatened by a number of abuses, particularly market-rigging and the promotion of fraudulent companies. These practices were, first of all, exposed in the press; then investigated by the Lord Chief Justice and later, the London Chamber of Commerce, the Board of Trade, and a Select Committee of the House of Lords; and eventually outlawed by Parliament.

Scandals, of course, did not stop, but "the British scandalmongers had a very highly developed sense of the State and a lofty conception of public duty," according to Searle (1987, 427). While this may mean that the British elite is less entrepreneurial than the elite of other industrial countries, it also may be more sensitive to charges of corruption.

The fact that under primary corruption, the worse manifestations of corruption are somewhat mitigated, does not mean that a heavy price is not paid for it. In the three countries that are here examined, those without the funds to buy power are particularly vulnerable.

An OECD study noted that more than 17 percent of Americans earn less than half the median income, creating an underclass two to three times that of any other industrialized nation (Wolff 1992, C4). A more recent OECD study (Bradsher 1995, D2) concluded that the gap between the incomes of the rich and poor in the United States is wider than in 15 other industrial countries. These findings are, I think, partly the results of systemic corruption (though racial prejudice may be equally responsible).

Having taught American urban studies, I realize that I cannot prove that the neglect of the American inner cities is partly a result of systemic corruption, but I believe that there is a connection. How else can we account for the fact that the richer you are in America, the more the government subsidizes your house (by allowing tax deductions for mortgages and property taxes, two thirds of which go to households with incomes over $75,000)? These subsidies amount to an estimated four times more than is spent on subsidized housing (public housing and housing vouchers). Consequently, only about a fourth of those needing housing assistance actually get it (DeParle 1996).

According to Reid (1991, A9), "the Japanese pay more for housing and get less for their money than residents of other developed countries." This is largely because "the tremendous pent-up demand within Japan for better housing is frustrated by a land-use law that encourages using land for inefficient agriculture or financial speculation" (Johnson 1995, 76).

In Italy, health care was often so poor during the 1980s that, if a patient was to receive proper meals and nursing care, his family had "virtually to move into the hospital to provide it," Spotts and Wiser (1986, 134), pointed out, suggesting that this was because the medical system had become "embroiled in political patronage at every level, damaging its reputation and effectiveness." This situation caused Italian pharmaceutical products to be generally "regarded as useless by other European countries" (Gilbert 1995, 161). The impact of corruption (as noted later) remains most apparent in Italy's South.

Despite all this, I consider these countries to reveal primary (not secondary) corruption for the reasons indicated:

THE UNITED STATES. In the United States, as so many books suggest (see Green and Waldman 1984 and Smith 1988), money plays more of a role in political life than in any other major democracy. National elections in 1982 are estimated to have cost more than $300 million, as against $3 million for the British 1979 elections. Gunlicks (1993, 4) points out that from 1968 to 1988, spending for presidential elections went up by 268 percent in constant dollars.

In 1988 the average House winner spent about $400,000, while the average Senate winner, almost $4 million (which meant that he had to raise $13,000 every week for six years). Consequently, politicians have become increasingly concerned and preoccupied with fund-raising. As businesses compete with one-another in campaign contributions, the decision-making process inevitably becomes distorted.

The fact that money is so important in American elections gives tremendous advantage to wealthy individuals, corporations, and interest groups. Much of their work is now done through Political Action Committees (PACs), which jumped in number from about 600 in 1974 to over 4,000 by 1987, with annual expenditures rising during this time from $8.5 million to over $140 million (Smith 1988, 32). PACs were responsible for much of the estimated $1.5 billion spent by candidates in the 1988 federal elections and an estimated $3 billion in 1996 (Gunlicks 1993, 9; THE ECONOMIST, February 8, 1997, 23). Even reluctant Congressmen are forced to cooperate with wealthy PACs because of their fear of opponents picking up what is available.

Wealthy interest group support is important for, not simply campaign contributions, but also newspaper publicity, legal activities, assistance of colleagues, and neutralizing of enemies or unsympathetic elements. According to Drew (1996, C7), both political parties are estimated to have spent during the 1996 election campaign between $200 million and $300 million in "soft money" (unrestricted funds that individuals, businesses, and labor unions can contribute). Soft money in 1996 was estimated to amount to at least 25 times more than in 1982 and three times more than in the 1992 election.

So far, powerful political organizations, led by Republican politicians, have resisted some form of public political financing of legislative campaigns used by a majority of liberal democracies (Gunlicks 1993). While there are legitimate concerns about reform proposals, I consider the American system of political financing to be "corrupt," as here defined, inasmuch as partisanship prevails over statesmanship. Indeed, Gunlicks (1993, 5) cites a 1991 poll result, indicating that only about one-third of Americans consider politicians to be "honest." Yet, I doubt if Congress is ready for a proposal to have the public pay for television political advertisements (which have become so costly and troublesome).

Other reasons are sometimes given for the apparent higher levels of corruption in the United States than in most Western European countries: the separation of powers, the seniority system, weak political parties, the filibuster, and the power of Congressional committees and subcommittees. Because it is relatively easy to block legislation under the American system, powerful interest groups have a near veto power over proposed legislation. At the same time, Congressmen with seniority, particularly if also chairmen or senior members of important committees or subcommittees, are in a strong position, using "pork barrelling" or "logrolling," to push through projects or legislation of greater benefit to their constituents than the general public.

Corporations work the administrative and political system in all sorts of ways. Defense contractors, for example, often hire retired Pentagon officials as "consultants," who "operate at the very frontiers of the laws, and perhaps beyond them, . . . relying on long-standing friendships . . . where tips, winks and gossip can convey crucial meaning and vital competitive bidding information" (Tucker and Swardson 1988, A12).

These defense contractors, however, primarily use PAC funds and the porkbarrel-logrolling process to keep defense expenditure at about 8 percent of GDP (more than 20 percent of the federal budget), which is almost as much as the rest of the world combined (Korb 1995, C1, C4). At the same time, American cities are starved of federal assistance, with the spending authority of Housing and Urban Development (HUD) declining by 71 percent during the 1980s to less than two percent of annual U.S. budget outlays, with no recovery since then (Nenno 1989; Anderson 1989).

Many generations of scholars studying the United States have wondered, as did Max Weber, how the U.S. could flourish economically in spite of "its lack of political and administrative morality" (Heidenheimer 1988, 583). Yet, there were always (and increasingly) offsetting factors: the public education system, the free press, competitive elections, a powerful middle class, professional and specialized associations and organizations, constitutional restrictions and separation of powers, and multiple power points that can be used by discontented and well-organized interest groups. While Congressmen must cooperate with wealthy and powerful interest groups, they need to avoid such excessive ties to particular ones as to prevent them from reaching agreement with supporters of competing groups essential for legislation and administrative action.

In looking at the American "pork barrel" process, Hird (1991) shows that the nation suffered substantial economic losses as a result. However, he also suggests that efficiency and equity considerations were not neglected. This happened because: (a) the Army Corps of Engineers was careful to select viable projects; (b) recommendations of the Corps had to be included in the President's annual budget proposal; (c) a number of committees in both Houses of Congress had to agree; and (d) legislators were willing to substitute more viable projects or more equitable objectives when their original ones encountered opposition.

Evans (1994) estimates that less than 2 percent of the $88 billion authorized under the 1987 omnibus highway and urban mass transit bill went for "bribes" in the form of pork barrel projects to members of the House Public Works and Transportation Committee. While these projects were essential to build a successful coalition, they did not undermine the achievement of a general interest policy goal.

As we turn to American state and local government, we see additional factors reducing corruption. Federal grants reached over $90 billion by 1980, as against about $7 billion in 1960. These federal grants amounted by 1980 to over 25 percent of state and local expenditures, as against about 10 percent in 1950. With this growth has come a flood of federal mandates requiring local officials to comply with various statutes and directives, thereby also requiring a meritocratic civil service and appropriate organization and procedures. Also accompanying the federal funds are a swarm of regulators and federal enforcement agents who are often better prepared to deal with impropriety than their state and local counterparts.

In many cities, U.S. Attorney's offices and public corruption units keep busy investigating a variety of cases, sometimes using paid citizen informants and those in legal trouble as undercover agents, equipping them with wiretaps and marked money for "sting operations." Federal and state investigators also work with public interest groups, businesses, and others who are unhappy with a mayor or a local administration to force improvements, possibly enlisting the support of disgruntled members of the city council, the school board, and independent commissions.

Neighboring jurisdictions can also play a role in bringing about change. The fact that cities have to compete with one-another for businesses and investments can have a therapeutic effect. While many cities continue to give construction contracts to companies that financially support or even employ relatives of important politicians, they generally require these companies to be properly bonded or insured to guarantee "character, credit, and capability" (La Noue and Sullivan 1995).

In their book on American whistleblowers (Glazer and Glazer, 1989) emphasize the uphill struggle they face in exposing or challenging corruption. What they do is analogous to putting the brakes on a fast moving vehicle inasmuch as they are under tremendous pressure to conform to the requirements of their organizations, regardless of their personal feelings. Their actions would be even more difficult without the cooperation of sympathetic interest groups, investigative reporters, Congressional investigating committees, public interest lawyers, a free press, television broadcasts, independent agencies, and the legislative and judicial branches of government.

Whistleblowers have also been able to take advantage of such relatively recent developments as the Inspector General Act, the Civil Service Reform Act, and state protection laws and boards. The Justice Department recently used a whistleblower to impose a $100 million fine on the Archer Daniel Midland company for illegal price-fixing. The fact that such a huge food company, which had gained many advantages in recent years as a result of lavish political donations to both major political parties, was so penalized indicates that these donations do not always protect companies engaged in typical forms of corruption.

The struggle against corruption in the U.S. must remain a continual process. An article by Raab (1993, 23, 27) points out how officials in New York City "have tried a stew of strategems to undermine corruption while strictly enforcing the city's multitude of building, health, sanitation, environmental and traffic laws." The most recent remedies have included rotation systems with frequent transfers, random double-checking by supervisors, planting spies in inspection forces together with stings, computer systems to monitor performances for possible corruption patterns, and rapid approval or rejection to prevent inspectors from obtaining bribes through decision-making delays. However, until working conditions are improved, including higher salaries, stronger professionalization, and more careful promotion and supervision, corruption is unlikely to decline.

JAPAN. "Bribery is built into Japanese politics," Iga and Auerbach (1977, 556) wrote, referring to money which is made available extralegally to holders of political power. Members of the ruling faction of the Liberal Democratic Party (LDP) are estimated to have access to about ten times their official income and expenditure allowances. "The LDP," according to Martin and Stronach (1992, 219), "may well be the most scandal-ridden party in the developed world. . . ." Largely because of its corruption, the LDP was rejected by Japanese voters in 1993, before being more or less returned to power in 1996, hopefully somewhat chastened.

The Japanese have an elaborate system of gift-giving, which clearly affects the political process. Most Japanese politicians, according to van Wolferen (1989, 134), are tied into a system of contracts and favors.

When a Diet member helps someone obtain a government or private-sector contract, the beneficiary is expected to pay at least 10 percent of the total price of the contract, and sometimes as much as 20 percent. Japanese political parties, politicians, and political groups are estimated to receive from the Japanese people four times more per capita than any other nation (Johnson 1995, 215).

In Japan, there is "a pervasive and institutionalized system of bid-rigging" operating in the constuction industry (Woodall 1993, 297). This "DANGO system" includes secret deals or joint ventures, brokers who arrange for division of spoils, the hiring of retired officials, and gift-giving to politicians to lubricate the appropriate bureaucratic and political wheels. Despite criticism in the press, it is defended by top politicians: "What's wrong with bid-rigging that helps the construction industry operate smoothly and secures jobs?" (Johnson 1995, 216).

Johnson (1995) suggests that Japanese corruption is also linked to the AMAKUDARI system, under which retired officials are allowed to take important positions in the legislature (the Diet), local governments, banks, corporations, and construction companies. "The result was a system so corrupt that it seemed beyond reform, and that disillusioned many citizens with the promise of parliamentary democracy itself" (Johnson 1995, 211). Johnson (1995, 72–73) also suggests that the high cost of living in Japan (with Tokyo estimated in 1988 to be twice as expensive as New York) is deliberately induced to subsidize exports.

Yet, in Japan, as in the U.S., there are offsetting factors that minimize the impact of corruption (as also pointed out in Chapter 1). Among the most important of these factors is the integrity of the civil service. The Japanese upper level civil servants are carefully selected, largely from among the graduates of Tokyo University's law school, with only about half of the candidates eventually receiving appointments. As such, there are "an elite of the elite" (Campbell 1989, 115). Those who survive the competitive process to get into the civil service, particularly into such ministries as Finance and International Trade and Industry (MITI), "tend to be among the best that Japan's educational system has to offer to that country's perspective employers" (Koh 1989, 253).

Corruption in Japan is also reduced by the competitive process under which companies work together in associations, pushing up proposals that eventually are backed by the consensus of members before being taken to the advisory councils of MITI (Ouchi 1984). What prevents any one actor from gaining too much power is a process of careful restraint, mutual scrutiny, and a devotion to "WA" (harmony).

Thus, the competitive struggle is controlled by a strong conviction on the part of the Japanese people that "bureaucracy is a neutral instrument, a conviction bordering on religion (Koh 1989, 205). Bureaucrats recognize that their failure to maintain a degree of autonomy and neutrality in the face of special interests will damage their reputation with the public, undermining their relations with other agencies and their ability to carry out their duties.

The fact that Japan's various government departments are, not only competent, but also competitive with one another, "instills a strong dose of creativity and individual responsibility" (Pempel and Muramatsu 1993, 19). While top level civil servants consider their incomes to be between a half and two-thirds of what their peers in private firms are making, the frequency of corruption among Japanese civil servants, according to the National Personnel Authority, is remarkably low (Koh 1989, 223). Whereas in 1960, 6 of every 10,000 civil servants were disciplined for corrupt behavior, that figure dropped to 2 of every 10,000 during the 1970s and 1980s (though it may have risen in the 1990s, according to press reports). Officials who are indicted become the lead story in the newspapers.

The Board of Audit plays the primary role in investigating corruption and pointing out needed revisions of laws, regulations, and practices. These audit reports are available to the public, allowing scrutiny by the press and the Diet. Despite the one-party (LPD) dominance of the government (except for a short period during the 1990s), the law enforcement agencies and the courts have dealt harshly with administrative corruption.

With the decline of the LPD's political power in the 1990s, investigative journalists have become increasingly active in exposing corruption, with much more attention being paid to the AMAKUDARI system (Johnson 1995, 223). They have been ably assisted in this regard by the work of official investigators, particularly those working in the Tokyo District Public Prosecutor's Office.

While the Japanese tend to be very tolerant of influence-peddling by politicians, they strongly react to evidence of dishonesty among their meritocratic public bureaucracy (MacDougall 1988). Johnson (1995, 214), who finds corruption apparent in certain ministries or agencies, considers it relatively absent from such sectors as the environment, foreign affairs, science and technology, economic planning, and justice.

MacDougall (1988, 227), in analyzing the Japanese reaction to the Lockheed scandal, concludes that, despite Japanese tolerance of political impropriety, "clear violations of the law, personal enrichment through dishonest behavior, bureaucratic corruption, and unseemly behavior by national leaders . . . are seen by the public as detrimental to legitimate government."

ITALY. How Italy can be so prosperous and also so politically and administratively corrupt is even harder to understand than the situation in the United States and Japan because its quality of public services (education, health, social security, justice, transport, etc.) "is exceptionally low" (Hine 1993, 255). Michael Porter, in his 1990 book on comparative economic development, notes (p. 437), that, despite Italy's remarkable economic performance in recent years: "Telecommunications and postal services have been poor, financial services slow and archaic, and transportation and logistics often a nightmare."

Spotts and Wiser, in their 1986 book on Italy, wrote (pp. 130–1) that "the civil service and its operations have been shamelessly politicized," adding: "the government employee regards his position as a sinecure to be occupied rather than a job with responsibilities to fulfill." In comparison with other Western countries, the administrative elite were unqualified, poorly paid, and unmotivated. It was common for civil servants to retire with pensions in their late twenties or early thirties and/or to take a second "unregistered" job, on which they paid no taxes.

The country's poor administration, according to Spotts and Wiser (1986, 135), led inevitably to the "BUSTARELLA," the envelope filled with money. Furlong's more recent study of Italy (1994, 256) finds the same situation, accounting for "the individual's grudging efforts, backed up by a centralised administrative apparatus regarded as corrupt and arbitrary." In the South, particularly in Sicily, the Mafia grew up in response to the weakness of the state and the distrust of government (THE ECONOMIST, July 8, 1995, 52).

Corruption has taken many forms in Italy: bribes for contracts, contracts in return for political contributions, undeclared campaign contributions, collusion among contractors, padding on construction contracts, tax evasion, etc. In the words of a Socialist Party official, "bribes were extracted for everything from a contract to renovate a cemetery, to supplying a school's heating oil, to ordering pencils for the clerks" (quoted, Cowell 1993, A8).

The self-employed (a quarter of the workforce, compared with 13 percent in other European countries) have generally avoided taxes and social security contributions, as have the country's nearly one million shopkeepers (THE ECONOMIST, June 26, 1993, 16). "The black market in services and in cheap labour for small industry is now acknowledged to amount to about 30 per cent of the total value added in firms with under 20 employees, and about 8 per cent of GDP" (Furlong 1994, 222). Motivating much of this tolerance for corruption has been, until recently, uncritical support for the Christian Democratic and Socialist parties because of their "anti-communism."

While all parts of Italy have suffered from corruption, the price has largely been paid by the seven most southernly regions of the country, all of which had levels of per capita gross domestic product below 85 percent of the European Community average during the 1980s. In contrast, Italy's ten regions of the center-north had levels of per capita GDP above 115 percent of the Community average.

In recent years, unemployment in the South has been double that in the North, while incomes have been 50 percent less (Spotts and Wiser 1986; Hine 1993). With 40 percent of the land area and 35 percent of the people, Italy's South accounts for only a quarter of the country's economic output (THE ECONOMIST, June 26, 1993, 16). Italy's biggest scandals have been in the South: the Naples subway, where, after 18 years, only one section was completed; Calabria's useless steel plant; and the failure to clean up the Gulf of Naples despite an expenditure of $800 million. Much of this area has been allowed by the political elite "to deteriorate into a banana republic" (Gilbert 1995, 43).

What has enabled Italy to be economically so successful is that aspects of the administration work fairly well. Particularly useful has been the Bank of Italy. Recruitment is highly selective; training, rigorous; and research work, outstanding. Thus, the Bank remains "an island of excellence in a public administration where excellence is not always in abundant supply" (Hine 1993, 248).

Some ministries, such as Foreign Affairs, Justice, Interior, and Treasury, "generally discharge their responsibilities efficiently and creditably" (Spotts and Wiser 1986, 133). With the exception of the postal and railroad systems, most of the state corporations, which are responsible for 80 percent of banking, a quarter of industrial employment, and half of fixed investment, "are managed satisfactorily" (Spotts and Wiser 1986, 128, 136). Indeed, the entrepreneurial and sophisticated management style of the state enterprises has been "a model much admired and studied outside Italy" (Furlong 1994, 248).

Summarizing studies of Italian corruption, Gilbert (1995, 130) suggests that it cost the Italian economy about $1 trillion during the 1980s, making Italy "the sick man of Europe." However, when the Italian government woke up to its responsibilities during the 1990s, it could take effective action. The judiciary proved to be a powerful force, led by prosecutors who attacked corruption everywhere, with victories even in Sicily over the deeply rooted Mafia. When aroused by a persistent press, the public used referenda, elections, and demonstrations to sweep away "the whole stultifying apparatus of the old party system" (Gilbert 1995, 151). This has meant, in the words of an editor of a Milan newspaper (quoted, Bohlen 1995, A3): "Before, corruption was habitual, and society was convinced it was normal. Now people are more careful, they are more afraid of being caught."

With the end of the Communist challenge, there is hope that corruption can be increasingly controlled in Italy. One positive factor seems to be is the pressure of European Community membership: "Just as Japanese governments use foreign, especially American, pressure as a scapegoat for unpalatable domestic policy, so Italy is beginning to use the strictures of the European community" (THE ECONOMIST, June 26, 1993, 20). As a result, government deficits have been reduced from 12.1% of GDP in 1992 to an estimated 3.0% in 1997. Likewise, local governments and other public bodies have become more efficient, using trustworthy competitive tendering (THE ECONOMIST, November 8, 1997).

A final factor, according to Furlong (1994, 257), is the continued reliance on regional governments in the north and center with "technical management styles utterly different from the ossified rites of central government." Furlong, however, goes on (p. 263) to emphasize that, until the industrial development model reaches Southern Italy, "how Italy sustains itself in bad times and flourishes periodically can appear an affront to reason."

INTENSIFYING FACTORS

If the reader agrees with me that there are problems with the conventional definitions of corruption in MDCs, he/she will certainly agree that there are more problems with them in LDCs. After all, what does corruption mean, first of all, in Hobbes's "state of nature," where the life of man is so "solitary, poor, nasty, brutish and short" that survival is more important than legality and, subsequently, under his Leviathan, where those in authority are unchallengeable and, as such, law is illegitimate? These definitions do not adequately take into account that "greed," however repugnant in the abstract, cannot easily be judged "immoral," in the absence of civilized or institutionalized governance.

Is it too much to assert that the World Bank's call for "good governance" (accountability, transparency, rule of law, enlightened policymaking, human rights, etc.), as set forth in the 1994 GOVERNANCE publication (Operations Policy Department 1994), is nothing more than "commonsense?" I believe this to be so, as presented in previous chapters, emphasizing the importance of: establishing acceptable goals, hiring qualified personnel, encouraging training, delegating responsibility, stimulating motivation and competition, paying attention to morale, expanding two-way flows of communication, promoting legitimacy, maintaining supervision, cultivating contractors, protecting independent spheres of authority, and developing conflict-resolution procedures.

We can go on to underscore the point so often made in this book that the quality of relationships ("political software") between leaders and followers will suffer to the extent that the requisites for better governance are neglected or mismanaged. This is why secondary corruption (referring here simply to greed uncontrolled by governance) has a corrosive effect on political software (intensifying distrust of and hostility towards government). Thus, to quote Ouma (1991, 473), regarding Uganda: "political instability, corruption, and underdevelopment are mutually reinforcing." Let us see how this is so:

IMPROPER POLICIES. In many LDCs, policies are not intended to be taken seriously. In India, as shown by Wade (1985, 480), state ministers are less interested in making policy than in "modifying the application of rules and regulations on a particularist basis, in return for money and/or loyalty." Likewise, in Mexico, policy making is undertaken in such as way as to add "to the potential for corruption by inhibiting societal checks on state power and by forcing weaker social organizations into exploitable positions vis-a-vis state representatives" (Morris 1991, 49).

Even when policies are "officially" changed to meet the requirements of foreign donors (as in Liberia during the 1980s under President Doe), they may actually not be changed. Secondary corruption accounts for the fact that, when USAID sent in a team to Liberia in 1987 to control wasteful expenditure, giving as an incentive $40 million in economic and military aid, it could not prevent misuse of the budget, with massive kickbacks sent abroad (Werlin 1990). The same situation existed in Niger, according to Amuwo (1986, 301), causing "a yawning gap . . . between self-perception and self-reality, between proclamations of intentions and concrete results."

APPOINTMENT OF PERSONNEL. In Mexico, Cothran (1994, 219) points out, "the bureaucracy is highly politicized in the sense that virtually the entire public work force is subject to political appointment rather than merit." However, because about a third of officials are affected by the "SEXENIO" system (the change of governments every six years), those who gain power often consider it their right "to partake of the system's spoils" (Morris 1991, 73).

In Bangladesh, according to Dey (1989, 508), people "offer bribes to get jobs with high bribe potential." Thus, "the bribe here is similar to an entry fee that one has to pay to join a club and become entitled to its benefits and facilities." The same is true in the Dominican Republic, where government jobs are seen even by the public as a legitimate way of enriching oneself (Ruffing-Hilliard 1991, 309).

In most LDCs, local government revenue estimates tend to be unreliable and unrelated to priorities (Dillinger 1991). There is seldom any significant financial planning, and no meaningful accounting for sums expended. The effect of this mismanagement is to deepen public disrespect for public policy. Even when local governments employ large numbers of tax collectors, their success remains meagre. In Nuevo Laredo, Mexico, for example, it is alleged that three-quarters of the 1982 budget fell victim to corruption (Morris 1991, 70). When reform took place at the municipal level during the 1990s, including more training opportunities, it was undermined by the lack of a career civil service staff (Massolo 1996, 245). Consequently (assuming that this situation continues), few Mexicans get upset at reports that businesses generally fail to pay local taxes.

Under conditions of secondary corruption, shifting to a meritocracy becomes extremely difficult. While the rulers sometimes take action to prevent the petty functionaries from misappropriating public funds and resources, the upper cadres of both the military and civil bureaucracies are left free for political racketeering (Dey 1989). In some cases, governments hesitate to arrest lower-level bureaucrats for corruption when this could implicate the ruler's inner circle and family, strain the courts and penal system, alienate the bureaucracy, slow down the functioning of government, and generate public cynicism. "The higher the target," write Gillespie and Okruhlik (1988, 70), "the closer the association with the head of state."

MOTIVATION OF PERSONNEL. Barbara Nunberg and John Nellis (1990), among others, have shown clearly that in most LDCs, civil service inefficiency and ineffectiveness stem from excessive wage bills, surplus numbers, inadequate salaries, and wage compression. Gould (1980) found that in Zaire in 1978 less than 10 percent of civil servants earned enough to feed their families. In Uganda, Battiata (1988, A15) reported that civil servants were paid barely enough to cover "the cost of a large bunch of bananas." Even when their salaries were raised in the early 1990s, they covered "barely three days of living per month" for the average civil servant (Gombay and O'Manique 1996, 104). Outside of Africa, the same situation of poorly paid civil servants is so common that Klitgaard (1989a) refers to it as "Incentive Myopia."

When civil servants are paid poorly, they will find numerous ways to "corrupt" the system. This situation was recognized by President Mobutu who advised Zairian civil servants: "if you want to steal a little, do so in a nice way" (Gould 1980, 71–72). One way to do so is to arrange for extra salaries, using fictitious names. Two-thirds of Zairian civil servants in 1979 were "ghosts" (fictitious employees), drawing an estimated 20 percent of the budget in 1978.

In Lusaka, only half of the employees were actually working, according to that city's senior governor (THE ECONOMIST, September 15, 1990, 28). In Uganda, most of the country's estimated 300,000 civil servants in 1988 spent "office hours" tending private agricultural plots or trading goods in order to make ends meet (Battiata 1988, A15). In Tanzania, Liebenow (1987a, 2) found salaries to be so low that "absenteeism, rather than shoddy performance alone, is a key element in the problem of productivity."

With the motivation of Zairian civil servants so low, Gould (1980, 122) pointed out, they could not be expected to provide needed services: "Instead of stimulating productivity, the state bureaucracy incarnates nonproductivity and indeed counterproductivity. . . ." Since officials here were allowed to keep any unspent budgetary funds at the end of the fiscal year, they had no incentive to spend these funds on what they were budgeted for.

In Uganda, Battiata (1988, A15) quotes the government's inspector general as saying that "senior civil servants have become accustomed to siphoning off most, in not all, of the public money that flows through their offices. As a result, nothing new is built and old things fall apart." A more recent study of Uganda (Langseth 1994, 7) suggests that, as a result of political breakdown during the 1970s and 1980s, corruption and malingering "were no longer punished but became an intrinsic part of the reward system, fully exploited by everyone."

Klitgaard (1991, 92) notes that the public administration ills found in Africa prevail in much of the world. In Bolivia, for example, "the incentives facing public employees erode, and this results in a brain drain, inefficiency, moonlighting, demoralization, and corruption."

THE INADEQUACY OF SUPERVISION. In Zaire under Mobotu, as in many countries, supervision was impossible because of nonexistent telephone service, impassable roads, unavailable vehicles or automobile parts and gasoline, and travel funds (Gould 1980). In Uganda, government offices try to manage "without the most basic equipment and ordinary office furniture such as chairs, tables, functional typewriters or copying equipment" (Langseth 1994, 6).

Lack of supervision is also a result of what Dey (1989, 507) calls, "asymmetry of information between subordinates and superiors . . ." In regard to sales taxes, for example, it is easy to manipulate tax rates when the technical characteristics of the goods are not rigidly defined, or cannot be ascertained in a foodproof fashion." Klitgaard (1991, 30) also insists on the importance of information "about the quality of goods and services, labor and housing, risks and portfolios, or whatever happens to be traded."

Since administrative performance is seldom measured or recognized, various forms of corruption become encouraged. For example, administrators are inclined to cooperate with the importers of contraband goods, to withhold funds that are collected, or to extract bribes from innocent citizens (Dey 1989, 506). In the Ivory Coast, officials "often turn a blind eye to customs regulations in exchange for a bribe..."

(Cabogo 1993, 167). And we could go on with examples from many parts of the world.

The impact of corruption on humanitarian assistance is most tragic. In Uganda, Ouma (1991, 481) reported that, during the 1980s, it was very difficult to get relief supplies into rural areas without a high percentage ending up for sale in urban markets. In the 1990s, those helping refugees in Zaire encountered even more severe manifestations of this official thievery.

Ahmed and Bamberger (1991) note that good Monitoring and Evaluation (M&E) systems are rare in LDCs. In South Asia, M&E efforts have been undermined by duplication of effort, lack of contact with top policymakers, intimidation of line agencies, unrealistic or irrelevant data, and excessive cost. Here and elsewhere, there seems to be little damand for, or interest in, monitoring data.

The World Bank is currently financing a large number of water and sanitation projects in Latin America and the Caribbean. However, to be effective, there must be appropriate institutions for metering and collecting water charges. "In Caracas and Mexico City, 30 percent of water connections are not even registered," indicating the poor quality here of M&E (World Bank 1992, 14).

To expect good supervision when it might embarrass those in power, including the head of state, is clearly to expect too much in many countries. During the 1980s, both Uganda and Tanzania investigated acts of corruption, but very little happened as a result. In regard to Francophone Africa, Laleye (1993, 250) points out that authorities are rarely committed to implementing corrective measures and enforcing sanctions. While some hope exists in Senegal following the introduction of an Ombudsman-like institution, modeled on French lines, "it will not be easy to allow it to make a significant impact" (Laleye 1993, 252). Kpundeh (1993, 239–240) makes the same point in regard to Sierra Leone, noting that during the 24 years of All People's Congress (APC) rule, "accountability was only to the President and his top party officials."

THE ILLEGITIMACY OF LAWS AND REGULATIONS. Legislation in LDCs is often designed, not to be universalistic, but to benefit particular regions, groups, and individuals, particularly the dominant ruling class (Alam 1989). In Latin America and the Caribbean, Maingot (1994, 58) points out, the concept of legality is so vague that legality becomes "an arbitrary point" across a range of behavior. In Mexico, for example, inspectors are bribed to ignore environmental controls, and judges are bribed to deflect "the impact of land reform legislation" (Morris 1991, 67).

While there may not be a ruling class in Africa, as in Latin America, leaders exercise a personalized form of control so that legislation and regulations become "whimsical," shifting from day to day in accord with the presidential mood to benefit those in power. (Hyden 1983, 453). Thus, the "rule of law" does not carry with it public respect.

In China, excessive regulations are combined with bureaucratic discretion to provide opportunities and incentives for civil servants to extract "rent." Consequently, the saying that goes back to classical China continues to be repeated: "Money is the horse that leads the way, gifts are the troops that overwhelm the fortress" (Harris 1988, 4).

LACK OF INDEPENDENT SPHERES OF POWER. In Africa, Jackson and Rosberg (1985, 34) pointed out, "since independence most constitutions have been honored in the breach—either by civilian rulers attempting to retain power or by soldiers attempting to seize power by unconstitutional means." In Sierra Leone during the 1980s, for example, decisions on pending cases were made by "political judges" before they were tried in accordance with governmental directives (Kpundeh 1993, 242). When the top banking official here resisted corrupt pressures during this period, he was assassinated.

In the case of Kenya, Cohen (1993, 442) notes, the situation has worsened since President Kenyatta's death: "In a perverse way, the apathy, irrationality, and incompetence that characterizes many of Kenya's public servants is a direct result of their seeking to survive in a fragmented bureaucracy that has been cowed by Moi and his faithful supporters, fragmented by very competitive tribal and regional cliques, and affected by increasing tolerance of public servants reaping personal benefits while balancing these competing pressures." Under these circumstances, to expect either the legislature or the judiciary to reduce corruption is clearly wishful thinking.

As a generalization, we can say that the more impoverished a country is, the more likely the press is to be suppressed, intimidated, or undermined in various ways. Wherever a government is hostile to the development process, it discourages an independent press. In 1994, for example, Richburg (1994, All) reported that the Kenyan press, which was considered among Africa's "liveliest and freest" in 1993, "is now one of the most harassed." Even in Pakistan, where the press has played a useful role in combatting corruption during the country's half-century of existence, "government censors have closed papers and spiked stories while reporters and editors have been physically and verbally attacked and their offices ramsacked" (Anderson 1995, A16). In Mexico, journalists, editors, and newspaper publishers are often paid (or given financial inducements) by the government to exercise "self-censorship," according to Morris (1991, 54), who adds: "members of the press find it rational to follow the corruption-paved avenue to mobility offered by members of the state rather than attack the system." The price for resistance may include murder, as encountered by more than thirty reporters during the late 1980s.

CONCLUSION: FINAL QUESTIONS

In addition to the questions already considered, there are many others that remain perplexing. One of them—what to do about corruption—will have to await the final chapter of this book. Others, however, can be addressed, using the definition of corruption presented here and the distinction between primary and secondary corruption, including the following:

1. How important is it to do cost-benefit or functional-dysfunctional analyses of corruption? Caiden (1990, 150–151) summarizes the arguments of analysts, indicating that corruption may at times be functional: (a) to speed up the administrative and legislative process; (b) to make the bureaucracy more humane and approachable for those who have not yet adjusted to the modern way of life; (c) to overcome excessive bureaucratic inflexibility, sluggishness, and bungling; (d) to integrate otherwise alienated groups (particularly, politically weak ethnic, religious, and racial elements) and, thereby, be an alternative to violence; and (e) to enable entrepreneurs to function within a difficult business environment.

In his 1967 article Nye suggested using a cost-benefit matrix, within which corruption can be considered harmful or helpful based on its impact on (1) economic development; (2) national integration; and (3) governmental capacity. In 1986 Nas, Price, and Weber used the Nye approach to suggest that, if corruption has a positive impact on social welfare, it should be considered beneficial; otherwise, detrimental.

Using the distinction presented here between primary and secondary corruption, it appears that such analyses are far more likely to be meaningful under primary than secondary corruption. For example, while the bribery of senior civil servants, judges, or Members of Parliament is unheard of in England, "the granting of planning permissions yields a steady stream of abuse" (THE ECONOMIST, July 3, 1993, 58). Under these circumstances, it is possible for a businessperson to do a cost-benefit analysis with regard to a possible "financial contribution" or "arrangement." (Doig, 1984, explains the corrupt methods used in contemporary British politics.)

In Russia, however, according to an article by Marshall Goldman (1994, F9), simple forms of bribery are useless. Secondary corruption manifests itself in more than 4,000 racketeering gangs; unfair legal and commercial rules; a dizzying array of arbitrary taxes; the unreliability of local banks and currency; etc. Goldman therefore concludes: "unless a company has answers to or high tolerance for these difficulties, now is not the time to invest." (This situation, which persists at the end of 1997, underscores the difference between paying a service charge or tip at a good restaurant and having to pay a bribe for each item of food at a terrible restaurant, for which we have no guarantee of delivery or quality.)

Caiden (1990, 152) suggests that corruption is a "functional dysfunction." What is indicated here is that, under conditions of secondary corruption, the more functional corruption appears in the short run, the more ultimately dysfunctional it is. In many countries, for example, businesses need to bribe bank officials to get a loan (de Juan 1991). Because these businesses are seldom forced to repay their loans, "zombie banks" are not uncommon in LDCs (see Chapter 1). This situation is most likely in countries where leaders are unwilling to distinguish "the public purse from their private holdings" (Smith 1997, 59). This is because leaders who rob their national banks by "coercive borrowing" or inducement often encourage their powerful subordinates to do likewise to engender their loyalty. Under these circumstances, efforts of foreign agencies to foster credit programs for business development usually end in failure.

2. Is rent-seeking a form of corruption? The concept of "rent-seeking" is increasingly used in World Bank reports in place of the word, "corruption." This is partly because, to quote Klitgaard (1989, 18): "Within the

Bank itself, the subject verges on the forbidden." (This situation may be changing, as noted in Chapter 10.) It is also because of the fact that, as here pointed out, secondary corruption prevails in most of the countries that the Bank is active in. Consequently, corruption as "greed" is concealed within the many manifestations of bad or weak governance.

If the argument presented here is meaningful, much of World Bank literature referring to "mistaken policies," "weak implementation," "inadequate bureaucracies, "dubious commitment," etc. indicates manifestations of secondary corruption. As such, these manifestations are "deliberate," rather than "accidental" results of existing systems of government. To hide them within the term, "rent-seeking," referring to "the direct use or waste of economic resources for non-economic gain" (Gallagher 1991, 31), can be misleading.

In several World Bank reports on Senegal (Morin 1993; World Bank 1993), the word, "corruption," is seldom mentioned. Yet, manifestations of secondary corruption are clearly evident:

- During the 1980s, most of the major sectors of the economy were highly protected, costing the state annually an estimated $173 million, representing about 20% of current budgetary receipts. This meant that cement was twice as high as in France; fuel and electricity, five times higher. The cost of protecting a government-supported sugar monopoly amounted to about US $55 million annually.
- Until recently, the Senegalese Labor Code put severe restrictions on wages, hiring, and dismissal. While reform of this Labor Code has been attempted, remaining restrictions necessitate the bribing of officials for "favorable interpretations."
- Until 1986, extensive quantitative restrictions and high tariffs affected imports. Since then, trade barriers have been supposedly removed and distortions eliminated. However, a degree of discretionary power has been given to customs officials, "allowing substantive protection to return through the back door." Consequently, smuggling, distortions, and the necessity for extra payments continue.
- Irrational intervention by the state has made it difficult for businesses to operate efficiently. For example, existing industrial and export processing zones have been undermined by high user fees, restrictions on ownership of buildings and land, inadequate political and commercial risk coverage, weak financial services, and the other problems already mentioned.

- Senegal's legal system is complex and unrealistic. Its judicial system is inefficient, confusing, and contradictory. Investors are doubtful about their claims being respected or enforced. Investors are subject to sudden and sharp increases in tax levies and elimination of incentives.
- While twenty public enterprises (PEs) have been privatized since 1988, those that remain continue to be mismanaged and a heavy burden on the national budget. The real estate PE may never be privatized because it owns dwellings occupied by officials and civil servants. Performance contracts are seldom taken seriously either by the government or by PE management, and there is no "genuine political will" to reform.

Why these and other "distortions" of the Senegalese economy should be considered "purposeful" and therefore, "corrupt" is explained in a 1990 article by Catherine Boone. She points out (p. 427) that "rentierism is an activity open to the political class," reflecting "patterns of access to politically mediated resources." Using grants from the state, contracts, kickbacks, and other illicit sources of wealth, rentiers channel their income into various state-mediated non-productive activities. Because they are dependent on inducements and sanctions meted out by state agents, they become part of the "clientelistic system of political control."

Insofar as this system is supported by France, it may be considered as "neocolonial." At the same time, because it is counter-productive, it may ultimately endanger those in power.

By recognizing rent-seeking behavior as a form of systemic corruption (characteristic of secondary corruption, though also apparent under primary corruption), we can also see how it endangers World Bank projects. Let us take the Nairobi City Council as an example.

Under colonial rule and for some years thereafter, Kenyan municipalities had relied on a progressive personal tax. Because Central Government officials accused local officials of corruption, they disallowed this tax, with the promise of grants instead. Since these grants were not forthcoming, the municipalities were left bankrupt and demoralized.

As part of a World Bank urban development project in Kenya, Bank officials insisted on a revaluation and an increase of property tax rates to enable municipalities to pay for the project. Because African property owners refused to pay for public services (also noted in Chapter 4), they undermined the project.

In the case of Nairobi, the Kenyan government took over the functioning of the City Council in 1983, claiming that it was corrupt and mismanaged (Stren 1989, 33). However, much of the city's problem stemmed from being deeply in debt (with rate arrears amounting to the then annual total recurrent expenditures) caused by the unwillingness of anyone to pay property taxes, including powerful politicians, senior bureaucrats, the Kenya Railways, and the Commissioner of Lands.

Since the BWANA KUBWA (the powerful people) were not paying charges and taxes, residents of the Bank-sponsored Dandora site/service project strongly objected to paying the dues levied under this project. (Indeed, their rioting forced the mayor and the entire city council to resign!)

Under central government control, the financial situation in Nairobi became much worse, particularly after a fire destroyed important records. In 1994, cumulative arrears in loan repayments from tenants of the municipal housing projects were below 60 percent of the amount due that year (OED 1996, 4). Yet, these projects are considered somewhat successful, despite persistent problems. As a result, there is a greater availability in parts of Nairobi of potable water, sanitation, and affordable housing (with beneficiaries increasing the supply of rental units, leading to a decline in average rent between 1985 and 1995). But without cost-recovery, it is difficult for the Bank to sponsor more urban projects here.

3. Should those in MDCs criticize the corruption of LDCs? This question includes several underlying questions, one of which is raised by Dey (1989, 506): "what is dishonesty in an environment where the possibility of punishment is remote?" Smuggling, he argues, can hardly be considered as an abuse of power when the border police are lazy, understaffed, or incompetent? However, based on the analysis here presented, I suggest that, in the absence of statesmanship, corruption, even when it is seldom punishable or reprehensible, must be seen as having dire consequences. Thus, I agree with Ouma (1991, 489): "Corruption has such far-reaching political and economic implications for development that it becomes unwise to take it too lightly."

The dysfunctional impact of corruption can be most clearly seen in Africa. (The material presented in Chapter 10 underscores this situation.) Sub-Saharan Africa (excluding South Africa), with some 450 million people and an estimated 30 percent of the world's mineral resources, had in 1987 a GDP about that of Belgium, with only 10 million people (World Bank 1989, 16; World Bank 1994).

Whereas severe food shortages were unusual in 1960, about one-fourth of the population now face chronic food insecurity (World Bank 1989, 7). Many of Africa's most educated and qualified people are leaving Africa. Only a small percentage of the 34,000 African students in the United States and the 70,000 in Europe (as of 1985) are expected to return. At the same time, Africans, with one-tenth of the world's population, now comprise about one-third of global refugees (World Bank 1989, 22, 81).

Turning to a country, such as Mexico, which appears to have reached a middle-income level of $2,000 annual per-capita income and 3 to 4 percent annual growth (at least during much of the 1980s), we can see how secondary corruption undermines the real wages and living conditions of most of the population (Cothran 1994). The payment of bribes here is so common that it is difficult to determine if this practice results more from "extortion" or voluntary "gift-giving" (Morris 1991, 52). Because the police and judiciary are often corrupt or incompetent, the wealthier one is, the more likely one is to escape punishment. According to Kenneth Johnson, this explains "why countries like Mexico seem to be always 'developing' but somehow never really develop" (quoted in Morris 1991, 70).

A second, perhaps more difficult, underlying question has to do with cultural relativism. While the relationship of culture to corruption will be examined in Chapter 8, we need to consider here the question of how appropriate it is for cultural "outsiders" to label as "corrupt" LDC favoritism, nepotism, and graft (Maingot 1994, 53).

The answer, as I see it, has to do with the effectiveness of foreign aid. Insofar as secondary corruption is preventing foreign aid from being useful, those of us in MDCs who have worked on foreign aid delivery have a right to be concerned about counterproductive factors.

The concept of "political illness," as used here in connection with secondary corruption, may seem to the reader farfetched. Yet, what if you observed someone who, after taking his car to a mechanic for repair, reacted to an analysis of the car's problems by accusing the mechanic of "an insult" in presenting these problems? Surely, this reaction would appear so irrational as to be considered paranoid, particularly if it led to avoiding local mechanics in favor of foreign ones or neglecting repair work altogether in the hope of a new car (particularly in the form of a gift).

Yet, this is exactly what Klitgaard (1990) observed when, following a seminar of leading officials concerned with the problems of Equatorial Guinea, one of the participants accused the others of "criticizing the government." Other manifestations of political illness observed by Klitgaard include:

PURGING OF THE EDUCATED. Under Francisco Marcias Nguema, who ruled from 1968 to 1979, from one-quarter to one-third of the population were killed or forced to leave, including a high percentage of the most qualified and educated. The greater affluence of the educated, combined with ethnic differences, made them more independent and, therefore, more dangerous. Poor pay, limited economic and professional opportunities, and dismal living conditions contributed to the persistent brain drain.

UNDERMINING OF THE BANKS AND BUSINESSES. Top politicians and officials seized much of the most highly productive land (though actual land-ownership remained doubtful). They then demanded loans from the banks to use this land, but they never bothered to repay these loans. Likewise, they never paid for electricity and other products or services, undermining parastatals and private businesses. Prosecution and punishment for nonpayment were inconceivable because to do so would have been politically destabilizing.

DISCOURAGEMENT OF COMPETENT PERFORMANCE. Those with integrity and competence tended to find themselves in trouble with the existing power elite, ending up imprisoned and sometimes tortured or killed. This happened to several of the most highly respected ministers and a leading auditor. Inter-ethnic and factional conflicts contributed to this situation. Consequently, governmental taxation and import-export regulations, among other activities, were hopelessly corrupt. Much foreign currency was wasted on liquor (occupying nearly half of market space) or on drugs and medical equipment that were ultimately stolen for sale abroad.

So widespread is the political illness described here that, according to Peter Eigen of Transparency International (1992), LDCs may be giving more foreign aid to MDCs than they are receiving, particularly if the impact of "brain drain," drug profits, and "laundered money" is taken into account. Baker (1995, C2) estimates that flight capital amounts to between $50 billion and $80 billion annually.

Much of "capital flight" is manifested in trade mispricing, combined with "kickbacks." "Manipulation of trade values occurs on some 30 to 60 percent of import and export transactions of many countries, especially in Latin America and Africa" (Baker 1995, C2). Baker's estimates and examples are supported by the publications of Transparency International.

Capital flight results from a combination of MDC primary corruption and LDC secondary corruption. Eigen (1992) suggests that Swiss banks may be holding in excess of $20 billion on behalf of African leaders. According to recent Sierre Leone commissions of inquiry, ex-president Momoh had about 170 million pounds sterling in a UK bank, which amounted to more than seven times the annual support level obtained by Sierra Leone from the IMF during the late 1980s (Kpundeh 1993, 242). The public sectors and private sectors of LDCs place more than $80 billion annually into the U.S. economy (Bradsher 1994, A1, A4).

Those who benefit from international corruption are not simply heads of states. Various amounts are distributed according to one's position in the hierarchy. This is made possible by the practice of donor countries guaranteeing the sale of entire industries, products, and technology to LDCs, with the understanding that appropriate bribes will be paid to middlemen or "helpful" officials.

Many governments have well-established arrangements in this regard. In the case of the Ivory Coast, these arrangements allowed President Houphouet (the "Old Man" until his 1993 death) to use gifts "as a system of government and a mode of development" (Cabogo 1993, 169). Thus, it has not been unusual for donor countries "to look the other way when their favored clients diverted money given as aid" (Harsch 1993, 39). Liberia is an example of a country ruined by secondary corruption, intensified by American foreign aid during the Cold War. As noted in Chapter 4, Egypt continues to a victim of counterproductive American foreign aid.

Baker (1995, C2) points out that the bleeding over the years of perhaps a half-trillion dollars from the world's poor, not only distorts free trade and negates foreign aid, but also "worsens inflation, diminishes tax revenues, undermines structural adjustment, delays and imperils democracy and firmly entrenches poverty." The debt that is being built up to many donor countries, amounting to about 40 percent of sub-Saharan Africa's debt structure, as of 1989 (but much more so in 1996, as noted in Chapter 10), is increasingly seen as a "gift." Altogether, 25 sub-Saharan countries rescheduled their debts 105 times during 1980–1988" (Cheru 1992, 503).

LDC leaders must be asking themselves, "why worry about business development when funds will flow to us automatically from kickbacks?" However, in the process, capitalism, in the form of productive use of assets, rather than non-productive activities dependent on state privileges, has become discredited.

African protesters often insist that governments should "repatriate the funds of those who have enriched themselves," rather than agree to the taxation and other economic reform measures demanded by the World Bank and the IMF (Harsch 1993, 45). Inasmuch as MDCs secretly hold African funds, thee protesters argue that they should be responsible for whatever debt has been incurred. Moreover, these protesters increasingly blame the World Bank and the IMF for being "complicit in the corrupt dealings of their clients" (Harsch 1993, 40). They therefore insist that the International Financial Institutions undertake a large debt reduction program.

Yet, if it is true that secondary corruption is similar to alcoholism or drug addiction, to substantially retire the debt of countries to multilateral institutions and foreign donors without requiring fundamental reform would simply be "to feed the habit," and thereby more certainly harm those being assisted. This is why I suggest in Chapter 10 that those countries considered eligible for debt relief be required to compete for the funds potentially made available to them.

CHAPTER 7

Democracy and Development
The Case for a Linkage

INTRODUCTION

Since the end of the Cold War, particularly since 1989, the promotion of democracy has become "something of a growth industry," pushed directly and indirectly by foreign assistance agencies (Barkan 1994, 2). The supposition, as explained by Sklar (1995, 20), is that "countries with less democratic political systems can (and should) modernize by emulating the example of countries classified as democratic."

Barkan (1994, 13) suggests that about 10 percent of total aid budgets are spent to support democratization. The United States Agency for International Development (USAID) has been at the forefront of this effort, providing an estimated $400 million in fiscal year (FY) 1994 to promote democracy around the world (Diamond 1994, 6).

Because More Developed Countries (MDCs) are putting so much pressure on Less Developed Countries (LDCs) to democratize, we have to ask the question: what is the relationship between democracy and development? While MDCs are generally considered "democratic," with the exception of the United States, they did not start out this way. "Democracy emerged only slowly in the West, and was not generally an outcome for which political actors actually strove" (Pinkney 1994, 37). Moreover, the countries that have developed most rapidly in recent years, particularly the Asian Newly Industrialized Countries (NICs), have hardly been "models of democracy." Does this mean that democracy has no relationship to development—that MDCs are wasting their money in their efforts to promote democracy?

In trying to link democracy to development, we come across two

201

problems: (1) that of priority (Is economic development essential for democracy or vice-versa?) and (2) that of definition (Is liberal democracy the only acceptable form of democracy?). In this chapter we will have to address both problems inasmuch as they are tied together.

While there is strong evidence that economic development causes democracy, it does not follow that democracy causes economic development (Burkhart and Lewis-Beck 1994, 903). To suggest otherwise goes against modernization theory which, until recently, had assumed that democratization required prior economic and social development, particularly industrialization (Leftwich 1993, 605). Georg Sorenson (1993, 20) asserts that "it is only for the period after World War II that one can talk about extended, stable democratic rule in the industrialized countries of Western Europe and North America." Yet, it was in the nineteenth century that industrialization took place in European constitutional monarchies despite the fact that their elected parliaments (under highly restricted suffrage in most cases) had very limited control over their governments.

Modernization theorists generally have in mind only "liberal democracy," which emphasizes representative government chosen through competitive elections (Pinkney 1994, 10). Yet, the relationship between democracy (defined as "liberal democracy") and development has never been established. Indeed, many scholars, officials, and political leaders or administrators are dubious that such a relationship exists.

Robert Dahl, who many consider the leading theoretician on democracy and who was my professor at Yale in 1956–57, points out, towards the end of his 1971 book (p. 213), that the relationship between "polyarchy" (his term for democracy) and socioeconomic development "is very far from simple, direct, or well-understood." This assertion is supported by many scholars.

After reviewing 17 studies that generated 20 findings, Adam Przeworski (1992, 52–53) concluded, "we do not know whether democracy promotes economic development, hinders it, or is irrelevant to it." Joan Nelson (1992, 14) adds that analysts in the late 1980s "comparing economic performance in many countries found no clear evidence of any link between authoritarian or democratic forms of government and either long-term growth or short-term ability to carry out stabilization measures."

An article in THE NEW YORK TIMES (Kristoff 1993, A1, A10) notes that a Chinese woman is almost twice as likely to be literate as an Indian woman and her baby, twice as likely to survive its first year of life as that of her Indian counterpart. Considering that India has had a much longer and better established democratic history than other Asian countries, its slow economic progress is discouraging. World Bank statistics indicate that India's per-capita growth rate between 1965 and 1990 was about one-third that of China (1.9% versus 5.8%). While this lag behind China may have lessened, it apparently persists.

India's economic development, according to Kohli (1990) is undermined by demagogic, rather than programmatic, leaders, using violence, corruption, and societal cleavages to gain and maintain power. Similarly, in relatively democratic Jamaica, Stone (1986) found a system of clientelism, combined with intolerant partisanship, undermining efforts to promote professionalism, accountability, and responsible public expenditure.

While most Latin American countries have carried out fraud-free elections, according to the November 30, 1996 issue of THE ECONOMIST (pp. 15-16, 19-21), there remains extensive cynicism and discontent because of persistent corruption, incompetent bureaucracies, great inequality of wealth, inadequate social services, miserable living conditions, high unemployment, and fiscal laxity. "Civilian rulers, in short, are failing to strike a balance between democracy and efficiency— and the answer, some people think, is to have less democracy" (p. 21).

Lord Acton's famous aphorism, "Power tends to corrupt, and absolute power tends to corrupt absolutely," is often quoted in the literature on corruption. Why this is so may be explained by neoclassical economics (Grabowski 1994). The power elite, inasmuch as it monopolizes the use of violence, is in a position to extract wealth to support its interests at the expense of the majority of society.

It would follow from this explanation that democratization is essential to reduce corruption. Unfortunately, as I have indicated in the previous chapter, this is not true. Charlick (1993, 178) notes that few analysts "would contend that liberalization or democratization in and of itself is sufficient to curb systemic corruption," adding: "Clearly improved governance and democratization are not identical or necessarily synchronous processes." In the case of Russia, where "absolute power" has been most obviously reduced, corruption may have actually intensified, according to a World Bank study (Sheppard 1995).

Leftwich (1995, 401) points out that development requires "developmental states," which he defines as "states whose politics have concentrated sufficient power, autonomy and capacity at the center to shape, pursue, and encourage the achievement of explicit developmental objectives...." He goes on to note (pp. 418–419) that these developmental states tend to be nondemocratic, combining repression and legitimacy in ways that effectively bring public services to an expanding circle of people.

Reviewing the data on economic performance, Leftwich (1993, 613) concludes: "there is no necessary relationship between democracy and development nor, more generally, between any regime type and economic performance." The fact that so few of the more than thirty countries that democratized between 1970 and 1990 have made much economic progress makes us wonder if insisting upon democratization as a "political conditionality" is appropriate (Brauer 1990, 3). It also raises the question of the usefulness of foreign assistance for this purpose.

Nelson (1992, 23) notes "not all aid agency staff share the new perspective that political reforms are crucial to promote economic and social development." At both the World Bank and USAID, staff are concerned about the extent to which political reform efforts may conflict with economic reform efforts. After all, economic reform, including stabilization of the currency, removal of price supports and controls, privatization, cost recovery for public services, and downsizing of the civil service, can be a very painful and unpopular process. To what extent should democratization be sacrificed for economic reform, or vice-versa?

On the one hand, World Bank officials insist upon the following medicine: "take one teaspoonsful each of free trade and private investment, plus a dram of property rights and the rule of law; and wash down with a swig of multi-party democracy" (Edward Mortimer, quoted in Van Arkadie 1994, 45). On the other hand, World Bank officials pointed out in the 1991 WORLD DEVELOPMENT REPORT (133–134): "the democratic-authoritarian distinction itself fails to explain adequately whether or not countries initiate reform, implement it effectively, or survive its political fall-out."

As Schmitter (1994, 62) emphasizes, people expect the end of tyranny to bring better living conditions. If not, "more and more people begin to question whether democracy is really worth so much anxiety and uncertainty." Pinkney (1994, 105) makes this point somewhat differently, suggesting that, while continued poverty may permit free elections, "it is uncertain whether such moves represent a transition to any durable form of democracy or merely the retreat of one group of authoritarians who have lost their power base while other groups wait in the wings until the democrats prove equally ineffective in dealing with the intractable problems."

IS DEMOCRACY DESIRABLE? THE AFRICAN DEBATE

While the debate over the desirability of liberal democracy can be heard wherever economic liberalization and political reform seem incompatible, it has perhaps reached higher levels of controversy and confusion in Africa than elsewhere. However, I might note my special sensitivity to the African debate, having studied it since my graduate days at the University of California/Berkeley in the 1960s and my teaching of African studies at the State University of New York/Stony Brook and the University of Maryland/College Park in the 1960s and 1970s.

The first generation of African post-colonial leaders opposed democracy (except within a one-party framework), arguing, not only that it is impractical and dangerous under existing conditions, but also that it would undermine the unity essential for socialism and rapid development. Strong government, in other words, not the weak or "limited government" advocated by liberal democrats, is essential. "Silence. We are developing." is the message heard in Africa, according to Claude Ake (quoted in Lancaster 1991–92, 150).

The failure of most African countries to develop economically during the three decades following independence has led many experts on Africa to question the justification for authoritarianism put forward by African leaders. "Whereas one can speak of a political economy of the European princely state, one is inclined to speak of a political dyseconomy of the African personal regime" (Jackson and Rosberg 1994, 297).

Because African rulers tend to be far more interested in enriching themselves than their people, "the state has now become THE PROBLEM in Africa and the ENEMY of development" (Ayittey 1994, 174). Pluralist democracy is increasingly being attempted in African countries, Ndue (1994, 54) argues, because, if they can achieve it, "pluralistic democracy will set them on the path toward the comprehensive modernization of their political systems and make them competitive in international terms."

I sympathize with those who suggest that liberal democracy is the only viable alternative to the misrule that so many African countries have suffered under since independence. I have Kenya particularly in mind because I spent almost ten years writing a book (Werlin 1974) about that beautiful country. Considering high levels of inflation (27.5 percent in 1992), unemployment (estimated to affect the majority of the adult population), and crumbling infrastructure, the lives of most people have worsened in recent years. Bad conditions in rural areas have contributed to increasingly volatile conditions in urban areas: begging, homelessness, malnourishment, crime, interethnic fighting, etc.

The inept and predatory nature of the Kenyan government (stemming from "secondary corruption," as defined in the previous chapter) is well known (Holmquist and Ford 1994, 17; Lorch 1995, A3). By August 1997, corruption had become so flagrant as to cause the IMF to take the unprecedented step of suspending a US $220 million loan program. "The signal sent to Kenya's investors and donors is that the president's cronies are pocketing the profits from economic reform and thus making a mockery of the reform process itself" (THE ECONOMIST, August 9, 1997, 38). Yet, for the following reasons, I fear the consequences of liberal democracy in Kenya, as well as in Africa as a whole, and (even if my fear is excessive), I doubt that life will really be better for most people:

THE ABSENCE OF PRECONDITIONS. Sorenson (1993, 27) points out that "for every factor seen as conducive to democracy, counterexamples can be put forward." Nevertheless, in More Developed Countries (MDCs) we can accept the view expressed in Milton's AEROPAGITICA that out of extensive and free debate, the best ideas will eventually emerge triumphant. But what about in Less Developed Countries (LDCs)?

"At the other end of the scale," to quote the Kenyan scholar, Afrifa Gitonga (1988, 16), "the illiteracy, ignorance and poverty of Third World masses, plus such factors as poor communication facilities, militate to a large extent against the full development of the democratic process." These people are considered, "unreasonable," and, as such, prone to demagogic appeal. Without considerable socio-economic development, political participation is likely to be manipulated, mobilized, and/or ineffective (Huntington and Nelson 1976, 166).

In regard to Africa, Lancaster (1991–92) notes the absence of the generally considered requisites for democracy: widespread literacy, high levels of per-capita income, a sizeable middle class, strong public institutions, nationally based political parties, a tolerant political culture, etc. Thus, while three-fourths of African countries are in various stages of political liberalization, there is much doubt about the durability and significance of this development. Joseph (1997a) describes them as "virtual," rather than "real" democracies inasmuch as existing political liberalization is very constrained in practice.

THE MEANINGLESSNESS OF ELECTIONS. In August, 1997, Herbst summarized the literature on African elections, using reports from Freedom House, the U.S. Department of State, and the Inter-Parliamentary Union. He concluded that only four countries had managed two transitions of power, indicating well-established civil rights. Many African elections appear to be nothing more than "a person competing against a frog" (Nyang'oro 1994, 134).

In 1994, Aaron Segal (1995, 6) points out, there were "20 contested elections in Africa but none resulted in a succession," adding (p. 20): "Contested elections featuring managed outcomes and co-opted opposition parties are becoming the new norm in much of Africa." By the end of 1996, half of the countries of West and Central Africa were ruled by "elected" ex-soldiers, who had learned how to carry out elections to please aid-givers and, otherwise, to practice "donor democracy" (THE ECONOMIST, November 23, 1996, 20).

Even when an African government does not overtly interfere with the conducting of an election, it seldom can properly handle the mechanics of an election. In the case of the 1992 Kenya multiparty elections, problems included a short period of registration, an inability to provide identity cards to more than a million eligible voters, and delays in both voting and the count (Holmquist and Ford 1994, 7–8). The handling of the December, 1997 general eletion there "made the delays and the foul play of its 1992 predecessor seem mere blips" (THE ECONOMIST, January 3, 1998, 44).

In the October 1995 Tanzanian national elections, foreign donors covered nearly half of their estimated $50 million cost (Buckley 1995, A22). Yet, even in the capital, where the most politically active citizens live, many of the polling stations did not open, opened late, had no presiding officials, and not enough ballots or materials. Consequently, the results had to be annulled, with the opposition threatening to boycott a rescheduled election.

Of course, African governments are hardly ever neutral in the electoral process. In the case of the Ivory Coast's 1990 elections, "the PDCI {the ruling party} and the president retained monopoly control of critical electoral resources, which made it difficult for the quickly formed alternative parties to build constituencies in the rural areas" (Widner 1994, 136). The persistence of this practice of allowing "Government-appointed officials to run the elections and determine the results" caused the Ivory Coast's main opposition parties to pull out of the 1995 elections (French 1995, A9).

African governments find many ways of manipulating the electoral process. During the 1980s, the Kenyan government replaced the secret ballot "by a queuing system in which voters have to line up behind the candidate they favored in order to be counted" (Widner 1994, 142). This obviously facilitated the buying of votes.

During the 1992 Kenyan elections, the government expanded the national money supply, enabling it to provide generous gifts and favors to the constituencies that were considered loyal to the regime. At the same time, it carefully monitored the activities of opposition leaders, reduced their access to credit and services, and used the police to harass their supporters. Moreover, opposition parties were often prevented from holding rallies, opening party branches, and gaining access to the press and the electronic media (Holmquist and Ford 1994, 8).

Summarizing Africa's experience with elections, Segal (1995, 7) concluded that they have so far not been "a guarantee of democracy and/or opportunities for non-violent political succession." In Senegal, for example, there are regular elections; but because the poor either do not participate or are controlled by religious leaders, "there is little public debate on poverty despite its being widespread" (Marc, Graham, and Schacter 1993, 32).

The government's monopoly of the electronic media, control over major newspapers, ability to buy favorable articles, and willingness to threaten or undermine opposition newspapers or journalists are other reasons for discounting election results. Consequently, to quote Pinkney (1994, 159): "once people have discovered that little has changed, or can be changed, as a result of their votes, why should they be anxious to defend democracy if an ambitious young major decides to bring the edifice down again?"

THE DANGER OF CIVIL WAR AND ANARCHY. African countries tend to be politically very fragile. The World Bank's Africa Region (1995, 4–5) reported that six countries, containing about one-fifth of sub-Saharan Africa's population, had become lost to the development process "owing to complete breakdown of order through civil war and social unrest." How much can be blamed on the democratization process is hard to say. In the case of Rwanda, democratization programs, according to Newbury (1995, 17), "contributed to, rather than alleviated, the crisis."

Even when elections do not lead to anarchy, they can lead to extensive violence and disorder. This was the situation in Congo-Brazzaville, where, following the October 1993 elections, opposition parties, using army deserters, village conscripts, unemployed urban youth, and mercenaries, ignited extensive ethnic violence to control the country's oil wealth (Clark 1994, 57). The inter-ethnic fighting that reemerged in Brazzaville in June of 1997 can be partly linked to these 1993 elections and to the presidential election scheduled for July 27, 1997.

It is common for politicians everywhere to arouse racial, ethnic, or religious animosities to generate political support. Countries, such as Yugoslavia, Sri Lanka, and Rwanda (to name just a few), functioned reasonably well under colonial or authoritarian rule before political liberalization tore them apart.

What worsens the situation is when political parties become "particularistic," confined to single ethnic groups, regions, religions, or racial categories. In regard to Africa, Ndue (1994, 53) writes: "Democracy cannot function in a tribalist society and any common attitude or policy is bound to fail in such a context."

When capitalism is not well established, there may be no alternative to using the public sector for employment and income. "Thus, competition over the state's resources often results in intense conflict, contributing to the problems of democratic consolidation" (Kohli 1993, 677). The "frenzy of competition for the spoils of office both within and among parties" that followed President Ndadaye of Burundi's assassination can easily lead to "moral justification for genocide" (Lemarchand 1995, 10).

In the Islamic world, the struggle for democracy is combined with a struggle for secularism, according to Khashan (1992, 20). This is why we read (Ibrahim 1995, A4) that "Islamic militants have threatened to kill anyone who goes to the polls for Algeria's presidential elections." Because political parties here are dominated by either Islamists or secularists, the country's security forces will probably continue to rule, despite relatively peaceful 1995 elections.

How much to push liberal democracy in a country such as Kenya, where inter-ethnic warfare is always a possibility, is hard to say (see

Ndegwa 1997). If the government were cooperative, it might not be so difficult. As it is, according to Holmquist and Ford (1994, 12), the regime wants "to show Kenyans and the world that multiparty democracy would only fan ethnic flames leading to civil disorder." Consequently, it has sanctioned ethnic cleansing in and around the Rift Valley and has promoted or encouraged inter-ethnic urban clashes. In August, 1997, this violence threatened tourism, the country's leading industry, worth nearly US $500 million annually.

THE FAILURE OF DEMOCRACY TO LEAD TO BETTER GOVERNANCE. The Gambia (along with Botswana and Mauritius) was, until the 1994 military coup, considered to be the only continuous democracy in Africa (Pinkney 1994, 89). Since it was extremely impoverished, its ability to conduct reasonably fair elections within a one-party framework was quite remarkable. There were several opposition parties allowed and a commitment to human rights. Yet, it was also very corrupt and poorly administered and, as such, similar to its more authoritarian neighbors.

Between 1975 and 1985, while the Gambian economy was stagnating, the government allowed its civil service to expand from about 6,000 to more than 15,000 (de Merode and Thomas 1994). A 1993 article in a Gambian newspaper revealed how weak the bureaucracy had become, "so befuddled with role conflicts and apathy . . . that there seems to be a total aversion to work within it" (Quoted in Kelm 1993, 36). Partly this situation resulted from the patrimonial system within which it operated, dividing positions among politically important groups. Partly it resulted from declining budgartary outlays for operation and maintenance and for salaries, which declined by 50 percent in real terms between 1980 and 1985.

As pointed out earlier, democratization may actually intensify corruption. However, confining our attention to Africa, we have to agree "that there may not be an ineluctable connection between democracy and limiting corruption" (Le Vine 1993, 272). Corruption was a major factor in explaining Gambia's poor economic performance and the 1994 coup.

While Gambian soldiers were not being paid their promised salaries for peace keeping operations in Liberia, several internal reports revealed substantial undercollection of customs duties caused by mismanagement (see Dia 1995, 31, 75). According to a 1992 study prepared by the

Harvard Institute for International Development, about 70 percent of revenue from taxes owed the government was lost because of widespread evasion. Even when judgments were sustained by courts, they were ignored because they were never enforced and "no personal or professional stigma is attached to not paying taxes." While the President's Office urged the tax commissioner to prosecute tax evaders, it undermined efforts to do so, particular when the elite ("big fish") were involved (Pinto and Mrope 1994).

Zambia is one of the few countries in Africa where a change in government occurred (October, 1991) as a result of a peaceful competitive election, thereby ousting Kenneth Kaunda, who had misruled the country for more than 25 years. Under the new president (Frederick Chiluba), there has been considerable economic reform: privatization, reduction of subsidies and price controls, lowering of inflation, convertibility of currency, and downsizing of the civil service (THE ECONOMIST, November 23, 1996, 46).

Yet, most people have not benefited from the Structural Adjustment Program (SAP). The persistence of corruption caused bilateral donors at the end of 1993 to withhold $300 million of the $1.1 billion support requested by the Zambian government, despite continued international goodwill toward what was considered to be a "new model" of democratic transition in Africa. "As of October 1994, almost half of Chiluba's original cabinet members had either resigned (and joined the opposition) due to what is seen as the absence of good governance; or left to facilitate investigations into their alleged involvement in corruption and related charges; or were simply dismissed by Chiluba following mounting pressure to cleanse his government" (Saasa 1994, 37). Because of the likelihood of Kaunda's returning to power by election, Chiluba had him banned from standing (and later arrested), causing his United National Independence Party to boycott the November 1996 vote.

Various studies find poverty rates in Zambia to range from a high of 77 percent to a low of 56 percent, with the prevalance, depth, and severity of poverty greater in rural Zambia (Southern African Department 1994, 4). Household survey results show a worsening of poverty between 1991 and 1993.

There is a tendency to blame the country's SAP for this, particularly for a 40-fold increase in the price of maize in the 1990s following the end of price controls (Duke 1995, A12). However, World Bank studies point to the weakness of governance in Zambia. The persistent malaise of the civil service, despite constant promises of administrative reform, is described by Bryant (1993, 2):

> Scarcity characterizes the work environment; buildings are not maintained, toilets do not work, nor do the telephones work reliably. There are no internal newspapers, few copiers and computers, and little paper. It is hard to know what is going on, where the history of a problem can be learned, or how to proceed to solve it. There are no workprograms, statement of objectives for bureaus, or mission statements for ministries.

The relationship of inadequate governance to rural poverty has been examined in a 1994 World Bank study of Zambia (Southern African Department 1994). Despite attempts at decentralization, there is virtually no involvement of local populations in decision-making and implementation. Disbursements from the Budget Office are often slow; and, even when they are made, the allocations get diverted to non-primary service delivery (e.g., to universities and hospitals rather than to primary education and district health services). Much of the responsibility for credit, seeds and fertilizer, transport, and payment for crops remains with inefficient parastatal organizations.

The failure to maintain roads is estimated to increase freight costs by 17 percent, as well as increasing breakage of goods and vehicles (Africa Region 1995, 53). "The poor condition of rural institutions, combined with deteriorating infrastructure, means that liberalization and reform has the potential for deteriorating the prospects of the already vulnerable rural poor" (Southern African Department 1994, 8l). Consequently, rural living conditions are unlikely to improve, despite the fact that only about 10 percent of Zambia's extensive tracts of cultivatible land is fully utilized.

THE DISCOURAGEMENT OF ECONOMIC REFORM. While by 1994 the majority of African countries had legalized a political opposition and either held or moved toward holding elections, "most African countries will not enter the middle income category for another half century" (African Region 1995, 4, 39). A 1994 World Bank report indicates that almost two-thirds of African countries had improved their macroeconomic and agricultural policies during the 1980s. Yet, no African country had achieved a combination of low inflation (under 10 percent), a low budget deficit, and a competitive exchange rate (World

Bank 1994, 1–2). In the case of Tanzania, for example, Van Arkadie (1994, 33) finds, on the one hand, that "the modest success achieved looks impressive against the sorry background of the depths to which the economy had sunk," but, on the other hand, "it is not yet evident that the material and institutional basis has been laid for sustained growth over the longer term."

As noted earlier, many experts now argue that strong leadership, rather than democracy, is essential for economic development. In regard to Africa, Husain (1994) does not preclude the emergence of a relationship between liberal democracy and strong economic performance, but he does indicate the following problems:

(1) The opposition of the elite to reform. Political leaders, regardless of the origins of their power, must maintain the support of such powerful groups as the military, the civil service, large business owners, trade unions, and journalists. Often these groups are more interested in rent-seeking opportunities than in anything else. The civil service, for example, is likely to oppose the curtailment of its power through privatization, deregulation, elimination of central planning, and reduction in the work force.

(2) The danger of appearing unpopular. The more democratic a government is, the more it is expected to use a participatory and consultative approach. Yet, it is difficult to use such an approach in justifying such requisites for reform as downsizing the civil service, reducing consumer subsidies and scholarships, cost recovery, privatization, and trade liberalization.

While the need for economic reform can be explained to small audiences of educated and well informed groups and individuals, it may not be possible to do so with the urban masses who have previously benefited from public policies and subsidies. The fact that the urban masses are likely to be led by such middle and upper income beneficiaries as university students demanding free education and automobile owners wanting cheap gasoline may make even more difficult consensus building for economic reform. It should be remembered in this regard that socialism remains a powerful ideology in Africa and that, among intellectuals, there is a widespread belief that markets "are anti-social, create inequities, hurt the poor and are repressive" (Husain 1994, 18).

(3) The lack of capacity for reform. Those who pretend to support economic reform may only be interested in a change in government which will bring to them opportunities for self-enrichment. The

clientelistic nature of politics, within which leaders view the public administration as their personal property and consider loyalty to be more important than competence, does not change with elections. Likewise, the demand for public sector jobs when there are limited private sector opportunities is far more powerful than the demand for a meritocratic bureaucracy.

We need not be so cynical about liberal democracy as Simon Bolivar, as quoted by Huntington (1971, 258): "Treaties are paper; constitutions, books; elections, battles; liberty, anarchy; and life, a torment." Yet, to go back to our question about the usefulness of pushing liberal democracy in a country such as Kenya, we have to wonder if much good will come of it, based upon the experience of other African countries. In Nigeria, for example, which has gone back and forth several times, from democracy to military rule, what can we expect of liberal democracy, assuming that the military allows it to come to fruition? Despite the poor quality of military government since 1983 (see Chapter 1), the danger of another civil war or even anarchy following democratization can never be underestimated here (Gboyega 1991).

Nigeria's First Republic (1960–1966) could not overcome interethnic conflict, eventually leading to the terrible Biafra War; and its Second Republic (1979–1983) proved to be hopelessly corrupt and inept. "Ethnic and primordial interests were once again at play confronting one another over the distribution of the national cake," Olugbabe (1989, 248-249), points out, adding (253): "Thus it was with open arms and jubilation that Nigerians welcomed the military."

THE PRIMARY/SECONDARY DEMOCRACY DISTINCTION

The increasing international pressure for democratization forces us to examine more carefully, not simply the relationship between democracy and development, but also the meaning of democracy. Unless we do so, we may find ourselves agreeing with the Korean scholar, Sung Moon Pae (1992a, 81) that studying democracy is like "walking in a jungle with no clear sense of direction."

Just as sportsmanship is essential for competitive sports, statesmanship is necessary for liberal democracy. This rather obvious assertion, which I followed with a distinction between primary and secondary democracy, was greeted with some misunderstanding when it was presented at an American Political Science Association workshop on democratization headed by Gabriel Almond (1993 Annual Meeting).

Since this distinction appears to be controversial, let me defend it here as a way: (1) to overcome some of the quandaries found in the literature on democracy; (2) to link democracy to development; and (3) to suggest more fruitful approaches to encouraging democracy than "the holding of free and fair multiparty elections as the litmus test of democratic transitions" (Barkan 1994, 6). Professor Almond's response to my primary/secondary democracy distinction was to assert that those participating in his workshop had used a definition of democracy presented by Dahl (1971) in his book on "polyarchy," emphasizing two dimensions: widespread participation and contestation (including competition and conflict). However, both of these dimensions seem to be sources of confusion.

With regard to participation, Huntington and Nelson (1976, 7–8) point out that, inasmuch as it is mobilized or manipulated, rather than spontaneous and autonomous, it may neither contribute to nor result from democracy. While the concept of "contestation" comes close to the standard definition of liberal democracy noted earlier (focusing almost exclusively on what I call, "primary democracy"), it omits the aspects emerging from secondary democracy: a mutual respect among competing groups and between leaders and followers and consensus on governmental goals and procedures.

Without secondary democracy, primary democracy tends to be meaningless, much like an Olympics without the necessary conditions for sporting events and rules for participating, competing, and officiating. Another way of making the distinction here presented would be the "two ideals of democracy" suggested by Mansbridge (1991, 7): "one based on conflict, the other on commonality." Until politicians are prepared to ask, "how can we work out our disagreements?," they are unlikely to reach "democracy," as defined by Diamond, Linz, and Lipset (1989, xvi): "meaningful and extensive competition among individuals and organized groups. . . ."

In the Introduction, I defined politics, using Wolin's 1960 book, as "the relationship between leadership and followership for the purpose of governance." The distinction between primary and secondary democracy arises from subdividing this definition into the two sides of politics presented in the previous chapter: the struggle for competitive advantage (partisanship, in other words) and the struggle for consensus (essentially, statesmanship).

Primary democracy is what academic writers and journalists pay most attention to, including: popular participation, elections, majority rule, empowerment, confrontation, conflict and dissent. (Behaviorists particularly stress those aspects that are easy to quantify.)

Those of us in the liberal tradition see primary democracy as our ultimate goal; but, to reach it, we may have to start with secondary democracy, which is, after all, closer to the Athenian conception of community or polis: continuous discussion in various forums, political education in civic virtue, and recognition of a shared fate (Euben 1993, 479). Under secondary democracy, "rule by the people" takes the form, not of domination, but of persuasion, including: influence of the people, respect for the people, and acceptance by the people. Thus, I stress "the five C's" put forward by Adebayo Adedeji, the former head of the Economic Commission for Africa: consent, consensus, conviction, commitment, and compassion (Lemarchand 1992, 99).

By distinguishing primary and secondary democracy, I believe it is possible to reduce the confusion emerging from the literature on democracy. Let us examine some examples of this confusion:

THE CONCEPT OF REPRESENTATION. As David Held (1992, 12) notes, we remain uncertain as to whether democracy should mean some kind of popular power or a procedure for decision-making. I insist that, without a balance between primary and secondary democracy, neither of these conceptions is meaningful. What is essential to the democratic process is a "reaching out" for approval—a process that goes far beyond the results of periodic elections or the enactment of legislation.

Verba (1991, 75) points out that the term "democratic government" is internally contradictory. After all, people cannot rule themselves in any meaningful way. They have to do so through government (i.e., the state). Otherwise, the result would be anarchy. How do we enable society (followership) to give itself leadership (a state) without undermining the society? Both Plato and Jean-Jacques Rousseau were disturbed by this question. Their answers—Plato's "philosopher king" and Rousseau's "the general will"—have at times been used or misused to attack representative democracy.

"One of the enduring mysteries of established democracies," Schmitter (1994, 68) points out, "is their source of political obligation." While primary democracy emphasizes competitive elections, it does not carry with it a necessity for "losers" to obey the dictates of "winners." This is why secondary democracy is so important, giving legitimacy to the decision-making process. Otherwise, democracies can easily become anarchies.

"Democracy will not be valued by the people unless it deals effectively with social and economic problems and achieves a modicum of order and justice," Diamond (1990, 49) writes. Yet, we so far have very few success stories. The sad truth seems to be, according to Schmitter and Karl (1993, 49), that "democracies are not likely to appear more orderly, consensual, stable, or governable than the autocracies they replace." That being the case, liberal democracy is hard to justify.

The Westminster model proved unworkable in most of the places where the British introduced it, as has the American presidential model in much of Central and South America (Ware 1992, 141). Consequently, debates in the pages of THE JOURNAL OF DEMOCRACY as to the superiority of parliamentary or presidential systems of government (i.e., political hardware) seem to me less relevant to governmental performance than the quality of relationships among legislators, executives, central government bureaucrats, local government officials, business groups, organizations, and ordinary citizens (i.e, political software). This is why Switzerland is a successful political system, despite its bizarre form of government, emphasizing rotating leadership, collegial decision-making, and popular participation (Baylis 1980).

MICHELS' "IRON LAW OF OLIGARCHY." For many reasons (expertise, wealth, tradition, family position, charisma, etc.), political power tends to fall into the hands of a few individuals or groups, as pointed out by Robert Michels (1958). The inevitability of oligarchy predicted by Michels is most likely when liberty leads to greater inequality.

Barrington Moore emphasized in 1966, "No bourgeois, no democracy" (quoted in Sorenson 1993, 27). This assertion suggests that, unless people have the economic freedom to be entrepreneurial, they will lack the political freedom essential for democratic government. But such freedom inevitably brings about inequality. The debate between liberals, emphasizing the need to prevent excessive bureaucratic control, and socialists, stressing the dangers of domination by wealthy individuals and irresponsible market forces, is well summarized by Beetham (1992). This debate raises the question: to what extent is economic inequality compatible with democracy?

In many Latin American countries, according to Diamond (1990, 57), violent political polarization is intensified by large landholders who depend upon cheap labor. Land reform may be necessary to reduce this polarization; but "to moderate class conflict in the long run, a political system may need to risk aggravating it in the short run." In Africa and Southeast Asia, economic disparities are often combined with racial and religious differences, causing a clustering of diversities. Under these circumstances, much of the opposition to privatization and other economic reform programs stems from fear of the majority that they will become even more economically subjugated. At the same time, minorities (e.g., Europeans in Zimbabwe and South Africa; Chinese in Indonesia and Malaysia) fear the radical pressures that might come from greater democratization.

As Pinkney (1994, 110) notes, the masses may insist on democracy during periods of economic decline, but they will not defend it if conditions do not improve: "Taken to extremes, the market and the ballot box appear to offer conflicting rather than complementary means of deciding on the allocation of resources."

Does "the iron law of oligarchy" make democracy impossible? I do not think so, even under limited electoral participation or nonpartisan elections, assuming adequate two-way flows of communication, problem-solving mechanisms, and acceptable and understandable rules. Insofar as leaders govern for the BENEFIT of those governed, they are more likely to do so with the CONSENT of the governed. In other words, so long as there is secondary democracy, organizations can effectively function under the control of a small group of directors and managers, with few members bothering to vote in the nonadverserial elections that are periodically held.

Most of us who have taught for many years are uncomfortable when the chairmanship of our department is the product of partisan politics. We much prefer a rotational system among those who are respected and interested. What we are really concerned about is having our needs and problems dealt with fairly and carefully. This, for us, is democracy, even if it doesn't appear to be to an outsider. Of course, we want the right to turn to a more confrontational approach when serious disagreements and divisions emerge.

EMPOWERMENT CONTROL. If we accept Lincoln's definition of democracy as "government of the people, by the people, and for the people," we run into the danger that decisions "by the people" may not be "of the people" or "for the people." Liberals insist that democracy must be "limited government," with respect for minorities and human rights, including the opportunity for minorites to become majorities. This is where an acceptable constitution comes in, with agreed-upon procedures, norms, regulations, and rights; but the more we insist upon limited government, the more we diminish the concept of majority rule.

Berry, Portney, and Thomson (1993) summarize criticisms and fears having to do with community empowerment proposals. Particularly when communities consist largely of impoverished and uneducated people and when there are deep-rooted social and ideological divisions, there is a danger of an "excess of democracy," tyranny of the majority, undermining of business and the functioning of government, and unreasonable expectations.

However, in their case studies of American participatory democracy, these authors found such fears to be exaggerated. When "citizens and governmental advocates combined a firm refusal to let partisan politics become part of the participation process with an equally firm insistence that policy issues . . . become part and parcel of the system's daily operation (p. 50), neighborhood associations become "mechanisms that resolve rather than exacerbate differences." (p. 202). The authors add: "Few people want to get involved in organizations that are highly conflictual and leave participants in an antagonized state."

Turning to LDCs, the dangers of excessive democracy are more apparent; but, as I see it, these stem more from the inadequacy of secondary democracy than of primary democracy. The truth is, according to Sangmpam (1992) that, while democratization is highly desirable, its benefits cannot be realized under the conditions of an "overpoliticized state," characterized by lack of compromise, use of violence, and manipulation of the state apparatus. Until oppression, exploitation, and discrimination are significantly reduced, democracy will remain "pro-forma," even when it includes various types of elections (Imam and Ibrahim 1992, 17).

BUREAUCRACY AND DEMOCRACY. Dwight Waldo (1980, 82) describes bureaucracy and democracy "as two major forces shaping the twentieth century." Yet, he points out (p. 91) that the task of reconciling them seems "an insoluble problem" because of the need to harmonize the apparently conflicting values of each, with democracy pushing us in one way, and bureaucracy in the opposite direction. As I pointed out in the Introduction, Waldo's bureaucracy/democracy dichotomy can be linked to the scientific/ humanistic management dichotomy.

Without a well-functioning bureaucracy, democracy cannot survive. The reason is simple, as Denis Thompson pointed out in 1983: "No-one has yet shown that the quality of life that citizens in modern democracies demand can be sustained without bureaucracy, or a form or organization very much like it" (quoted in Pollitt 1986, 158).

While effective bureaucracies may be essential for a high standard of living, do the advantages of bureaucracy predispose countries towards authoritarianism? This was a question first raised by Max Weber, who is generally considered the most seminal thinker in the field (Mommsen 1989).

If, as Weber pointed out, bureaucratic procedures have the same advantage over non-bureaucratic ones as machine production over hand labor, authoritarian regimes which inhibit democratic interference with bureaucracy will inevitably come out ahead. In such regimes, democratic tendencies will, according to Weber, be increasingly stifled: "The bureaucratic organization is, together with lifeless machinery, about to produce the iron cage of future serfdom in which men will have to live helplessly, like the fellahin in Egypt . . ." (quoted in Mommsen 1989, 117).

If bureaucracy and democracy are so irreconcilable, should experts who value democracy be assisting LDCs in improving their public administration, thereby endangering democratic tendencies? Heady (1979, 387–397) summarizes the debate over this question that emerged during the 1960s and to some extent persists (see Smith 1996).

While an efficient bureaucracy is generally considered essential for economic development, it may undermine political development inasmuch as civil servants become "a new kind of politically and economically dominant class" (Smith 1996, 242) and, as such, consider representative institutions as endangering their power. Moreover, the process of strengthening public administration may make bureaucrats more corrupt by enabling them to give preference to their own group interests at the expense of the population as a whole.

Another dilemma can be added to intensify our confusion: that, while strong bureaucracies are dangerous without various countervailing institutions (legislatures, courts, political parties, interest groups, free newspapers, etc.), weak bureaucracies can retard the development of a strong governmental framework essential for such institutions. This confusion causes scholars to describe Third World bureaucracies as being simultaneously "overdeveloped" and "underdeveloped"—too powerful in relation to other political institutions but not powerful enough to strengthen these other institutions (Smith 1996, Ch. 7).

My emphasis on secondary democracy suggests why it is that, contrary to Weberian theory, successful bureaucracies cannot be altogether undemocratic. In other words, using political elasticity (PE) theory, as explained in previous chapters, we can link bureaucracy and democracy in a way that is impossible under Weberian theory. This is because political elasticity requires a high quality of "political software," referring to the social or human relationships essential for "political hardware" (organizational forms) to work effectively.

Developing and maintaining a high quality of political software does not require primary democracy, but it does necessitate secondary democracy, including: setting acceptable goals, selecting qualified subordinates, developing legitimate and understandable rules, allowing widespread participation in decision making, delegating authority, building morale and motivation, overcoming conflict, protecting experts and independent spheres of authority, and maintaining accountability. Consequently, neither administrative nor political leaders can simply impose their will to attain political elasticity, and, thereby, the Weberian goals of precision, speed, certainty, continuity, and impartiality. Instead, they must consider the needs and desires of subordinates and followers.

Without secondary democracy, political inelasticity inevitably characterizes the relationship of leaders to followers, as pointed out in previous chapters. Political inelasticity, however, is not simply a phenomenon found in the so-called "Third World." A brief look at manifestations of political inelasticity in the Former Soviet Union (FSU) in regard to agricultural development may be useful in exposing the following myths: (1) that democracy is unnecessary for development; (2) that development can be coerced; and (3) that liberalization will automatically bring about development.

Soviet agriculture never fully recovered from Stalin's "war against the peasantry," which was most brutally conducted during the early 1930s, including coercive collectivization, closing of free markets, compulsory contracts specifying prices and deliveries of crops, heavy penalties for refusal to deliver, high taxes, and payment in low fixed prices or worthless government bonds (Hedlund 1984). Political inelasticity thereby became apparent inasmuch as, by 1932, grain delivery quotas had to be reduced by more than one-third, and the crop of grain in 1933–37 was actually about one-fourth less than published.

However, judging by the experience of the Ukraine, liberal democracy has not yet led to greater productivity: "Despite significant producer and credit subsidies, agricultural output has declined by about 22% since 1990" (World Bank 1994c, ix). Existing problems include high inflation, worsening terms of trade, decline of real wages and domestic demand, lack of vital inputs, slow privatization of land, inadequate financial and rural social services, unsatisfactory technical information, and the collapse of marketing opportunities. Thus, the political system remains "inelastic," despite the introduction of primary democracy, without the capacity to generate a positive response from agricultural producers.

PE theory also enables us to address the question posed in the next section, raised by Kohli (1990, 398): "why authoritarianism in many African countries has failed to create developmental dynamics whereas the results of authoritarianism in East Asian countries like South Korea have been nearly the opposite?" By examining the Asian Newly Industrialized Countries (NICs) in the next section, using PE theory and the distinction between primary and secondary democracy, we may be able to illustrate the linkage between democracy and development.

SECONDARY DEMOCRACY: THE ASIAN NIC EXPERIENCE

As we look at the political economies of the Asian NICs, two facts stand out: (1) extraordinarily high levels of economic growth and (2) rejection, until recently, of forms of political pluralism, combined with repression of governmental opposition. These two facts have not been easy to reconcile. While the economic success of the Asian NICs has been well described in a number of books (e.g., Hofheinz and Calder 1982; Wade 1990; Campos and Root 1996), the political explanation for this success remains somewhat murky.

With an average 5.5 percent annual per-capita real income growth from 1960 to 1990, the Asian NICs more than quadrupled their GNP per-capita during these years (World Bank 1993a, 2, 28). There are, of course, dark spots to dim the brilliance of this achievement: environmental degradation, discrimination against women workers in the labor market, exploitation of foreign labor, and repression of independent labor unions (see Bello and Rosenfeld 1990).

However, even the harshest critics of the Asian NICs recognize the difference between authoritarianism and totalitarianism, as manifested in differences between South Korea and North Korea and between Taiwan (ROC) and the People's Republic of China (PRC). Despite indications of recent economic progress in China and Vietnam, the high levels of poverty, corruption, and governmental mismanagement in Communist Asia cannot be hidden (Chang 1991; Sanger 1992).

During the 1970s, South Korea appeared to combine the most extensive political repression with the most rapid economic growth (Clifford 1994, 77).President Park Chung Hee used a number of different security agencies, particularly the KCIA, to investigate private companies, universities, the media, and any other possible source of trouble. In addition to overt repression, the president did not hesitate to use his control over the economy to impose pressures and sanctions on those who might be uncooperative or disloyal.

Writing about Taiwan, Fei (1991, 106) points out that, until 1986, efforts to end martial law, grant freedom to the press, permit street demonstrations, and legalize opposition parties had made little progress. However, it was during 1947, following a revolt of the "Mainlanders," that we find the highest levels of repression imposed, including the execution of thousands and the imprisonment of the intellectual and political elite (Wachman 1994, 47). For the next three decades, the Kuomintang Party (KMT) "faced a very unorganized and weak political opposition consisting primarily of defiant local factions that had no national political aims and posed little threat to the KMT's dominant position" (Chu 1994, 102). While the KMT did not hesitate to suppress political discontent, it managed largely by a combination of indoctrination, cooptation, and clientelism. Moreover, "thought control was pervasive in schools as everywhere else in the society" (Lu 1994, 290).

Singapore has been described as a "sub-fascist state," in which the "vulnerability" of the island republic is used as a pretext "to crack down on democratic critics" (Haas 1990, 39). Despite periodic elections, the government has used a one-party system to suppress dissent, detain without trial, intimidate newspapers and radical trade unions, and enact anti-democratic laws and administrative regulations (Beng-Huat 1994). While the regime does employ overt repression, it prefers to use "the bankrupting libel suit" as a tool to discourage political dissent (Crane 1995, A24).

Lee Kwan Yew, Singapore's only prime minister until his 1990 resignation, always made clear his hostility to liberal democracy, concluding in a 1987 speech: "We decide what is right. Never mind what the people think. That's another problem" (quoted, Bello and Rosenfeld 1990, 318).

At the beginning of 1997, the ruling People's Action Party (PAP) increased its seats (81 of 83) in Parliament and its share of the vote (65 percent) over 1991. It did so, however, by threatening to delay the upgrading of public housing estates and planned infrastructure projects in opposition-supporting constituencies. These tactics, which were denounced by the U.S. State Department, were defended as well-established "pork-barrel politics" (THE ECONOMIST, January 11, 1997, 33). Yet, they were a crude manifestation of "hard politics": "what you get depends upon how you vote!"

While there is no doubt that primary democracy is a very recent development in the Asian NICs (with Singapore still hesitant to move in this direction), I believe that secondary democracy has been apparent in these countries. In other words, unlike the situation in totalitarian states or in the incompetent states that we so often find in Latin America and Africa, the governments of the NICs have reached out in the following ways to build popular support:

1. EQUALIZATION OF OPPORTUNITY. Measuring income inequality by the proportion of national income which the poorest 20 to 40 percent of all households receive, South Korea has maintained a good performance and Taiwan, an outstanding one (Barrett and Chin 1987, 20). Whereas in 1979, the poorest 40 percent of Korean families received 21 percent of total income, this same proportion in Mexico received only 10 percent. World Bank figures (1993a, 30–31) suggest that, for all the NICs in 1989, the ratio of the income share of the top quintile to that of the bottom quintile was less than 10, as against more than 20 in such African countries as Kenya and the Ivory Coast and more than 25 in Brazil.

2. BETTER LIVING CONDITIONS. Along with efforts to equitably distribute wealth, the Asian NICs have made a "heavy and continuing investment in education for everyone" (Johnson 1987, 145). Between 1970 and 1989, real expenditure per pupil rose by 355 percent in Korea, whereas during this same period, it rose by only 64 percent in Mexico and less than 15 percent in Pakistan (World Bank 1993a, 45).

By the mid-1980s, middle school enrollment in South Korea was approaching 100 percent, and high school enrollment had surpassed 75 percent (Cho and Breazeale 1991, 569). During the 1970s, the percentage of Korean high school graduates reaching colleges and universities more than doubled to 16 percent (Kwack 1987, 68). Taipei and Singapore were not far behind Seoul in reaching levels of literacy and proportions of enrolled school-age population comparable to the United States, Japan, and Western Europe (Hofheinz and Calder 1982, 114). Indeed, their students are usually within the top group in international competitive examinations, particularly in mathematics.

Health conditions improved greatly in South Korea and Singapore between 1960 and 1990, with life expectancy estimated to reach 73 or 74, nearly 20 years more than in 1960 (World Bank 1993a). By the end of the 1980s, nearly 83 percent of the regularly employed Korean labor force was covered by medical insurance, despite inherent weaknesses and shortcomings in the system (Park 1991, 345–6). Likewise, by 1990, the quality of life in Taiwan "had improve immensely," Myers (1986, 26) writes, adding: "Better diet and medical care led to a vast improvement in the overall health of the population."

3. A HIGH QUALITY OF GOVERNANCE. It is generally acknowledged that the Asian NICs possess well-trained, efficient, and relatively uncorrupt bureaucracies (Pei 1994, 95). "The political systems are held together by technocrats of varying expertise but of uniformly great influence" (Hofheinz and Calder 1982, 72).

Whereas in 1960, the Korean civil service was viewed "as a corrupt and inept institution," by the late 1970s, it had "become one of the most reputable in the developing world" (World Bank 1993a, 176). In explaining the high reputation of Singapore's civil service, Quah (1995, 135) notes the following policies: anti-corruption measures, selective recruitment, competitive pay, computerization, and the establishment of a Service Improvement Unit. In addition to using a civil service examination system, Taiwan recruits heavily from academia, bringing in those with advanced degrees from major universities for fixed periods ranging from three to six years (World Bank 1993a, 175).

Respect for Asian NIC bureaucracies enables governments in these countries to use "soft authoritarianism" in influencing the private sector (Johnson 1987, 138). This takes the form, not so much of direct commands or coercion, but of politically elastic incentives and disincentives. Thus, in Singapore, firms that upgrade technology and skills are rewarded, while those that do not are punished. In the case of Taiwan, according to Wade (1990, 285), the government can certainly enforce its power over firms, but it "has a variety of more or less subtle ways to make life awkward if they do not respond." In both South Korea and Taiwan, the bureaucracies were able to develop acceptable rewards, rules, and referees, allowing access to credit and foreign exchange for businesses competing in government-sponsored export contests (World Bank 1993a, 93–94).

4. TWO-WAY COMMUNICATION. Despite the repression of overt opposition in the Asian NICs, various forms of two-way communication have been allowed and even encouraged. In South Korea, for example, effective labor-management councils were sometimes established in lieu of labor unions (Kim 1994, 636). In Taiwan, during the 1980s, the government increased its efforts "to seek comment from private sector groups on draft legislation before submitting it to the Cabinet" (Wade 1990, 293). Moreover, bills coming from the Cabinet "are now closely examined, heatedly debated, and often rejected, or passed only after major amendment" (Ya-li 1991, 120).

In Singapore, according to Chee (1986, 161), there is "vocal and frank comment on all public policies" carried out in the press, parliament, public forums, and grass roots institutions. Chee provides a number of 1985 examples of governmental reversals of policy (having to do with education and the operation of taxis) as a result of public pressure, suggesting the need to rexamine Wilkinson's assertion (1988, 184) "that criticism of government policy was taboo" during the 1980s.

From my own visit to several of the Asian NICs (Taiwan and Singapore) in 1990, I came away impressed, not only with the economic progress found, but also with the quality of their bureaucracies, their seriousness about development, and their capacity to be innovative. I began to understand that development in Asia is not simply a matter of Confucian culture or enlightened paternalism. Thus, I agree with Campos and Root (1996, 177) that, despite inadequate primary democracy, the successful Asian countries have established a "commitment to shared growth," which is carried out through "narrow, highly controlled channels for representation and dialogue between state and society."

I was told in Singapore, for example, about the request in 1985 or 1986 by the employees of a profitable American firm for the REDUCTION of their salaries by about 12 percent in accord with governmental guidelines because of a recession. Such manifestations of patriotism cannot be taken for granted or seen as automatic responses to dictatorial proclamations (Rigg 1988; Soon and Tan 1992, 17; Campos and Root 1996, 70, 81). This action resulted from the "tripartism"—the unanimous recommendation of an advisory council, created in 1970, composed of representatives of government, employees, and labor. According to Campos and Root (1996, 8l), "the council has given the government the capacity to credibly commit to a stable, rational policymaking process."

The case studies presented below of secondary democracy in action may be seen as my effort to explain what Pei (1994) refers to as "the puzzle of East Asian exceptionalism:" the fact that economic reforms occurred before rather than after democratization. (In the next few chapters, I present more case studies having to do with Singapore and South Korea inasmuch as they are relevant to my explorations of the "mysteries of development.")

TAIWAN'S AGRICULTURAL DEVELOPMENT. What is remarkable about Taiwan, is the prosperity of its rural areas, despite the fact that the average farm (as of 1984) was only 1.12 hectare, which was too small to make a living from. Yet, according to Williams (1994, 218), "farmers in Taiwan are well off, and the island is a bountiful producer of a rich variety of agricultural commodities, sufficient to maintain the people in a well-fed condition." By the mid-1980s, the island had achieved 70 percent food self-sufficiency, with a surplus of rice, sugar, fruits and vegetables, eggs and fish.

The Nationalist government, from its early days of control over Taiwan, took a number of steps to motivate farmers by gaining their political support: a compulsory rent-reduction program in 1949, the sale of public lands in 1951, the land-to-tiller program in 1953, and the redistribution of all land above 1.7 acres of paddy and 7.2 acres of dry land (Huang 1993, 50; Myers 1986, 44). Farmers received government loans to purchase their land, which could be repaid over a fifteen-year period at low interest rates. Thus, between 1949 and 1953, a quarter of Taiwan's private farmland changed hands as a result of one of the world's most successful land reform efforts.

By 1989, 86 percent of farm households were owner-cultivators, as against 36 percent in 1949. "Learning from its disastrous experience on the Chinese mainland, the KMT sought to use land reform to blunt the appeal of Communism among the peasantry as well as eliminating the Taiwanese landlord class as a competing elite" (Bello and Rosenfeld 1990, 184). However, the government compensated landowners with bonds that could be used to develop urban industry and services, thereby facilitating their becoming successful entrepreneurs.

Because of the small size of Taiwanese farms, profitable agricultural production (particularly for export) has been difficult. The agricultural labor force has declined from about 50 percent of the country's work force in the early 1960s to less than 15 percent by the 1990s, with 87 percent working in agriculture on a part-time basis (Huang 1993, 51). Whereas agricultural exports comprised of more than 60 percent of the value of Taiwan's total exports in the early 1960s, they accounted for less than 7 percent in the late 1980s.

However, some Taiwanese agricultural products have remained competitive because of the ability to shift from the traditional exports of sugar and rice to processed and canned or frozen fruits and vegetables, pork, and pond-raised fish. What has facilitated these new forms of rural productivity in Taiwan is a close working relationship between Farmer Associations (FAs) and a network of agricultural research institutes, credit programs, and improvement stations, efficiently linking agricultural planning, credit, research, and extension. In other words, the government has recognized that its development plans "cannot be effectively implemented without the active support of well-organized farmers" (Mao 1992, 85). As a result, Taiwanese farmers receive from 75 to 90 percent of the terminal market price for their products, as against less than 60 percent in Africa (Campos and Root 1996, 52).

Since the 1940s, the KMT has used FAs and Irrigation Associations (IAs) as "corporatist control mechanisms in the countryside" (Hsiao 1994, 204). While the FAs and the IAs remain quasi-governmental organizations (with roots going back to the days of Japanese occupation, early in the Twentieth Century), members have many ways to exercise power: the election of boards of directors and supervisors; the determination of activities and use of profits; the financing of operations and staff expenses; the determination of membership fee rates; etc. (Mao 1991, 77; Stavis 1982, 214).

Fruit-Marketing Cooperatives are similarly democratically organized, with members electing boards of directors, who subsequently employ managers to carry out their decisions and policies. Consequently, these organizations can be looked at from two directions. On the one hand, they are institutions "for corrupting and co-opting rural elites in every locality" (Hsiao 1994, 204). On the other hand, they have become schools for democracy, training Taiwan's politicians at every level and carrying "the view of peasants into the highest Government councils in Taipeh" (Stavis 1982, 243). While farmers may complain bitterly about taxes and fees and the reduction of import barriers, their cooperation has been eagerly sought.

Taiwan's agricultural associations are linked to other aspects of secondary democracy. Since the land reform program of 1949, village councils have been democratically organized to discuss local land and market management issues. Even when KMT party members controlled villages, ordinary Taiwanese had a significant influence over local decision-making. Moreover, "mayors could introduce policies to make their jurisdictions attractive to small-scale, and sometimes medium-scale enterprises" (Campos and Root 1996, 120).

SOUTH KOREA'S COMMUNITY DEVELOPMENT. Under President Rhee, several community development programs were initiated, but they were largely ineffective because they were considered irrelevant, inadequately supported, or too dictatorial. In the case of the National Movement for Reconciliation, which was established in 1961, villagers resented "the officious attitude of the administrators, the alleged use of the training centers for military propaganda, and the attacks upon their ancient customs" (Turner, Hesli, Bark, and Yu 1993, 74).

Because of President Park's rural background, he recognized that community development (which he called "Saemaul Undong" in a 1970 speech) would have to "create and cultivate the spirit of self-reliance and independence and hard work" (quoted, Turner, Hesli, Bark, and Yu 1993, 75). However, what became known as the Saemaul Undong Movement (SUM) may have begun somewhat accidentally in 1971 when the government found itself with an excessive inventory of cement, allowing it to give 335 bags of cement to each of about 33,000 villages (Moon 1991a, 408).

Based upon the effective use of this cement, the government selected 16,600 villages in 1972 for an additional 500 bags of cement, together with one ton of steel rods, to improve farm roads, water and sanitation systems, and irrigation or laundry facilities. This encouraged other villages to begin similar projects in the hope or expectation of governmental assistance. At the same time, President Park became an enthusiastic supporter of the SUM (even allegedly composing a song for it), seeing it as a way to generate popularity as well as to promote modernization.

There is no doubt that a "heavy top-down approach" was used in some of the SUM programs. For example, the costly "home improvement" program, under which an estimated one-third of all Koreans replaced their thatched roofs with composition or tile, was at least partly a response to coercive techniques (Bello and Rosenfeld 1990, 84). However, Doug Kyun Kim (1991, 188–189), who is critical of the government's authoritarianism, points out that local governments also engaged in extensive information, education, and communication activities in motivating and stimulating private initiative and the commitment of local resources, adding: "In this respect, the Korean experience is a worthwhile example for other developing countries."

The Park government soon realized that a bottom-up national movement was essential for a coordinated top-down approach to be successful (Boyer and Ahn 1991, 38). President Park himself, despite his dictatorial propensity, recognized that, "Projects should be determined by the general consensus of the villagers" (quoted, Turner, Hesli, Bark and Yu 1993, 79). While elected but unpaid Saemaul leaders (including female leaders and youth leaders) usually had to share power with appointed village heads (who were also paid civil servants), the government accepted the lesson emerging from its early implementation efforts: "leadership is a prerequisite for self-reliant and self-sustaining community development" (Moon 1991a, 413).

Of course, the government attempted to influence the selection process and, above all, the orientation of leaders, establishing for guidance purposes a number of central-level and provincial-level training institutions, together with various types of informal training programs at the county and village level. However, the training pragrams were expanded to include many levels of politicians, religious leaders, academics, journalists, and business managers, thereby facilitating two-way flows of communication.

To motivate local participation, the Ministry of Home Affairs classified the country's villages into three categories: (1) basic or undeveloped; (2) self-help or developing; and (3) self-reliant or developed (Moon 1991a, 408). On the basis of this classification, the government gave more assistance to higher-level villages, thereby stimulating those in the two lower categories to make an effort to advance in the classification scheme.

While initially villages were judged on the basis of their rural environment achievements (particularly water supply and sanitation), they were later encouraged to emphasize income-augmentation and social-development programs (e.g., infrastructure building, marketing facilities, education, and health projects). The government assisted with various forms of financial, material, and technical assistance, ordinarily matching whatever cash or labor had been mobilized by villagers. On a daily basis, television programs highlighted the SUM success stories, and Saemaul leaders were presented at publicized ceremonies with medals and awards by national, provincial, or local politicians.

By 1980, 97 percent of villages were ranked as "developed" (as against only 7 percent in 1972), and no village remained in the "undeveloped" category (whereas 53 percent were so classified in 1972). Between 1972 and 1982, total investment in the SUM projects increased five times in real prices (Moon 1991a, 418–419).

While it is difficult to isolate the SUM contributions to rural development from other modernizing factors, the SUM clearly had a major socio-economic impact, thereby, not only bettering the farmers' financial condition, but also reducing the cultural gap between rural and urban areas (Moon 1991a, 419; Turner, Hesli, Bark and Yu 1993, 85). For example, by 1982, almost all farm households had access to electrification and a telephone system, whereas only 20 percent of them had electric lighting in 1971. Inasmuch as every rural village was affected by the movement, the massive scale of participation "is probably unprecedented in the history of community development" (Moon 1991a, 414).

The extent to which the SUM can be considered "democratic" remains somewhat controversial. Corruption certainly undermined the SUM projects during the 1980s, particularly from 1981 to 1987 when Kyung-hwan Chun (the brother of President Doo-hwan Chun) was head of the Saemaul organization. According to Boyer and Ahn (1991, 70), "it appears clear in retrospect that the movement was conducted top-down, counter to the quest of Korean peasants for equity, integrity, and dignity. . . ." Yet, these authors also suggest (1991, 52) that Saemaul Undong did, at least unwittingly, plant the seeds of decentralization and democratic development.

In his study of the SUM, Moon (1991a, 415) points out that the identication of projects, project planning, and the approval of plans are undertaken by consensus, adding (p. 417): "The Saemaul leader must try to obtain a consensus, which contributes both to village solidarity and to a democratic way of thinking." Despite the authoritarian nature of the regime during the 1970s, I believe that Cochrane (1983, 31–33) is correct in asserting that greater reliance was placed on tangible rewards than on blatant forms of coercion in obtaining results. While administrators may have wanted a "command-obedience relationship," they came to realize, in the words of Turner, Hesli, Bark, and Yu (1993, 86): "People have to be consulted; administrators have to listen to their concerns."

SINGAPORE'S PUBLIC HOUSING PROGRAM. Under this program, more than 80 percent of the 2.7 million population live in government-financed and subsidized apartments, which are clustered into seventeen estates or towns (Field and Ofari 1989). Residents are encouraged to buy and improve their apartments, using funds from the Central Provident Fund (CPF), which somewhat resembles the American social security system. The estates are designed to be attractive, safe, and exciting, surrounded by parks, shopping centers, and playgrounds, and linked by an excellent rapid transit system and expressways to one-another, the industrial areas, and the central business district.

In handling its more than 600,000 apartments, the Housing and Development Board (HDB) maintains an island-wide network of area offices operating under the guidance of its headquarters. In 1983, a local management system called "TEAMS" was introduced, under which the performance of every area office in routine functions and in special projects is evaluated, with cash awards and other incentives given for special efforts, productivity, and initiative. Based upon external assessments, the HDB has been ranked "on par with organizations well-known for their service excellence" (HDB 1993/94 ANNUAL REPORT, 55).

The HDB's efforts to motivate staff are, in my view, a form of secondary democracy inasmuch as top administrators seek (rather than impose) cooperation and responsiveness. The HDB pays more attention to training than other governmental agencies (with each staff member receiving more than twice the national average of training days).

The HDB was also among the first agencies in Singapore (beginning in 1982) to launch a Quality Control Circle (QCC) Movement. As a result, its ability to make rapid or emergency repairs is remarkable, with particular attention paid to elevators, using an automatic telemonitoring system. At the 1993 International Exposition of QCCs, the HDB received the Outstanding QCC of the Year Award. It also has an effective Staff Suggestion Scheme, with nearly 12,000 suggestions received in 1993/94, of which 44 percent were accepted.

To improve contact with public housing residents, Singapore's government has experimented with various forms of residential representation (Hill 1987). While each of these arrangements has to some extent been coopted by the administration, residents with serious grievances can usually make themselves heard through the FORUM PAGE of the leading newspaper (the STRAITS TIMES), the business and professional associations, Members of Parliament, and the judicial system, all of which maintain considerable autonomy. HDB regularly monitors residents' satisfaction with its services, maintains an award-winning newsletter, and a computerized interactive facility to handle information requests and applications to sell, purchase, or rent apartments.

Even during the 1970s, when HDB's staff had less experience handling the problems of low-income residents, 90 percent of those who had come into contact with the staff reported that they were "satisfied" with the services received, despite a certain amount of fear and avoidance (Hassan 1977, 56). Particularly appreciated was the high quality of HDB maintenance services.

Since the 1970s, HDB staff have made a greater effort to appear "compassionate," allowing unemployed households to go into arrears, with the arrangements for recovery delayed until after re-employment (Chua 1991, 36). Because the HDB staff is respected, it is able to use advice and persuasion, instead of stronger measures, in dealing with problems.

As a result of various forms of secondary democracy, as here defined, the HDB has modified its policies over the years, according to Yong (1992). These policy changes have resulted in an overall deregulation of financial markets affecting, among other things: the price of HDB apartments, the household income ceiling for HDB apartments, the phasing out of rent control, the use of CPF savings, the subletting of rooms, governmental acquisition of land in relationship to its market value, and the decontrol of commercial land within the central business district.

The HDB continues to pay attention to changing needs and demands by upgrading its housing stock, demolishing smaller apartments, and converting unsold three and four-room flats into five and six-room ones. In trying to prevent older HDB buildings from degenerating into slums and to keep attracting an increasingly affluent population, the Urban Redevelopment Authority (URA) has gone to great lengths to hold press hearings, dialogue sessions, seminars, exhibitions and small group discussions, particularly in regard to its Master Plan for Housing and National Development. The URA is especially proud of its success in responding to more than 88% of complaints and appeals within two weeks (URA 1986/1987, 22).

University planning professors, in 1990 interviews that I had with them, were impressed, not only by the willingness of officials to listen to their criticisms and suggestions, but also by their willingness to fund research on existing or emerging problems. Eng (1996) supports this observation in noting that potential residents of forthcoming new towns are asked to rank their priorities, and independent architects are invited to evaluate HDB's proposals. While HDB planners are limited in their ability to meet the conflicting objectives of satisfying everyone and cost-effectiveness, "the recent more open policy towards resident involvement in the decision-making process augurs well for future town planning" (Eng 1996, 279).

CONCLUSIONS

In linking democracy to development, I believe three conclusions are appropriate: (1) as countries achieve at least a "middle income category," primary democracy is more likely to facilitate further development; (2) while primary democracy may be counterproductive for impoverished countries, secondary democracy is essential for all stages of development; and (3) requests for economic assistance should be tied to a willingness to implement secondary democracy.

While I will leave to the final chapter considerations of ways to promote secondary democracy, I will here follow-up the sections that have been presented, suggesting: (1) that the Asian NICs will probably benefit from more primary democracy; (2) that in African countries, where leaders are facilitating economic progress, no effort should be made to push them into primary democracy before they are ready for it; and (3) where governments are either incapable of or clearly opposed to secondary democracy, donor countries or agencies will have to find ways of replacing or reforming these governments, if they wish to assist them effectively. In supporting these conclusions, I will use the following case studies:

THE CASE OF TAIWAN. In writing about the politics of Taiwan, Chu (1994, 99) asserts that, since the beginning of the 1980s, "the political landscape of the island has changed almost beyond recognition." For example, in 1987, newspapers reported several incidents a day of citizen petitions, demonstrations, wildcat strikes, civil disobedience, and riots. Despite the efforts of KMT politicians to buy votes, to misuse or undermine the legal system, and to discourage various forms of opposition, they were unable to prevent the rise of a strong opposition party (the Democratic Progressive Party—DPP), the legislative expulsion in 1991 of the so-called "old thieves" (powerful politicians who had accompanied Chiang Kai-shek to Taiwan in the 1940s), the termination of martial law, the privatization of government-owned corporations, and the growing participation in political life of various intellectual and voluntary organizations (Arrigo 1994).

Taiwan has had seven important elections since 1980. Each of them has contributed to the democratization process, particularly the 1986 election, which was the first ever two-party election in a Chinese nation (Tien 1994). In the 1992 general election, the DPP won nearly a third of the popular vote and representation in the legislature (the Legislative Yuan). In the December 1995 general election, opposition parties gained a much larger percentage of popular votes, leaving the ruling party with a legislative majority of only three seats. Based upon elections in November, 1997, the DPP won the majority of elections for county chiefs, receiving for the first time more seats than the KMT. Consequently, Taiwan has emerged as "one of Asia's liveliest democracies, and the world's freest and most democratic Chinese society" (Richburg 1995, A31).

In describing Taiwan's 1994 sub-national election, Cooper (1995) notes how impressed he was at the high voter turnout, the education level and youthfulness of the candidates, the number of women participating as candidates, the lack of attention to ideological considerations, the extent of vote splitting, and the professional handling of the election. The most recent book on democratization in Taiwan (Hood 1997, 163) points out that, while some aspects of democracy have been damaged by corruption, intimidation, and intolerance, other aspects (particularly, the judicial system, press, and local government) are increasingly respected and effective.

Assuming that political trends continue, the KMT is likely to lose its majority status in 1998 national elections. While relations with mainland China could deteriorate if a declaration of independence follows, there could also be more effective administration in regard to persistent problems of crime, corruption, public health, and safety. Political turmoil has become a reality in Taiwan along with democratization; and political leaders can no longer either ignore or repress the massive demonstrations that are occurring, together with other forms of public discontent.

Perhaps the most important impact that greater primary democracy has had in Taiwan has been growing attention to the environmental crisis. Because of the inadequacy of sewage treatment, "Taiwan has among the highest incidence of hepatitis B in the world" (Williams and Chang 1994, 241). Most of its rivers and reservoirs suffer from eutrophication.

According to Taiwan's Environmental Protection Agency, 30 percent of rivers are moderately or heavily polluted (Devlin and Yap 1994, 54).

Air pollution is a serious problem in all of Taiwan's big cities, caused largely by motor vehicles, particularly two-stroke motorcycles. "In Taipei, for example, the vehicular density is ten times greater than that of Los Angeles" (Williams and Chang 1994, 245). This caused Taipei's air to be rated unhealthy or very unhealthy 61 times in 1991 (Devlin and Yap 1994, 54).

Inadequate urban planning, garbage recycling, enforcement of pollution regulations, and public transportation, among other factors, worsen the situation. "Factories, whose numbers grew by an annual rate of 7.5 percent in the 1980s, belched wastes into the water, the air, and the earth, almost at will and without any governmental reproach" (Chen 1994, 259).

Since the lifting of martial law in July 1987, grass roots environmentalists "have employed confrontational tactics and direct action, with notable success" (Bello and Rosenfeld 1990, 212). Because of the growing environmental protection movement, the government has had to modify its nuclear power and petrochemical plans. The Du Pont company, under public opposition, gave up a proposal to build a titanium dioxide plant. Likewise, popular opposition prevented the planned damming of Toroko Gorge (the country's most impressive geological sight) and the exploitation of its few remaining wilderness areas. While most Taiwan residents remain passive about the environment, "media coverage of the controversial cleanup plans for two of Taiwan's worst-stinking rivers, the Tamsui in Taipei and the Love in Kaohsiung, garnered more publicity than had been anticipated" (Chen 1994, 262). Likewise, Earth Day activities are receiving far more attention than ever before.

The impact of primary democracy on environmental protection will, of course, remain problematic. Taiwanese citizens are as likely to protest environmental taxes, restrictions on use of motor vehicles, and solid waste recycling requirements as those in other wealthy countries. Yet, as Chen (1994, 278) points out: "As a result of political liberalization and a more enlightened media, those with the strongest convictions have spoken up," adding: "An environmental consciousness has definitely emerged." Indeed, solid waste management was "a big issue" in the 1997 local elections (THE ECONOMIST, December 6, 1997, 43).

THE CASE OF UGANDA. Since taking power in 1986, the Museveni government has indicated enough seriousness about development to suggest that foreign donors can expedite the introduction of secondary democracy. According to Brett (1995), the military has been removed as a direct player in setting the political agenda; the country has been relatively pacified; the army and the civil service have been significantly reduced in size; the government, as well as the military, have become "broad based" and multi-ethnic; the traditional "royal chiefs" have been given more authority and status; there is increasing freedom of the press; and "the system as a whole has become increasingly open and inclusive over time" (p. 152). The result has been significant economic progress and an impressive inflow of foreign aid. In April, 1997, Uganda became the first country to be approved for debt relief (see Chapter 10).

The assertion in THE ECONOMIST (July 22, 1995, 43) that Uganda's economy "is growing faster than any other on the continent" is, however, a sad commentary on economic progress in Africa as a whole. While a recent World Bank report on Uganda (Eastern African Department 1995, i) suggests a per-capita GDP growth averaging about 3 percent since 1987, its annual per-capita income of about US $220 indicates greater poverty and worse living conditions than under colonialism. Nevertheless, as pointed out in Chapter 10, Uganda has had considerable success in achieving administrative reform.

Despite its willingness to follow structural adjustment lending requirements, the Museveni government has resisted international pressure to introduce multiparty democracy. The President has argued that, while liberal democracy might be suitable for countries where class differences prevail, it would deepen Uganda's existing regional and ethnic differences. Consequently, in announcing his new constitution in October, 1995, he banned political party activity for five years, allowing instead non-party presidential and general elections, beginning in 1996. In the 1996 national election, Museveni received 75 percent of the vote under rather undemocratic conditions (see Oloka-Onyango 1997).

The American government has vigorously denounced Museveni's position on liberal democracy, while financially supporting his regime. Is its protest justified? Brett (1995, 151–2) supports Museveni's action on the grounds that "copies of western parliaments, parties, and electoral systems . . . failed in a society with deep ethnic cleavages, an illiterate electorate, and a political elite that had not yet learned to respect the requirements of democratic processes."

Based upon a general study of African politics, Moss (1995, 205) gives intellectual support to the Museveni position, arguing that, contrary to American liberal theory, legitimacy does not require democracy, and, in the case of Africa, is rarely based upon it. Because American officials do not understand African political realities, it is unlikely "that democracy can be successfully exported by the United States" (Moss 1995, 204).

Following the logic of this chapter, I would agree with Moss (1995, 209) that liberal democracy may be inappropriate for most African governments. Yet, I would disagree with his suggestion that democracy is unnecessary for or irrelevant to economic development. Of course, I have in mind secondary democracy. Without it, I insist, there can be little progress in Uganda or anywhere else.

Under colonialism, for example, Ugandan cooperatives were highly successful. They could again be very helpful in rural development. Ugandan officials recognize that member control is essential in this regard, including democratic elections, participation by members in defining by-laws and rules, and "conducting of regular meetings of members to enforce performance control and accountability..."(Hussi ET AL. 1993, 23).

Unfortunately, cooperatives continue to be undermined by counterproductive parastatals as well as by inadequate infrastructure, education, technical assistance, and financial support (Brett 1994; Eastern African Department 1995). They have also suffered from the weakness of decentralization. Whereas China has greatly improved its rural infrastructure by allowing administrative and fiscal decentralization, Uganda remains a highly centralized country, with only 5 percent of public expenditure covered by local revenue (Eastern African Department, 1995, 9, 61).

While the government in theory has strongly supported decentralization (holding local elections since 1989), local governments have been given very little control over use of revenue, selection of local officials, and delivery of local services (Brett 1994, 67–68). Consequently, rural development has been seriously retarded; and "service delivery in urban areas, where it exists, has been effectively, if not legally, privatized" (Gombay and O'Manique 1996, 95).

Uganda is heavily dependent on foreign donors. Counterpart funds covered about 40 percent of the country's total nonproject outflows and 90 percent of its development expenditure in its 1993/94 budget (Eastern African Department 1995, 6). Consequently, the Ugandan government may be pressured by donors into taking political steps essential for economic development. This is, of course, not an easy thing to do (see Chapter 10).

Since political liberalization is such a long and difficult process, "turning aid on and off interrupts the long run processes underpinning democratization" and intensifies the problems of administering an effective program of economic development (Nelson 1992, 45). Nevertheless, in the case of Uganda, the government seems interested enough in development that "political conditionality" can perhaps be used to promote secondary democracy.

Brett (1994) gives an example of the use of foreign political pressure to force the Ugandan government to liberalize its economy, thereby facilitating secondary democracy. During much of the 1970s and 1980s, the overstaffed and inefficient Coffee Marketing Board (CMB) discouraged farmers from improving their trees and harvesting their crops by reducing prices to a minimum, paying late, and mismanaging exports.

Following World Bank threats to withhold aid disbursements, an independent export authority was established and licenses were extended to private processors and exporters. By 1992–93, the CMB's share of the crop had declined from more than 80 percent to a little over 30 percent, and farmers were left with a much larger share of the final price.

There are now over 100 coffee exporters in Uganda, and they no longer have to surrender proceeds to the Bank of Uganda (Eastern African Department 1995, 40). While much more reform needs to take place, there has been "a positive redistribution of income to poor farmers, and a reduction in monopoly power and rents" (Brett 1994, 74).

In 1993 the World Bank made the elimination of all monopolies a condition for the renewal of its structural adjustment credit. Fortunately, President Museveni himself recognizes the heavy cost endured by producers and consumers resulting from "the stranglehold by the corrupt parastatal bureaucracy over so many elements of the means of production" (quoted by Brett 1994, 78). However, Museveni may not have much room for reform inasmuch as the parastatal sector, which contributes 7–8 percent of GDP, gives formal employment and financial support to many powerful politicians. At the same time, a majority of the private traders and processors either are Kenyan Asians or Africans financed by Asians and, as such, are subject to racial prejudice and discrimination.

Because of the weakness of institutions, together with incentive distortions, it is uncertain how rapidly Uganda can move toward secondary democracy. Fortunately, enough progress is being made to justify continued international support for what the Ugandan scholar Oloka-Onyango (1997) calls a "benevolent dictatorship," defective as it may be.

THE CASE OF BENIN. There are still many countries in Africa where the political systems are so overwhelmed by corruption, ineptitude, inter-ethnic conflict, and illegitimacy that promoting secondary democracy is impossible. What then is the international donor community to do?

In a few cases, such as Zambia under Kaunda and Malawi under Banda, it may be possible to expedite change through the ballot-box. However, one cannot be hopeful about electoral succession because, in the words of Aaron Segal (1995, 9): "The odds are so stacked against most opposition parties in Africa that their victory at the polls represents an extraordinary achievement."

In addition to reform via elections, Luckham (1994, 60) notes transitions to democracy through negotiated settlements, "as part of national reconciliation, as attempted (with varying success) in Namibia, Angola, and Mozambique." When countries have reached a certain stage of economic collapse and political paralysis, foreign assistance donors may be able to use this approach for political reform . This is apparently what happened in Benin in 1989, according to Richard Westebbe (1994), who was then the World Bank's senior economist responsible for West Africa.

The World Bank is precluded by its Articles of Agreement from directly promoting democratization, though, as noted Chapter 10, there is confusion about how far the Bank can go in this regard. However, in the case of Benin, there was so much corruption and mismanagement that, by the end of 1989, civil servants and teachers were no longer being paid and much of the business community practically ceased operating or investing.

When the World Bank and the IMF refused to assist the government without fundamental political changes taking place, President Kerekou was forced in early 1990 to convene a national conference to consider a new constitution. This led initially to an interim government under an internationally respected economist, Nicephore Soglo, together with a supreme council headed by Monseigneur de Souza of the Catholic Church. Under this arrangement, the way was paved in 1992 for a new constitution and a multiparty election, under which Soglo won an overwhelming victory.

Under Soglo's administration, significant economic progress and institutional reforms became possible, despite many persistent problems. Because of widespread opposition to these reforms, Kerekou was fairly reelected in 1996.

While there continues to be fear that Kerekou will undermine or reverse the reforms undertaken by Soglo, there has so far been no retrogression. According to Bruce Magnusson, governance remains strong, with the constitutional court effectively resolving disputes (cited in Joseph 1997, 8).

A FINAL NOTE

What the analysis presented here suggests is that, it may be possible for foreign donors to promote secondary democracy, leaving the form of political change and the movement toward primary democracy up to those in power. By widening our conception of democracy, the problems of dysfunctional elections and multiparty competition can be at least postponed until countries are ready for them.

This analysis seems to be supported by a growing number of experts, according to a 1997 conference on democratization in Africa at the Massachusetts Institute of Technology (Joseph 1997). John Harbeson of the City University of New York expressed concern about the overemphasis on elections, suggesting the need for comprehensive agreements before electoral competition. Joel Barkan of the University of Iowa pointed out that this emphasis on the holding of elections to resolve problems has often proved counterproductive. Dele Olowu of the United Nations Economic Commission for Africa added that democracy needed to begin with the development of local government and decentralization.

Interestingly enough, Herman Cohen, a former U.S. Assistant Secretary of State, pointed out at the MIT conference that good governance may be an alternate framework to democratization. While I hope that his viewpoint will influence Congress and the State Department, I also believe that there is a relationship between good governance and democratization. That relationship is, of course, what I have attempted to clarify (using political elasticity theory) in this chapter and in this book. That is also why I would disagree with the position of Professors Crawford Young and Larry Diamond at the MIT conference that the East Asian "developmental dictatorships" are inapplicable to Africa. In other words, insofar as African countries become serious about development, they must find the same linkage as exists in East Asia between "good governance," "a high quality of political software," and "secondary democracy."

CHAPTER 8

Politics Versus Culture
Which Is Stronger?

INTRODUCTION

A number of years ago I entered into a debate in the AMERICAN POLITICAL SCIENCE REVIEW with Professor Harry Eckstein regarding the relationship of political culture to political change (Werlin and Eckstein 1990). Eckstein (1988) had presented three propositions in regard to the possibilities of rapid cultural change: (1) the older the cultural practice, the harder it is to undo; (2) rapid cultural change requires a political revolution; and (3) the faster the pace of cultural reform, the more problematic the consequences are likely to be.

The primary thrust of Eckstein's article was to suggest that, while slow cultural change is normal, understandable, and perhaps useful, rapid cultural change is unusual, unsustainable, and dangerous. Because this conclusion is discouraging for those attempting to facilitate rapid socioeconomic development, I felt it important to examine the culturalist case.

Without denying the seriousness of cultural barriers to political development in various parts of the world, I raised a number of questions having to do with "cultural discontinuity" (the ability of people to rapidly add or drop cultural attributes in response to new situations); causation (the priority of various factors: ideological, socioeconomic, historic, as well as political); and definition (the extent to which patterns of behavior and belief must be interrelated and persistent to have a cultural dimension). The debate essentially came down to a "chicken or egg" question of which comes first: the power of politicians to manipulate cultural attributes or the ability of politicians to free themselves from cultural conditioning and constraints.

Readers may have come away from my debate with Eckstein believing that I was trivializing political culture. This was not my intention. Indeed, I am convinced that the secondary corruption which I discuss in Chapter 6 is largely the result of political culture—the deep rooted beliefs and practices of sycophantism. I mean by this the determination of leaders and their subordinates to have parasites and flattering people around them, believing that their political survival depends upon it and fearing anyone else.

Under these circumstances, the requisites for political elasticity or a high quality of political software (hiring qualified people, delegation of authority, establishing legitimate laws and independent spheres of authority, etc.) cannot emerge. Until political development (rather than personal enrichment and survival) is taken seriously, the political culture associated with a patrimonial or clientelistic system is unlikely to change.

The purpose of this chapter (which is a revision of Werlin 1994b) is to dig deeper into the widespread belief that cultural factors, more than anything else, explain the rapid economic progress of Asian countries in recent years, as against the slow progress (and even retrogression) of African countries. Whereas in East Asia, per capita economic growth rate was between five and six percent annually between 1965 and 1990, the growth rate was almost negative during these years in Sub-Saharan Africa (World Bank 1993a, 2). "As a result, the average African is poorer today than in 1970" (Carapetis, Levy, and Wolden 1991, 10).

In considering the dysfunctional impact of political culture on Africa and other parts of the world, I will try to make three points: (1) However powerful the cultural impediments to development, we must recognize their political roots. (2) We should avoid both "cultural fixity," exaggerating the rigidity and persistence of culture, and "cultural nullity," ignoring or underestimating cultural manifestations (Jones 1995). (3) If political programs are properly implemented, they can change culture. In any case, to change political culture, we must understand it as well as take it into account.

THE POLITICAL NATURE OF CULTURE

It was out of my concern that there were "cultural impediments" to African development that I studied corruption in Ghana from 1966 to

1972. David Apter (1963) and W. E. Abraham (1962), among others, had attributed nepotism, excessive gift-giving, and extreme family or clan ties to the persistence of counterproductive traditional values.

Aspects of the so-called "traditional way of life," influenced by the work of Talcott Parsons (1951), include: ethnocentricity; primordial rather than functional associations; the sanctification of customs, beliefs, and practices; the discouragement of individualism; the emphasis on authority by birth rather than merit; customary rather than contractual relations; supernaturalism; the unwillingness to accept personal responsibility for development; and social rather than legal sanctions. While acknowledging the relationship of traditional values to corruption, I concluded that it was less important than the relationship of politics to corruption (Werlin 1972).

In considering the relationship of politics to culture, we need to begin by examining the following quandaries:

THE MEANING OF CULTURE. What makes culture such a difficult phenomenon to describe, according to Smelser (1992, 23), is that it "is in large part a construct about the society or group under study rather than a simple empirical attribute to be apprehended, recorded, and described." In other words, we need to be concerned, not simply with an empirical description of ideas, values, beliefs, symbols, practices, and other characteristics, but also with the conceptual apparatus that the investigator brings to the study (e.g., Marxist, Freudian, or some other conception of behavior and the possibilities of behavioral modification.)

The anthropological approach, Nolan (1986, 98–99) points out, trains students to analyze cultures as integrated ensembles, with isolated acts being reasonable within a holistic setting. Thus, in looking at the concept of culture (much like a novelist describing a personality), anthropologists tend to see it as more than the patterns of behavior, belief, value, and emotion that we associate with it. They therefore view actions as purposeful and functional, however counterproductive they might appear.

Because of the amorphous characteristics of culture (including significant variations of behavior within a particular culture), we can never separate relevant independent from dependent variables (Klitgaard 1991a). Nevertheless, cultures are often more than "piles of innumerable behaviors, customs, tastes, and values" (Jones 1995, 271). For both orthodox Jews and Muslims, for example, religious law regulates many aspects of culture. "The Koran tells Moslems what names they may and may not give themselves, musical instuments they may not play, and deals also with such matters as clothing, sports, sexual intercourse, and the suckling of children" (Berger 1964, 14).

The uncertainty about the meaning of culture causes it to be used as a catch-all explanation, much as the psychosomatic one in medicine (Papenek 1988). As such, its explanatory value is doubtful. For example, a 1973 study of Japan described the cultural traits as including hypocrisy, factionalism, immaturity, and selfishness (Takeo Doi, cited in Klitgaard 1991, 20–21). Yet, Japan's culture is often given credit for its national development. However, Chalmers Johnson, a leading American expert on Japan, points out that, while Japan's culture was not an obstacle to development, "neither was it an obstacle to militarism, elitism, emperor worship, colonialism, or many other things that the Japanese prefer to forget" (quoted in Redding 1988, 100).

Max Weber concluded early in this century "that Asian cultures and religious traditions were deeply uncongenial to modernization" (Berger 1988, 7). Pye (1985) found a far greater degree of counterproductive paternalism, authoritarianism, ethnocentricity, selfishness, and xenophobia in Asia than in the West, despite great cultural differences within these parts of the world. Nevertheless, in explaining the rapid development of the East Asian countries, many writers point to basic Confucian cultural values, particularly respect for authority, education, and meritocratic administration.

These Confucian cultural values, however, were not evident during the Chinese cultural revolution from 1966 to 1976. While aspects of Chinese culture may have survived this revolution, it cannot be used to explain Chinese history. Taiwan's Kuomintang and the Chinese Communist party (CCP), Liu (1987) points out, grew out of the same cultural tradition but (until recently) have moved in quite divergent political directions, with profound implications for all aspects of life.

Townsend (1974, 2–3) notes in regard to China: "At various times it was thought that China could never gain true unity and independence; that Chinese Communism could never become a significant political force; that China would necessarily develop as a pro-Western power; that the Chinese peasant could not be collectivized; that the Sino-Soviet alliance could not be broken; that the authority of the CCP could not be seriously threatened from within." While judgments and predictions may be possible, he concludes, they require "an expanded vision of what is politically possible."

THE CAUSES AND MANIFESTATIONS OF CULTURE. If we stick to the widespread definition of culture as persistent patterns or systems of behavior and belief characteristic of particular social and ethnic groups (Goodman 1967), we encounter serious disagreements about causation. To what extent are the causes situational (not directly affected by government) or political in origin? While situational factors tend to be emphasized, culturalists remain uncertain about the priority among possible causes: ideological (prejudices, fears, values, beliefs, goals); socioeconomic (class structure, inter-ethnic rivalry, standard of living, occupation, technology, geography); and historical (impact of conquest, religion, colonialism, nationalism, industrialization, war, revolution, international relations).

Culturalists, however, have the most trouble with political factors. "Culture," according to Eckstein (1988, 803), "is the instinctive, variable set of ways in which societies normatively regulate social behavior;" but where does politics fit in? While leaders are clearly guided by societies, they can also manipulate them?

For example, the Malawi government in the 1960s banned the use of modern contraceptives following widespread fears that they would cause sterility, but it reinforced these fears in doing so (Kalipeni and Zulu 1993, 116). After 1984, when it changed policies toward family planning, it was both reflecting and encouraging the revision of public opinion. Unfortunately, its slow actions in reducing population may mean that the population could reach twelve million by the year 2000 (as against less than one million in 1900), undermining efforts to improve the standard of living (House and Zimalirana 1992).

As recently as 1956, the Thai government offered bonuses for large families, thereby both reflecting and supporting traditional pronatalist attitudes (Knodel, Chamratrithirong and Debavalya 1987). Under World Bank persuasion, the government gradually reversed its position, declaring in 1970 that it was official policy to reduce population growth.

Using innovative contraceptive methods and distribution systems, the government within only a decade (1969–1979) facilitated a 40 percent reduction in marital fertility, with contraceptive prevalence among married women in their reproductive ages expanding from 15 percent to approximately 50 percent. While Knodel, Chamratrithirong and Debavalya (1987, 8) point out that it is difficult to separate the impact of socioeconomic changes from organizational efforts, the "transformation in reproductive attitudes and behavior that has been taking place in

Thailand over the last several decades is so far-sweeping and profound that it can aptly be called a reproductive revolution."

A recent World Bank comparison of the legal and regulatory environment of Brazil and Chile provides another example of how political systems affect culture (Stone, Levy, and Paredes 1992). In Brazil, firms had to contend with numerous problems: rapid and unstable inflation; a maze of contradictory, rapidly changing, and unknowable regulations; over 50 federal, state, and municipal taxes; and numerous filing and payment requirements. This results in a dualistic system, in which an "informal system" of bribery is used to get around the complex and expensive formal legal system. Thus, in Brazil, according to da Matta (1993, A17), "it is necessary to understand this profoundly negative relationship between a state that is considered above society and a society that wants to be insulated from the state that rules it."

In Chile, in contrast, there has been an effort to deregulate and privatize the economy, establishing well-defined property rights, rationalizing tax and labor regulations, and reducing constraints on capital mobility and competition. This has resulted in much easier contracting and operating procedures, greater legal simplicity, more certain enforcement of contracts, and a far better environment for business. Above all, the culture of corruption, which once existed in Chile and seems so deep-rooted in Brazil, is no longer part of the Chilean way of life.

In considering Africa's slow economic progress, we cannot easily dismiss the assertion that cultural barriers are primarily responsible. In describing the bureaucracy prevalent in most African countries, Mamadou Dia, a World Bank economist from Senegal, writes (1993, 20): "The whole system encourages lethargy and clientelism rather than dynamism and entrepreneurship."

The cultural barriers that Dia refers to have their origins in traditional institutions and management systems, based essentially on ethnicity, under which "paternalistic, tutelary habits and patronage imbue the civil service/bureaucracy" (Dia 1993, 12). Over the years, according to Dia (IBID, 12–15), colonialism, the post-colonial "revolution of rising expectations," single-party systems, military rule, and declining official remuneration have combined with traditional forms of authority to reward political and personal loyalty, rather than merit.

However, the question of whether Africa's economic problems are primarily political or cultural in nature remains a source of confusion and contradiction. David Leonard, for example, in a 1987 article (p.

905), pointed out that "Africans are unusual among the world's elites in the extent of their patronage obligations to poorer people and the strength of the moral pressures which they feel to fulfill them."

Yet, in his more recent study (1991) of four successful Kenyan rural development managers, Leonard found that, under President Kenyatta, they could resist pressures for tribalism, nepotism, excessive staff, irresponsible Africanization, and corruption. The four administrators "had very well defined organizational missions they wanted to accomplish, were activist and entrepreneurial in their pursuit, devoted considerable attention to the public policies affecting them, and were concerned that the resources they managed served the public interest" (IBID., 259).

Leonard goes on to note (1991, 300) that various factors eventually undermined the Kenyan civil service so that here, as elsewhere in Africa, "it is unlikely to be resurrected as a positive force in the near future." But the factors mentioned (economic difficulties, political insecurity, and policy confusion) are essentially "political," rather than "cultural." Moreover, inasmuch as these factors are found in various parts of the world, their cultural roots cannot be seen as uniquely African or Kenyan.

According to John Cohen (1993, 458), senior politicians and civil servants in Kenya are apathetic about bureaucratic performance "for reasons that lie deep in culture and colonial experience." But what are these reasons? While it is true that colonialism left Kenya with institutions for which the cultural premises "were alien to the vast majority of Africans," (Landell-Mills 1992, 473), it also produced a country with a growing Westernized middle class and an elite "who share a desire for the best that modernity has to offer for themselves and their children" (Miller and Yeager 1994, 78).

Marris and Somerset (1971) pointed out that Kenyan African business owners were quite prepared to disregard family and ethnic obligations in developing their businesses. A more recent article on Kenya's successful export of horticultural commodities (Schapiro and Wainaina 1991) shows how quickly African farmers respond to economic opportunities, regardless of their traditional way of life. African smallholders now account for the majority of coffee, tea, and sugar produced in the country, as against a small fraction in the 1960s (Miller and Yeager 1994, 132). Unfortunately, the incompetence of the Moi government and its opposition to structural adjustment demands seriously threatened export producers during the early 1990s.

In noting that 20 percent of the Kenyan population, including a large urban sector, suffer from extensive poverty, Miller and Yeager (1994, 182) emphasize that most of the fault can be ascribed, not to culture, but to "mismanagement and abuses of power on the part of an essentially autonomous national leadership." Himbara (1994, 72), for example, points out that, during the mid-1980s, a potential entrepreneur had to receive as many as thirty approvals from the Ministry of Commerce and Industry, requiring possibly a three year waiting period. Because the state has become such a counterproductive factor, it is hard to blame Kenyan or African "culture" for the fact that African entrepreneurs in Kenya "have been largely discredited by their inability to sustain themselves in the marketplace" (Himbara 1994, 88).

ACCULTURATION AND WESTERNIZATION. "People cling to their cultural ways, not because of some vague feeling for their historical legacies and traditions, but because their culture is part and parcel of their personalities," Pye (1985, 20) asserts, adding: "we know from psychoanalysis how hard (and expensive) it is to change a personality." If we combine this position with the "culture-of-poverty" concept associated with the writing of Oscar Lewis, we face an overwhelming barrier to development.

According to Lewis (1968), the culture-of-poverty concept contains within it some seventy interrelated social, economic, and psychological traits (including early initiation into sex, informal marriages, abandonment of wives and children, female or mother-centered families, authoritarianism, impulsive behavior, and fatalism) that are combined into a way of life passed down from generation to generation in many parts of the world. Yet, even if we agree with William Julius Wilson (1987) that the "culture of poverty" concept is relevant to understanding inner-city African-Americans, we must also agree with him that it is confusing and misleading inasmuch as their problems may also stem from the decreasing availability of well-paid employment opportunities for the unskilled.

In comparing culture to personality, Pye's analysis is based on Freudian theory that has come to be discredited. E. Fuller Torrey, a psychiatrist and anthropologist, notes (1986, 75) that there is no evidence that early childhood experiences are crucial in determining later behavior or that there are distinct stages of personality development.

Rogowski (1974), in writing about German political culture, questions, not only the extent to which early learning conditions later learning but also the durability of early learning and its coherence. He points out that there is no agreement, as to which cultural values are most durable or basic, that learned behavior can be distinguished from other behavior, and that norms and values need to be congruent with those stressed by the political system.

Lederer (1993, 188) found that, as a result of the discouragement of authority and obedience in German schools during the 1970s, German adolescents in 1978–79 scored higher than their American counterparts in support of democratic values. While for reasons mentioned in Chapter 2, I distrust this effort to quantify political values, I accept her conclusion, based upon a variety of evidence, that German authoritarianism as a cultural attribute is far less fixed and durable than the authors of THE AUTHORITARIAN PERSONALITY (Adorno ET AL. 1950) had assumed.

Pye's position also seems to suggest that acculturation requires a slow evolutionary process. However, the rapid rise of nationalism in Africa and Asia would have been impossible without an equally rapid process of Westernization (Emerson 1960). The impact on African traditional culture of urbanization, capitalism, mass party systems, and technological changes has been well researched. The same rapid acculturation process has been observed in many parts of the world (Southall 1973).

Acculturation can be molded as well as hastened by political processes. Within a relatively short time at the end of the eighteenth century, Josiah Wedgwood had turned a traditionalistic work force (used to drinking on the job, working flexible hours, and working at their own discretion) into an efficient, diligent, and reliable work force (Langton 1984).

A more recent example of politically accelerated acculturation can be found along the Mexican-United States border, where Mexican workers, thought by Oscar Lewis to be affected by a "culture of poverty," have proved highly productive and internationally competitive in "maquilas," when properly trained and organized (Rivera and Goodman 1981). This finding is supported by the study of a US auto assembler in Mexico (Posthuma 1995, 109). Because this assembler used appropriate recruiting and training methods, it achieved better levels of productivity and product quality than in its US and Canadian factories.

"One cannot simply take the institutions and developmental patterns that worked for one country, plop them down elsewhere, and hope to achieve the same results," Leonard (1991, 298) argues. Yet, with appropriate political nurturing, this can happen. For example, based upon a study of 18 firms in Brazil, Humphrey (1993) shows that Japanese style management methods can be effective when an adequate effort has been made to address employee concerns and problems. "The Brazilian case also shows that a history of poor industrial relations is not an insuperable barrier to the introduction of production systems which rely on some degree of worker involvement" (IBID., 112).

It should be pointed out that the so-called "Japanese management model," as described in Chapter 1, is a relatively recent development in Japan. A visitor to a typical Japanese silk or cotton factory a century ago, during the Meiji period, would have found workers, particularly girls, treated so brutally as to make the current system of production appear "culturally impossible" (Tsurumi 1990).

In any case, the Japanization of production will be effective only to the extent that the political software considerations emphasized in Chapter 2 are taken into account, according to studies in Indonesia (Harriss 1995) and Zimbabwe (Posthuma 1995). For example, good results were obtained in South Africa by Nissan "based upon a comprehensive program which linked elements such as vocational training and job rotation to form a basic career development plan for manual workers" (Posthuma 1995, 113).

The extent to which Westernization should be pushed is another subject of considerable controversy. Verhelst (1990, 158–159), a Belgian analyst, emphasizes the danger of Westernization because it "constitutes a dreadful threat when it imposes or even suggests a change that denies the cultural identity of a people." Even in the Western world, he asserts, the existing way of life has brought cultural alienation and spiritual impoverishment; and, in the form of "Western cultural imperialism," it undermines the capacity of a people "to forge its own identity, its own new response to present-day challenges."

Warren (1991, 7) presents a less polemical version of this argument—that the traditional ways of doing things are often highly effective "adaptations to local agroecosystems." Even when their technologies are simple, indigenous peoples sometimes have very sophisticated knowledge about their natural resources and productive organizational systems. Therefore, it is foolish, if not counterproductive, to ignore local approaches to local problems. Moreover, in the words of Dolores Koenig (1986, 54), an applied anthropologist: "An approach that allows villagers themselves to define the problem can uncover information that otherwise would have been ignored."

However, applied anthropologists often find themselves in a "damned it you do, damned if you don't" situation. If they push change too aggressively, they are accused of "neocolonialism;" if, too conservatively, of perpetuating backwardness and cultural differences (Klitgaard 1991a, 108). Some of the current problems of Nigeria are said to stem from Lord Lugard's colonial rule, in which he attempted to protect the way of life of the Hausa-Fulani peoples, thereby keeping them from progressing as rapidly as the Ibo and Yoruba (Melson and Wolpe 1971).

In considering the plight of 300 million indigenous people in 70 countries, anthropologists tend to argue in favor of maintaining their culture, whereas economists emphasize the danger of holding up development (Wilford 1994, D1). Whereas anthropologists consider the economy as "a child of culture," economists assume the reverse, "that cultures will adapt to prevailing incentive structures" (Jones 1995, 269, 276).

Fortunately, in many cases, tradition and modernity are not antithetical. Randall and Theobald 1985, 35–37) point out that traditional societies are not static, monolithic, or incompatible with Westernization. Indeed, "the process of modernization may actually revitalize dormant traditional institutions and practices." More common is the coexistence of traditional and modern forms of culture—e.g., superstition with science or witchcraft with modern medicine. According to an article in THE ECONOMIST (January 6, 1996, 21), a third of Italians believe that you can communicate with the dead, that curses work, and that you should "watch out for the evil eye."

It should also be noted that the most Westernized groups can also be the most counterproductive—the most likely to be corrupt, wasteful, socially disruptive (using alcohol and drugs or committing crime), and harmful to the environment. Dove (1988, 16) points out, in the case of Indonesia, that, while peasants are often accused of illegally felling trees from state forests because of their way of life, their actions are promoted by city-based entrepreneurs who (without a cultural excuse) send in trucks, corrupt forest department personnel, and offer irresistible sums of money to the peasantry.

THE IMPORTANCE OF LEADERSHIP

Cultural barriers to development are certainly difficult to overcome. Yet, from what we have here indicated, these barriers are often politically created and, as such, susceptible to political action. This can be clearly seen by looking at some of the foreign aid success stories where significant behavioral modication was brought about by strong leaders serious about development and by well-established organizations (Paul 1986). A comparison of the equally impoverished neighboring countries of Tanzania and Malawi in regard to road maintenance and repair can perhaps illustrate the point being made here (Moeller 1990).

In Tanzania, as of 1990, about 45 percent of paved roads and 60 percent of unpaved roads were in poor condition, making reconstruction costs and vehicle operating costs far higher than would otherwise be the case. A World Bank study of the situation found inept management to be largely responsible: "The organization remains unmotivated as a result of weak accountability, low salaries, and recurrent reorganizations which have eroded the definition of organizational objectives and designation of responsibilities" (Moeller 1990, 41). The fact that infrastructure created by British colonial institutions deteriorated so rapidly after independence in Tanzania seems to support Landell-Mills's point (1992, 473) "that the underlying cultural premises of these institutions were alien to the vast majority of Africans. . . ."

In Malawi, on the other hand, President Banda made it clear that "there should be no potholes in my roads" (quoted, Moeller 1990, 15). Under the President's direction, workshops were established to set objectives for the implementation of all repair activities. There were then quarterly reviews, with the monitoring of performance at all levels. A management system was installed, using micro-computers to provide needed information at various levels of organization. In addition, there was a comparison of work performance between districts, creating a spirit of competition and an incentive for supervisors to perform as well as or better than others doing similar work (Msalomba 1991, 87).

As a result of all this, only 6 percent of Malawi's paved roads and 16 percent of its unpaved roads were in bad shape, as of 1990. Considering that in Sub-Saharan Africa as a whole an estimated one-quarter of paved roads and 40 percent of unpaved roads are in bad shape, this was quite an achievement. In other words, Banda's leadership, at least in this sector, significantly modified the counterproductive administrative culture that is so prevalent in Africa.

African national airlines tend to be inefficient, unreliable, and even dangerous because of paternalistic cultural practices. An exception is the Ethiopian Airlines Corporation (EAL), which was created by imperial charter in 1945 under a contract with Trans-World Airlines (TWA). By the mid-1970s, when the TWA contract was terminated, EAL was, not only completely Ethiopianized, but also highly professional, efficient, and profitable. As of 1991, it had 3,200 employees worldwide, two pilot schools, the best repair and maintenance depot in Africa, and annual profits of about $25 million.

Educated Africans are often thought to lack an entrepreneurial spirit, preferring to work for the government than to develop independent businesses. "With regard to culture," Berman (1994, 247) notes, "there is no evidence that a hegemonic bourgeois culture of instrumental rationality has developed within any society or state in Africa."

In the Ivory Coast, however, under Houphouet-Boigny, the state, according to Rapley (1994, 39), "generously favored the continued development of the domestic bourgeoisie." Consequently, educated Africans here are, not only active in all segments of the economy, but also are more aggressive in seeking out new markets and more technologically innovative and sophisticated than European settlers. In particular, they prefer running plantations to being civil servants. Inasmuch as Ivorian capitalists intermix freely with one another in Lions and Rotary clubs and similar social gatherings, with little apparent regard to ethnicity, "one sees that Ivorian business culture resembles those of advanced capitalist countries to a considerable extent" (Rapley 1994, 57).

While it may be apparent that governments with the power to implement policies can have a profound impact upon culture, we lack a theory to explain why this is so. This is because, according to Vernon Ruttan (1991, 277–278), political scientists remain uncertain about the sources and meaning of political power. In this regard, Ruttan's assertion (derived from the writing of Robert Dahl) that "A has power over B to the extent that he can get B to do something that B would not otherwise do" is misleading because it does not distinguish coercive from persuasive power.

In using political elasticity theory as a way of explaining the capacity of leaders to influence and change political culture, I need to remind readers of my distinction between political hardware (the objective forms, rules, procedures, and methods of organization) and political software (the subjective relationship between leaders and followers). Political software, as I have been using the concept, has both psychological and cultural implications, affecting attitudes, prejudices, emotions, and other motivational factors. While I include a "cultural" dimension in political elasticity theory, I avoid a rigid concept of "culture," denying that beliefs and behavior are always tightly interrelated and passed from generation to generation without significant modification.

To what extent are the political software requisites (establishing acceptable goals, hiring qualified personnel, etc.) here emphasized free from a particularly Western connotation? I fear that I am open to the charge of "Western utopianism": attempting "to reproduce and sustain the paradigm of modernity throughout the world" (Berman 1994, 253).

My defense is to agree with the African scholar Adjibolosoo (1995, 34) that, to be productive, "the people of a nation must also acquire unique human qualities and/or characteristics that encourage and promote economic progress (such as integrity, discipline, dedication, responsibility, diligence, insightfulness, accountability and the like)." This is why I have tried in this book to suggest a single direction for development to take place, regardless of culture or form of government (but, at the same time, possibly affecting culture and government in the process). However, the ability to move in this direction requires effective leadership, as the following case studies will hopefully illustrate:

SINGAPORE'S CULTURAL ENGINEERING. During the 1950's prior to independence, the majority of the adult population lacked a primary-level education; and only about 20 percent were literate in English. Less than 7 percent were in professional, technical, or managerial occupations (Swee-Hock 1967). In 1958, about 25 percent of the population were considered below the poverty level (unable to afford essential goods and services). There was much underemployment, drug addiction, petty criminal activities, gambling and prostitution organized by secret societies, and the traditional practice of medicine (Huat 1989). Families were large (with seven children, on average) and extended, often with several wives. During the decade from 1947 to 1957 there was an annual population growth rate of 4.4 percent, of which 3.4 percent represented a natural increase (LePoer 1991, 73).

Nearly three-quarters of the population, estimated in 1959 to be about 1.5 million, were packed into the central area of the city. Much of the population lived in ethnic communities, with ten or more families often living above the traditional low-rise shophouses (Field 1987). At the same time, between 250,000 and 300,000 people were living on the city's outskirts in squatter settlements, usually without sanitation and other essential services.

Singapore's living conditions are now very different, much of which has to be attributed to cultural engineering: (1) information dissemination; (2) indoctrination or persuasion; (3) incentives; (4) disincentives; and (5) sanctions or harsher forms of coercion (Quah and Quah 1989, 113). "Probably nowhere else in the world are state policies to organize a country's people and to influence its values and attitudes so extensive and pervasive" (Fong, Huat, and May 1989, 129).

Of course, cultural engineering was also attempted in Eastern Europe; but, according to Jowitt (1992, 209), "Leninist rule reinforced many of the most salient features of traditional culture throughout Eastern Europe (the Soviet Union and elsewhere)." This is because, unlike the practice in Singapore, coercive, rather than persuasive, power tended to be exercised, creating psychological and political estrangement.

Singapore's capacity to undertake cultural engineering has required a "cultural change" within the bureaucracy (Quah 1994, 205). To fight the corruption and apathy that had emerged during the colonial and postwar periods, the Lee Kuan Yew government (as noted in the previous chapter) recruited the "best and brightest" in Singapore, improved salaries and working conditions, accelerated promotion for "high-flyers," prevented overstaffing, reduced incentives for corruption, and changed the values of the civil servants. "The Singapore civil service today is a far cry from what it was during the colonial period because of changes in the basic assumptions or values that influence the behavior of its members today" (Quah 1994, 215).

While Singapore's government can be considered a relatively authoritarian one-party system (as noted in the previous chapter), ordinary citizens, professionals, and businesses have been able to influence policy-making, despite excessive controls, resulting in policies that have been generally pragmatic and flexible. In Singapore, respect stems from, not only the government's integrity, but also from its success, particularly its public housing program, described in Chapter 7.

The country's annual per capita GDP growth rate between 1960 and 1985 averaged over 6 percent. Per-capita income was (as of 1989) about US $15,000, as against US $1,600 in 1965, with unemployment only 3 percent, one-third the 1965 level (Cheung 1990, 36). THE ECONOMIST (January 13, 1996, 37) reports the average income of Singaporeans to be US $24,000, higher than that of the British.

The government's effect on culture has been most obvious in regard to birth control. Singapore's fertility rate fell by almost 70 percent in about 20 years, from 4.66 in 1965 to 1.44 in 1986 (Cheung 1990, 35). Thus, the population remains at about 2.7 million, instead of the 3.3 million predicted to be reached by 1990 (Swee-Hoek 1967). Between 1965 and 1989, the percentage of children (below 14 years of age) fell from 44 to 24 (World Bank 1993a).

However, it may well be, based upon the Hong Kong experience, that greater female educational and occupational opportunities are more effective than birth control programs in lowering population growth. Because Hong Kong's fertility rate also declined below replacement level by 1980, without any official anti-natalist policy, we have to recognize that only part of Singapore's fertility decline can be attributed directly to governmental policies (Leete 1994, 817).

I doubt that we can ever completely determine what is more important in affecting behavioral modification—new and better policy implementation or socio-economic changes. Nevertheless, in accounting for this fertility transition, Singapore's use of elastic forms of political power should be noted, including: a national campaign to highlight the negative effects of a large family and the benefits of a two-child family; the making available free of charge of contraceptives, abortions, and sterilizations; cash grants for mothers under thirty years of age willing to be sterilized or ligated after their first or second child; and paid medical leave for those agreeing to sterilization. Disincentives included: higher fees for delivery services and prenatal care for each child beyond the second; denial of maternity leave and income tax relief; and discrimination in availability of public housing apartments.

The following changes between 1970 and 1990 were at least indirectly affected by these governmental policies: a doubling of the percentage of females aged 25–29 with secondary or higher education (reaching 61 per cent); a shift in the female participation rate in wage-earning employment from less than 30 percent to nearly 50 percent; the postponing of marriage from an average age of 23.7 years to 26 years; and the doubling of the percentage of unmarried females in the 30–34 year age group (Cheung 1990).

Although the cultural consequences of low fertility in Singapore have been largely positive (more resources for children, greater educational opportunity, the rising status of daughters, and a higher standard of living), there have been problems: a labor shortage, a growing demand by single people for apartments or rooms, the need for more day-care facilities, an influx of foreign workers, and greater difficulty in caring for the elderly. "Women's social emancipation through better education and increased participation in the work force, it became clear, had become the fly in the technocratic ointment" (Bello and Rosenfeld 1990, 322).

Since 1987, the government has reversed its anti-natalist policy, providing various incentives for well-educated women to enlarge their families: tax rebates or reductions (amounting to an annual US $10,600 in 1990, good for seven years, for couples who have a second child before the mother is twenty-eight), priority for children to enter elite schools, larger apartments, leave to be with sick children, and assistance with child care. However, the efforts of the Social Development Unit, established in the mid-1980s, to encourage the better educated to marry earlier and have more children have been "a conspicuous failure" (Leete 1994, 815). In 1990, almost one-quarter of Singaporean women aged 30–34 (and 12 percent of those aged 40–44) were unmarried.

While this shift in policy may be having little success (particularly in equalizing the reproduction rates of the majority Chinese with the minority Malays), it has been criticized as paternalistic, racist, and elitest, indicating limits to cultural engineering methods (Bellows 1990; Cheung 1990). Indeed, the government's "love boat" ocean cruises, which attempt "match-making" among the educated elite, is seen as bringing "a little tragi-comic relief to the community at large" (Bello and Rosenfeld 1990, 323).

Singapore has found that turning back the cultural clock is extremely difficult. Despite official encouragement, the tradition of arranged marriages is unlikely to reappear. Whether the government will have more success with its effort to require adults to care for elderly and handicapped parents remains to be seen.

INDONESIA'S CULTURAL GUIDANCE. While a number of Asian countries have been able to lower birth and death rates in two decades (from 1970 to 1990) faster than Europe and North America were able to do in two centuries, Indonesia is the first Islamic country to achieve less than a 2.0 average annual growth of population (World Bank 1993a, 38–40). Part of this has been due to various factors in addition to those already mentioned: higher income, better nutrition, improved housing and health, greater participation in wage labor, major increases in mass media communications, higher levels of female education, fewer arranged marriages, and an increase in the age of marriage (Cobb and Boediono 1993, 13; World Bank 1992a, 27). Greater female literacy seems to be most closely correlated here with a desire for fewer children.

However, the most important direct cause of Indonesia's 40 percent fertility decline between 1967 and 1987 was the contraceptive prevalence rate, which rose from less than 10 percent in the 1960s to nearly 50 percent by 1990 (World Bank 1992a). Based upon experience in Bangladesh, socio-economic development, without a strong family planning program, is not likely to be very successful in reducing fertility (Khuda, Harbison and Robinson 1990).

Following the enthusiastic support of President Suharto, the government created in 1970 a strong family planning program (the BKKBN) which operated effectively throughout the country, directly implementing a variety of activities and coordinating the efforts of responsible ministries. By 1988 there were family planning posts in virtually every village and in most hamlets which, in addition to facilitating basic health care, organized and supervised family planning workers and village volunteers.

The central government, not only provided financial resources and technical assistance (with considerable help from international donor agencies), but also put pressure on officials at every administrative level. Failure to meet targets was quickly followed by steps to correct the situation. This meant that the hostility of line agencies, jealous of their authority and prerogatives, was largely overcome.

The BKKBN was also remarkably successful in gaining the cooperation of village heads and Muslim religious leaders even where Muslim fundamentalism is relatively strong (Warwick 1986, 477). Without this effort, it is unlikely that so many poor, uneducated, and rural couples in Indonesia would have become as interested in birth control as surveys showed (indicating in 1987 that 94 percent of adults knew about at least one modern method).

BOTSWANA'S CULTURAL FAVORITISM. We should not think of cultural change as being entirely positive. It can lead to great socio-economic disparities among ethnic groups, the intensification of inter-ethnic conflict, and civil war. This is what happened in Liberia as road and rail lines were built throughout the country from 1950 to 1980 (Liebenow 1987). Under Presidents Tubman and Tolbert, the elite used its economic resources and political power to take control of large sections of land, undermining traditional agricultural and social systems and forcing many of the tribal people into urban misery.

In Kenya also, the political favoring of certain ethnic groups has led to increasingly violent inter-ethnic land disputes (Miller and Yeager 1993, 110). Likewise, this seems to be happening in Botswana, despite its democratic characteristics, meritocratic administration, and remarkable educational and economic success.

At the time of its independence in 1966, Botswana was classified as one of the world's least developed countries (Southern Africa Department 1993). By 1992, its per capita income had reached almost US $3,000 (a middle income level), with a growth of GDP averaging nearly 10 percent annually during its post-colonial history (perhaps the fastest economic growth in the world between 1970 and 1990), stemming largely from the export of diamonds and other minerals. Unlike other African countries, it has not wasted its export earnings, using them to develop an extensive tarred road system and reliable (though expensive) utilities, while maintaining enough foreign reserves to cover about a year of imports.

A 1984 World Bank study of Botswana's public sector management (Raphaeli, Roumani, and MacKellar) found it to be unusually efficient and pragmatic, with commendable attention to detail, discipline, and accountability. Unlike the situation in other African countries, hiring is in accord with strict merit criteria and promotion is directly linked to performance (Wescott 1994, 220). Moreover, civil servants have remained firmly under the control of an elected legislature and district councils, with officers held personally accountable for the correctness of expenditure.

In developing many different training programs, citizen participation, and management systems to reward and retain outstanding civil servants, the government has largely avoided wasteful corruption, parastatals, and public works (Gulhati 1990, 33–35). "The strategy has been one of constant, incremental improvements on many fronts" (Wescott 1994, 221).

Along with Botswana's economic development has come an extraordinary cultural transformation. Whereas over 90 percent of the population was rural and nomadic (raising cattle) prior to 1970, it is now 30 percent urban, with nearly universal basic education (covering nine years), expanding higher education facilities, and life expectancy up from 48 years to over 60 years. Formal sector employment rose from only 14,000 in 1965 to over 220,000 by 1990. All sizable population centers now have potable water, electricity, and telephone service; and the the transport system has brought cultural continuity between rural and urban areas (Abucar and Molutsi 1993, 64–65).

The effectiveness of Botswana's government is indicated by the fact that, whereas Ethiopia lost thousands of people from drought during the 1980s, Botswana lost not a single life during this period from drought. The ability to feed 60 percent of the total population during a five-year period of drought within the 1980s is considered, "a major logistical feat in Africa's most sparsely populated country" (Lewis 1993, 19).

Despite this success, the Botswana government may have planted the seeds for future disaster (Good 1992, 1993; Abucar and Molutsi 1993). According to a World Bank 1991 survey of 41 countries, the highest 20 percent of the population in Botswana during 1985–86 obtained more than 23 times the income accruing to the lowest 20 percent (with only Brazil matching this disparity).

Whereas in the 1940s less than 10 percent of the population were estimated to have no cattle, about 45 percent were in this position by 1980. A recent estimate suggests that 75 percent of the cattle industry is owned by five percent of the population. Those without cattle also lack land.

This situation has reinforced a feudalistic system, under which the Basarwa or Bushmen have become increasingly impoverished (with decreasing opportunity also for hunting and gathering) and subservient to the Tswana elite. As Bushmen move into the urban areas, they also face legal, political, and educational discrimination because their language is not recognized. Consequently, there is increasing urban violence as well as environmental degradation, intensified by the rapid annual population increase of 3.5 percent. In regard to the country as a whole, Good (1992, 94) writes: "apathy or inchoate violence could result."

Botswana, according to Yeager (1993), has also failed to address increasing problems of resource conservation and environmental protection. An estimated fifteen percent of the country's total area is now overgrazed, bringing about "a tragedy of the commons." This situation cannot be easily corrected because many of the large-scale ranchers are also senior officials in the central government and the ruling party. They see efforts to protect the environment as threatening their cattle-based hegemony.

With declining revenue from the diamond market, careless environmental exploitation might spread, with horrific results. "Unless ecological balances are restored, rural inequality and poverty will widen and deepen, problems of forced urbanization and unemployment will worsen, and the regime's political base of support will recede and finally vanish in cities and countryside alike" (Yeager 1993, 130).

An optimistic view of Botswana, however, can be found in a recent article (Holm, Molutsi, and Somolekae 1996), suggesting that slow progress is being made toward a civil society. While political parties continue to focus on ethnic concerns, "social groups appear in a number of cases to be teaching politicians and civil servants the importance of debating policy issues in public" (p. 66). If so, Botswana could become a much needed model for other African countries.

Several developments, according to Holm, Molutsi, and Somolekae (1996, 48), have enhanced the democratic character of the regime: (1) the greater willingness of the three private newspapers to critically report on failed policies, corruption, and political conflicts and (2) the allocation of as much as one-third of the government's budget on such social justice concerns as mass education, preventive health, and drought relief. Although Botswana remains a system dominated by one party, the judiciary and the civil service function more effectively than in other African countries, thereby allowing social organizations "to avoid capture by politicians" (IBID., p. 58).

CONCLUSION: THE PLIGHT OF AFRICAN WOMEN

The case studies presented here call into question the amount of time necessary to change culture. Inglehart (1990, 424) emphasizes the "inherent slowness of cultural change," pointing out: "The worldviews that prevail in given societies can change—but these change gradually in large part through intergenerational replacement." I would agree with him that, where leadership is obstinate or indecisive and administration is weak, cultural change is a slow process. In India, for example, Breman (1993, 362) found in his study of rural life in South Gujarat that, despite some improvements in social conditions, "official policies have been instrumental in augmenting caste consciousness."

Yet, culture can within a generation change if leadership will allow or facilitate the change. In the United States, where civil rights legislation has been more effectively implemented than in India (despite lingering racial inequality and segregation), more than 80 percent of whites (as against less than 40 percent in the 1940s) now support integrated schools, fair employment practices, and nondiscrimination in housing (Carmines and Merriman 1993, 237). Even in the South, racial viewpoints have changed. Consequently, the racist culture of Houston, Texas (where I am from) has been significantly transformed, judging by the willingness of its citizens in 1997 to vote to maintain affirmative action in the city's contracting and hiring policies and for its first African American mayor.

As indicated in the Introduction, I cannot use PE theory for rigorous or definite prediction. For example, I do not forsee a change in the antiquated culture of the Catholic Church (e.g., allowing only celibate men to serve as priests), regardless of declining membership support for such a culture. However, I also did not forsee the totalitarian Soviet culture or the apartheid South African culture changing so rapidly since the mid-1980s.

While one cannot take rapid cultural change for granted, one should also not be surprised by it. Moreover, we must recognize that rapid cultural change, such as the appalling rise of single-parent families in America and elsewhere, may be quite dysfunctional. That rapid cultural change can have simultaneously both bad and good consequences is not precluded by PE theory. What the theory does suggest is that, when a political system is responsible, the government can do something to reduce the worst manifestations of cultural change.

What is being advocated in this chapter is, not simply taking culture into account, but going beyond it into the political requisites for changing culture. I have in mind attacking the patrimonial system which, as noted in the introduction to this chapter, is deeply ensconced in the political systems of much of the world. While I will leave a study of possibilities until the final chapter, I am convinced that these possibilities are realistic, based upon the theme of this chapter—that politics is more powerful than culture.

In Latin America, for example, the ministries of education, health, and the environment tend to be far weaker than the finance or economics ministries (Husain 1994, 10). Most of the ministries delivering social services to the poor are "staffed by poorly paid and unmotivated personnel—often political appointees . . ." (Glaessner ET AL., 1994, 2).

Tendler and Fredheim (1994) found a surprising exception to this situation in Ceara, one of Brazil's most impoverished states. Here reformist governors who ran the state during 1987–1994 introduced merit hiring for health care workers, instead of the clientelistic procedures that had been customary in Northeast Brazil. Largely because of meritocratic selection and training, "both workers and supervisors saw their jobs as giving them more prestige and status than they normally had" (Tendler and Fredheim 1994, 1773).

Within a few years of operation, this preventive health program tripled vaccination coverage for measles and polio and contributed to a 36 percent reduction in infant deaths. As a result of these and other achievements, Ceara's health system became the first Latin American governmental agency to win the UNICEF Maurice Pate prize for child support programs. We can see as a result how a simple improvement in governance, can have a profound impact on political culture. This is why I assert in Chapter 10: "Anything that improves governance is a step in the right direction."

In accord with Edmund Burke, I see political culture as a mixture of ideas and forms of behavior that have evolved over time and, as such, unlikely to be easily manipulated. I am also somewhat fearful of the results of careless political interference. Yet, assuming that we understand what we are trying to change (which, of course, requires a careful research effort), PE theory suggests the possibility of combining soft and hard forms of power to transform culture that might appear unmalleable, especially, African culture.

Evidence of the relationship of African culture to changing socio-economic and political conditions comes from studies of African rural and urban life. In regard to rural life, it was once thought that Africans were opposed to new agricultural methods (particularly terracing) because it conflicted with their traditional way of life, as well as being very laborious (Young and Fosbrooke 1960). The truth is, according to Paul Harrison (1987, 57), colonial administrators seldom bothered to understand why African peasants and pastoralists did what they did and, therefore, condemned them out of hand." What is essential is that researchers pay more attention "to what might prove attractive to farmers and less to what is agronomically optimal" (Jones and Egli 1984, 98).

The flexibility and adaptability of African culture can be seen in a CARE windbreak project in Niger (Thomson ET AL. 1989, 34–37). At first, villagers opposed the project, fearing that, if the government was involved in the planting of trees, it might take over their land. After government foresters assured the villagers that their land was safe, they got their cooperation in return for "Food for Work." Consequently, a ban on grazing was introduced, allowing increased crop yields and consumable timber products. As village farmers saw the benefits of the windbreaks, their way of life became less counterproductive.

Although I believe that promoting cultural change is not only possible but also in some cases essential for development, determining what exactly will be the consequences goes far beyond what my theory (or any theory, for that matter) is capable of. Yet, I am not afraid of a certain amount of experimentation.

I have particularly in mind the sad condition of African rural women, caught as they are within dysfunctional cultural manifestations: discouragement of education, teenage marriage and pregnancy, polygamy, continuous child-bearing during the reproductive years, economic dependence, heavy agricultural and domestic duties, sex-segregated labor markets, etc. (Adepoju 1994; Gordon 1996). According to Cleaver and Schreiber (1994, 1–2), there is a strong linkage connecting "rapid population growth, degradation of the environmental resource base, and poor agricultural production performance."

Whereas in East Asia, birth rates declined by 40–50 percent between 1965 and 1980, they declined only 2–10 percent in Sub-Saharan Africa (World Bank 1993a, 39). African women have on average 6.5 children, as against less than 4 in other developing areas (Cleaver and Schreiber 1994, 7).

The factors encouraging smaller families in rural Asia are not yet so important in Africa: the "Green Revolution," increasing mechanization and irrigation, improved communication and transportation, more use of credit, and greater demand for fertilizer and pesticides (Campbell 1990). As rural Asian families have more income and leisure, their daughters stay at school longer, marry later, are more knowledgeable, and have higher social and economic expectations—all of which leads to smaller families.

Yet, we cannot entirely blame African culture for the apparent failure of African family planning programs. While women are primarily responsible for crop production in many parts of Africa, they have limited access to land tenure, capital, extension advice, transportation, and improved technology. The resulting increasing workloads, particularly fetching water and wood and headloading produce, may cause African women to seek assistance from their children. The need to have sons for potential financial support is an additional factor in this regard.

To change this situation is going to require the convergence of Western and African family systems. This is, of course, already happening in African urban areas, including later marriages, more sexual freedom, decreasing polygamy, looser control by husbands, more frequent separations, growing female autonomy and consensual unions, increasing unplanned pregnancies, and greater family instability (Lauras-Lecoh 1990). If we can believe THE ECONOMIST (March 16, 1996, 33), the most rapid forms of African acculturation may be taking place in the United States where, according to recent census figures, the median household income of African immigrants is higher than that of immigrants from Europe and Korea.

The reform of African family life will certainly be extremely difficult in rural areas. Until African women in rural areas (where 80 percent of them still live under traditional family arrangements) have more opportunity for education and decreased work burdens, they may not be able to resist the social pressure for large families, particularly in the absence of family planning services. Yet, reform could be promoted by: (1) greatly expanding female educational opportunity; (2) compulsory education for girls; (3) the privatization of land; (4) joint ownership of land for married couples and individual ownership for single women; (5) discouragement of polygamy; and (6) enactment and enforcement of equal rights and opportunities.

Eritrea, which gained its independence from Ethiopia in 1991, may be leading the way in African cultural reform affecting women (Joireman 1996). Under 1994 legislation, women have the same right as men to possess their own land under a lifetime lease. Land that is allocated by the government to a married couple is to be divided, so that husbands and wives share equally. In marriage, a woman's right to farm her own land and to keep the profits from it is preserved. Divorce does not diminish a woman's property rights. Because this reform is seen as revolutionary, it is to be slowly enacted, after an educational campaign and testing in four areas of the country.

The result of this cultural experimentation could of course be negative, according to some leading African fiction writers, with African wives becoming as materialistic and selfish as their Western counterparts (Gordon 1996, 178). However, I am more in agreement with those who point out that, until the conditions of African women improve, particularly in rural areas, development will remain impossible (Adepoju 1994, 17).

The epidemic of AIDS in Africa is perhaps by itself increasing the need for cultural experimentation. In other words, as African women become more liberated, they may be able to resist the sexual exploitation which promotes the spread of AIDS.

In any case, I believe strongly that, even in Africa, politics may be more powerful than culture. Skeptics might argue, for example, that it is impossible to eliminate female circumcision or genital mutilation in Africa where it is imposed upon a majority of women, according to a 1993 report by Fran Hosken (cited in Snyder and Tadese 1995, 196). Russell-Robinson (1997, 54) goes so far as to suggest that "female circumcision in African culture is clearly adaptive, in that it is culturally and morally purposeful."

While I consider female circumcision to be cruel and dysfunctional, I would point to the fact that the equally iniquitous and deep-rooted practice of female footbinding is no longer practiced in China or Taiwan. Political as well as social forces clearly combined to have this effect, and they could be just as powerful in Africa as in Asia.

CHAPTER 9

Ghana and South Korea
Explaining Development Disparities

INTRODUCTION

In its September 23, 1989 issue, THE ECONOMIST pointed out that, in 1957, Ghana, then the wealthiest nation in Sub-Saharan Africa, had a per capita income almost equal to that of South Korea (US $490 against US 491 in 1980 dollars). By the early 1980s, Ghana's annual income per head had fallen by nearly 20 percent to US $400, while South Korea's per capita GDP was, by then, over US $2,000. The UNDP's 1990 HUMAN DEVELOPMENT REPORT suggests that South Korea had an annual purchasing power per head ten times greater than Ghana (US $4,832 vs US $481), based upon 1987 statistics (THE ECONOMIST, May 26, 1990, p. 81).

With the declining value of the Ghanaian currency (the cedi), the World Bank in 1996 put Ghana's per capita income at about US $430 (where it was in 1966), placing it among the poorest countries (Buckley 1996, A12). Meanwhile, South Korea's per capita income has reached over US $6,000 (Pae 1992, 77). The most recent statistics indicate that South Korea's real per capita annual growth rate has been more than twice that of Ghana (between 4 and 5 percent in S. Korea, as against 2 to 3 percent in Ghana).

Whereas South Korea is now the eleventh largest trading nation in the world economy, with a great diversity of industrial exports, Ghana remains dependent on logs, cocoa, and gold for most of its export earnings, with gold becoming the largest export earner in 1994, overtaking cocoa (West Central Africa Department 1995, iii). The value of Ghana's exports more than doubled between 1984 and 1994, reaching US $1.2

billion by 1994. However, between 1970 and 1990, the value of Korea's exports rose from $800 million to $65 billion (Cho 1994, 3). Ghana's industrial production has been stagnant in recent years, largely because of the domination of some 300 highly inefficient but protected public enterprises (Leechor 1994, 180–181). In Korea, on the other hand, output per worker in manufacturing nearly tripled during the 1980s (Cho 1994, 4).

Ghana's high fertility rate causes the population (now about 16 million or one-third that of S. Korea) to rise by about 3 percent annually, thereby also reducing per-capita income growth and putting an enormous burden on every aspect of the economy. At the same time, S. Korea's fertility rate is at about replacement level (2.2 children being the average for each Korean woman, as against nearly three times that number for each Ghanaian woman).

By 1985, using a variety of social welfare indicators to measure the physical quality of life (PQLI), the Washington-based Overseas Development Council had given S. Korea a PQLI of 86, as against only 38 for Ghana. The infant mortality rate in Ghana that year was estimated to be 91 per 1,000 live births, about three times S. Korea's rate. According to a 1993 Ghanaian study, almost 30 percent of two-year old children are affected by acute malnutrition, putting Ghana near the bottom of African countries in this regard (Vieta 1995, 999). The condition is much more prevalent in rural than in urban areas, which contain 30 percent of the population. However, poverty is now estimated to affect nearly a fourth of Accra's population, as against less than 10 percent during 1987–88, due to an increase in inflation (West Central African Department 1995, 27).

What is particularly disturbing is that, at the rate of its per capita GNP growth (about 2 per cent per annum), Ghana will not reach the status of a lower middle income country for another 20 years and the average poor person will not cross over the poverty line for another half a century (Chhibber et al. 1993, 1). Meanwhile, assuming that its record of growth persists, "by the early twenty-first century South Korea will be as rich as Britain and Italy are today" (Johnson 1994, 64).

Having studied public administration in Ghana in the late 1960s and early 1970s (Werlin 1972, 1973), I became acquainted with some of the reasons for Ghana's economic problems. My continuing effort to understand Ghana's difficulties led to a 1991 article, comparing Ghana and South Korea, using largely World Bank sources. In this revision (which also builds upon a 1994 effort), I have widened my research to examine certain generalizations about development generally and African development particularly.

Most of us who studied under Carl Rosberg in the early 1960s at the University of California/Berkeley shared his optimism about the future of Africa. It is therefore with great sadness that many of us, who continued to be his students until his 1996 death, began to share his growing pessimism about Africa. Being in the first group at Berkeley to receive a Ph.D. under his guidance, I write this chapter as a little memorial to him. (Werlin, 1994, was also dedicated to him.) Yet, in comparing Ghana and South Korea, I question some of the political factors stressed in the 1982 and 1994 Jackson and Rosberg analysis (political insecurity, authoritarianism, corruption, and clientelism) as being primarily responsible for Africa's retrogression. After all, these factors also have affected S. Korea (see Clifford 1994).

Indeed, Ghana's current President, Jerry Rawlings, seems to be far less corrupt and tyrannical than his recent Korean contemporaries, Presidents Roh and Chun, both of whom were convicted of accepting at least US $300 million each in bribes and for 1980 massacres in Kwangju Province (Pollack 1996, All). Based upon the 1992 and 1996 election results, which independent observers consider relatively valid (Jeffries and Thomas 1993; Rupert 1996), most Ghanaians have respected his leadership. According to Chazan (1991, 28), Rawlings enjoys "a reputation for honesty, dedication, and commitment to justice."

The implications of the Jackson and Rosberg analysis are here explored in regard to IMF and World Bank loans made to Ghana since 1983 for its Economic Recovery Program (ERP). These "conditionality" loans, which have been made to many African countries, have been criticized as intensifying economic dependency on primary products, discouraging non-traditional agriculture and industry, and hurting the poor (see Stewart, Lall and Wangwe 1992 and Anunobi 1992).

Using Ghana as my example, I will try to show that the debate on the usefulness and fairness of the IMF/World Bank approach seems far removed from what is happening. In other words, Ghanaian leaders are not yet taking the requisites for development seriously, particularly those having to do with public administration. Until they do (with implementation in mind, rather than simply policy-making), the effort to facilitate economic and social development will remain hopeless.

I end agreeing with Jackson and Rosberg that leadership in Africa is personalistic rather than developmental, but I remain perplexed regarding the reasons for this. Indeed, based upon the narrow focus of the research presented here, I find it hard to understand why Ghanaian leaders, in contrast to their South Korean counterparts, have failed to make the same rational association of their political success with the steps essential for development.

Acheampong, for example, who ruled Ghana during much of the 1970s, was so disdainful of the advice of international, as well as local economists, that, in the words of an observer, he "reminds one of a drunk on a motorway driving against the flow of traffic: the crash was only a question of time" (Huq 1989, 28). While Rawlings is much more rational and courageous than Acheampong or Nkrumah in this regard, his political commitment to development appears far less than that of his South Korean counterparts. Thus, practical problems in Ghana continue to be seen as insurmountable rather than merely challenging.

There is a large body of literature which suggests the importance of cultural factors. For reasons indicated in the previous chapter, I discount these factors. African scholars are more likely to stress the dysfunctional impact of colonialism. Claude Ake (1996—he died in a plane crash in Nigeria in November, 1996), for example, argued that colonialism undermined nationalism (causing therefore factionalism and strong centrifugal tendencies) through its absolute, arbitrary, and statist practices. While I have written (1974) very critically of British colonial practices, I have serious reservations about this explanation for reasons suggested in the following section.

HISTORICAL COMPARISONS

GHANA'S RETROGRESSION. Ghana came into independence under Kwame Nkrumah in 1957 with more advantages than perhaps any other country in Sub-Saharan Africa. It exported about one-third of the world's cocoa (far more than any other country) and 10 per cent of the world's gold. It also exported significant quantities of diamonds, bauxite, manganese and mahogany. It had reserves amounting to an estimated US $532 million, or US $83.1 per head in 1955—enough to pay for one-year's import requirements (Fieldhouse 1986). Its liquid assets were more than seven times its long-term debt. Ghana's transport infrastructure was considered among the best in Africa (Huq 1989, 62).

In addition to its economic assets, Ghana had at the time of independence a higher percentage of well-educated, professionally qualified, and technically trained and experienced people than any other Sub-Saharan African country. At this time, Ghana's investment in education as a percentage of GDP was far higher than that of any other tropical African country (Huq 1989, 71). While the rural masses had limited educational opportunities under colonialism, urban educational institutions at primary, secondary, and tertiary levels were judged "the best in Africa" (World Bank OED 1995, 17).

According to the book by Ake (1996, 3) earlier mentioned, colonial officials "showed hardly any interest in transforming domination into hegemony, beyond the notion that their domination was also a civilizing mission." However, a strong argument can be made that Ghana was more democratic under colonialism than afterwards. Ghanaians, not only participated in all of the country's governing bodies, but also exercised real authority. "This system of rule gave Ghanaians experience with modern, representative government to a degree unparalleled elsewhere in sub-Saharan Africa" (Berry 1995, xxxi).

On my first research day in Ghana in 1967, I attended a session of the Committee on Enquiry into the State Furniture and Joinery Corporation. The dismal story was here revealed (Anon. 1968) of a productive and profitable private company being reduced to anarchy when nationalized by Nkrumah through unqualified political appointees, kickback arrangements, misuse of funds and equipment, failure to collect debts, and allowing of assets to be "drained into the sea." My effort to understand what had happened led me to the same explanations found in the 1982 and 1994 writings of Jackson and Rosberg:

- SOCIALISM. Nkrumah's concept of socialism caused him to see government as a source of employment and control rather than an engine of productivity and development.
- CLIENTELISM. Nkrumah relied upon an elaborate patronage system—linking officials, with their tribes, friends, and extended families into webs of corruption—with favors (rather than performance) as the output in return for bribes and other gifts (Le Vine 1975).
- AUTHORITARIANISM. Nkrumah so effectively undermined all the political institutions of the country (legislature, judiciary, civil service, political parties, interest groups, the press, the universities, etc.) that "the learning capacity of Ghana was reduced to the learning capacity of Kwame Nkrumah" (Bretton 1966, 142).

Nkrumah's economic mistakes seriously eroded Ghana's living standards. The real value of Ghana's minimum wage, on which public wages were based, declined by nearly 45 percent between 1960 and 1966; public sector monthly earnings, by 20 percent; and industrial earnings, by 25 percent (Fieldhouse 1986). The income of cocoa farmers dropped in 1966 to about one-third of what it had been in 1960. In 1968 the lower half of income-earners received only about one-quarter of national income, as against one-third in 1956.

By 1966, when Nkrumah was overthrown, Ghana's economy was already in bad shape (Younger 1989). Between 1959 and 1964, Nkrumah increased Ghana's total debt to nearly US $1.0 billion, wiping out in the process the country's foreign reserves (Fieldhouse 1986). Its credit rating had deteriorated to such an extent that suppliers were willing to give credit only at exorbitant rates or under international barter arrangements. In 1965, the government began negotiating with the IMF for assistance.

Despite Nkrumah's mismanagement, the economy still had considerable potential for rapid recovery at the end of the 1960s. A 1970 report found Ghana's transport system to be essentially adequate, including the rail system, roads, airline and shipping services, and ports (Huq 1989, 62). As of 1972, there were 16 automatic telephone exchanges in the country. And the electricity supply was still considered the best in West Africa.

With over 5 percent of GDP being spent by government on education in 1965, Ghana's education system continued to be of good quality, enrolling nearly 75 percent of primary-age children by 1974 (Cobbe 1991, 101; World Bank OED 1994a, 1). Throughout the 1960s and until 1975, the average annual rate of increase in the output of trained teachers was more than 10 percent (Huq 1989, 72). As of 1970, there were more than 12,000 students enrolled in technical schools and higher educational institutions; and there was an average annual rate of growth in enrollment for secondary schools of 8.3 percent and for higher educational institutions of 6.1 percent between 1965 and 1980.

The period from 1972 to 1982 (beginning with Busia's overthrow) can be considered a disaster for Ghana from almost every point of view. The average Ghanaian "in 1982 was much worse off than he was in 1957" (Huq 1989, 2). Nearly 10 percent of the 13 million population were estimated to have left Ghana during the 1970s to escape impoverishment (Kraus 1991, 124; Huq 1989, 229). Since they included between half and two-thirds of the country's educated, experienced, and affluent elite, its institutions could hardly function.

By the early 1980s, more than 80 percent of the working population were self-employed (outside the formal sector); and nearly one-third of the economy was conducted without regard for official exchange rates and price controls (Chazan 1991, 33; Nugent 1991, 74). Smuggling became standard operating procedure for farmers. By 1981 one cedi commanded only one-tenth of its 1971 purchasing power (Huq 1989, 5). "By 1982, the government of Ghana had become inexorably separated from its people, acting like a switchboard without connections; the lights blinked, but the wires led nowhere and the interaction between force and order, delicate in any society, had completely collapsed" (Smillie 1986, 24).

How did Ghana get into such a dismal situation? The reasons, according to various scholars (Younger 1989; Huq 1989), include:

1. INFLATION. Ghana allowed inflation to get out of control, with prices rising by nearly 35 per cent annually between 1970 and 1982. By 1982, the exchange rate was overvalued by an estimated 816 percent. This inflation was caused by the need to print money to finance growing government deficits, which rose from 2.3 percent in 1970 to 12 percent of GDP by 1976. Such drastic overvaluation devastated exports, which declined at a rate of 5.3 percent per year during the 1970s.

2. OVERREGULATION. With the rise of inflation, the government had to rely upon an inefficient system of price controls, licensing, and administrative allocations to deal with the demands and needs of the public. Petroleum and certain other imports became excessively subsidized, causing the flourishing of black markets, as only small amounts of imports were possible.

Because nearly 50 percent of foreign exchange was used to import petroleum, there was little left for other needed imports. Thus, the country found itself without foreign exchange to close the food supply gap (amounting to an estimated one-third of what it needed). Corruption flourished under these conditions, with a high percentage of goods illegally diverted from the controlled to the parallel market. This situation also undermined the banking system, which was considered untrustworthy by most Ghanaians and useless to the business community.

3. PRODUCTIVITY DISINCENTIVES. Because of the overvaluation of the currency, there was little incentive to produce. By 1982 farmers were receiving only 60 percent of 1970s prices in real terms. And other producers were similarly affected. Manufacturing declined to less than 4 percent of GDP by the early 1980s, as against nearly 14 percent in the

early 1970s. By 1982 the gross output of the industrial sector was about half of what it had been in 1975 (Smillie 1986, 21).

From a peak of 538,000 metric tons in 1965, production of cocoa dropped to a mere 179,000 metric tons in 1983 (with the decline caused by a combination of drought conditions and smuggling abroad). Thus, Ghana's share of the world cocoa market dropped from 30 percent in 1970 to about 10 percent. By 1983, the production of tobacco was down by more than 20 percent from its high, and cotton, to only 5 percent of its 1977 high (Smillie 1986, 22). From 1970 to 1980, the export value of gold fell 7 percent annually and of timber, 14 percent annually.

4. INFRASTRUCTURE COLLAPSE. Because access to spare parts became impossible, about 70 percent of the transport fleet was out of commission by 1982. Whereas the average vehicle was only 3.5 years old in 1960, its estimated age was 10–15 years by 1985 (Kraus 1991, 136). As the age of engines increased and the condition of tracks declined, the railway system no longer functioned reliably.

At the same time, only about 22 percent of the major roads were considered usable throughout the year (Huq 1989, 64). The telephone service had so deteriorated that the Cocoa Marketing Board had to use morse code to convey information to its various offices. Trucks going into the interior had often to return empty because of poor communication facilities outside of Accra. The postal service also became almost useless. And there were frequent stoppages of water and electricity in urban areas. Conditions in these areas were made more appalling by declining sanitation and garbage collection.

5. INSTITUTIONAL DEMORALIZATION. By 1972, the public sector was already bloated, containing nearly 75 percent of those in wage-earning employment. It continued to grow at 14 percent per annum between 1975 and 1982. Employment in public enterprises (PEs) expanded from 11,000 at independence to 240,000 in 1984. Thus, 60 percent of the government's non-debt current expenditure went for wages. However, by 1983, the value of real wages had fallen to one-third of their 1977 value.

Since senior civil servants were in the early 1980s earning only about twice as much as unskilled civil servants (compared to a 10:1 ratio in the private sector), they found themselves below the poverty line. When realistic exchange rates started to be used in 1983, even an upper level civil servant earned less than one-fifth of the amount needed for a minimum acceptable diet for a family of five (Stewart, Lall and Wangwe

1992, 35). Consequently, the public sector had difficulty keeping qualified personnel. The Ghana Water and Sewage Corporation, which had 90 engineers in 1979, had only 20 in 1984 and no accountants.

6. PUBLIC SECTOR MISMANAGEMENT. Gyimah-Boadi (1991, 195) describes the weaknesses of Ghanaian agencies, particularly its PEs, as including: inept planning, overstaffing, inadequate capitalization, undue political interference, lack of experts, corruption, and inefficiency. This was most apparent during the 1970s. For example, the Central Bureau of Statistics, which in earlier years published annual ECONOMIC SURVEYS, failed to do so any longer because it lacked adequate personnel and other requirements (Huq 1989, 77).

The Ghana Cocoa Marketing Board (COCOBOD) was reported to have had twice as many employees as needed in the 1970s. Of its more than 100,000 employees in 1979, an estimated 30,000 were "ghost workers" (on the payroll, but not actually at work.) Farmers often refused to deal with the COCOBOD because of the staff practice of paying with phony checks and misusing funds.

7. DETERIORATION OF HUMAN SERVICES. Expenditure on education and health declined during the 1970s, partly because (as was then typical of African countries), more was spent on the military than on education and health. Expenditure on education fell to only 1 percent of GDP by 1983, compared to 5.2 percent in all of Sub-Saharan Africa as a whole (and 9 percent in South Korea).

The education ministry lost up to 10,000 staff during the 1970s, including 13 percent of all teachers. By 1982/83 the proportion of unqualified teachers was estimated to be nearly 50 percent at the elementary school level and 20 percent at the secondary school level; and most schools (which by then were in terrible physical condition) also lacked textbooks and other needed supplies, as well as stable electricity and telephones (Cobbe 1991, 105). Even Ghana's top university (the University at Legon) had only one functioning telephone—in the Vice Chancellor's office—in 1993 (Peil 1996, 53).

Because schools were so miserable, primary enrollment rates dropped to the level of the 1950s as parents withdrew their children (World Bank OED 1994a, 1). This situation has most adversely affected females. According to a 1991 survey (Canagarajah and Thomas 1997, 10–11), only 16 percent of females were then literate enough to read a newspaper, whereas over 26 percent of males could do so. This was clearly one of the factors accounting for the low participation (29 percent) of females in wage employment between 1987 and 1992. However, lack of educational opportunity for males, as well as females, made it difficult for the country to reduce the percentage of the population (more than one-third in 1991) living below the poverty level.

With the departure of so many medical personnel, facilities could not offer even the most basic services during the early 1980s. The lack of these services, combined with unsanitary conditions, caused infant mortality to rise from 80 per 1,000 to 120 per 1,000 between 1975 and 1983 (Chazan 1991, 27).

SOUTH KOREA'S MARCH TO PROSPERITY. In 1961, when its GNP per capita was only US $85 and its GNP growth, less than 1 percent, South Korea seemed economically far less likely to succeed than Ghana (de Franco ET AL. 1988). It was one of the most densely populated countries in the world, made more so by the fact that 60 percent of S. Korea is mountainous.

The 36 years of Japanese colonial rule can hardly be considered more beneficial to Korea than British colonial rule to Ghana. While the Japanese may have stimulated a greater enthusiasm for development than the British, they were certainly more heavyhanded.

Japan did leave Korea with extensive chemical, machinery, and textile enterprises; communication and transportation networks; universal primary education; and a centralized administrative structure (Clifford 1994, 306; Cho and Kim 1991, 6–7). However, the objectives were "to train a subservient workforce of subjects loyal to Japan and capable of filling the growing number of menial and low-paying jobs for the benefit of the imperial economy" (Cho 1994, 35). The departure of 70,000 Japanese administrators after World War II left the nation's political and administrative apparatus "virtually paralyzed," according to Cho and Kim (1991, 10).

Koreans emerged exhausted from World War II, during which an estimated 10 percent of the population were uprooted and forced to work for the Japanese military effort in East Asia, starting in the early 1930s (Gibney 1992, 126–127). And their misery was immeasureably intensified during the Korean War of the early 1950s, suffering terrible destruction of housing and infrastructure, death or wounding of hundreds of thousands, and displacement of millions of people.

"Between the end of World War II and the end of the Korean War, over 2 million refugees flooded into the South" (Mason and Cho 1991,

303). Much of the country's industry and natural resources was lost to North Korea, including most power plants. Without access to fuel or electricity, poverty was intensified because of Korea's harsh climate. "In 1960, the entire country had only 627 public telephones" (Clifford 1994, 43).

While agriculture generated nearly 40 percent of national income during the 1950s, Korea had little comparative advantage in many aspects of agricultural production: rice, corn, soybeans, beef, etc. (Steinberg 1984, 2–3). President Syngman Rhee's policies of import substitution, high tariffs and restrictive quotas, and overvalued currency worsened the situation. Without considerable U.S. foreign aid during the 1950s and 1960s (amounting annually to US $12 per capita), the country would have been in deeper economic trouble. However, corruption (in the form of kickbacks to Rhee's Liberal Party) seriously reduced the value of the $4.3 billion given by the Americans between 1953 and 1961 (Gibney 1992, 40).

General Park Chung Hee (who ruled between 1961 and 1979) is generally given credit for Korea's economic ascent, beginning with a 100 percent nominal devaluation of the currency in 1964 and the adoption of a unified floating exchange rate (de Franco ET AL., 1988; Corbo and Nam 1992). However, it was President Park's enthusiastic and persistent encouragement of exports which primarily accounted for South Korea's extraordinarily high GNP growth rate, averaging almost 10 percent annually during much of his 18-year rule, despite the drastic reduction of US foreign aid, the oil shocks of the 1970s, various world recessions, and droughts affecting agricultural production.

In carrying out his policies, President Park defied his country's historical tradition and orthodox economic thinking. He also undermined dependency theory accepted by many scholars in the 1960s, that because Less Developed Countries (LDCs) were dependent on the export of primary products and the import of manufactured products, they were doomed to deteriorating terms of trade, low standards of living, and educational underdevelopment.

World Bank economists, who discouraged South Korea's shift from light to heavy industry (ship building, steel production, automobile manufacturing, etc.) are still trying to understand the "vital lessons that could be learned here for other industrializing countries . . ." (World Bank OED 1991, 54). The reasons appear to me to stem from the following practices:

1. PRIORITIZING EXPORTS. Traditionally in Korea, industrial and export activities had little social prestige. Indeed, Korean traditional antipathy toward business is somewhat similar to that found in Ghana inasmuch as "it is rooted in a primitive notion of equality"—that all "should share equally in the fruits of prosperity" (Clifford 1994, 326). Moreover, as in Ghana, "the unhappiness with business also stems from the fact that most leading businessmen were political entrepreneurs, dependent on their political skills as much as their business acumen" (Clifford 1994, 326–7).

While certain aspects of Confucianism (particularly, its meritocratic orientation) have been conducive to development, President Park had to change its anti-business bias by honoring exporters and exalting them as patriots. November 30 was declared as "export day" and made a national holiday. Thus, international profiteering was considered a worthy and legitimate activity rather than as "wicked capitalism." Park attended ceremonies for project launchings, the opening of industrial parks, and press conferences concerned with exports and economic growth, which came to be the hallmark of his presidency. Every ambassador was assigned a quota of exports, with the understanding that assistance would be forthcoming from the highest levels of government.

2. COORDINATION OF EFFORT. Park established the Export Promotion Conference, a joint body of economic ministries, major economic institutions, and leading businessmen, over which he presided once a month. In addition to official policy forums and working committees, there were perhaps more important informal channels through which the business community worked together with leading government officials to plan economic development (Whang 1992, 318).

Park personally followed up emerging problems, even using the Korea Central Intelligence Agency for this purpose, as well as the Economic Planning Board (EPB). To encourage coordination, Park, not only selected key officials, but also promoted the interchange of personnel among the EPB, the Budget Bureau, and the Ministry of Finance.

3. CORPORATISM. In South Korea, as in other Asian NICs, the public and private sectors are linked in a variety of ways, sometimes referred to as "corporatism"—with the government as "script-writer;" and the actors drawn from the private sector (see Johnson 1987). For example, the government recognized the potential of the wig trade, using synthetic hair, and helped to develop it. In doing so, it "picked and created" industrial winners (contrary to prevailing economic wisdom),

rather than simply providing "an environment in which winners emerge and thrive" (World Bank OED 1991, 41).

Under Park, the government used at least 38 different market sustaining incentives and disincentives, with new ones invented when old ones proved ineffective or internationally unacceptable (Johnson 1987). "The government quietly prescribes a solution to problems, constantly monitors its progress, and adjusts the policy direction as necessary" (Whang 1992, 308). The most important incentives were foreign exchange allocations, tax rebates on imported raw materials used for export, low-interest loans, and a domestic market cushion for certain exporters (Campos and Root 1996, 166–7).

Korea's ability to integrate soft and hard forms of power was evident in all of President Park's undertakings. For example, Korean enterprises willing to conform to national priorities could borrow all the funds that they needed. Incentives, however, could be quickly withdrawn from non-performing firms. While businesses were allowed high profit rates, they were increasingly forced to compete in domestic markets by import liberalization. And, in the words of a leading businessman: "If an entrepreneur failed—well, he might even be imprisoned" (Gibney 1992, 57). In any case, the "rules of the game" have been understood, accepted, and maintained.

Government-guaranteed funds for export activities obviously required a strong banking system, which supplied an estimated 80 percent of funds for business development (as against 50 percent in the US). By establishing the trustworthiness of the financial system, the government could attract and utilize savings (Y. C. Park 1991, 48–49). Between 1965 and 1969, there was a 700 percent increase in deposits, and total bank deposits rose from 10 percent to 30 percent of GNP. Money from corruption therefore tended to stay in Korea, whereas in Ghana, it went abroad. The tax system was also greatly improved during the 1960s, thereby mobilizing domestic resources, improving savings, and making the system "more responsive to changing rates of inflation and economic growth" (C. K, Park 1991a, 247).

4. USE OF ADMINISTRATIVE EXPERTISE. The South Korean government, in its promotion of economic growth, used a process of trial and error. Such an approach, according to Whang (1992, 308) of the Korea Development Institute, "can work only when the bureaucracy is under the control of highly motivated and competent administrators." Whang goes on to note (1992, 321) that the use by government of

highly respected technocrats and economists was essential to make the process of economic planning and implementation "acceptable and credible to the public."

South Korea has followed the Japanese "best product" policy in public employment practices, selecting graduates of Seoul National University for the majority of the senior positions in politically and economically important agencies (Kim 1992, 321). The use of meritocratic examinations in Korea goes back five centuries, according to Gibney (1992, 19). However, such examinations did not prevent the prevailing corruption of the 1950s, noted in Chapter 7. To raise morale, President Park introduced a great variety of allowances, amounting to half of a typical civil servant's income, so that public sector compensation was (and continues to be) close to private sector levels (Campos and Root 1996, 146).

Despite the tendency of "the moral predominance of the bureaucratic elite culture over the masses," many civil servants think of themselves as "modernizing agents," anxious to facilitate the efforts of development-oriented presidential leadership (Kim 1992, 322). While President Park during the 1960s and 1970s and President Chun during the 1980s surrounded themselves with "palace guards" (particularly classmates from the Korean Military Academy) and patron-client networks, both balanced them with highly qualified civilians with advanced degrees, usually from the United States (Gibney 1992, 72–73; Pae 1992, 309).

5. GROWTH WITH DEVELOPMENT. World Bank studies during the 1970s found South Korea to be relatively egalitarian, with the bottom 40 percent of the population earning 18 percent of the national income, as against about 10 percent in Brazil and Mexico (Leipziger ET AL. 1992, 9). Later studies by the Korean Development Institute, which take into consideration legally allowed "hidden income" and the distinction between income and assets, indicate that, as of 1988, the bottom 40 percent of the population owned only 8 percent of financial assets (Leipziger ET AL. 1992, 99). Nevertheless, the Korean distribution of personal wealth does not appear to be out of line with more developed countries "when allowance is made for Korea's stage of development" (IBID., 37).

While the rich in Korea may have become richer over the years, the poor became less poor. Whereas in 1970, nearly a fourth of families were impoverished, less than 10 percent of families were unable to purchase basic needs in 1980 (Leipziger ET AL. 1992, 8). And, contrary to the situation in most countries, there was no large disparity between urban and rural income levels.

Education and health statistics (also noted in Chapter 7) are consistent with the conclusion that poverty has greatly declined in South Korea. It is reported that 98 percent of the population are literate, with nearly 80 percent of students reaching high school (as of 1985), compared to only about 30 percent in 1970 (Pye 1992, 17; Leipziger ET AL. 1992, 4). By the end of the 1980s, 37 percent of Koreans (as against only 22 percent of Britons) received some form of higher education (THE ECONOMIST, July 14, 1990).

A South Korean born in 1988 could expect to live 70 years, as against only 58 years in 1965. Health insurance, which was nonexistent in 1970, covered the entire population by 1989. Between 1976 and 1985, there was almost a 20 percent drop in infant mortality and almost a 30 percent drop in maternal mortality rates (Suh and Yeon 1992, 296–297). Calorie intake, which went up nearly 15 percent during these years, and the piped water supply (which reached about 75 percent of the population in 1989, as against only one-third in 1970) were important factors in this regard.

6. LABOR INCENTIVES. "Confucian benevolence" is the term sometimes used to characterize the socioeconomic policies of South Korea and the other Asian NICs, accounting to some extent for an average rate of annual productivity increase of about 10 percent during the 1970s and 1980s (Hofheinz and Calder 1982). It would, however, be a mistake to think that labor-management relations have always been harmonious in South Korea, despite legislation protecting employees from arbitrary dismissal (Castaneda and Park 1992). Labor unions and strikes have been discouraged, accounting perhaps for the long average work week (54 hours) and relatively low unit labor costs in certain industries. When the repressive system of industrial relations was relaxed in 1987, nearly 70 percent of all but the smallest manufacturing firms experienced some form of labor dispute (Sakong 1993, 86).

The surge of strikes at the end of 1996, together with the government's inept response to it, indicates that labor relations remain troublesome in South Korea. Yet, the government has encouraged the introduction of various labor incentives: 7 percent per year average wage increases; overtime pay; annual and seasonal bonuses; profit-sharing arrangements; and large lump-sum severance payments at retirement.

In addition to supplemental monetary incentives (which in certain years amount to nearly 30 percent of income), the larger Korean industries provide subsidized housing and medical care, sports and educational facilities, dormitories, and paid vacations. The bonus system facilitates good working relations in some industries by sharing profits in good years and reducing costs in bad years. It has also helped to keep unemployment rates to between about 3 and 5 percent, thereby reducing opposition to import liberalization and the loss of labor-intensive manufacturing jobs. However, the law guaranteeing to workers "a lifetime right to jobs" has become controversial following the East Asian financial crisis of November, 1997, noted later in this chapter.

COMPARING PROGRAM IMPLEMENTATION

Chalmers Johnson (1994, 80) describes South Korea's political system before 1987 as a "hard authoritarian" regime, meaning by that: "single-party rule, rigged elections (if they are held at all), and de facto dictatorship or oligarchy, regardless of what attempts may be made at legitimization." The trouble with this description, in explaining development disparities, is that Ghana, for much of its post-colonial history, can also be described this way. What then is the difference?

Ghana would seem to fit Jackson and Rosberg's characterization (1994, 300–301) of the African "princely state," where operations are "affected by norms of personalism, familism, and ethnic favoritism." Such a "princely state," as I see it, is incapable of exercising the "carrot and stick" methods so effectively used by South Korea's "authoritarian state." But even a distinction between a "princely state" and an "authoritarian state" would not adequately explain the greater capacity of South Korea than North Korea for development.

The difference, as I see it, brings us again to political elasticity theory, as used in the other chapters of this book. Korea's capacity to develop stems clearly from "political elasticity," whereas Ghana has remained "politically inelastic." In the abridged case studies below, the reader should be able to clearly see manifestations of political elasticity in South Korea and of political inelasticity in Ghana:

RURAL DEVELOPMENT: S. KOREA. It was not until the late 1960s that the Korean government became seriously concerned about the income gap between rural and urban workers which, as of 1971, amounted to about 20 percent (Pye 1988, 91). To overcome this gap, the government expanded four programs: price supports for producers of food grain; assistance for rural roads and other forms of infrastructure; the encouragement of high-yielding rice and scientific agriculture; and support for the SAEMAUL UNDONG MOVEMENT (SUM, discussed in Chapter 7).

Later programs were added to expand land consolidation, diversified farming, mechanization, new storage technology, high-yield breeds of livestock, agricultural credit, and rural industry. Between 1965 and 1975, the consumption of chemical fertilizer more than doubled, with almost all of it locally produced (as against 20 percent in 1965).

David Steinberg, a USAID official, describes the Korean government's rural development efforts as "the invisible hand in the iron glove" (1984, D-3). Under President Park, all aspects of grain productivity and distribution, including procurement, transport, storage, milling, and sale, were controlled by government. This control has persisted. "The government has the authority to import or export grain and can give orders to grain dealers, shippers, and processors, and to hotels and restaurents whenever deemed necessary" (Moon 1991, 381). Yet, while President Park gave rural development continuous personal attention, he realized that "people need to be persuaded to work with the government for the good of the country" (Kim and Leipziger 1992, 31).

By 1986, farmers were earning about 88 percent as much as urban dwellers, indicating considerable progress despite continuing problems (Song and Ryu 1992, 162). The difficulty of increasing rural income beyond this was by then apparent inasmuch as it ran into the need for expensive price supports, subsidies, schools, and medical facilities. Whereas agriculture comprised almost 50 percent of GNP in 1960, it was down to about 12 percent in 1990 (Song and Ryu 1992, 167).

Nevertheless, the Korean government continues to make the effort to equalize urban and rural incomes, most recently establishing a green-house farming system, using Dutch methods (Gibney 1992, 128). With the shift of population to urban areas (from more than two-thirds of the population on farms in 1960 to less than one-third by 1990), there is likely to be more mechanization, a shift to higher value crops, and greater off-farm employment. As this happens, rural development here will increasingly resemble that of Europe and Japan.

Even wealthy countries have much to learn from Korean farmers. Korea's land productivity is among the highest in the world, while the availability of cultivatable land per person is among the world's lowest (Moon 1991, 371). Its farmers can produce double the rice yields of their Southeast Asian competitors. The fact that Koreans are able to maintain self-sufficiency for rice is attributable to high price supports and a wide diffusion of credit, fertilizer, and high yield varieties (see Moon 1991).

While the protection of rice farmers is becoming more difficult, particularly because of American opposition, the country has a great willingness and capacity to deal with emerging problems. One has only to look across the border to North Korea, where rural misery and starvation seem to be persistent, to realize how remarkable is rural development in South Korea.

GHANA. In contrast to South Korea, Ghana remains dependent on agriculture for nearly half of GDP and export earnings and 70 percent of employment (Chhibber ET AL. 1993, 29). While rural poverty has somewhat diminished, it is much higher than the national average, affecting about one-third of the rural population (West Central African Department 1995, 27). In 1988, more than three-fourths of Accra's population had access to electricity in their homes, but less than 10 percent of those in rural areas had this service (Rothchild 1991, 11–12). Educational opportunity in rural areas is also very inadequate, with only 47 percent completing elementary school and thus achieving functional literacy. In rural areas, the infant mortality rate is 30 percent higher and child mortality, 20 percent higher than in urban areas. Lack of medical facilities in rural areas is only part of the reason for this. Of far greater importance is the fact that only 20 percent of the rural population (as against about 70 percent of the urban population) has access to safe water (Bahal ET AL., 1993, 25).

Agricultural output has risen in recent years at an average rate of only 2 percent. The growth of food crops, livestock, and fishing catch has been particularly slow. Cocoa production is still far below its 1970 share of GDP, causing an estimated US $125 million to be lost in 1993 (West Central African Department 1995, 61).

The inability of the government to significantly expand agricultural productivity clearly stems from underlying bottlenecks to rural development (Chhibber ET AL. 1993; Bahal ET AL. 1993). Perhaps most serious of all is the lack of decent roads, of which an estimated 60 percent are in poor condition. This means that rural Ghana remains a "footpath economy," with farmers (most of whom are women) having to spend much of their time head-loading commodities. The government has not even helped provide small carts, wheelbarrows, and bicycles, which could also promote local artisanal and small-scale industry.

There is also an inadequate availability of simple equipment for conditioning, processing, and preserving of crops. And very few farmers have access to irrigation, credit, fertilizer, insecticides, and other inputs taken for granted in South Korea. Fertilizer consumption actually declined from 40,000 tons in 1988 to 23,000 in 1991. Because of the traditional tenure system (without individual ownership of land), there is little incentive for land improvement and credit provision.

The research and extension systems remain uncoordinated and ineffective. Much of their staff is untrained or without funds and vehicles to get to the rural areas. Thus, horticultural export, which could be profitably expanded, is discouraged. And more severe problems, such as soil fertility loss, soil erosion, and deforestation (estimated to cost 4 percent of GDP per year) cannot be addressed. Farmers are also hampered by high marketing costs (17 percent of the export price, as against 10 percent in Brazil and the Far East) and an export tax amounting to 25 percent of what is received.

The Ghanaian government, unlike that of South Korea, has failed to mobilize the self-help efforts of rural areas. Although it embarked in 1988 on an extensive program of decentralization to District Assemblies (DAs), it remains an extremely centralized country. All but about 2 percent of DA revenue comes from the central government. DAs generally lack qualified staff to do financial planning, budgeting, revenue collection, expenditure control, and accounting. The staff sent by the central government tends to be inadequate in number, unqualified, poorly paid, and rotated every few years without regard for local needs and personal preferences. And their work is seldom audited or supervised. Consultations with DAs are rare, even on priorities and budgetary needs. Even when DAs are provided resources, they maintain "a poor and erratic commitment to development and services as demonstrated by their actual expenditure patterns and widespread corruption" (Ayee 1997, 41).

Civil servants generally consider being posted in rural areas a hardship because of the lack of adequate housing, infrastructure, family services, and resources to carry out their assigned tasks. Rural life continues to be miserable, characterized by "poor sanitation, inaccessible roads, polluted water, unhygienic markets, and dilapidated school buildings" (Ayee 1997, 51). Especially unhappy are secondary and university graduates who are required to spend a year in villages doing low-level jobs

(Peil 1996, 56). They are seldom paid enough even to cover accommodation and food.

Because of these conditions, officials are unable to inspire or facilitate the sort of cooperation essential for improving rural conditions that is normal in South Korea. Over the years, the Ghanaian government has attempted a variety of programs, using many institutions, to help farmers. But none has worked very well.

For example, a non-profit NGO began a pilot project in 1986 to help 40 farmers with improved technology, credit, and marketing (Chhibber ET AL 1993, 8). Because its approach initially appeared successful, the government expanded it to 85,000 farmers in 1989. Problems, particularly with credit repayment, caused the government to scale back the project to 20,000 farmers in 1990. Likewise, rehabilitation of feeder roads went slowly during the late 1980s and early 1990s, with work being done on only 5 percent of these roads. Only a few districts had funds allocated for routine maintenance, and only one of them had a Senior Technical Roads Officer in place.

Without a better linkage between the assignment of responsibilities and the capacity to carry out these responsibilities, rural Ghanaians will continue to be frustrated and apathetic. This means that agricultural export opportunities will be missed. For example, while Ghana could be exporting more and better pineapples than Costa Rica, it managed to sell only $5 million worth in 1994, as against $45 million worth for Costa Rica in 1994 (Buckley 1996, A12).

This situation could cause more serious political trouble. The growing scarcity of fertile land and consequent tension over land rights led to dangerous tribal strife in the Northern region early in 1994 (World Bank OED 1995, 121).

INDUSTRIAL PARKS: S. KOREA. During the 1970s, both Ghana and South Korea attempted to link technical education to industrial development, thereby making higher education more useful to the economy, reducing the problem of unemployed graduates, and recovering some of the high costs of universities. This effort was also partly a reaction to the criticism of higher education in both countries: that universities were elitist and that the study of science or technology involved too much passive memorization and not enough problem-solving and experimentation.

In 1969, the South Korean government borrowed from the World

Bank to create a network of vocational training institutions near industries, so that instructors could analyze the needs of these industries and experts from the industries could serve as part-time tutors. A Curriculum Research and Development Department within the Ministry of Education was created to facilitate the introduction of computer technology, new textbooks and equipment, a national testing service, and a "models of excellence" approach. By tying their vocational education system to five-year economic development plans and to manpower projections, the schools were able to find employment for 81 percent of their graduates and to keep drop-out rates low.

The development of industrial parks in S. Korea has been facilitated by the domination of a small number of conglomerates (the chaebol) along German and Japanese lines, together with a close partnership among government agencies, universities, and corporations. President Park developed a "reverse brain drain," attracting Koreans studying and working abroad to fill the top ranks of industries and research institutes (Clifford 1994, 110).

Several of the industrial parks are described by Gibney (1992, 128–129). One of them—the Korean Advanced Institute for Science and Technology—is particularly concerned with the expansion of electronics, where Korea now ranks fourth in the world. Pae (1992, 126, 484) points out that the Daeduck Science and Research Center over a 20 year period expanded to accommodate about 40 research institutes and three universities. During the 1990s, the government and the private sector have each contributed about US $1 billion to research in more than 900 strategically important target areas.

Korea's greatest success with industrial parks or estates may have been in its Cholla region (World Bank 1997, 74). Prior to 1980, Cholla accounted for less than 10 percent of Korea's industrial land. With the assistance of the central government, local authorities learned how to plan, finance, build, and operate large-scale industrial estates, overcoming in the process existing bureaucratic obstacles to public-private partnerships. Consequently, Cholla's rate of regional manufacturing was above the national average during much of the 1980s, and it accounted for 15 percent of the nation's industrial land by 1991.

GHANA. Ghana's Technology Consultancy Center (TCC) was set up in 1972 as an autonomous unit within the Kumasi University of Science and Technology (KUST). It received assistance from a number of sources, particularly the London-based Intermediate Technology Development Group. Much of its effort was directed at assisting a huge informal industrial area near Kumasi called Suame Magazine. Smillie (1986, 10–12) described it as a dismal place where more than 40,000 workers struggled without reliable credit, water, sanitation, electricity, and roads, using rudimentary buildings, techniques, and equipment.

Employees in the small establishments (typically consisting of a master with three or four assistants) were industrious and enterprising but seldom knew much about materials, safety, or engineering. According to Smillie (1986, ll), "none of the workers understood how an internal combustion engine worked, making simple diagnosis, testing and maintenance virtually impossible."

Despite TCC's many difficulties, it was successful during its early years in introducing a large array of products and techniques, creating numerous jobs and enterprises, and in saving considerable foreign exchange. What prevented it from being more successful were the overwhelming problems of Ghana combined with the lack of support so evident in comparable Korean programs.

TCC achieved a small measure of success "mostly despite, rather than because of policies, attitudes, and programmes of university, government, and the international development community" (Smillie 1986, 197). For example, in the case of a TCC-invented glue made from locally available cassava starch, a government chemist withheld certification of the invention and then stole it for his own profit-making venture. There was no effective legal recourse.

Smillie (1986) gives several examples of Canadian and American foreign aid projects to expand or improve Ghanaian industrial parks during the 1970s and early 1980s that were frustrated or delayed by various factors, the most important of which stemmed from governmental indifference. Ghanaian officials never even bothered to meet with a visiting Canadian team in 1982.

This same discouraging situation persists, according to Chhibber ET AL., 1993. As of 1988, only a third of Tema's industrial area (which was developed during the 1960s) was occupied. The share of manufacturing in Ghana's GDP remains at around 10 percent, whereas in Malaysia (with a similar level of industrialization in the 1960s), the share of manufacturing in the GDP has more than doubled in the last thirty years.

Between 1988 and 1991, manufacturing production grew at an average of only 2.8 percent annually (Leechor 1994, 170). This slow growth is attributed to governmental discouragement, according to a 1994 survey (Jebuni 1994, 65). "Business opportunities were constrained by the presence of public enterprises with powerful political connections" (Leechor 1994, 177).

Without a well-functioning legal system, Herbst (1993, 162) points out, which can ensure individual rights and provide a credible means of resolving conflicts, the Ghanaian investment climate remains unattractive. After the 1992 election, the President urged Ghanaians to avoid products made by companies supporting opposition parties, indicating his persistent disdain for the private sector (Buckley 1996, A13). Several of these companies were nationalized, including the nation's largest tobacco company, with some 1,000 workers. The ability of owners to legally fight such actions is doubtful considering that the legal system remains, according to its Chief Justice, not only "chaotic," but also, "dilatory, time-consuming and expensive" (Gocking 1996, 223).

The inadequacy of the banking system is indicated by the fact that Ghana's "savings performance is notably poor in comparison to all low-income countries" (Armstrong 1996, 37). While leaders constantly urge local businesses to undertake more investment, they have yet to establish a trustworthy banking system. "Many people in Ghana have discovered that it is better to keep savable money in hard foreign currency than in cedi savings accounts or treasury bills because of the fast depreciation of the cedi" (Vorkeh 1995, 922).

Moreover, the sort of "export mentality" that exists in South Korea has not emerged, indicated by the lack of an export credit facility, an export bank, and a system for exempting duties on imports needed for expanding exports (Armstrong 1996, 97). This partly explains the low level of foreign investment—about 4 percent of Ghana's GDP, as against 18 percent in South Korea and between 12 and 18 percent in Southeast Asia (Campos and Root 1996, 123). Consequently, the government cannot provide employment opportunity and a stimulating learning environment for the nearly 25,000 students enrolled in its three universities, six polytechnics, and seven colleges. According to recent estimates, only about 15 percent of the 250,000 young people annually coming out of the school system will find jobs (Chhibber 1993, 25). They face the fact that, in urban areas, unemployment is estimated to exceed 25 percent (Buckley 1996, A12). Even those with degrees in business, science and engineering are discouraged (Peil 1996).

PUBLIC ENTERPRISES (PEs): S. KOREA. While both South Korea and Ghana initially developed PEs for manufacturing, financial services, and public utilities, South Korea, unlike Ghana, eventually turned over almost all but public utilities (postal service, electricity, telecommunications, and railways) to the private sector (Shirley 1989; Pae 1992, 384). Whereas Ghana's 329 PEs provide employment for about 25 percent of its formal sector, S. Korea's 90 PEs account for less than 2 percent of total employment.

Despite extensive privatization, S. Korea's PEs continued (as of 1986) to possess about 15 percent of the country's fixed capital assets (Sakong 1993, 80). To motivate a higher level of performance, the government introduced a bonus system (amounting to as much as three months' salary) in 1983, with the assistance of the Korea Development Institute.

This bonus system included: (1) annual performance reports; (2) agreed-upon criteria and a system of scoring each criterion; (3) the use of outside experts, primarily from universities, as evaluators; (4) the publishing of rankings in the press; and (5) the use of the results to flag problems and deficient departments or divisions (Shirley 1989).

This system is considered so successful that it is now being used in Pakistan and other countries. However, Sakong (1993, 81–82), who helped develop the system, notes that other reforms were also essential, including more promotion opportunities for middle-level managers, greater autonomy and accountability, and elimination of redundant and rigid administrative controls and regulations. Otherwise, managers would not have felt so personally responsible for results.

GHANA. Ghana's privatization program, which goes back to 1988 (longer than any other African country), has been slow, with only 54 of 300 PEs fully divested by 1993, though others have been partially sold. The 1994 privatization of the Ashanti Goldfields Corporation was highly successful. While the Ghana stock market has become more active, the "results, in terms of private investment levels, remain to be seen" (Armstrong 1996, 101). Among the barriers to privatization are: shortage of financing and an active capital market, political interference, administrative obstruction, lack of accounting information, large liabilities, mutual fears and mistrust, and concern about restrictions and conditions (Drum ET AL., 1991; Sherif, 1993).

The redeployment effort has also largely failed, with PEs continuing to employ about 200,000, of which four-fifths in some cases have been identified as redundant (Leechor 1995, 179). Lack of funds for expensive end-of-service benefits (with US $25 million still owed, as of 1995, to the 16 percent retrenched between 1986 and 1990) is considered a major impediment to downsizing.

A 1990–91 survey of 127 PEs showed their 1989 losses to be about US $62 million (Drum ET AL., 1991. Among the reasons given for poor performance include: lack of management autonomy to make decisions; arbitrary and unpredictable political interference; inability to select and control staff; inadequate expertise and respect for professionals; useless grade and occupational classifications; irrational use of personnel (e.g., 18 drivers for 5 cars); deficiencies in financial and cost accounting; and failure to audit transactions.

While, as in Korea, there are performance contracts and incentive bonuses, they tend to be meaningless because performance remains unmeasured and bonuses are given automatically. Indeed, PEs here survive in a discombobulated atmosphere, without much control over (or knowledge about) debts, loans, taxes, dividends, arrears, grants, or other forms of governmental assistance and reimbursement requirements.

CONCLUSION: POLITICS VERSUS ECONOMICS

In Chapter 2, I argued that, if we focus on political software (the relationship between leadership and followership), politics has more explanatory power than administration (conceived only as political hardware and, particularly, forms of government or organization). In the previous chapter I asserted that, if politics is properly understood (including appropriate "political hardware" as well as "political software"), it is more powerful than culture.

I also believe that politics is more powerful than economics (as typically presented), much as I respect the work of economists. Using S. Korea and Ghana as my examples, I will, in this concluding section, try to show that this is so.

Because economists seldom understand the power of politics, their analysis of economic problems and opportunities can be quite misleading. When political leaders are as firmly committed to economic development, as they were (and still are) in Korea, they can cause the most rational recommendations stemming from comparative advantage, cost-benefit, and other forms of analysis to appear mistaken and even ridiculous. In other words, they can make economic progress by disregarding the prevailing economic advice.

On the other hand, when political leaders (as in Ghana) are opposed to rational economic management, they are quite capable of sabotaging it. Thus, they too manage to disregard economic advice, while paying "lip-service" to it. For example, in 1990, according to a World Bank division chief responsible for Ghana, the Country Strategy Paper "was endorsed by senior management one day but the next day it was back to business as usual" (Armstrong 1996, 127). In the case of Ghana, the "dirigiste/statist policies" are considered primarily responsible for the failure of economic development (World Bank OED 1995, 18). Yet, Ghanaians, in resisting World Bank/IMF economic ideology, might, oddly enough, look to Korean experience for support. "Government-business relations in Korea have been characterized by strong leadership from a government that did not hesitate to intervene directly with markets by means of commands and discretionary measures" (Cho 1994, 15).

Amsden (1994, 96) points out that state-guided capitalism has become controverial in South Korea, particularly because of the criticism of Korean economists influenced by the "conservative, antigovernment Chicago school." The truth is, she concludes (1994, 113), there is no scientific evidence to back up the contention that either Japan or Korea could have grown faster with less government intervention. Chalmers Johnson (1994, 74) notes in this regard that neo-classical economic theorists who prevail at the World Bank and other international organizations remain very defensive about the achievements of state-guided capitalism, "which they did not anticipate and still cannot fully explain using their purely economic concepts."

The financial crisis that struck Asia, particularly South Korea, in November, 1997, rekindled the debate among economists as to the efficacy of state-guided capitalism. All probably agree with THE ECONOMIST (November 29, 1997, 21) that there has been too much bank "lending on the basis of political whim rather than proper risk-assessment." On the other hand, Amsden and Euh, in an article in THE NEW YORK TIMES (November 27, 1997, A39), argue that careless deregulation in Korea, rather than excessive administrative control, caused the situation requiring the most expensive IMF rescue operation (amounting in December, 1997, to an estimated $55 billion) ever undertaken: "Indeed, it was the Government's decision to allow banks and other financial institutions to borrow and lend without interference that created the current crisis."

While I am unable to resolve this debate, I do believe, based upon what is here presented, that South Korea, unlike Ghana, has the requisite political determination to reform its financial institutions and industrial enterprises. The contrast between Ghana's "cannot do" spirit and Korea's "can do" orientation is most apparent in the history of Korea's steel-making venture, the Pohang Integrated Steel Mill (POSCO). Both the World Bank and the American Export-Import Bank, as well as the public loan authorities of other countries, rejected Korea's loan applications during the late 1960s for this project, emphasizing the country's lack of comparative advantage for such an undertaking and the failure of integrated steel mills in Brazil, India, Mexico, and Turkey (C-y Kim 1994, 53). Eventually Japan agreed to provide $500 million in loans and grants for POSCO.

Under the dynamic and meticulous leadership of General Park Tae Joon, POSCO became by the mid-1980s the world's single largest steel production site, reaching nine million tons a year. "It has maintained extremely high quality standards and at the same time consistently managed to shatter international records with its rapid construction schedule" (Clifford 1994, 71). By 1995, POSCO was able to produce 23 million tons of crude steel (second only to Japan's Nippon Steel) at about 20 percent less per ton of cold-rolled steel than its Japanese competitor (THE ECONOMIST, March 2, 1996, 62). While there is pressure to completely privatize POSCO and to allow rival CHAEBOL to compete with it, these two precepts of contemporary capitalism (privatization and free competition) run up against the adage: "if it is not broken, don't fix it!"

In comparing Korea's industrialization with that of India, S-C. Lee (1991, 470) notes that Korean leaders were able to free themselves from orthodox or classical economic thinking only because they respected it. In other words, Korean leaders often distorted market incentives and disincentives to compete in the world market; but they were "pragmatic and bold enough to reform the entire incentive and economic management regime when circumstances dictated it."

Ghanaian officials generally acknowledge the usefulness of the World Bank/IMF-sponsored Economic Reform Program (ERP) begun in 1984. With the assistance of the World Bank group and other donors, inflation was brought down from more than 75 percent to 10 percent between 1982 and 1992 (World Bank OED 1995).

296   The Mysteries of Development

Whereas real income per capita fell by one-third during the 1970s, it rose by an average of 2 percent annually after 1983 (Leechor 1994, 155). Indeed, for a decade following the ERP, average annual GDP growth was nearly 5 percent, which was far better than the economic performance of most other African countries. Yet, many senior Ghanaian officials continue to view the ERP as "externally driven," and, consequently, to deny it their full commitment (World Bank OED 1994, 26).

This begrudging attitude was expressed by a senior Ghanaian official: "When we know what we want and take the initiative, things go okay. But when the World Bank takes the initiative, things don't work so well" (World Bank OED 1995, 11).

According to Armstrong (1996, 125), the World Bank does a disservice in "overselling Ghana as a success case," in its external relations activities. While Ghana may have achieved a higher compliance with World Bank/IMF conditionalities during the 1980s than many other countries, it appears recently to have sabotaged economic reform in the following ways:

IRRESPONSIBLE EXPENDITURE. Expenditure overruns have become increasingly common. While there are rules governing the authorization of transactions and for purchases of supplies, recent reviews have found that expenditure control machanisms have not been operating as they should (Jebuni 1994, 53).

The World Bank made a major effort between 1987 and 1993 to improve the capacity of Ghana's Ministry of Finance and Economic Planning to control expenditure; but, according to the Bank's Operations Evaluation Department, it was largely unsuccessful in doing do, encountering "resentments, rent-seeking and other behaviors" not conducive to long-term institutional development (World Bank OED 1994, ix). In 1993, the Ghanaian government admitted that it lacked an ability to control expenditure, "especially expenditure on its multi-year contracts for building roads and buildings" (Country Operations Division 1995, 15).

IRRESPONSIBLE PAY INCREASES. While between 1988 and 1992, the Ghanaian government managed to link public sector pay increases to a measure of productivity, it ceased to do so prior to the 1992 elections, with the implicit justification: "if the international community wants us to have elections, it will have to pay for them." In October 1992, the government agreed to raise the average government service pay by about 80 percent, causing average real wages to go up 20 times the gain in per capita GDP and a deficit of about 5 percent of GDP (Leechor 1994, 165). Benefits were also increased for non-civil service workers in agencies funded by the budget.

In January 1995, the government granted a 52 percent increase in the minimum wage under labor union pressure (Berry 1995, xxxvii). These additional "wage shocks" were again given, not to facilitate better administration, but to gain popularity in anticipation of the 1996 elections, regardless of the need for fiscal discipline and tighter monetary control (West Africa Central Department 1995, 48).

DOWNSIZING FAILURES. While the Ghanaian government officially reduced public sector employment by 50,000 between 1987 and 1993, public sector wage and wage-related expenditures remain at about 9 percent of GDP, thereby doubling the the GDP percentage for these expenditures reported in 1990 (World Bank OED 1995, 94). If the 1992 salary increases had been used to provide financial and motivational incentives, the World Bank would not have been so discouraged by the result. Instead, downsizing has been largely circumvented by giving contracts to pensioned employees "on a temporary, renewable basis" (Abban 1994, 1350).

PERSISTENT INFLATION. Largely because of the 1992 "wage shock," inflation, which was down to 10.1 percent in 1992, went up to about 25 percent in 1993 and 1994, instead of the anticipated 15 percent (West Central Africa Department 1995, 9). Irresponsible increases in the money supply caused a 58 percent increase in inflation in 1995. This has undermined the financial system, discouraging savings in bank accounts, bank lending to the private sector, private sector investments, and improved banking services.

Ghana's trade deficit in 1995 was estimated to be about US $200 million, and its foreign debt, about US $5 billion (Berry 1995, xxxvii). The fall in the value of the cedi was reflected in the need of the government to raise gasoline and kerosene prices by about 25 percent at the beginning of 1995 (Yeboah-Afari 1995, 220). In 1996, the price of rice was 20 times higher than in 1992 (Buckley 1996, A13).

One can understand the frustration of Ghanaians who see the World Bank's enthusiasm for privatization as undermining their potential for industrialization. Abban (1994, 1350), for example, points out that, while Ghana has huge deposits of bauxite, the Kaiser Aluminium and Chemical Corporation (which has in Ghana an aluminium processing subsidiary) finds it economically advantageous to convert bauxite into alumina in Jamaica rather than in Ghana. Yet, knowing how poorly PEs function in Ghana (as noted earlier in this chapter), it would be irresponsible to advocate a Ghanaian PE for aluminum production.

While Korean leaders have been able to deviate from conventional economic advice because of their respect for it and their careful implementation, Ghanaian leaders have shown neither respect for this advice nor attention to implementation. Consequently, on the whole, efforts to improve the capacity of the bureaucracy have failed. During the 1980s, an effort was made to reduce the power of the Cocoa Marketing Board (COCOBOD) through downsizing and restructuring; but COCOBOB continues to monopolize export marketing as well as research, extension work, and quality control to the detriment of cocoa producers (World Bank OED 1995, 72–73). Various expenditure control mechanisms introduced by expatriate staff and consultants have seldom operated as intended (Jebuni 1994, 53). "Other reforms such as the automated payroll system and job evaluation and planned links of pay to performance have so far been ineffectual" (World Bank OED 1995, 94). Consequently, there has been no significant civil service reform. Moreover, there seems little interest in reform, judging by the refusal of the Ghanaian government to participate in a recent UNDP-financed program to improve its capacity to do long-term development planning (Armstrong 1996, 121).

African scholars often see the outside world as a "hostile force," preventing Africa from developing, as I noted in Chapter 1 (see, for example, Anunobi 1992). The so-called "blame game" appears especially absurd when one considers the refusal of Ghanaian officials to keep meaningful financial records, using the excuse that there are "too few managers of high training and skill in the public sector, e.g. qualified accountants" (Vorkeh 1995, 922).

The truth of course is that there are plenty of qualified Ghanaian managers and accountants, though many have emigrated or work in Ghana for foreign corporations. According to Peil (1996, 54), about 15 percent of Ghanaians emigrating to the United States have professional, technical, or executive qualifications, indicating university training. During the 1980s, Ghana is estimated to have lost about 3,000 qualified teachers and about 60 percent of young doctors. Periodic efforts to reverse this "brain drain" have been unsuccessful because of the low pay and poor working conditions of available positions.

"In African countries," Jackson and Rosberg (1982, 18) noted, "governance is more a matter of seamanship and less one of navigation— that is staying afloat rather than going somewhere." While this appears to be a valid conclusion, I remain perplexed as to why it should be so. In other words, while the following reasons given in the literature for the apathy and carelessness that one finds in Ghana ring true, they do not fully account for the contrast between Ghana and Korea in their motivation:

- THE PATRIMONIAL SYSTEM. Over the years, Ghanaian leaders created a supportive monstrosity of politicians, traders, military officers, bureaucrats, managers and employees of protected state industries, and urban interest groups. This monstrosity eventually controlled those who had created it and prevented reform (Jebuni 1994, 3). While governments find it politically expedient to hire on the basis of patronage, they also find it politically dangerous to dismiss these appointees, regardless of international pressure to do so (Mills ET AL., 1994, 4). The public sector remains at nearly 600,000—"an extremely large number by a comparative standard," undermining efforts to control the deficit (Armstrong 1996, 97).
- HISTORICAL EXPERIENCE. In Ghana memories of the overthrow of Professor Busia in 1966 (when he attempted administrative and financial reform) remain vivid (Jebuni 1994, 11–13). As pointed out in the next chapter, Ghana is much like other African countries in this regard because the majority of employees in the modern sector work in the public sector, even though they comprise only about 2 percent of the population (Leechor 1994, 179). Yet, efforts at downsizing have not led, as feared, to an impoverished, embittered coterie of ex-civil servants because many of them never stopped deriving income from numerous sources (Mills ET AL., 1994, 41–42).
- FEAR OF PROMOTING POLITICAL OPPOSITION. There may continue to be some fear of a large entrepreneurial class because of its possible political independence. This may explain why, according to a study, about three-fourths of firms in Ghana, according to a study, regarded government attitude towards business to be problematic (Jebuni 1994, 65). In any case, it is easier for leaders to remain de-

pendent on foreign donors (using whatever tricks that are necessary to augment donations) than to undertake real reform.
- CORRUPTION. Secondary corruption, as explained in Chapter 6 (partisanship in the absence of statesmanship), may also be an important explanatory factor in accounting for Ghana's persistent poverty. The failure to keep accounts, combined with mismanagement, facilitates the theft of public funds. The "root causes," according to Armstrong (1996, 124), "may lie in the environment and governance frameworks in which the institutions function."

While reports of the Auditor-General reveal substantial evidence of embezzlements of funds and failure to comply with established procedures for the purchase of supplies and equipment, judicial or administrative measures to correct the situation are seldom taken. Government reports also acknowledge that "blatant collusion between importers and officials have sadly become rather pervasive" (1994 budget statement reported in Jebuni 1994, 70). Thus, "failure to take public action on allegations of abuses creates a credibility problem for government," thereby reducing its capacity to control the irresponsible behavior of office holders (Jebuni 1994, 69).

When Ghanaian leaders want to reform administration, they can do so. Between 1983 and 1988, tax revenues went up from 4.6 percent of GDP to about 12 percent (Jebuni 1994). While this reform partly resulted from reorganization and more rational policies, it also benefited from employment of people committed to the program, using a bonus system that was tied to a certain proportion of the additional revenues collected.

However, with so much government funds being stolen or wasted, business leaders often see the increased efforts to raise taxes as a form of thievery. "Today, private businesses are still concerned about losing property and being subject to arbitrary tax audits" (Leechor 1994, 189). During the 1980s, Ghanaian local authorities were given tax collecting powers with soldiers used for enforcement; but, because they failed to provide promised services, "citizens do not see why they should pay for services they do not receive" (Garnett, Merrill, and Miller 1988, 25). Even in parts of Accra, electricity is sporadic and water is unavailable most of each week (Buckley 1996, A12).

"It is difficult," for example, "to fire a teacher for chronic absence or drunkenness, let alone for being a poor teacher" (World Bank OED

1994a, 10). This may partly explain why it is, according to a recent USAID study, that only some 2 percent of sixth grade primary students were able to answer correctly more than 60 percent of relatively simple mathematics and English questions (Armstrong 1996, 87).

Corruption and mismanagement also exist in South Korea. A small business owner often needs to bribe bankers to get loans (Aliber 1994, 347). The use of "false-names" for financial transactions remains widespread, despite efforts of recent presidents to stop the practice (Park 1994, 198). "At present, wealth-related taxes affect only a small proportion of taxpayers because wealth is unevenly distributed, and many people who should be paying taxes are able to avoid them" (Park 1994, 216). The underutilization of property taxes in Korea is both a cause and a consequence of corruption. Likewise, the persistent demand for political contributions ("quasi-taxes") is used by businesses to justify underreporting of income (Park 1994, 221).

Nevertheless, reform efforts have been persistent enough in Korea, combined with strong governance, to keep corruption somewhat under control. For example, according to Whalley (1994, 246), "the tax system has slowly matured toward that of an OECD country. . . ." The latest scandal involving President Kim Young Sam, his son (Kim Hyun Chul), and the collapse of the Hanbo steel company, includes accusations of bribery, dubious business and bank transactions, and tax fraud. As noted earlier, a combination of governmental carelessness and corruption probably contributed to the economic crisis of November, 1997. Yet, what is significant is that the press is now willing and able to investigate and report on these accusations. Cabinet members are no longer mere functionaries; and state prosecutors "have shown a strong degree of independence from political control" (THE ECONOMIST, May 24, 1997, 37–8).

Although authoritarianism, patronage, and corruption may be no less evident in South Korea than Ghana, they appear to be less dysfunctional. The reasons, as here indicated, include: (1) the use of soft forms of power (persuasion and incentives) along with coercion and intimidation; (2) the combining of meritocracy with patron-client relationships; and (3) the acceptance and enforcement of rules to control corruption. Likewise, while South Korea may have depended just as much as Ghana on the public sector, "self-reliance and ultimately internationally competitive performance were expected, and the authorities were not patient with non-performers" (Kim and Leipziger 1992, 27).

Ultimately, I have no other explanation for Ghana's poverty than the one presented here: that Ghana lacks South Korea's strong commitment to development. Evidence for this point (if more is needed) can be seen in the following examples:

THE VALUE ADDED TAX (VAT). The effort to introduce a VAT (set at 17.5 percent of the price of many commodities and services) by Ghana's Minister of Finance Dr. Kwesi Botchwey in February 1995 could be considered quite rational. However, it was done carelessly, without proper consultation with business and community groups (Berry 1995, xxxvii). It led on May 11, 1995 to the largest protest demonstration in Accra since the Rawlings regime came to power. Five people were killed, and many others were injured. Eventually (June, 1995), the government was forced to return to a national sales tax.

South Korea, in contrast, introduced a VAT in 1977; but the government took two years to prepare for its implementation (Choi 1991). Nationwide tryout exercises were carried out on three separate occasions before the changeover to VAT. Along with a consultation and information program, it expanded and retrained its tax administration staff. A staff handbook was prepared in anticipation of questions by staff and taxpayers.

While difficulties and criticisms remain, the VAT is considered relatively successful and an improvement over the indirect taxes it replaced. In the process, however, the government had to do what would even be more difficult in Ghana—replace the practice of bargaining with a system of record keeping and attaching price tags. Otherwise, there is no way to avoid large-scale tax evasion, such as exists in Ghana, while decreasing in South Korea.

PAMSCAD. Considering the lackadaisical attitude apparent among Ghana's leaders, efforts to shift blame for the problems and inadequate progress from these leaders to the IMF, the World Bank, and the international economy are misdirected (Herbst 1993). While it is certainly true that the government has had to cut back on subsidies and programs for the poor, it is also true that Ghana's major effort to help the poor (PAMSCAD) was so poorly administered that it had to be largely abandoned, despite the commitment by 13 donors in 1988 of nearly US $85 million. A 1990 multi-donor evaluation found the efforts of PAMSCAD to have been relatively ineffective in "mitigating the social cost of adjustment" (World Bank OED 1995, 99).

URBAN SANITATION. My conclusion—that it is governmental lethargy more than anything else that is undermining progress in Ghana—can also be supported by reference to urban health. Ghana's urban poor are clearly in bad health, with employed adults (primarily urban) in 1988/89 reporting 3.6 days of illness each month, whereas adults in Indonesia (who are also very poor and deprived of public utilities) claimed illness only 1.0 days/month in 1978 (Chhibber ET AL. 1993, 23). While much more might be spent on curative health care in Ghana, this would be largely wasted without major improvements in water and sanitation.

In Kumasi, where there are almost no sewerage systems for about 600,000 people, conditions are especially bad (Whittington ET AL. 1992). Although waterborne sanitation remains too expensive, a potentially effective system of improved pit latrines was introduced during the 1980s by a local government-supported political organization, charging a small fee for management and expansion of the system. However, because about half of the funds received were lost by mismanagement, not enough was spent to maintain and expand the system. This was then another example of a "lost opportunity." The broader question of what can be done to stimulate more enthusiasm for development within unmotivated countries will be left to the next and final chapter of this book. However, I will end here with this narrower question: how much should foreign aid donors be pushing Ghana for reform?

The World Bank's Evaluation Department (OED 1995, 41) notes that, while Ghana's economic performance has been in many respects counterproductive, it is impossible to know the potential impact of a tougher Bank approach. It therefore concludes that "it is better to have a relatively 'soft' program that is owned by the Government than a 'harder' one not so owned." Consequently, there is some indication that Bank staff are "giving higher priority to getting new projects launched than to getting ongoing projects implemented satisfactorily" (World Bank OED 1995, 41). For example, in several of its projects, the Bank has relaxed its requirement that the Ghanaian government provide appropriate counterpart funds. While this practice may be an expedient response to Ghana's economic difficulties and slow project disbursement, it goes "against sustainability and accountability objectives" (Armstrong 1996, 124).

While I agree that a heavyhanded approach would be counterproductive, I believe we should recognize that governments will respond to reasonable pressure, if public opinion can also be reached. Gyimah-Boadi (1994, 84) points out that, within Ghana, supporters of democratization have been encouraged when political conditions, such as transparency, accountability, and good governance, are attached to loans and foreign assistance by international financial institutions and Western donors.

Because I believe Ghana's apathy to be inexcuseable, I see no reason to let it off the hook. If the possibilities presented in the next chapter are relevant to Ghana, more effective foreign aid might then be useful because, as it is, Ghana's bureaucracy is so weak that it cannot productively use more foreign aid. "By end 1992 the undisbursed aid pipeline exceeded US $1 billion" (World Bank OED 1995, 46). When Ghana's leaders eventually become serious about development, they will hopefully find relevant the Korean experience, as here presented.

CHAPTER 10

Conclusion
Treating Political Illness

INTRODUCTION

In Chapter 6, I introduced the concept of "political illness," which, as I see it, is a manifestation or form of secondary corruption—the situation under which governance is too weak to control excessive partisanship or greed. In using the concept of political illness, my thinking has been affected by teaching American urban studies and studying the problem of homelessness or vagrancy.

As I often told my students during my professorial years, "it is as difficult to help highly impoverished countries as it is to help the vagrants in American urban centers." Inasmuch as many vagrants suffer from various forms of mental illness or social pathology (alcoholism, drug addiction, schizophrenia, retardation, etc.), it is impossible to help them become self-supporting without getting deep into their psychological and social problems. Going beyond charity may be impossible in most cases, as Jencks (1994, 122) points out; but we have to try to balance compassion and prudence, using a mixture of experimentation, incentives, persuasion, medical and psychological care, educational opportunities, and occasional coercion.

Likewise, we need to be equally realistic in dealing with the poorest countries of the world, particularly the 79 countries that (as of 1996) received World Bank International Development Association (IDA) funding, amounting to between $6 and $7 billion a year (for which about half goes to Africa) on highly concessional terms (practically no interest charges and repayment over fifty years). The average per capita income of these countries is about $400—just over one dollar a day. About half

305

of these countries are in Africa, and nearly one-third of the beneficiaries are in South Asia.

The nations eligible for IDA funds make up 57 percent of the world's population. However, if we include Latin America, particularly Brazil and Central America, where a poverty line of US $2 per person per day is often used, we find ourselves thinking about nations with about perhaps two-thirds of the world's population. Altogether, according to OECD calculations, 80 percent of the world's population will be living in developing countries in the year 2000, of which about 16 percent (more than a billion) will be in absolute poverty and despair.

Of course, there is an affluent minority in even the poorest countries. However, the World Bank estimates about 30 percent of the World's population to be living below US $1 a day in developing and transitional economies (World Bank 1996, 4). Despite evidence of economic improvement in many countries, the gap between LDCs and MDCs may be growing (Korten 1995). During the 1980s, the number of people living in poverty increased by 42 percent, while the population increased by only 22 percent. In 1950, the wealthiest 20 percent of the world's population had an income that was 30 times higher than that of the poorest 20 percent. By 1990, this ratio had increased to 60. While the richest fifth has more than 80 percent of the world's wealth, the poorest fifth has less than 1.5 percent.

In this book, as noted in the Introduction, I have tried to avoid definite or unqualified predictions. Nevertheless, I believe that qualified predictions, taking into consideration many factors and dimensions, are quite appropriate and even essential, if the social sciences are to be useful. Let me, therefore, make such a qualified prediction:

If those of us in MDCs fail to effectively facilitate the development of LDCs (as explained in Chapter 1), the following consequences, among others, are likely: (1) the gap between MDCs and LDCs will grow; (2) there will be dysfunctional emigration pressures and immigration difficulties; (3) the need to deal with such problems as civil war, terrorism, and international criminal behavior will increase; (4) economic opportunities for both rich and poor countries will be lost; and (5) there will be a greater likelihood of international conflicts affecting all countries in an increasingly interconnected world. Yet, providing effective foreign aid means treating political illness.

Using the concept of political illness, I will concentrate on perhaps the most perplexing "mystery of development" examined in this book:

what can be done to help these countries that suffer from it? My thinking about this question was facilitated by my independent research at the World Bank in the spring and summer of 1996, during which I presented to between 70 and 80 Bank staff members a memorandum, entitiled, "Finding Results Oriented Approaches."

The objective of this memo was to follow-up President Wolfensohn's efforts "to make the Bank a more effective, results-oriented institution," as reported in the March 30, 1996 WASHINGTON POST. According to Blustein (1996, 11, 26), Wolfensohn has been particularly disturbed by the determination of the Bank's evaluators that a majority of its projects are unlikely to prove sustainable (especially after a long period without foreign assistance) and that the share of projects judged unsatisfactory has risen since the beginning of the 1980s from 15 percent to 37.5 percent.

In meeting Wolfensohn's challenge, I included examples of "proactive" projects and approaches, hoping thereby to expand my understanding of possibilities. I also wanted to facilitate the meetings of the Washington D.C. Chapter of the Society for International Development, particularly its Development Administration Workgroup, for which I am responsible.

The proactive approaches I had in mind included variations of ideas stemming from the famous 1992 book by Osborne and Gaebler. Mike Stevens, whom I had worked for in 1994 in doing a study for the Bank on political corruption (which I eventually took advantage of for Chapter 6), emphasized the need for a "framework for analysis." Such a framework is also essential in overcoming the theoretical weakness of the "reinventing government" approach popularized by Osborne and Gaebler (see Fox 1996).

Using political elasticity (PE) theory (as presented in this book), I suggest that what is valid about the Osborne and Gaebler approach is its emphasis on intensifying and integrating or alternating incentives and disincentives. As such, foreign aid should never be an "entitlement." It should be wanted and worked for—demand, rather than supply driven. Requiring competition at all levels and in every way (among countries, cities, communities, private and public organizations, etc.) for available assistance is therefore appropriate. And assistance should be reduced or terminated when confronted by persistent or egregious failure, mismanagement, and contractual violation.

Yet, there is another aspect of PE theory that must be emphasized— the importance of political software or the quality of relations between leaders and followers. For example, in Chapter 7, I noted that, under World Bank pressure, the Ugandan government was forced to allow private traders to compete with the inefficient Coffee Marketing Board. This action proved very helpful to Uganda's coffee growers, particularly its poor farmers.

However, in many countries, these private traders are so poorly regulated and supervised that farmers suffer dreadfully. In the Ivory Coast, for example, farmers are often cheated in various ways by traders, according to a 1993 study: "Absent an umpire to guard against collusion among merchants, the farmers had no way to trust that the prices offered were fair market prices, and resentment over real or imagined cheating boiled right below the surface" (Widner 1993, 310).

Enthusiasts for reinventing government often neglect the role that the public sector must play for any progress to be made, as noted in Chapter 5. This is why I insist that any "success story" having to do with managed competition or private sector sponsorship include the need for political software development. After all, to give another example, why should a private contractor in Bangladesh undertake a public sector contract when there are likely to be long delays (amounting to two years) in getting approval and payment for the work, combined with corruption and confusion (Hasan and Saadat 1996, 113)?

Let me therefore mention again (and, I promise, for the last time) the commonsensical steps required for better governance, including acceptable goals, qualified personnel, training, legitimacy, delegation of responsibility, motivation and competition, supervision, independent spheres of authority, and conflict-resolution procedures. While I agree with David Gordon (1993, 126) that "nowhere in the world has fundamental reform ever been substantially driven by external actors," I believe that ANYTHING WHICH IMPROVES GOVERNANCE IS A STEP IN THE RIGHT DIRECTION. This assertion, stemming from PE theory, suggests small windows of opportunity that might at least be investigated. (Inasmuch as this chapter is a review as well as a conclusion, I will occasionally hark back to points and examples previously presented.)

THE POLITICAL WALLS OF NATIONAL IMPOVERISHMENT

In 1993, the useful book, HEMMED IN, edited by Thomas Callaghy and John Ravenhill, appeared, having to do with the political constraints limiting the possibilities for African development. I believe these constraints also undermine the efforts of impoverished countries generally to improve their standard of living. At the same time, foreign aid donors (with the World Bank particularly in mind) are also "hemmed in" by various constraints. Until the following interacting constraints are adequately understood, we cannot expect to effectively treat political illness:

A SUFFOCATING PUBLIC SECTOR. In Africa, Ravenhill points out (1993, 35), politicians have long relied upon "the state's patronage network, especially its ability to provide employment to urban schoolleavers." In Kenya, for example, "there are severe political pressures to use government employment as a means of coping with the country's growing unemployment problem" (Lofchie 1993, 415). In Cameroon, public sector employment grew from 1960 to 1990 by about 9% a year, expanding from 20,000 in the early 1960s to nearly 200,000 by the end of the 1980s (van de Walle 1993, 362).

Outside of Africa, we have the same situation, with the civil service frequently accounting for 30 percent of total employment. In Bangladesh, employment in the public sector more than doubled between 1971 and 1992, amounting to an annual compounded growth rate of 3.6 percent, compared to the population growth rate of about 2.5 percent (Hasan and Saadat 1996, 18). In Egypt in the 1980s, State Owned Enterprises (SOEs) accounted for about 14 percent of total employment, with nearly 40 percent employed in the public sector.

Whereas the average industrial public sector spends about 20 percent of its income on wages and 10 percent on general administration, governments in Africa and many other parts of the world spend about 30 percent of their income on wages and 25 percent on general administration (World Bank OED 16040 1996, 77). LDCs typically devote twice as much of their total public expenditure on capital projects (often neglecting maintenance in the process) as MDCs do, and half as much on such basic services as health. Many countries devote more of their budgets to their military concerns than to their education and health sectors.

In the world's poorest countries, SOEs account for an average of 14 percent of GDP. In Bangladesh, in FY 1992/93, the combined losses of SOEs were about US $500 million, which would have enabled expenditures on education to go up from 0.9 to 3 percent of GDP or health expenditures from 0.2 to 2.3 percent of GDP. "Diverting SOE operating subsidies to basic education, for example, would increase central government education expenditures by 50 percent in Mexico, 74 percent in Tanzania, 160 percent in Tunisia, and 550 percent in India" (Shirley ET AL. 1995, 47).

There is, of course, a relationship between a "bloated bureaucracy" and an "inept bureaucracy." To describe a typical LDC bureaucracy as a "civil service" is to stretch unrealistically the meaning of that term inasmuch as such a bureaucracy tends to be "precivil" and, as such, primarily concerned with maximizing budget share rather than the public interest (Boyle and Silsby 1996). The proper handling of performance contracts is "hard to achieve where civil service pay is low and responsibilities are often shifted around for political reasons, a common situation in developing countries" (Shirley ET AL. 1995, 256). In 1988 in Uganda, for example, the salary of a permanent secretary was only three percent of what it had been in 1977. Under these circumstances, training could not be taken seriously. The World Bank found that it was necessary to send 3–4 Kenyan civil servants abroad to ensure that one would return.

CRONY STATISM. In the Callaghy and Ravenhill book, we find frequent mention of "crony statism," emphasizing import orientation, overvalued exchange rates, black markets for foreign exchange, favoring of importers over exporters, and the maintenance of urban support at the expense of rural development (Gordon 1993, 96–97). Because these arrangements are intended to enrich those in power, they obviously discourage reform.

In understanding the relationship of crony statism to political illness, we might use as an example (also see Chapter 1) the relationahip between "vampire states" (see Ravenhill 1993, 23) and "zombie banks," as pointed out in a 1996 World Bank study of Tanzania (Eastern Africa Department 1996). According to this study, the National Bank of Commerce lost about US $186 million in FY 94 largely as a result of bad loans to parastatals. Checks were often cleared through a kickback arrangement with bank clerks. This meant that development expenditure (including desparately needed counterpart funds for better living conditions) declined from 4.6 percent of GDP in FY94 to 2.8 percent in FY95. Consequently, education expenditure was during the early 1990s among the lowest in Africa (l.9 percent of GDP), with public secondary school enrollment stagnant at about 5 percent. Shirley ET AL. (1995,

2) point out that in Egypt, Peru, Senegal, and Turkey, "a mere 5 percent reduction in SOE operating costs would reduce the fiscal deficit by about one-third." However, there is seldom a strong constituency in favor of SOE reform. In regard to Bangladesh, Hasan and Saadat 1996, 7) note the "raw" power of the state: "Consumers and citizens are too scared to complain as there is little redress if the monopoly provider harasses."

In Latin America, Persaud and Malik (1994, 246) ask, how can those who benefit from corrupt arrangements be convinced to undertake reform? "How does one convince city council members to vote for improved tax collection or increases in such taxes when these members are the owners of most of the lands which would be so taxed?" Boyle (1996, 4) poses a similar question in regard to Karachi, Pakistan where "the bureaucracy was bloated, public enterprises were heavily subsidized, and financial management and reporting practices were weak, as was political leadership." Because of the disconnection between what society wanted and needed and the organizations created to carry out these desires and needs, "many of those seeking solutions have become frustrated" (Boyle 1996, 2).

DISCOURAGEMENT OF THE PRIVATE SECTOR. With the public sector so bloated and inefficient, the private sector becomes undermined in various ways. "In the 1980s," Berry (1993, 251) points out, "African governments found themselves unable to maintain basic infrastructure and services, such as transportation, education and health." This meant, in the case of Zambia in 1985, that as much as one-third of the maize purchased from farmers was never collected. At the same time, foreign exchange intended for imports of diesel fuels, tires, and jute bags was "inexplicably diverted at the last minute" (Berry 1993, 252).

Farmers in Africa are generally discouraged when prices are low or when they cannot predict what prices are likely to be or whether payments are likely to be made. But even when prices are "right," Herbst (1993a, 337) suggests, farmers cannot overcome bottlenecks in transportation systems for such basic inputs as seed and fertilizer. In Cameroon, as in Nigeria (noted in Chapter 1), the state sector was so parasitic that the oil windfall, beginning in 1978, actually hindered productivity growth in the agricultural sector (van de Walle 1993, 358).

With the financial sector so weak and unreliable, manufacturing is just as hampered as agriculture. "Low on the agenda of priorities are the costs of importing the machinery required, the technical and managerial skills needed to operate factories, the technology used, the costs of production, the degree of protection needed, current and future levels of demand, and the degree of subsidy required for the products to be purchased" (Riddell 1993, 219). In Tanzania, for example, the share of the industrial sector in GDP remains at about 13 percent, which is a lower percentage than in the 1970s because of the inadequacy of infrastructure, market information, and entrepreneural skills and training (Eastern Africa Department 1996, 23).

In recent years, the World Bank has pushed privatization. However, private firms are not necessarily more efficient in the absence of a competitive market system. Private firms may encounter the same difficulties as encountered by SOEs—e.g., an inability to shed excess workers, to purchase needed inputs from the best or least expensive sources, and to ensure that agreed-upon payments are made. In the absence of a respected independent judiciary, who can compel a governmentally favored private organization to keep promises and contractual obligations? "In the case of privatized, regulated monopolies, new buyers who doubt government commitment may withhold needed investments because they fear that their assets will be expropriated" (Shirley ET AL., 1995, 111).

DECENTRALIZATION IMPEDIMENTS. In Chapter 4, I point out that in LDCs, suffering from political inelasticity, leaders fear decentralization and, at the same time, create conditions under which forms of centralization and decentralization become ineffective. Decentralization, for example, requires an ability and willingness of central governments to pay for contracted services. Yet, commitment is often doubtful in LDCs (Shirley ET AL. 1995, 256). This means that it is difficult for foreign-sponsored reform efforts to bypass central governments to utilize or improve the operations of local governments and Private Voluntary Organizations (PVOs) or Non-Governmental Organizations (NGOs).

Because problems of local government have been analyzed in previous chapters, particularly Chapter 4, I will not here say much more about them. However, insofar as foreign aid agencies rely increasingly upon PVOs and NGOs, the difficulties of doing so should be emphasized. As a generalization, we can say that, the weaker and more insecure a government is, the more problematic the relationships are likely to be between this government and NGOs or PVOs. This generalization is increasingly linked to a relationship between the quality of governance and the quality of civil society, referring to the extent or nature of organizational life. In regard to Sub-Saharan Africa, van de Walle (1993, 388) points out that "there are fewer independent civic organizations . . . than anywhere else in the developing world."

Examples of problems likely to be encountered by World Bank staff in utilizing NGOs is found in a 1996 Bank publication by Carroll, Schmidt, and Bebbington. In Brazil an important micro-enterprise NGO encountered a staff revolt and was forced into bankruptcy because of prolonged delays in government payments. In Pakistan, the founders of two successful NGOs were forced out as their boards were packed with government appointees. In India, the successful AMUL dairy cooperative model has at various times and places been threatened by the reluctance of state governments to support fully the concept of farmer control. In the Philippines, community development was undermined by the unanticipated replacement of a senior official in the Department of Environment and Natural Resources sympathetic to NGO participation with one that "wanted to dictate to the NGO and the indigenous groups what they should be doing under the project" (Carroll, Schmidt, and Bebbington 1996, 41).

On the one hand, Bank staff need government support to enforce standards, contracts, and loan repayments. On the other hand, there is a danger of "dancing with the state," insofar as the state attempts, directly, a takeover or, indirectly, an excessive reduction of or interference with autonomy (Carroll, Schmidt, and Bebbington 1996, 48).

Official corruption can challenge NGOs and PVOs in various ways. In Cameroon, for example, members of cooperatives have lost their interest in arabica coffee because of fraud and the waste of money on prestige expenditures (van der Walle 1993, 370–1). In India, the rural cooperative credit system has been undermined by "political interference in the form of promises to write off loans or to waive interest dues" (Guhan 1995, 50–51).

ETHNIC, RACIAL, AND RELIGIOUS DIVERSITY. A recent World Bank publication (Easterly and Levine 1995, 13) notes that, while three of East Asia's most economically successful countries are relatively homogenous, "fourteen out of the fifteen most ethnically diverse societies in the world are in Africa." Of course, one can point to economically and politically distressed countries lacking such ethnic diversity, such as Somalia in Africa and Haiti in Latin America. Yet, there is no doubt that, especially when ethnic or racial differences coincide with those of religion, occupation, and class, one is likely to find serious obstacles to economic and political development.

Nationalism is weakly developed in many parts of the world, causing officials to be much more concerned with particularistic interests than the general interest (Callaghy 1993, 474). "Consequently, upon getting into office, whether by democratic or other means, jobs and other benefits would generally be awarded to those affiliated with the group in power, with existing staff either shunted aside or fired" (Persaud and Malik 1994, 247).

In Kenya, according to Lofchie (1993, 442–443), governmental actions have been taken to redistribute the wealth and privilege of the Kikuyu to benefit the Kalenjin followers of President Moi. In Guyana, much of the opposition to economic liberalization has come about because of the fear of the dominant Afro-Guyanese party (the PNP) that this would benefit Asian entrepreneurs who also happened to be supporters of the opposition PPP (Harrigan, 1991, 385). "In Cameroon, the government twice turned down an offer to buy the national airlines because the buyers were from the wrong ethnic group" (World Bank OED Report No. 13273 1994, 29). Prejudice against the Chinese minority in Southeast Asia, against the Asian minority in East Africa, and against the Lebanese minority in West Africa have in various ways delayed or adversely affected privatization efforts.

DEMOCRATIZATION PRESSURES. In Chapter 7, I note the increasing international pressure for democratization. Turning back to this chapter, particularly to my summary of the World Bank publication by Husain (1994), I point to the following factors often discouraging economic reform: the opposition of the elite, the danger of appearing unpopular, and the lack of capacity for reform.

In Chapter 9, I show how Ghanaian leaders used elections in 1992 and 1996 as justification for irresponsible expenditures and pay increases, downsizing failures, and persistent inflation and mismanagement. In Cameroon, as in Ghana, there has been a pro-democracy movement; but, according to van de Walle (1993, 386), the leader (referring to Paul Biya) "has increasingly become little more than the prisoner of his ruling alliance." This ruling alliance includes: consumers of imported goods, urban groups opposed to reform, politically powerful state agents, and the social or ethnic elite favored by the leader.

In the Philippines, as in so many other countries, it was hoped that democratization would bring about reform in the telecommunications sector; but those who benefited from the statis quo "retained enough influence through political institutions (such as Congress) to forestall the introduction of competition or other reforms in the sector" (Shirley ET AL. 1995, 166). Here, as elsewhere, those who might gain from economic and institutional reform resulting from liberal democracy can seldom compete with those who could potentially be hurt by the effects of this reform. Because there is not yet a strong merit system or other forms of protection in the Philippines, civil servants continue to be under the pressure of politicians "to alter a decision that they do not like" (Campos and Root 1996, 154). Thus, politicians do not even have to justify their efforts to intercede on behalf of influential or wealthy groups.

The costs of reform, according to Gordon (1993, 116), tend to be far more sharp and focused than the benefits. In one Latin American country, for example, "fourteen government ministers were impeached and removed from office over a ten-year period because they advocated or supported proposals for such policies as increasing the price of petroleum and floating the exchange rate" (Persaud and Malik 1994, 249).

With 5–6 people dependent on each civil servant (as in Senegal), it is extremely difficult to persuade governments to reduce their public sectors (Dia 1993, 6). Where public sector employees are prepared to resort to strikes, demonstrations, or other forms of civil disobedience, the danger to the leadership may be so costly "that reform becomes unfeasible" (Shirley ET AL., 1995, 191). Moreover, according to Malcolm Holmes (1996, 36), the public service ethic is so weak that it is impossible for the World Bank or any other external body to "mandate a performance orientation if the government has little or no interest in following through on it."

If, at the same time, foreign donors are pushing democratization, reform is likely to become more difficult. Consequently, "political obstacles are the main reason that state-owned enterprise reform has made so little headway in the last decade" (Shirley ET AL., 1995, 23). In regard to Bangladesh, for example, Hasan and Saadat (1996, 143) write: "Why should bureaucrats and politicians reform a structure which allows them a secure and comfortable living in an environment full of uncertainty?"

THE LIMITATIONS OF FOREIGN ASSISTANCE

Peter Boone of the London School of Economics is among the leading critics of foreign aid (THE ECONOMIST December 10, 1994, 69). He argues that foreign aid is neither promoting growth nor improving the lives of the poorest. While Francophone countries have receive far higher levels of foreign support tnan their Anglophone neighbors, they have little to show for it. What Africa needs, according to Jeffrey Sachs (1996), the director of the Harvard Institute for International Development, is not more foreign aid, but rather, open markets for their exports.

I would agree with Professors Boone and Sachs that foreign assistance is not the answer to the problems of LDCs, particularly in Africa, if I were convinced that LDCs could be more productive if only there were profitable markets available. The truth is, however, (as this book continuously points out) what retards these countries is, not the absence of profitable markets for their goods, but the absence of the capacity to produce goods—in other words, the weakness of public administration and politics.

For example, Tanzania has far greater tourist potential than Kenya but earns only a fraction of Kenya's income from tourism because of the inadequacy of service staff, internal air transport, roads, power, hotels, and communication facilities (Eastern Africa Department 1996, 18). Until the government of Tanzania becomes serious about these problems, it cannot meet market demand.

This gets us back to Tanzania's political illness and to the question of how to overcome it. Judging by the fact that, under Robert McNamara during the 1970s, the World Bank lent more to Tanzania per person in IDA funds "than to any other country on earth," foreign aid clearly is not by itself a cure (Blustein 1996, 25).

As is the case with most people writing about development, I have mixed feelings about foreign assistance. While I am aware, for example, that foreign aid, including the "green revolution" of the 1960s, has significantly reduced starvation in South Asia, I must also acknowledge that "South Asia's social indicators are among the worst in the developing world" (World Bank 1996, 9). Surveys of India find that nearly half of the adult population remains illiterate and on calory-deficient diets (Burns 1996, A10). The situation in Bangladesh, as presented by Hasan and Saadat (1996), is summarized at the end of this chapter.

Because the World Bank is the most important source of foreign aid,

I believe it is important to understand the constraints under which its staff works. At the end of this section, I note the important contribution that Bank President Wolfensohn's "war on corruption" could make. However, the following indicate difficulties that go far beyond the proposals (reorganization, better public relations, more staff training, and faster loan approval) currently being considered by Mr. Wolfensohn (THE ECONOMIST, April 20, 1996, 63–64):

THE DISDAIN FOR POLITICS. There is, on the one hand, a growing attention to issues of governance at the World Bank, including human rights, the legal framework, a free press, civil service reform, military expenditure, and corruption. Between FY 1994 and FY 1996, Bank loans to improve public sector management tripled to nine percent of all loans (Blustein 1996, 26). Between FY 1987 and FY 1996, the Bank undertook 145 operations with major civil service components in 68 countries, two-third of them in Africa (Nunberg 1996, 2). On the other hand, staff members continue to be admonished "not to interfere in a country's internal political affairs" (Operations Policy Department 1993, 3).

The resulting confusion can be found in a book by Shihata (1991), the Bank's Vice President and General Counsel, suggesting, that, while considerations of "governance" should be taken into account in the Bank's operations, "politics" should not be. Yet, he defines governance (p. 56) as "the exercise of political power to manage a nation's affairs." Consequently, I have to agree with Rich (1994, 76) that the Bank's definition of "politics" and "political influence" seems to come out of ALICE IN WONDERLAND: "whatever it does is by definition not political because it says so."

Because Bank staff maintain an apolitical orientation, their understanding of reality can be quite naive. "The Bank has frequently supported technical administrative fixes for what are fundamentally political problems" (Nunberg 1996, 6). Even THE ECONOMIST (June 29, 1996, 81) criticized the 1996 WORLD DEVELOPMENT REPORT (FROM PLAN TO MARKET) for being one-dimensional in its analysis of the privatization efforts of post-communist countries.

To be fair to the Bank, however, there has been a recent realization of the importance of politics in analyzing economic development. The 1995 Bank study, BUREAUCRATS IN BUSINESS (Shirley ET AL), emphasizes the importance of political desirability, political feasibility, and political credibility in reforming state-owned enterprises. The unusual nature of this study is noted in the "Foreword" to this study by Michael Bruno, the Bank's Chief Economist: "While this is a significant contribution, we should also bear in mind that our analytical knowledge of political processes, though arguably older, is less complete than that of economic forces and motives."

The Bank's apolitical orientation may be due more to the fact that economics is the religion of the Bank than to the preclusion of politics by the Bank's Articles of Agreement. In any case, Bank staff feel more comfortable focusing their attention "almost entirely upon quantitative aspects of project design and implementation rather than on the underlying sociocultural and political context" (Persaud and Malik 1994, 247).

While Bank staff pay a great deal of attention to policy reform in their structural adjustment lending, Richard Moore (1995, 157) contends that they seldom focus on institutional development for successful implementation: "Often, limited groundwork is done with regard to a realistic understanding of the complexity of the institutional, political, and economic impacts that inhere in policy reform."

It is not very easy or pleasant for the client, as Boyle and Silsby (1996, 19) point out, "to probe beneath the waterline" into the institutional frameworks of governance; but, the failure to do so accounts for the fact that (p. 1), "after almost fifty years of development work in South Asia, the record on project sustainability and institutional development is not encouraging." Moreover, leaders in LDCs are quick to proclaim "political interference," when Bank staff go too deeply into the underlying reasons for mismanagement.

Ironically, as I will point out later in this chapter, Bank staff might be more effective if they were less anxious to determine the form and pace of projects. In other words, if assistance took the form of "flexible loans," with borrowing governments themselves deciding on their priorities and the amounts and timing of their inputs, the Bank might not be so vulnerable to "political interference" accusations. Of course, in subsidizing these inputs in the form of IDA loans, Bank staff would remain in a powerful position to influence decision-making.

STAFF WEAKNESSES. The lack of training of World Bank staff in fields other than economics, business administration, and technical subjects is often brought up as a reason for their failures of analysis and implementation. Bank staff, according to Gopal and Marc (1994, 34), are not trained to deal with "community participation or sensitized to the fact that supporting grassroots community related procurement has a number of implications for project design." Salmen (1995, 14) adds that "Bank management traditionally provided few incentives or rewards for culturally-sensitive project or policy work." Moreover, beneficiary assessment seems contrary to the Bank's dominant culture (which is top-down and quantitative rather than bottom-up and qualitative).

In searching for opportunities to improve governance, the World Bank may need to look more carefully at the way it operates. Coralie Bryant, in her 1993 study of Zambia pointed out that in the Africa Region, there were only ten Public Sector Management Staff. "Learning to work with indigenous institutions raises questions of staffing, capacity, research, and process," she wrote (p. 21), adding: "There are still too few Bank staff with management experience or professional education in management (and there are too few sociologists or anthropologists)."

Berkman (1995, 130) reports that management specialists remain a rarity on project preparation and appraisal missions. A 1995 OED study of monitoring and evaluation (Report No. 15222, 44) notes that few projects ever use specialist consultants for monitoring and that this aspect is usually underdesigned. In regard to the capacity to diagnose financial management systems, Siegelbaum (1996, 46) asserts that the Bankwide stock of professionally qualified financial management specialists "is now at a dangerously low level." Nunberg (1996, 15) adds that "staffing for civil service activities is often insufficient in numbers, inadequate in skills, and all too often, improvisational—utilizing staff from other disciplinary areas to pinch-hit as government reform specialists."

Stemming from my study of the relationship of politics to culture (presented in Chapter 8), I unsuccessfully advocated in 1992 the development of a "social science fund," using contributions from donor countries to hire social scientists (as against technical specialists) to work on World Bank projects. I was particularly influenced by the efforts of several Bank staff members. Larry Salmen (1987) had shown the usefulness of a "participation-observer-evaluation" approach, under which trained local evaluators study the perceptions, fears, and problems of a community undergoing a project. Michael Cernea had persuaded the Bank in 1984 to require that sociological appraisal be undertaken in the processing of projects (Kardam 1993).

According to a 1991 study by Cernea, projects that included social and cultural analysis had more than twice the economic rate of return as those with no or minimal social analysis. However, despite considerable funding for socio-cultural studies and for community participatory approaches, Bank staff continue to rely upon "econocratic or technocratic models" (Cernea 1991, 28, 30). "The professional culture of economists prevents them from seeing how culture matters at all" (Jones 1995, 273).

Most Bank staff continue to work out of Washington, D.C.; and they are shifted every three to five years. The fact that Bank field staff is so much smaller than that of the Agency for International Development, while financially far more important, is often a source of comment and criticism. In regard to agricultural reform in Ghana, Herbst (1993a, 352) argues that, only with a larger in-country staff, could the Bank develop the ties with society, institutional memory, and coordination with NGOs essential for long-term improvements.

The reliance on visiting missions meant, in the case of Mexico, that members were "fair game for everybody who wanted to to manipulate the missions—from project heads who warned staff not to relay bad news, to wily farmers who saw a chance to get a new round of concessions" (Environment Department 1995, 66). In South Asia, according to Guhan (1995, 69), Bank missions had to work almost exclusively with ministries of finance, which were reluctant to allow Bank staff to "run around."

The absence of appropriate staff, Bryant (1993, 11) points out, is only part of the problem: "At best, civil service reform is a slow process, not necessarily requiring much foreign exchange (which is what donors lend)." Therefore, this makes it unattractive to ambitious managers in Country Operations Departments.

Institutional Development (ID), according to Moore (1995, 159), "must be seen as a process." Because ID work in World Bank projects tends to be "an afterthought," implementation is often problematic. Moreover, the requisite "learning process" approach tends to be far more labor-intensive than the alternative "blueprint" approach and, as such, is generally considered unaffordable.

Without a considerable change in the incentive system, institutional and career goals will take precedence over the staff continuity required for the learning process approach (Bhatnagar 1992, 22). This incentive system particularly discourages attention to issues of poverty because of "a willingness on the part of the Bank's management to compromise a focus on poverty reduction in the name of maintaining good country relations and to be satisfied with lending operations that address aggregate growth with little attention to the distribution of growth" (Africa Region 1996, 110).

COUNTERPRODUCTIVE LENDING. The complaints of the Bank's own Staff Association regarding "an assembly-line approach to project preparation," the overemphasis on quantitative goals involving the lending of large sums and rapid disbursements, and the neglect of supervision and institutional development are found in an article by Clements (1993) but echoed in the World Bank OED 1992 EVALUATION RESULTS report. This is apparently an old problem.

Albert Hirschman (a highly respected economist) complained during the early 1950s that he had to come up "as soon as possible" with an ambitious economic development plan for Colombia, despite the fact that "no Colombian was to be found who had any inkling of how to go about it" (quoted in Rich 1994, 74). When Bank staff pointed out during the late 1970s and early 1980s that the Bank was lending more to Mexico than was consistent with its absorptive capacity, they found themselves "undercut by management tendency to over-rule them on appeal by the Mexicans" (World Bank OED Report No. 12923 1994, xxxiii).

In theory, Bank staff must avoid irresponsible lending. In practice, they often cannot do so. The Bank's country loan officers, Mosley, Harrigan, and Toye (1991, 72) explain, "are under intense pressure to meet country commitment targets, whatever the negotiating posture adopted by the recipient government, and to meet country disbursement targets however unpromising that government's subsequent implementation performance." The pressure on Bank managers comes simply from the fact that "those who fail to meet their projected loan volumes often find their budgets cut the following year" (Blustein 1996, 28). The need of the Bank to keep to a predictable lending schedule causes Bank staff, rather than officials in borrowing countries, to determine the selection, timing, and characteristics of projects. This practice partly results from the need to keep money flowing and partly from the fact that the Bank does not get enough good projects to appraise (Rich 1994, 68). The description of the World Bank as "a money-moving machine" (Rich 1994, 309) does not come simply from outraged Bank critics. It can be found in the famous 1992 critique of the Bank (OPTAINING RESULTS) by its then Vice President, Willi Wapenhans. As explained by Mosley, Harrigan, and Toye (1991), the pressure to lend arises because of its annual commitment to each borrowing country and its arrangements to procure these amounts from the world money markets.

Moreover, Bank project officers, international contractors and consultants, and host country personnel and organizations put pressure on Bank country staff to get projects approved and funds obligated as soon as possible and in a predictable way. "World Bank country desks are under strong pressure to spend, and thus earn a return on the money that has been budgeted for their use" (Harrigan 1991, 430). Consequently, there is no local ownership of projects. "The project-by-project, and donor-by-donor approach has sharply reduced government ownership of projects, which has proved fatal for the sustainability of many projects" (Harrold and Associates 1995, 3). An example of this can be found in a Philippine communal irrigation project, in which the task manager (Gunasekara 1995, 108) noted, "that because our country counterparts sometimes lacked commitment or capacity, we tended to seize the initiative and, with the borrower inadequately involved, we sometimes made most of the decisions and provided most of the expertise."

Another factor in this regard is the need to please powerful Bank shareholders, operating through their representatives on the board, who order: "Get such and such an amount of money to Mexico before the sun rises;" or, "You've got to get money to Russia, and if they can't find projects, you find them" (Blustein 1996, 28).

Counterproductive French foreign aid is often noted. For example, the World Bank's 1995 Country Strategy for Senegal "discusses the painful lessons learned from Senegal's easy access to external aid despite the inadequate implementation of improved policy" (Africa Region 1996, 78).

According to an informant, Bank staff were forbidden by an Egyptian education minister from even raising the possibility of examinations in an education project. Since American foreign aid was paying for this education project, no one objected, even though evaluation was impossible. Moreover, the real problem was overlooked—the fact that Egyptian teachers are paid so little that they manipulate examination results to force students to pay for private tutoring (THE ECONOMIST, January 25, 1997, 43).

The fact that so many of the Bank's borrowers are heavily in debt, not only to the World Bank itself, but also to the wealthy countries of the world, dynamically pushes the lending process. By the early 1990s, loans from the Bank and the IMF accounted for about a third of Africa's foreign debt (Rich 1994, 310). To keep these countries from massive default, the Bank had to keep increasing the volume of loans "so that net transfers over the short term from the Bank to the borrower remain positive" (Rich 1994, 79). (This situation is examined at the end of this chapter.)

Many governments recognize that the International Financial Institutions (IFIs) have "a vested interest in not declaring the countries to be in default" and, as such, to ignore threats of sanctions (Callaghy and Ravenhill 1993, 6). They therefore engage in "ritual dances" with the donor community, under which governments make "nominal commitments to programs" but have "little intention of carrying through the conditions" (Ravenhill 1993, 46). Conditionality becomes meaningless insofar as the IFIs "need both to lend and collect" and "do not really have the capabilities to monitor proliferating conditionality" (Callaghy and Ravenhill 1993, 526).

Because of the need to meet lending targets, "ultimatums are indeed rare in the history of policy-based lending" (Mosley, Harrigan and Toye 1991, 78). Officials in recipient countries are generally aware that "World Bank country desks are under strong pressure to spend, and thus earn a return on, the money that has been budgeted for their use" (Mosley 1991, 430). Consequently, violations of legal covenants tend to be ignored, according to a report on Bank projects in India (Guhan 1995, 44): "conditions are imposed and when the borrower fails to meet them, the conditions are relaxed or their deadlines are postponed."

During the 1980s, the Bank undertook "large, fast-disbursing adjustment loans to promote more rapid integration of borrowing countries into global markets so that they might earn still more hard currency to continue servicing their debt" (Rich 1994, 149). In some cases in Africa, structural adjustment has produced some real gains. However, according to Sachs (1996, 19), structural adjustment on the whole has been a failure: "For every case of a success story like Uganda, there are others in which democratisation and incipient market reforms have been reversed under the pressure of worsening economic conditions." International adjustment lending, according to Korten (1995, 165), has caused the international indebtedness of low-income countries to increase from $134 billion in 1980 to $473 billion in 1992, thereby nearly tripling their interest payment obligations.

The fact that adjustment lending is a fast-disbursing process is one of the reasons why it is often ineffective. This is pointed out in an evaluation study of the Bank's privatization efforts done by the World Bank

OED (Report No. 13273 1994, 69): "There is a mismatch between the timing of sale preparation (always time-consuming and frequently subject to factors outside the seller's control) and the fast-disbursing nature of adjustment loans."

Mosley (1991, 300) makes a similar point in reviewing the Bank's experience in Kenya during the 1980s: "institutional development is an objective which sits uncomfortably with quick-disbursing finance." While the World Bank constantly complained about Kenya's inadequate economic reform, there was no alternative to continuing the SAL program (Mosley 1991, 291).

THE NEGLECT OF IMPLEMENTATION. The dysfunctional impact of the Bank's need to meet annual resource transfer targets has often been noted. In regard to South Asia, Guhan (1995, 64) points out that "large investments and repeat projects have discouraged experimentation, lesson learning, and institution building, all of which would call for a more relaxed and reflective pace of lending." Moreover, the Bank's leverage in policy dialogue has been seriously reduced by its inflexibility.

Bank evaluation reports on Africa "suggest that the World Bank did not see, or played down, warning signs of inadequate commitment during implementation" (Schacter 1995, 341). In Latin America and the Caribbean, Persaud and Malik (1994, 249) assert that there is little attention to maintenance issues because "the tendency is to yield to borrowers' insistence upon financing for new operations."

Generalizing about the World Bank's "monitoring and evaluation," the Bank's Evaluation Department concludes: "overambitious demands; weak capacity; minimal institutional support; and poor follow-up lead to poor performance" (World Bank OED Report No. 15222 1995, 6). Yet, just as so many poor countries of the world are prevented from developing by handicaps of their own creation, the World Bank cannot escape the need to generate new projects and provide more funds rather than concentrate upon old projects and previous lending.

If the World Bank is to be more successful in institutional development, Schacter (1995, 343) writes, it is going to have "to address the issues in terms of what is motivating the relevant actors." This necessitates understanding and engaging top-level political actors. The failure to do so, according to de Regt (1995, 81), "has to do with the fact that until quite recently, the implementation culture had not really permeated the Bank."

The lack of emphasis on implementation is partly the result of the fact that "once it comes time to start implementation, reality sets in," Katherine Marshall, a manager in the Africa section, points out (quoted by Blustein 1996, 28). While Bank staff tend to be discouraged by problems of supervision, they are encouraged by the enthusiasm associated with new projects. In other words, it is more exciting to build bridges than to fix potholes. And there are often more funds available for developing new projects than for supervision.

An article by Picciotto and Weaving (1994) indicates that top Bank officials are encouraging staff to experiment with a "new project cycle" (called the "Picciotto cycle"), emphasizing adaptability, government commitment, capacity building, and effective monitoring. The first step of this cycle is to elicit the preferences and values of people who are to be affected by projects and policies. The second step is to fund a series of small pilot projects to test local leadership and provide information about the problems and tasks anticipated at a later stage. Based upon these first two steps, "mainstreaming" or nationwide implementation can be attempted, nurturing continued commitment of major stakeholders, decentralized methods, and reliance on markets and voluntary organizations.

It was hoped that the Picciotto cycle would reduce the percentage of Bank projects considered "unsustainable." However, as of 1996, efforts to use this approach were sporadic and dependent "largely on the initiatives of enterprising and committed individual staff members" (Carroll, Schmidt, and Bebbington (1996, 37).

A major impediment to the participatory approach, according to Carroll, Schmidt, and Bebbington (1996, 2), is "donor or government pressure to deliver services quickly." The fact that it can take several years to go through the approval process may actually intensify this pressure. The tendency of Bank staff to develop their projects quickly, confining their interactions largely to ministries of finance and, to a lesser extent, planning commissions and technical agencies, has meant that there is seldom "much sharing of the Bank's policy analyses and prescriptions with the media, nongovernmental organizations, and academia as part of a wider effort to mold opinion among the public at large, even in a country like India which offers good opportunities for doing so" (Guhan 1995, 68). In the case of a Structural Adjustment Loan to Guyana in the 1980s, Mosley (1991, 374) found that private sector groups, such as the Guyana Manufacturers' Association and the Guyana Electricity

Corporation, were ignored, "even though many important components of the program were aimed at this sector."

As I turn in the next section to possibilities of treating political illness, I want to share with readers my delight that President Wolfensohn is willing to confront the problems of corruption and governance. In his October, 1996 Annual Meeting Speech, his "focus on corruption was seen as the defining message of the speech and was interpreted as a significant shift in Bank policy" (Siegelbaum 1996, 2). The importance of better administration is the central theme of the 1997 WORLD DEVELOPMENT REPORT. For this purpose, a higher percentage of Bank staff are to be stationed in borrowing countries, and they are to be evaluated on the basis of project implementation. However, I agree with THE ECONOMIST (June 28, 1997, 77) that, while the Bank is making progress in analyzing the impediments to development, it "has not made as much progress with the answers."

POSSIBILITIES OF A PROACTIVE APPROACH

After the two previous sections, readers may understandably doubt that much can be done to treat political illness. In considering possibilities, I have been influenced by the writing of two World Bank experts on governance (Heaver and Israel 1986), in which they advocate breaking a project into small operations, with continuation of the project or future assistance dependent on results. Political commitment can be encouraged, they suggest, by: insisting upon commitment prior to a project; isolating opposition to reform; and evaluating progress based upon performance.

What Heaver and Israel advocate—turning aid off and on—is, of course, practically difficult because the World Bank does not have the same power over a sovereign country as a commercial bank over a private borrower. Consequently, many countries have been able to ignore Bank conditionality requirements, according to Mosley, Harrigan and Toye (1991, 67), "a fact of which other borrowers are well aware."

Moreover, it also intensifies problems of administering economic development (Nelson 1992, 45). The questions that are raised for Bank staff were most clearly presented in a 1994 World Bank OED study of industrial sector reform in East Africa (Report No. 12922, 128): "Should the Bank continue to support a vacilating and ineffectual political leadership whose policies are not working . . . ? Or, should the Bank retrench, question the wisdom of further involvement, and even suspend lending?"

As I indicated earlier, I believe that, using the Heaver and Israel approach (combined with that of Osborne and Gaebler), there are small windows of opportunity that need to be explored. In my search for them, I came across the following possibilities:

REQUIRING PRIOR REFORM. The standard Bank practice of developing Special Project Units after a project gets started has been often criticized (see Berg 1993). These units typically face resentment on the part of regular civil servants because of the salary premiums, training opportunities, and special privileges given to the unit staff and are therefore undermined or destroyed at the end of the project.

An alternative to using project units is suggested by the experience of Sunat, Peru's tax collecting agency (World Bank LAC 1994). With the assistance of the IMF and the Inter-American Development Bank, Sunat required in 1991 all of its staff (then, 3,025) to take a test to compete for 991 positions identified as essential. Those not taking or failing the test were transferred or encouraged to retire. Remaining staff were given salaries comparable to those in the private sector (US $1,000 monthly, as against only $50 prior to the reorganization). New applicants were subject to a very competitive exam (in which, less than 3 percent were successful). Currently nearly half of the staff are professional, as against less than one-fourth before 1991; and all are subject to a performance evaluation every six months and to rigorous competition for promotion.

The improved performance of Sunat is evident from its ability to collect in taxes nearly 14 percent of GDP, compared to only 4.5 percent in 1990. Moreover, corruption has been significantly reduced, according to THE ECONOMIST (August 5, 1995, 21): "Professionals such as doctors and lawyers are paying taxes for the first time."

The experience of the Peruvian Sunat project suggests the importance of requiring the country itself to create an appropriate project unit: identifying needed positions; requiring staff to take examinations to compete for these positions; and giving salaries comparable to those in the private sector. Only when the Bank is satisfied with the quality of this unit would the project begin.

The financing of a Sunat-type reform effort could be done through a World Bank-supported "Government Re-orientation Facility," advocated by Barbara Nunberg (1996, 10), a leading Bank governance expert. As explained by Nunberg, such a facility would be available to finance a wide variety of organizational reforms with monitorable performance benchmarks and outcomes. One of these might be the development of a meritocratic hiring system, such as introduced in Ceara, Brazil, for health care workers, noted in Chapter 8. "Progress on these and other jointly agreed indicators would be reviewed annually by the Bank to determine that the program was on track and that its financing should be continued" (Nunberg 1996, 10).

By requiring prior reform, it may be possible to avoid the problem identified by Berkman (1995)—an overreliance upon foreign experts. Berkman, therefore, argues for a "management by objectives" approach, with a phasing out process for foreign experts and a "phasing in" process for local counterparts. This might also enable better selection of staff for foreign training, instead of training costs becoming a "slush fund" for politically well-established individuals, as reported in the 1990 World Bank OED study of technical assistance in Africa (No. 8573, 40).

What is advocated here is nothing more than "borrower participation and consensus in project identification and design" to increase the chances for its sustainability and institutionalization (World Bank OED 9225 1990, 43). However, such a process will have to be combined with a sophisticated "institutional analysis" advocated by Steedman (1994, 18) "in the reality of socio-political, legal and bureaucratic contexts." This would mean paying special attention to the fact that civil servants "are, by and large, paid too little to motivate good work" (Schacter 1995, 343).

Dia (1996, 87–90) reports progress made in Ghana in the collection of tax and customs revenues which rose from 6.6 to 12.3 percent of GDP between 1984 and 1988 under international pressure. The agencies responsible for this work were given new leadership, independent status, additional allowances, better equipment, and the tying of incentives to output benchmarks. Highly qualified personnel were attracted to the new revenue institutions, a new grading structure was adopted, unqualified or corrupt staff were dismissed or retired, and salaries were made comparable to the private sector (with operational expenses funded from the revenue collected). While the rest of the civil service chafed at this preferential treatment, the political leadership gave its full backing to the venture.

The success of the Uganda Revenue Authority (URA) in raising tax collection (particularly import duties, with petrol topping the list) from

$90 million in 1990 to $522 million in 1995 is reported in THE ECONOMIST (July 27, 1996, 38). Much of this success is due to internationally supported programs to reduce corruption, including reduction of "ghost workers," higher salaries, review of job classifications, introduction of "Results-Oriented Management," and expanding the power of the Auditor General and the inspectorate system: "No other country on the continent has carried out a public sector reform initiative of this scale and with so many components" (Langseth, Stapenhurst, and Pope 1996, 43). Based upon the success of the URA, Schacter (1995, 343) advocates "small-scale experiments with motivational salary levels in selected units of the civil service."

Uganda's success in getting administrative reform has been partly due to the work of the Implementation and Monitoring Board (TIMB), consisting of Presidentially appointed senior citizens. The TIMB has evaluated the performance of every employee in certain central goverment ministries and in six districts, removing "ghost workers," "overdue leavers," and unacceptable performers (Langseth 1995, 5). It has also reinforced the President's efforts to use redundancy reviews, voluntary retirement schemes, and hiring freezes to downsize and reform the government. Yet, much remains to be done, considering that tax revenue in Uganda, as a percentage of GDP, "is the lowest among 26 African countries receiving World Bank structural adjustment credits and is three times lower than neighbouring Kenya" (Langseth, Stapenhurst, and Pope 1996, 34).

In Tanzania, the Ministry of Agriculture and Livestock Development (Kilimo) remains weak. Yet, a unit of Kilimo, the Marketing Development Bureau (MDB), has emerged since the 1970s as "a major training ground for senior Kilimo administrators" (Costello 1996, 142). Foreign donors, particularly the World Bank and the Food and Agricultural Organization, have been instrumental in providing higher salaries, training, operational resources, and political protection. As such, the MDB "has increasingly infiltrated the ministry with personnel it has trained and inculcated with norms of bureaucratic elitism" (Costello 1996, 142).

In requiring prior reform, it may be possible to do so through sponsoring elite schools of public administration, similar to the French ENA. Brazil's National School for Public Administration (ENAP) is a step in this direction; but, according to Marcelino (1994, 241), it has resulted in an internal culture in which "loyalty to the house" takes "precedence over the needs and demands of outside society." Hopefully this will change as the ENAP undertakes responsibility for a new National Program for

Training. In this regard, I noted in Chapter 4 the usefulness of the Brazilian Institute of Administration, which received significant assistance from USAID between 1962 and 1980.

If good institutes of management can be developed, they can be used to train personnel for the private as well as public sectors. The Ford Foundation in India has relied heavily upon the Indian Institutes of Management for programs to strengthen NGOs (Carroll, Schmidt and Bebbington 1996, 31).

Johnson (1996) presents a number of examples of useful international support for the education and training of accountants in Anglophone Africa. Under an IDA-funded Institutional Capacity Building Project, financing is being provided to the Institute of Certified Public Accountants of Uganda to introduce examinations and national accounting and auditing standards. In Lesotho, the Irish government has supported since the 1970s the Institute of Accountants and the Centre for Accounting Studies. By its support of the Zambian Centre for Accountancy Studies since 1988, the European Union is estimated to have saved Zambia over US $16 million in foreign exchange because it removed the need for students to go to the UK for professional training.

INTENSIFYING PRESSURE. The Terms of Reference of a project might include language that allows Bank staff to require the removal of uncooperative officials. It might also be used to prevent the high turnover of counterparts and trained staff and the failure to link training with improved career prospects. While leaders are likely to resent this interference, they might be won over by the promise of more projects and expanded funding.

Clark (1995) notes a situation in an Indian forestry project in Andhra Pradesh in which the manager of the Forestry Department (FD) kept undermining agreements reached with the World Bank for low-cost technologies for forest land treatments. By going over the head of this manager to the State Forest Secretary and by developing support from FD officials for appropriate technology through workshops, a change in leadership eventually came about. While this project required more time and money than anticipated, the participatory approach eventually was successful. "It built a large network of support for what in every respect is the best way we now know of protecting forests and helping poor fringe forest dwellers at the same time" (Clark 1995, 53).

Watson and Jagannathan (1995, 11) give an example of the World

Bank's bypassing of an uncooperative state agency in developing small, dispersed rural water projects. In this case, with the support of high level government officials, the Bank created a new, parallel agency that disbursed funds based on transparent criteria. In Brazil, the Bank located and cultivated reformers within resistant agencies and worked with them to forge alliances with other supporting sectors for expanding municipal water and sanitation services.

The World Bank has at times been most useful when it has been confrontational. In infrastructure projects, "the Bank's strict enforcement of fair and open procurement procedures has gone a long way toward preventing corruption, arbitrariness, and malpractice in the placement and enforcement of contracts" (Guhan 1995, 24). In Madras, the Bank suspended lending following the government's unwillingness to adjust bus fares as agreed to. "The adjustment was eventually made, to the relief of the nearly bankrupt local bus company" (World Bank OED Report 13117 1994, 35).

By working with bilateral foreign aid agencies and donor organizations within consultative groups, the World Bank has sometimes successfully pushed governance reform. The case of Benin was mentioned in Chapter 7. While former President Kerekou regained power through an election in 1996, "Benin's infrastructure is being rehabilitated, the banking system is back in order, the debt burden is falling, and foreign investors are discovering Benin" (Soglo 1996, A25). Although Kerekou talked about renationalization during the election, he has so far not undermined his country's respectable six percent growth rate.

At the end of 1993, the Bank used a consultative group to threaten to withhold nearly US $100 million from the US $860 million pledged Zambia unless effective action was taken against high-level drug trafficking and corruption (Lorch 1994, A10). In the case of Ghana, a consultative group provided "a starting point for a more concerted approach to policy advice and the negotiation of more solidly-based policy conditionality" (Toye 1991, 198). While (as noted in the previous chapter) progress remains slow in Ghana, there has also been, as a result of Bank pressure and guidance, significant economic and administrative reform, particularly in tax collection.

Since 1992, the Consultative Group of donors has also been putting pressure on Malawi to pursue simultaneously economic and political liberalization (Adamolekun, Kulemeka and Laleye 1997). Following the expression of concern about the lack of progress in the area of basic freedoms and human rights, donors "are seeking tangible and irreversible evidence of a basic transformation in the way Malawi approches these matters . . . ," Adamolekun, Kulemeka and Laleye (1996, 210–211), write, adding: "All this means is that henceforth, project implementation is likely to proceed more expeditiously" (p. 219).

There has been a similar effort in Bolivia, using a consultative group, to develop a Civil Service and Administrative Reform Program (CSARP). If successful, financial assistance would be contingent upon the development of a highly qualified professional and technical staff (competitively recruited and remunerated); the increase of tax revenues; and the reduction of unncessary expenditures. Each year the Bank would review the implementation of the CSARP and would present its findings to a session of the Consultative Group to ensure that commitments are met. The release of each aid tranche would be conditional on the government's willingness to finance an increasing share of the CSARP.

The pressure from donor countries on the World Bank to undertake irresponsible lending was noted in an earlier section of this chapter, together with the fact that much bilateral assistance has been counterproductive. The end of the Cold War is clearly a factor in causing donors to rethink their rationale for foreign aid. Moreover, Bank staff can more readily get the cooperation of Western diplomats in linking aid commitments to administrative reform. While, on the one hand, it may (as in the case of the United States) cause countries to be less generous, it may also facilitate a greater willingness to make foreign aid more effective. In any case, by probing into the changing motivation for foreign aid, Bank staff may be able to work with donors to intensify pressure for reform.

Harrold and Associates (1995, 41) give several examples of projects (in Zambia and Pakistan) which were carried out on a multi-donor basis, in which each donor specialized in a particular aspect. By coordinating donor supervision missions, the effectivenss and sustainability of operations were enhanced. In a project in Karachi, Boyle (1995, 94) notes the important contribution of a Japanese grant for participant observation, organizational study, and reorganizational work.

An example of changing attitudes to foreign aid comes from Canada (Stackhouse 1995, B1). Since 1978, Canada has provided more than $110 million of aid for Bangladesh's railroads, including locomotives, repairs, and training. However, following persistent loss of revenue ($35 million in 1994), the Canadian International Development Agency (CIDA) switched its emphasis from hardware to software. Instead of providing locomotives and other equipment, CIDA focuses on operations, preventive maintenance, and productivity. It has also been cooperating with the Asian Development Bank to significantly downsize the railroad's bloated bureaucracy.

While Canada's foreign aid commitments to Bangladesh in 1995–96 were only about 30 percent of what they had been ten years previously, it has become a major buyer of Bangladeshi-made garments. CIDA is also trying to become more effective by working with other donors to persuade the government to address the causes of poverty, such as excessive government landownership, and to support effective grassroots NGOs, such as Proshika, BRAC, and Grameen Bank.

PROMOTING COMPETITION. Being more confrontational with LDCs has obvious limitations in making foreign aid more effective. Mike Garn of the World Bank's Transportation, Water and Urban Development Department, is a strong supporter of a "demand-based approach" to foreign assistance. Instead of programs that emphasize need, affordability, charity, and central government personnel, he advocates the importance of providing services on the basis of demand, willingness to pay, cost-sharing, and local decision-making (Garn 1995). What governments can therefore most usefully provide are appropriate information, incentives, and arrangements for implementation so that there can be "a balance between the economic value of water to users, the cost of providing services to users, and the prices charged for these services" (Garn 1995, 9).

Briscoe and Garn (1994) provide several examples of successful "demand based" approaches. In Karachi, Pakistan, Akhter Hameed Khan has managed to provide over 600,000 poor people with sewerage by getting them to finance part of the costs, to participate in construction, and to elect neighborhood committees to manage the sewers and to bring pressure on the municipality to improve services. With a sewerage system, property values have increased, thereby stimulating demand for this service from other neighborhoods and communities. In Jakarta, a demand-based approach has led to the installation of 800,000 septic tanks by local contractors, fully financed by households, and maintained "by a vibrant and competitive service industry" (Briscoe and Garn 1994, 14).

The more competitive the mechanism is for financing activities that meet certain criteria, the better the results are likely to be. However, this may "require changes in established behavior patterns and attitudes on both the Bank and the Borrower's part, and might therefore be difficult to apply on a significant scale" (World Bank OED Report No. 12144 1993, 36). In the case of the Nigeria universities adjustment loan, the notion of competing for limited funds on the basis of reform proposals was not accepted. Nigeria was apparently allowed to get away with this on the grounds that "implementation is the responsibility of the borrower."

The problems with a solid waste management project in Lagos were presented in Chapter 1. Assuming that Bank staff are willing and able to design better projects, why not require cities to compete for this sort of project, with funding going only to cities that meet certain preconditions, such as successful tax collecting for this purpose? Several Russian Federation projects illustrate possibilities of requiring competition for Bank funding.

In a 1995 urban transport project, fifteen medium-sized cities requested financial assistance for replacement of their vehicle fleet; but only those that met the project's eligibility cost recovery target of 25 percent were to be selected (Europe and Central Asia Region 1995). At the time of appraisal, only ten of these cities were expected to be eligible for inclusion in the project. However, the nature of the project stimulated reform in all the project cities by encouraging them to raise fares in real terms, to reduce exemptions and stop fare evasions, and to develop cost-effective ways to cover exempt passengers (such as students, soldiers, and the elderly).

In the 1994 Management and Financial Training Project, Russian business schools and educational institutions were invited to compete for funding to develop or expand training programs in accounting and corporate finance, including computer-based case studies, textbooks, training modules, distance learning, and training of teachers. The loan was to finance about 190 contracts, costing altogether about US $40 million. In the process of stimulating competition for funding, the project hoped to achieve "a major shift from academic to active, problem-oriented methodology" (Europe and Central Asia Region 1994, 68).

In Chapter 5, I noted the success of Kenya's "harambee schools," in which communities are expected to build and maintain their own schools. This approach is being examined by World Bank officials in an effort to increase the percentage of education policies and projects (estimated in the case of Africa to be less than 10 percent) that are successfully implemented (see Colletta and Perkins 1995). In Kenya, it has been found that, when there is community participation in the operations and maintenance of constructed facilities, there is likely to be far more cooperation for infrastructural development (Watson and Jagannathan 1995, 14).

COMBINING DECENTRALIZATION WITH CENTRALIZATION. In Chapter 4, I emphasized the importance of combining centralization and decentralization. With the right combinations of political hardware and political software, "political elasticity" becomes possible. Returning to the theme of this book, I am, of course, referring to the delegation of responsibility from central governments to local governments, community organization, and private-sector companies in such a way as to (1) maximize autonomy without losing control and (2) expand influence to reliably and predictably affect the behavior of wider circles of citizens, participants, and subordinates.

Where soft and hard forms of power (incentives and disincentives) are properly used, development is likely to take place. For example, in Paraguay, the Ministry of Health provides financing, technical support, and construction assistance to communities willing and able to comply with the requirements for a rural sanitation program (Watson and Jagannathan 1995, 16). Communities are expected to contribute to cover 60 percent of capital costs, of which 25 percent may be in cash or labor and materials at the time of implementation. So far, cost recovery has been good and recurrent costs have been covered.

In Indonesia's Kampung Improvement Program (KIP), funds were provided to urban communities without a requirement for local cost-sharing (see Chapter 5). As a result, beneficiary communities did not feel enough "ownership" of investments to maintain or improve them. Building on this experience, more recent KIP projects use a combination of incentives and disincentives to "persuade" communities to maintain infrastructure and utility services provided (World Bank 1992, A7–16).

A similar approach is being used in Nepal where communities, in addition to contributing to capital costs, must deposit one year of Operations and Maintenance (O&M) costs in a bank account prior to the initiation of a water and sanitation project. While the success of this project remains uncertain, long term sustainability "requires that rules be set to address cost recovery and the financing of depreciation and replacement" (Boyle 1995, 13).

Unfortunately, in many countries, the national government is too weak to undertake effective decentralization. Consequently, the World

Bank may have to turn to respected NGOs, despite the problems mentioned in Chapter 5. The World Bank has had good experience in many countries (noted in previous chapters) with using NGOs, such as the Aga Khan Foundation in Pakistan, BRAC in Bangladesh, and FUNDASAL in El Salvador, for community development work. Beginning in 1991, supported by the Swedish International Development Authority, there has been increasing funding for World Bank participatory operations, guided by the Environment Department, and the Economic Development Institute (Yahie 1993).

Social Funds have been increasingly used by the World Bank to facilitate decentralization. Through them, NGOs help communities formulate projects, conduct participatory surveys and beneficiary assessments, and offer training in project management and organizational skills. In the Uttar Pradesh Basic Education Project, for example, funds are released to village chiefs on the following basis: "one-third to begin work, one-third on the completion of the foundation and one-third on completion of the walls" (Gopal and Marc 1994, 49). This project has been far more successful than one in Liberia where many of the schools built by an NGO deteriorated because villages were not involved in planning for maintenance (Carroll, Schmidt, and Bebbington 1996, 17).

While social funds are low cost and flexible arrangements for distributing resources to underserved communities in such a way as to encourage community participation, they may not reach the poorest communities, particularly when there is an emphasis upon rapid implementation of projects. "Where local ability is limited, additional resources for capacity building and institutional strengthening may be needed" (Africa Region 1996, 92). Nevertheless, Social Funds can be successfully implemented in highly impoverished countries.

A good example of possibilities is the Ethiopian Recovery and Rehabilitation Program (ERRP), begun at the end of 1992 (Eastern Africa Department 1996a). According to an evaluation carried out at the end of 1995, more than 2 million people had benefited from the ERRP, including projects for primary schooling, basic health services, rehabilitation of roads, improved water and sanitation, irrigation and micro-dam storage, and income generation. Despite shortages of qualified staff, local contractors, and financial resources, the communities on the whole seemed well enough organized to collect user fees, to supervise maintainence, and to undertake the other requirements for sustainability. Consequently, the World Bank agreed in 1996 to provide another US $120 million in IDA funding to continue the project for another five years.

Because of the frequent hostility between government and NGOs, the World Bank may have to mediate and convince both parties that cooperation is in their mutual interest. "Trust can be built in advance of project appraisal by creating a forum for NGO-government dialogue through training workshop, conferences, and consultation, and particularly by including both parties as stakeholders in project design" (Carroll, Schmidt and Bebbington 1996, 42). In the case of a rural development project in Bihar, India, a combined public sector/private sector "NGO Cell" was established to deal with NGOs throughout the project period. This facilitated the successful completion of a wide variety of activities through NGOs with active support of government agencies (Carroll, Schmidt and Bebbington 1996, 45).

In Bangladesh, where NGOs tend to be more effective than government agencies, there has been a long history of mutual distrust and animosity. Consequently, a recent independent study on government-NGO relations advocated a Government-NGO Consultative Council to enhance cooperation (Hasan and Saadat 1996, 46). Among the other recommendations of this study were to streamline the registration and approval process, disseminate information about good practices and performance potential, and provide for prompt appeal in cases of project disapproval or accusation of mismanagement.

USE OF BENCHMARKS. In More Developed Countries (MDCs), it is common for decentralization projects to allow local residents to write their own "benchmarks" or quantifiable goals, and only when they reach them them do they get the next installments of funds (see Chapter 4). Such benchmarks, of course, are useless if funds are given on the basis of political considerations and if monitoring and evaluation are neglected or mismanaged.

Harrold and Associates (1995) advocate a broad sector approach to World Bank lending. For this to be effective, there must be consensus on priorities and agreement among all parties on a limited number of outcome indicators. "Measuring progress in this will require establishing a base-line at the start of the projects and monitoring progress each year" (Harrold and Associates 1995, 39). Based upon audited financial reports and sample indicators (e.g., school enrollment or disease incidence), periodic visiting missions could analyze the details of project implementation and address particular constraints to implementation.

In regard to borrower financial management, Siegelbaum (1996, 57) emphasizes the importance of a well-staffed independent supreme audit institution, with responsibility to publish government accounts on an annual basis and to report periodically to the legislature during the fiscal year. In supporting economic reform, the World Bank could "condition lending on some benchmarks for government-wide sound financial management" (IBID.).

In the case of Uganda, the World Bank's Economic Development Institute has developed a survey to determine appropriate and useful indicators of service delivery for implementation of civil service reform and other programs. By developing a "baseline" description of pre-reform services at the district level, it will facilitate comparing the effects of different programs across the 39 districts. The service-delivery survey (which began in 1995) has an easy-to-read format, enabling policymakers to "determine which reforms yield the highest net marginal benefits and analyze the relation between inputs and outcomes" (Langseth 1995, 24).

In doing Monitoring and Evaluation (M & E), the World Bank's OED (Report No. 15222 1995, 21) emphasizes the importance of forcing design engineers and social workers "to work as a team, go into the community and listen to people." This can engender a variety of perspectives, a healthy competition among project teams and communities, and a willingness to confront (rather than hide) failure so that new solutions can be found. By reinforcing borrower ownership, the "fear of failure which inhibits so much evaluation can be overcome" (p. 22).

If M & E can be combined with an emphasis on institutional reform, some interesting possibilities emerge. I advocated such an approach in evaluating an urban project in Monrovia. This would have meant insisting upon tax reform and cost recovery prior to beginning what was really wanted by the government -infrastructure improvements (Werlin 1990, 259).

If a step-by-step approach had been used in the Monrovia project, step one would have included the institutional reforms essential for the sustainability of step two, consisting of infrastructural investments and capital works. Step three could then have included traffic management, education, microenterprise development, and other components left out of the project. The entire project, accordingly, could have been presented as a multi-sectoral urban loan package, with funds released, based upon progress in institutional development. During each step, the project could be reconsidered, allowing for unanticipated contingencies and additional experimentation.

UNLOCKING DOORS TO REFORM

There is a saying that the more impoverished a country (or individual) is, the more tightly closed is the door to reform, with the lock having to be opened from the inside. While I believe (as here indicated) that governments, as well as individuals, respond to incentives and disincentives, I also believe that we have to understand what might trigger or expand motivation. The following are various ways to possibly unlock the doors to reform:

THE IMPORTANCE OF SOCIAL SCIENCE RESEARCH. I already mentioned the work of the World Bank sociologist Michael Cernea. A good example of the success of social science research, combined with a participatory approach, is the development of Pakistan's Water User Associations (WUAs). According to Cernea (1993, 27), "these WUAs hold an attractive promise of taking over a share of the responsibilities currently vested in governmental agencies, and of expanding their participation in system management beyond the watercourse."

Using sociologists is, of course, not the only way of getting useful information about a project's possibilities. In Russia, land reform has been stalled by Russia's parliament, supported by politically powerful collectives. However, in the region of Nizhny Novgorod, the World Bank has found a way to use "cashless auctions" to allocate ownership (THE ECONOMIST, June 29, 1996, 79). While this system has been supported by the region's reformist governor, it required considerable research by Bank staff to facilitate implementation. As a result, production has gone up by more than one-third on the private farms, joint-stock companies, and mixed partnerships that have emerged since 1993 from this program.

THE QUALITATIVE RESEARCH APPROACH. I also earlier noted Larry Salmen's 1987 book, LISTEN TO THE PEOPLE. Using his "qualitative research" approach, the World Bank or some other sponsoring organization hires trained local social workers to live in areas being assisted for extended periods, enabling them to engage in confidential discussions with members of the community about their perceptions, fears, and problems.

Salmen, in the most recent update (1995) of this approach, notes that it is being used used in 59 projects in 34 countries. In Malawi, a beneficiary assessment has helped make the electricity utility more responsive to its consumers. It showed that, while people were often willing and able to pay for ongoing charges, they were unhappy with high installment costs, the delays in connecting houses, and complicated electricity bills. In Lesotho, as a result of a beneficiary assessment, traditional healers were brought into the national health system and given courses in basic health; contraceptives were made more accessible to women; and cost-recovery fees were made more rational and acceptable.

In Pakistan, participant observers studied the performance of provincial and municipal institutions over a nine year period as part of several World Bank-financed projects (Boyle and Silsby 1996, 2). As a result of this work, institutional weaknesses were identified, and the TRIAD of stakeholders (elected officials, bureaucracy, and various interest groups) were encouraged to cooperate for implementation of fiscal and administrative reforms. "Once they arrived at some mutual truths, patterns emerged; and they were able to identify corrective actions that addressed not only physical and financial concerns, but social and political, as well" (Boyle 1996, 9).

In thinking about the potential usefulness of World Bank participant-evaluation research, I remain concerned about the lack of (or decreasing) funds for such research. One possibility that needs to be explored is the idea of a Donor Implementation Fund, using contributions and perhaps experts from donor countries, to study ways of overcoming the problems of implementing projects. For example, anthropologists hired under the U.S. Peace Corps might be quite helpful in harmonizing community with institutional development objectives.

PROTECTING INDEPENDENT SPHERES OF AUTHORITY. In Uganda, the World Bank's Economic Development Institute (EDI), in cooperation with Transparency International, has sponsored a course for journalists to encourage them to be more vigorous in self-regulation and conveying news objectively and fairly (Langseth 1995, 19). EDI has also held regional seminars for investigative journalists in other parts of Sub-Saharan Africa.

Conclusion 341

Based upon my distinction between primary and secondary politics, I believe that the World Bank should avoid "primary politics" and, instead, emphasize "secondary politics." In other words, I do not think that the World Bank should be insisting upon competitive elections and multi-party system; but I do believe that the Bank can legitimately demand that governments allow the mass media to investigate and publicize allegations of fraud and corruption (Siegelbaum 1996, 60). I also suggest that the Bank can be more assertive in regard to independent ombudsman offices and anti-corruption agencies. Thus, I do not agree with the assertion that there are "limits to what the Bank can do in this area . . . without infringing the Articles" (Siegelbaum 1996, 60).

A 1995 World Bank publication (THE WORLD BANK AND LEGAL TECHNICAL ASSISTANCE: INITIAL LESSONS) summarizes the work of the Bank's Legal Department. In a number of countries (e.g., Bolivia, Dominican Republic, and China), Japan has been quite generous in assisting legal reform work. In Africa, European countries and USAID have often co-financed these efforts.

A 1992 US $30 million project in Venezuela is typical of the Bank's efforts to make the judiciary more effective and legitimate. It attempts to improve administration of the court system by computerizing operations, raising salaries, introducing a pilot model court, and providing better information about laws and legal requirements. Unfortunately, this project has had only limited success, according to THE ECONOMIST (September 14, 1996, 44–45).

The difficulties of this Venezuela project (particularly, persistent corruption) underscore the need of Bank staff to deal with underlying political realities. While the publication on legal technical assistance earlier referred to (p. 18) emphasizes that legal reform "cannot, and at any rate, should not be imposed on a country," it points out that the Bank required the Ghanaian government "to clearly demonstrate its commitment to legal reform by establishing a Private Sector Advisory Group which would set the agenda for law reform." In Benin, Bolivia, and the Philippines, structural adjustment credits called for legal reform, indicating that "legal conditionality in adjustment loans has become more specific and frequent" (p. 3).

OTHER POSSIBILITIES. The usefulness of Project Launch was mentioned in the 1994 OED EVALUATION RESULTS (pp. 22–23), in which the objectives of a project are presented to the public media. What about having PROJECT MIDWAY REVIEWS, allowing and perhaps requiring the problems of a project to be discussed before the media? In Liberia, despite the country's political turmoil during the mid-1980s, an open discussion of the difficulties of a Bank-funded Monrovia project was at least enlightening (Werlin 1990). Based upon this sort of open discussion, it might be possible to develop acceptable ways of redirecting or invigorating a project that may be misguided or unsustainable. It would, of course, have to be understood and accepted by officials from the very beginning of a project that this approach might be used.

The situation in Nigeria, described by Agbese (1990, 244), in which force is the "prevalent method of governance" and the police and soldiers are society's "mad dogs" was noted in Chapter 1. It is unfortunately so widespread in LDCs as to be almost taken for granted. To get governments to shift from coercive to persuasive forms of power is, of course, extremely difficult; but there are examples of useful efforts being made.

To encourage a softening of political power and a reduction in civil violence, the World Bank has conducted surveys in many countries, showing how unnecessarily burdensome certain tax and labor regulations are, taking up more than one-fourth of senior management time in one instance (Operations Policy Department 1994, 8). Based upon these surveys in Latin America, the Bank has supported revenue administrative reforms to make tax and customs regulations more easily comprehensible as well as acceptable.

In Nicaragua a major impediment to advancing both democracy and development has been the government's inability to resolve most of the ownership claims on property seized by the Sandanistas (Golden 1993, A6). This is where foreign assistance could be useful, including land registration, an arbitration arrangement, and appropriate compensation.

A successful land reform program was carried out in Kenya after independence, transferring land from European settlers to African farmers through British assistance. However, according to THE ECONOMIST (December 6, 1997, 48–49), a similar effort in Zimbabwe has been undermined by the government in various ways, causing Britain to reject necessary financial assistance, fearing particularly that much of the land will go, not, as intended, to small-scale commercial farmers, but to those who are politically powerful. An earlier program here failed because of the lack of tenure, credit, training and farm support services.

Bryant (1997) suggests the possibility of the World Bank supporting a land fund in Brazil to buy land which could then be sold for distribution to small farmers. To be successful, she points out (p. 3), the weakness of land registration, debt collection, and land adjudication, (especially in the Northeast), would have to be overcome (getting us back to the importance of political software).

CONCLUSION: ACCELERATING REFORM

By 1996, it was recognized that about 20 countries had reached unsustainable debt levels, absorbing, in the case of Uganda, over one-quarter of government revenue collection and ten percent of its export earnings. In 1994, the most indebted countries made debt payments of some $3.3 billion, of which around one-half went to the World Bank.

As noted earlier, the total foreign debt of the world's low-income countries more than tripled during the 1980s. The seriousness of this problem has become undeniable, reaching between 200 and 250 percent of export earnings of the 20 most heavily indebted countries. For example, in 1993–94, the US $155 million spent by Tanzania on debt repayments was more than its budget for clean water and health combined (OXFAM 1996, 10). Uganda spends more than five times more each year on debt repayment to industrialized countries than it does on health care for its citizens.

As a group, the heavily indebted countries have foreign exchange reserves covering only forty-days worth of imports, with many African countries having less than half of this coverage. (Ideally, these countries should have foreign exchange reserves to cover at least six months of imports to protect themselves against emergencies and external shocks.)

Moreover, these countries are shut out of international capital markets. Many have stopped paying bilateral creditors to keep up their debt repayments to mulilateral ones. However, at least ten countries now face almost impossible arrears problems with either the IMF or the World Bank, or both.

The World Bank's most recent proposal is to set aside $500 million for an initial contribution to a special Trust Fund. The I.M.F. would sell a small portion of its gold stock, invest the proceeds and use the income from the investments to reduce the debt payments of some of the most severely indebted borrowers. The Bank and the Fund would also pressure donor countries to write off between 67 and 90 percent of their loans to these countries. Altogether this is expected to cost between $5.6 and $7.7 billion over six years.

According to the World Bank's "Framework for Action to Resolve the Debt Problems of the Heavily Indebted Poor Countries," a case-by-case approach is to be used, with action "only when the debtor has shown, through a track record of reform and sound policies, the ability to put to good use whatever exceptional support is provided to achieve a sustainable outcome." However, my fear is that debt relief will eventually become "a gift to be waited for," rather than "a prize to be worked for." This is because of the frequent failure of conditionality to be effective, as pointed out earlier in this chapter. If so, the results will be as disappointing as, in so many cases, IDA funding and structural adjustment loans.

To stimulate impoverished countries to make the sort of effort that some of them did in 1996 to win Olympic medals, I suggest requiring countries being assisted to compete for the amounts available, using Bank country studies or sector reports, to determine the current situation and existing problems. Countries might be given four years to reform (using the concept of an "Olympics of Economic Reform"), and encouraged to apply for available IDA funding and the assistance of international donors in so doing.

Countries would be invited to apply for debt relief, with each country offered a potential amount. They would then be requested to determine their own quantifiable goals, strategies for achieving them, and timetables for doing so. (They could not therefore easily claim "political interference.") When they were ready, they would have to invite in donor-selected evaluators including representatives from multilateral and bilateral organizations, NGOs, United Nations agencies, potential investors or business organizations (such as Chambers of Commerce), women's and humanitarian associations, etc.

In determining what percentage of the potential debt relief available to each country would actually be given, evaluations would have to consider: (1) the extent to which a country had met its own quantifiable goals; (2) the achievements of this country in comparison to those of other highly indebted or impoverished countries; and (3) how well this country had addressed its problems as initially presented. The evaluators would publicly announce their decisions, together with justifications. Funds for debt relief denied to a particular country would be put back into a financial pool and made available to countries competing for debt relief within the next four-year economic reform cycle.

Based upon a recent World Bank study of Bangladesh's public sector

(Hasan and Saadat 1996), I propose that the following factors, among others, be taken into account:

INFRASTRUCTURE. Electricity is available to only 15 percent of the population; telephone access, to only two per thousand (one of the world's lowest); and sanitary latrines in rural areas, to only 26 percent. Most utilities are unable to keep up with applications for connections, and long waiting periods are common, unless one is willing to pay "speed money."

PUBLIC SERVICES. Only 4 percent of students entering grade one complete 12 years of general education. The adult literacy rate is only 44 percent for males and 26 percent for females. The teacher:pupil ratio is 1:70.

The quality of health services is dismal and access is extremely poor. In the rural areas, only 16 percent of the sick population use government-provided services. Consequently life-expectancy is only 57 years and infant mortality, 91 per thousand live births.

BUREAUCRATIC EFFICIENCY. The number of ministries in Bangladesh (35) is more than twice that of Thailand (14), Japan (14) and the UK (16) and significantly more than Malaysia and South Korea. Generally GOB agencies perform badly, without performance standards, financial discipline, or serious scrutiny by the legislature or legal institutions.State-Owned Enterprises (SOEs) continue to employ more than 400,000, causing colossal losses to the taxpayer, undermining the budget and the banking system, and crowding out private sector credit.

Because of their lack of accountability, agencies tend to be inefficient and corrupt, and citizens lack any effective means for redress. It takes 3 to 4 months to get connection to water, and payoffs come to US $340–$500 to be connected within a week. Unless one pays US $125–$200, a municipal trade licence might require a year to go through the numerous steps (some of them renewable annually). In the case of a garments exporter, it was found that necessary illegal payments amounted to more than seven times the official initial costs.

Some of the criteria that could be used in determining administrative improvement include: customer satisfaction; transparency; timeliness and adequacy of services; and redress of grievances. Progress toward privatization or commercialization of SOEs would also have to be evaluated. Likewise, studies would have to be undertaken to determine downsizing, the employment of qualified civil servants, and the payment of reasonable salaries to bureaucrats.

LEGITIMACY. Everything conducive to legitimacy is weak in Bangladesh: the legislature works under poor conditions; legislation is badly designed and outdated; judicial procedures are cumbersome; court facilities are inadequate; the legal education system and judicial training facilities are poor; there are too few well-trained judges; and there is no arrangement for monitoring and reform.

In judging improvements of the legal system, a variety of factors would have to be taken into account: physical facilities in the courts; overload; quality and timeliness of justice; legal education; training opportunities for judges; etc. The basic question would have to be addressed: the extent to which the legal system can be trusted and used.

A FINAL NOTE

In suggesting this competitive process for countries seeking debt reduction, evaluators from the private sector might be in a better position than those from the World Bank and the donor community to emphasize the importance of an environment that will attract private investment. After all, in 1995 private investors poured $170 billion into developing countries, as against only $21.5 from the World Bank (THE ECONOMIST, July 27, 1996, 61).

Until low-income countries become good places to do business, they will remain hopelessly impoverished, regardless of how much debt reduction they receive. In other words, these countries must get the message that "the political walls of national impoverishment" are ultimately of their own making. The "blame game" (blaming International Financial Institutions, foreign countries, colonialism, and international capitalism for problems), which so many LDC leaders and intellectuals love to play, as noted in previous chapters, is decreasingly playable.

While recognizing the limitations of the World Bank's ability to promote development, I am encouraged by the fact that foreign aid donors and recipients are at least formally receptive to President Wolfensohn's anti-corruption effort. Assuming that World Bank staff can overcome their fear of "rocking the boat and the impact it would have on processing loans" (Siegelbaum 1996, 2), they can, as here suggested, not so much directly confront corruption, as, indirectly, through strengthening governance. As I see it, this is only effective way of treating political illness and, in so doing, improving the political software essential for political elasticity.

References and Citation Index

This citation index is intended to facilitate research by enabling readers, first of all, to identify references of interest to them and, then, to examine how these references are used in the text. Bracketed numbers refer to text pages containing the citation.

Abban, Charles Moses 1994. "Why Isn't Ghana Working?," WEST AFRICA, 1–7 August: 1350 [297].
Abney, Glenn and Thomas P. Lauth 1982. "Influence of the Chief Executive on City Line Agencies." PUBLIC ADMINISTRATION REVIEW, Vol. 42 (March/April): 136–142 [63].
Abraham, W. E. 1962. THE MIND OF AFRICA. Chicago: U. of Chicago [245].
Abucar, Mohamed H. and Patrick Molutsi. 1993. "Environmental Policy in Botswana: A Critique." AFRICA TODAY 40(1): 63–69 [262].
Adamolekun, Ladipo. 1991. "Introduction: Federalism in Nigeria." PUBLIUS: THE JOURNAL OF FEDERALISM. Vol. 21 (4): 1–12 [52].
Adamolekun, Ladipo; Noel Kulemeka, and Mouftaou Laleye 1997. "Political Transition, Economic Liberalization and Civil Service Reform in Malawi." PUBLIC ADMINISTRATION AND DEVELOPMENT 17: 209–222 [332].
Adams, Dale W. 1991. "Taking a Fresh Look at Informal Finance." In Philippe Callier, ed., FINANCIAL SYSTEMS AND DEVELOPMENT IN AFRICA. Washington, DC: The World Bank [31].
Adepoju, Aderanti 1994. "The Demographic Profile: Sustained High Mortality & Fertility & Migration for Employment." In Aderanti Adepoju and Christine Oppong, eds., GENDER, WORK & POPULATION IN SUB-SAHARAN AFRICA. Portsmouth, N.H.: Heinemann [266, 267].
Adjibolosoo, Senyo B-S.K. 1995. THE HUMAN FACTOR IN DEVELOPING AFRICA. Westport, CN: Praeger [256].
Adorno, Theodor W., ET AL. 1950. THE AUTHORITARIAN PERSONALITY. New York: Harper [251].
Africa Region. 1995. A CONTINENT IN TRANSITION IN THE MID-1990's. Washington, DC: World Bank Unpublished Report [208].
Africa Region 1996, TAKING ACTION FOR POVERTY REDUCTION IN SUB-SAHARAN AFRICA. Washington DC: World Bank [322, 336].

Agbese, Pita O. 1990. "The Military and the Privatization of Repression in Nigeria." CONFLICT. Vol. 10 (3): 239–266 [43, 342].

Aharoni, Yair 1991. "On Measuring the Success of Privatization." In Ravi Ramanurti and Raymond Vernon, eds., PRIVATIZATION AND CONTROL OF STATE-OWNED ENTERPRISES. Washington, DC: The World Bank [152].

Ahmed, Viqar and Michael Bamberger, 1991. "Monitoring and Evaluation (M&E): The South Asian Experience." PUBLIC ADMINISTRATION AND DEVELOPMENT, Vol. ll (May/June): 281–284 [77, 189].

Ahsan, E. ET AL. 1991. "Bangladesh's Second Extension and Research Project." PUBLIC ADMINISTRATION AND DEVELOPMENT. Vol ll (3): 207–210 [87, 98].

Aina, Tade Akin, Florence Bam Etta, and Cyril I. Obi. 1994. "The Search for Sustainable Urban Development in Metropolitan Lagos, Nigeria." THIRD WORLD PLANNING REVIEW. Vol 16 (2): 202–216 [33, 42].

Ake, Claude 1996. DEMOCRACY AND DEVELOPMENT IN AFRICA. Washington, DC: Brookings Institution [272, 273].

Al-Sayyid, Mustapha K. 1993. "A Civil Society in Egypt." THE MIDDLE EAST JOURNAL 47(2): 228–242 [121}. Alam, M. Shahid 1989. "Anatomy of Corruption: An Approach to the Political Economy of Underdevelopment." AMERICAN JOURNAL OF ECONOMICS AND SOCIOLOGY 48 (4): 441–453 [189].

Aliber, Robert Z. 1994. "Financial Reform in South Korea." In Lee-Jay Cho and Yoon Hyung Kim, eds., KOREA'S POLITICAL ECONOMY: AN INSTITUTIONAL PERSPECTIVE. Boulder, CO: Westview Press [301].

Almond, Gabriel A. and James S. Coleman 1960. "Introduction;" "Conclusion." In Gabriel A. Almond and James S. Coleman, eds., THE POLITICS OF DEVELOPING AREAS. Princeton, N.J.: Princeton University Press [23].

Amaral, Maria Ruth de Sampaio 1994. "Community Organization, Housing Improvements and Income Generation." HABITAT INTERNATIONAL 18(4): 81–97 [137].

Ambler, John S. 1991. "Ideas, Interests, and the French Welfare State." In THE FRENCH WELFARE STATE, ed. John S. Ambler. New York and London: New York University Press [123].

Ameur, Charles 1994. AGRICULTURAL EXTENSION: A STEP BEYOND THE NEXT STEP. Washington, DC: World Bank Technical Paper No. 247 [84, 90, 93].

Amsden, Alice H. 1994. "The Specter of Anglo-Saxonization is Haunting South Korea." In Lee-Jay Cho and Yoon Hyung Kim, eds., KOREA'S POLITICAL ECONOMY: AN INSTITUTIONAL PERSPECTIVE. Boulder, CO: Westview Press [11, 294].

Amsden, Alice H. and Yoon-Dae Euh 1997. "Behind Korea's Plunge." THE NEW YORK TIMES (November 27): A39 [294].

Amuwo, Kunle 1986. "Military-Inspired Anti-Bureaucratic Corruption Campaigns: An Appraisal of Niger's Experience." THE JOURNAL OF MODERN AFRICAN STUDIES 24(2): 285–301 [186].

Anderson, Eric 1989. "HUD: The Real Scandal." JOURNAL OF POLITICS. Nov/Dec: 287–292 [177].

References and Citation Index   351

Anderson, Jack and Michael Binstein 1995. "A Shifting Line on Job Corps Violence." THE WASHINGTON POST. February 16: B23 [71].
Anderson, John Ward 1995. "Pakistani Journalists Face Official Pressures as 6 Papers Are Banned." THE WASHINGTON POST. July 4: A16 [191].
Annis, Sheldon. 1987. "Can Small-Scale Development Be a Large-Scale Policy? The Case of Latin America." WORLD DEVELOPMENT 15:128–135 [152].
Anon. 1968. REPORT OF THE COMMITTEE OF ENQUIRY INTO THE STATE FURNITURE AND JOINERY CORPORATION. Accra-Tema, Ghana: State Publishing Corp. [273].
Antholt, Charles H. 1992. RELEVANCY, RESPONSIVENESS AND COST-EFFECTIVENESS: ISSUES FOR AGRICULTURAL EXTENSION IN THE 21ST CENTURY. Washington, DC: World Bank Discussion Paper [87, 89, 95, 98].
Antholt, Charles H. 1994. GETTING READY FOR THE TWENTY FIRST CENTURY: TECHNICAL CHANGE AND INSTITUTIONAL MODERNIZATION IN AGRICULTURE. Washington, DC: World Bank Technical Paper No. 217 [84, 87, 89, 90, 99].
Anunobi, Fredoline O. 1992. THE IMPLICATIONS OF CONDITIONALITY: THE I.M.F. AND AFRICA. Lanham, MD: University Press of America [298].
Applegate, Jane 1992. "Customers Are a Driving Force Behind Auto Repair Shops." THE WASHINGTON POST. September 14: E6 [171].
Apter, David E. 1963. GHANA IN TRANSITION. New York: Atheneum [245].
Apter, David E. and Carl G. Rosberg. 1994. "Changing African Perspectives." In David E. Apter and Carl G. Rosberg, eds., POLITICAL DEVELOPMENT AND THE NEW REALISM IN SUB-SAHARAN AFRICA. Charlottesville and London: University Press of Virginia [24].
Argyriades, Demetrios. 1991. "Bureaucracy and Debureaucratization." In Ali Farazmand, ed., HANDBOOK OF COMPARATIVE AND DEVELOPMENT PUBLIC ADMINISTRATION. New York: Marcel Dekker [85].
Armstrong, Robert P. 1996. GHANA: COUNTRY ASSISTANCE REVIEW; A STUDY IN DEVELOPMENT EFFECTIVENESS. Washington, DC: World Bank OED Study [291, 292, 294, 296, 298, 299, 303].
Arrigo, Linda Gail. 1994. "From Democratic Movement to Bourgeois Democracy: The Internal Politics of the Taiwan Democratic Progressive Party in 1991." In Murray E. Rubinstein, ed., THE OTHER TAIWAN: 1945 to the Present. Armonk, NY: M.E. Sharpe [235].
Ashford, Douglas E. 1980. "Introduction: Political Choices and Local Finance." In FINANCING URBAN GOVERNMENT IN THE WELFARE STATE, ed. Douglas E. Ashford. New York: St. Martin's Press [110].
Ashford, Douglas E. 1989. "British Dogmatism and French Pragmatism Revisited." In Colin Crouch and David Marquand, eds, THE NEW CENTRALISM: BRITAIN OUT OF STEP IN EUROPE? Cambridge, MA: Blackwell [111].
Assie-Lumumba, N'Dri T. 1993. HIGHER EDUCATION IN FRANCOPHONE AFRICA. Washington, DC: The World Bank [103].
Atkinson, Michael M. and Maureen Mancuso 1985. "Do We Need a Code of Conduct for Politics? The Search for an Elite Political Culture in Canada." CANADIAN JOURNAL OF POLITICAL SCIENCE 18(3): 461–470 [163].

Atlas, John and Peter Dreier, 1993. "From Projects to Communities: Redeeming Public Housing." JOURNAL OF HOUSING, Vol. 50 (January/February): 21–38 [70].

Attahi, Koffie, 1997. "Decentralisation and Participatory Urban Governance in Fracophone Africa." In Mark Swilling, ed, GOVERNING AFRICA'S CITIES. Johannesburg, South Africa: Witwatersrand University Press [105, 123, 125}.

Axinn, George H. 1988. "T&V (Tragic and Vain) Extension?" INTERPAKS INTERCHANGE (November): 6–7 [84].

Ayee, Joseph R. A. 1997. "The Adjustment of Central Bodies to Decentralization: The Case of the Ghanaian Bureaucracy." AFRICAN STUDIES 40 (2): 37–58 [287].

Ayittey, George B. N. 1994. "The Failure of Development Planning in Africa." In Peter J. Boettke, ed., THE COLLAPSE OF DEVELOPMENT PLANNING. New York: New York University Press [205].

Bahal, Jagdish ET AL. 1993. STRENGTHENING LOCAL INITIATIVE AND BUILDING LOCAL CAPACITY IN GHANA. Washington, DC: World Bank Internal Document [286].

Bahl, Roy and Johannes Linn. 1992. URBAN PUBLIC FINANCE FOR DEVELOPING COUNTRIES. Washington, DC: The World Bank [108, 115].

Baken, Robert-Ian and Jan van der Linden, 1993. "Getting the Incentives Right: Banking on the Formal Private Sector." THIRD WORLD PLANNING REVIEW, Vol. 15 (ll): 2–18 [77].

Baker, Randall. 1991. "The Role of the State and the Bureaucracy in Developing Countries Since World War II." In Ali Farazmand, ed., HANDBOOK OF COMPARATIVE AND DEVELOPMENT PUBLIC ADMINISTRATION. New York: Marcel Dekker [89].

Baker, Raymond W. 1995. "Riding the Rivers of Dirty Money." THE WASHINGTON POST. June 4: C2 [197, 198].

Bammeke, A.O. and M. K. C. Sridhar. 1989. "Market Wastes in Ibadan, Nigeria." WASTE MANAGEMENT & RESEARCH. Vol. 7: 115–120 [49].

Bannerjee, Tridib and Sanjoy Chakrovorty 1994. "Transfer of Planning Technology and Local Political Economy: A Retrospective Analysis of Calcutta." JOURNAL OF THE AMERICAN PLANNING ASSOCIATION 60(1): 71–82 [134, 140].

Barkan, Joel D. 1994. "Can Established Democracies Nurture Democracy Abroad? Lessons from Africa." Annual Meeting of the American Political Science Association, New York City [200, 215].

Barkan, Joel D. 1994a. "Resurrecting Modernization Theory and the Emergence of Civil Society in Kenya and Nigeria." In David E. Apter and Carl G. Rosberg, eds., POLITICAL DEVELOPMENT AND THE NEW REALISM IN SUB-SAHARAN AFRICA. Charlottsville and London: University Press of Virginia [22].

Barnekov, Timothy and Douglas Hart, 1993. "The Changing Nature of US Urban Policy: The Case of the Urban Development Action Grant." URBAN STUDIES, Vol 30 (9): 1469–1483 [60].

Barnett, W. Stevens, 1992. "Benefits of Compensatory Preschool Education." THE JOURNAL OF HUMAN RESOURCES, Vol. 27 (2): 279–313 [70, 71].

Bartone, Carl 1990. "Economic and Policy Issues in Resource Recovery from Municipal Solid Wastes." RESOURCES, CONSERVATION, AND RECYCLING, 4: 7–23 [32].
Bartone, Carl ET AL. 1994. TOWARD ENVIRONMENTAL STRATEGIES FOR CITIES. Washington, DC: The World Bank [124, 135].
Bartone, Carl, Janice Bernstein, and Frederick Wright. 1990. INVESTMENTS IN SOLID WASTE MANAGEMENT: OPPORTUNITIES FOR ENVIRONMENTAL IMPROVEMENT. Washington, D.C.: The World Bank [33].
Bates, Robert H. 1996. "The Death of Comparative Politics." APSA-CP. Vol. 7 (2): 1–2 [4].
Battiata, Mary 1988. "Graft Hobbles Uganda's Comeback." THE WASHINGTON POST. June 27: A15 [187, 188].
Baylis, Thomas A. 1980. "Collegial Leadership in Advanced Industrial Societies: The Relevance of the Swiss Experience." POLITY (Fall): 34–54 [217] Beetham, David. 1992. "Liberal Democracy and the Limits to Democratization." In David Held, ed., PROSPECTS FOR DEMOCRACY. Oxford, England: Blackwell Publishers [217].
Behn, Robert D. 1992. "Management and the Neutrino: The Search for Meaningful Metaphors." PUBLIC ADMINISTRATION REVIEW. Vol. 52 (5): 409–419 [18].
Bello, Walden and Stephanie Rosenfeld 1990. DRAGONS IN DISTRESS: ASIA'S MIRACLE ECONOMIES IN CRISIS. San Francisco: Institute for Food and Development Policy [222, 223, 227, 229, 236, 259].
Bellows, Thomas J. 1990. "Singapore in 1989: Progress in a Search for Roots." ASIAN SURVEY 30(2): 201–210 [259].
Ben-Ari, Eyal. 1990. "A Bureaucrat in Every Japanese Kitchen?: On Cultural Assumptions and Coproduction. ADMINISTRATION AND SOCIETY. Vol. 21(4): 472–492 [40].
Bendavid-Val, Avrom and Jeanne Downing. 1991. MOBILIZING SAVINGS AND RURAL FINANCE; THE A.I.D. EXPERIENCE. Washington, DC: USAID [29, 31].
Bendick, Jr., Mark. 1989. "Privatizing the Delivery of Social Welfare Services: An Idea To Be Taken Seriously." In PRIVATIZATION AND THE WELFARE STATE, eds. Sheila B. Kamerman and Alfred J. Kahn. Princeton, NJ: Princeton University Press [148].
Beng-Huat, Chua. 1994. "Arrested Development: Democratisation in Singapore." THIRD WORLD QUARTERLY 15(4): 655–667 [223].
Bennett, Robert J. and Gunter Krebs. 1991. LOCAL ECONOMIC DEVELOPMENT: PUBLIC-PRIVATE PARTNERSHIP INITIATION IN BRITAIN AND GERMANY. London and New York: Belhaven Press [106].
Bennis, William G. 1966. CHANGING ORGANIZATIONS. New York: McGraw-Hill [130].
Berg, Elliot. 1988. "Introduction." In Elliot Berg, ed., POLICY REFORM & EQUITY: EXTENDING THE BENEFITS OF DEVELOPMENT. San Francisco, CA: ICS Press [23].

Berg, Elliot J. 1993. RETHINKING TECHNICAL COOPERATION. New York: UNDP [327].
Berger, Morroe 1964. THE ARAB WORLD TODAY. Garden City, NY: Anchor Books [246].
Berger, Peter L 1988. "An East Asian Development Model." In IN SEARCH OF AN EAST ASIAN DEVELOPMENT MODEL, eds. Peter L. Berger and Hsinhuang Hsiao. New Brunswick, NJ: Transaction Books [246] Berkman, Stephen 1995. "Technical Assistance in Africa." THE INTERNATIONAL JOURNAL OF TECHNICAL COOPERATION l(1): 124–134 [319, 328].
Berman, Bruce J. 1994. "African Capitalism and the Paradigm of Modernity: Culture, Technology and the State." In AFRICAN CAPITALISTS IN AFRICAN DEVELOPMENT, eds. Bruce J. Berman and Colin Leys. Boulder and London: Lynne Rienner [255, 256].
Berman, Evan M. and Jonathan P. West 1995. "Municipal Commitment to Total Quality Management: A Survey of Recent Progress." PUBLIC ADMINISTRATION REVIEW. Vol. 55(1): 57–66 [77].
Berry, Jeffrey, Kent E. Portney, and Ken Thomson. 1993. THE REBIRTH OF URBAN DEMOCRACY. Washington, DC: The Brookings Institute [219].
Berry, LaVerle 1995. GHANA: A COUNTRY STUDY. Washington, DC: Library of Congress [273, 297, 302].
Berry, Sara 1993. "Coping with Confusion: African Farmers' Responses to Economic Instability in the 1970s and 1980s." In Thomas M. Callaghy and John Ravenhill, eds., HEMMED IN: RESPONSES TO AFRICA'S ECONOMIC DECLINE. New York: Columbia University Press [311].
Bestor, Theodore. 1989. NEIGHBORHOOD TOKYO. Stanford, CA: Stanford University Press [40, 48].
Bhatnagar, Bhuvan 1992. "Participatory Development and the World Bank: Opportunities and Concerns." In PARTICIPATORY DEVELOPMENT AND THE WORLD BANK: POTENTIAL DIRECTIONS FOR CHANGE, eds. Bhuvan Bhatnagar and Aubrey C. Williams. Washington D.C.: World Bank Discussion Paper 183 [320].
Bhattacharya, Amar and Mari Pangestu 1993. THE LESSONS OF EAST ASIA: INDONESIA DEVELOPMENT TRANSFORMATION AND PUBLIC POLICY. Washington, DC: The World Bank [52, 54].
Bindlish, Vishva and Robert Evenson 1993. EVALUATION OF THE PERFORMANCE OF T&V IN KENYA. Washington, DC: World Bank Technical Paper No. 208 [87, 89, 102].
Blackwell, Jonathan M, Rodger N. Goodwillie and Richard Webb. 1991. ENVIRONMENT AND DEVELOPMENT IN AFRICA. Washington, DC: The World Bank [96].
Blustein, Paul 1996. "Missionary Work," THE WASHINGTON POST MAGAZINE. November 10: 8–13; 24–30 [307, 322, 325].
Boddy, Martin. 1981. "The Public Implementation of Private Housing Policy: Relations Between Government and the Building Societies in the 1970s." In POLICY AND ACTION: ESSAYS ON THE IMPLEMENTATION OF PUBLIC POLICY, eds. Susan Barrett and Colin Fudge. London and New York: St. Methuen [111].

Bohlen, Celestine 1995. "Italy's Clean Hands' Judges Bite Their Nails." THE NEW YORK TIMES. June 25: A3 [184].
Bonomo, Luca and A.E. Higginson. 1988. INTERNATIONAL OVERVIEW ON SOLID WASTE MANAGEMENT. San Diego: Academic Press Limited [44, 50].
Boone, Catherine 1990. "The Making of a Rentier Class: Wealth Accumulation and Political Control in Senegal." JOURNAL OF DEVELOPMENT STUDIES 26(3): 426–445 [194].
Borja, Jordi. 1992. "Past, Present, and Future of Local Government in Latin America." In RETHINKING THE LATIN AMERICAN CITY, eds. Richard M. Morse and Jorge E. Hardoy. Baltimore and London: The Johns Hopkins University Press [108].
Bounin, O. and Ch. A. Michalet 1991. REBALANCING THE PUBLIC AND PRIVATE SECTORS: DEVELOPING COUNTRY EXPERIENCE. Paris: OECD [153].
Boyer, William W. and Ayong Man Ahn. 1991. RURAL DEVELOPMENT IN SOUTH KOREA: A SOCIOPOLITICAL ANALYSIS. Newark, DE: University of Delaware Press [230, 231].
Boyle, Neil 1995. "Pakistan: Sindh Special Development Project." In Environment Department, ed., WORLD BANK PARTICIPATION SOURCEBOOK. Washington, DC: The World Bank [88, 262].
Boyle, Neil 1996. EXPLORATIONS OF A THEORETICAL FRAMEWORK OF INSTITUTIONAL DEVELOPMENT. Washington, DC: World Bank Unpublished Report [310, 340].
Boyle, Neil and Susan Silsby 1996. MAPPING THE BLACK BOX OF INSTITUTIONAL DEVELOPMENT. Washington, DC: World Bank Unpublished Report [310, 318, 340].
Boyle, Philip. 1986. "On the Analysis of Organizational Culture in Development Project Planning." In U.S. Agency for International Development, ed., REPORT ON THE MANAGEMENT OF AGRICULTURAL PROJECTS IN AFRICA. Washington, DC: USAID [88].
Boyne, George A. 1993. "Central Policies and Local Autonomy: The Case of Wales." URBAN POLITICS 30: 87–101 [109].
Bozeman, Barry. 1987. ALL ORGANIZATIONS ARE PUBLIC. San Francisco: Jossey-Bass Publishers [47, 171].
Bradsher, Keith 1994. "U.S. is Attracting New Money Pool." THE NEW YORK TIMES. July 31: Al, A4 [198].
Bradsher, Keith 1995. "Widest Gap in Incomes? Research Points to U.S." October 27: D2 [174].
Bratton, Michael and Donald Rothchild 1992. "The Institutional Bases for Governance in Africa." In Goran Hyden and Michael Bratton, eds., GOVERNANCE AND POLITICS IN AFRICA. Boulder & London: Lynne Rienner Publishers [24].
Brauer, Dieter. 1990. "Tying Aid to Democracy." DEVELOPMENT FORUM (July-August): 3 [204].
Breman, Jan. 1993. BEYOND PATRONAGE AND EXPLOITATION: CHANGE IN AGRARIAN RELATIONS IN SOUTH GUJARAT. Oxford: Oxford University Press [263].

Bremmer, Joel F. and Herbert M. Franklin. 1977. RENT CONTROL IN NORTH AMERICA AND FOUR EUROPEAN COUNTRIES. Washington, DC: Council for International Urban Liaison [170].

Brett, E. A. 1994. "Rebuilding Organizational Capacity in Uganda Under the National Resistance Movement." JOURNAL OF MODERN AFRICAN STUDIES 32(1): 53–80 [237, 239].

Brett, E. A. 1995. "Neutralizing the Use of Force in Uganda: The Role of the Military in Politics." JOURNAL OF MODERN AFRICAN STUDIES 33(1): 129–152 [237, 239].

Bretton, Henry. 1966. THE RISE AND FALL OF KWAME NKRUMAH. New York: Callaway and Card [273].

Briscoe, John and Mike Garn 1994. FINANCING AGENDA 21: FRESHWATER. Washington, DC: The World Bank [333].

Brooke, James 1995 "Peru: On the Very Fast Track." THE NEW YORK TIMES. January 31: D1, D19 [57].

Brown, David S. 1982. MANAGING THE LARGE ORGANIZATION. Mt. Airy, MD: Lomond Books [129].

Brown, Frederick., 1990. "Creating More Dynamic Public Housing: A Modest Proposal." JOURNAL OF HOUSING, Vol. 47 (November/December): 309–314 [69].

Bryant, Coralie, 1991. "Sustainability Revisited: States, Institutions, and Economic Performance." Paper Presented at the Annual Meeting of the American Society of Public Administration, Washington, DC [85].

Bryant, Coralie 1993. OWNERSHIP OF PUBLIC SERVICES & MANAGEMENT REFORM. Washington, DC: World Bank Draft Report [212, 319, 320].

Bryant, Coralie 1997. "Market Assisted Land Reform: Private Property Rights for the Rural Poor." OCCASIONAL PAPER SERIES: SECTION ON INTERNATIONAL AND COMPARATIVE ADMINISTRATION [342].

Bryant, Coralie and Louise White 1982. MANAGING DEVELOPMENT IN THE THIRD WORLD. Boulder, CO: Westview Press [157].

Buckley, Stephen. 1995. "Confusion is Compounded In Marred Tanzania Election." THE WASHINGTON POST. November 21: A22 [207].

Buckley, Stephen 1996. "Wave of Trade Leaves Africa Parched." THE WASHINGTON POST. December 31: A1, A12–13 [288, 300].

Bullmann, Udo, Michael Goldsmith, and Edward C. Page. 1994. "Subnational Government Autonomy and Political Authority: Regions, Localities and the Shifting Balance of Authority in Europe." New York: Annual Meeting of the APSA [114].

Burkhart, Ross E. and Michael S. Lewis-Beck. 1994. "Comparative Democracy: The Economic Development Thesis." AMERICAN POLITICAL SCIENCE REVIEW 88 (4): 903–910 [201].

Burns, John F. 1996. "India Ruefully Takes Stock of 49 Years." NEW YORK TIMES. August 16: A10 [316].

Butler, Stuart and Anna Kondratas 1987. OUT OF THE POVERTY TRAP. New York: The Free Press [147].

Cabogo, Sarasoro H. 1993. "Civil Service Ethics and Corruption in Cote d'Ivoire." In Sadig Rasheed and Dele Olowu, eds., ETHICS AND ACCOUNTABILITY IN AFRICAN PUBLIC SERVICES. NY: United Nations [189, 198].

Caiden, Gerald E. 1982. PUBLIC ADMINISTRATION. Pacific Palisades, CA: Palisades Publishers [8].
Caiden, Gerald E. 1988. "Toward a General Theory of Official Corruption." ASIAN JOURNAL OF PUBLIC ADMINISTRATION 10 (1): 3–20 [165, 169, 172].
Caiden, Gerald E. 1990. "Official Corruption and Political Stability." SRI LANKA JOURNAL OF DEVELOPMENT ADMINISTRATION 7(1): 142–166 [191].
Caiden, Gerald E. 1991. ADMINISTRATIVE REFORM COMES OF AGE. Berlin: Walter de Gruyter [51, 56, 83].
Caiden, Gerald E., 1991a. "What Really is Public Maladministration?" PUBLIC ADMINISTRATION REVIEW, Vol. 56 (November/December): 486–493 [62].
Calder, Kent E. 1988. CRISIS AND COMPENSATION: PUBLIC POLICY AND POLITICAL STABILITY IN JAPAN: 1949–1986. Princeton, NJ: Princeton University Press [22].
Calibrone, W. 1985. "Scavenger Class Still Does India's Dirtiest Job." THE WASHINGTON POST, May 13: A-6 [100].
Callaghy, Thomas M. 1993. "Political Passions and Economic Interests." In Thomas M. Callaghy and John Ravenhill, eds., HEMMED IN. New York: Columbia University Press [314].
Callaghy, Thomas M. 1994. "State, Choice, and Context: Comparative Reflections on Reform and Intractability." In David E. Apter and Carl G. Rosberg, eds., POLITICAL DEVELOPMENT AND THE NEW REALISM IN SUB-SAHARAN AFRICA. Charlottesville and London: University Press of Virginia [23].
Callaghy, Thomas M. and John Ravenhill 1993, "Introduction," and "How Hemmed In?" In Thomas M. Callaghy and John Ravenhill, eds., HEMMED IN. New York: Columbia University Press [323].
Campbell, John C. 1989. "Democracy and Bureaucracy in Japan." In Takeshi Ishida and Ellis S. Krauss, eds., DEMOCRACY IN JAPAN. Pittsburgh, PA: University of Pittsburgh Press [38, 172, 180].
Campbell, M.J. 1990. "Technology and Rural Development: The Social Impact." In NEW TECHNOLOGY AND RURAL DEVELOPMENT: THE SOCIAL IMPACT, ed. M. J. Campbell. London: Routledge [266].
Campos, Jose Edgardo and Hilton L. Root 1996. THE KEY TO THE ASIAN MIRACLE. Washington, D.C.: The Brookings Institution [54, 222, 226, 229, 281, 291, 315].
Canagarajah, Sudharshan and Saji Thomas 1997. GHANA'S LABOR MARKET (1987–92). Washington, D.C.: The World Bank Policy Research Paper 1752 [277].
Carapetis, Steve, Herman Levy and Terje Wolden. 1991. THE ROAD MAINTENANCE INITIATIVE: VOL. l. Washington DC: The World Bank [244].
Carmichael, Paul. 1994. "Analyzing Political Choice in Local Government: A Comparative Case Study Approach." PUBLIC ADMINISTRATION. Vol. 72 (Summer): 241–262 [111].
Carmines, Edward G. and W. Richard Merriman, Jr. 1993. "The Changing American Dilemma: Liberal Values and Racial Policies," In PREJUDICE, POLITICS AND THE AMERICAN DILEMMA, eds. Paul M. Sniderman, Philip E. Tetlock, and Edward G. Carmines [264].

Carroll, Alan ET AL. 1995. RESTORING URBAN NIGERIA. Washington, DC: The World Bank [35, 43, 47, 49].

Carroll, Tom, Mary Schmidt and Tony Bebbington. 1996. PARTICIPATION THROUGH INTERMEDIARY NGOs. Washington, DC: World Bank Discussion Paper O31 [313, 325, 330, 337].

Cassandra, 1995. "The Impending Crisis in Egypt." THE MIDDLE EAST JOURNAL 49(1): 9–27 [121].

Casteneda, Tarsicio and Funkoo Park. 1992. "Structural Adjustment and the Role of the Labor Market." In Vittorio Corbo and Sang-Mok Suh, eds., STRUCTURAL ADJUSTMENT IN A NEWLY INDUSTRIALIZED COUNTRY: THE KOREAN EXPERIENCE. Washington, DC: The World Bank [283].

Cernea, Michael M., eds. 1985, 1991. PUTTING PEOPLE FIRST: SOCIOLOGICAL VARIABLES IN RURAL DEVELOPMENT. Washington, DC: The World Bank/ Oxford U. Press [152].

Cernea, Michael M. 1991. "Sociologists in a Development Agency: Observations from the World Bank." WORLD BANK REPRINT SERIES, No. 463 [76].

Cernea, Michael M. 1991a. "The Social Actors of Participatory Afforestation Strategies." In Michael M. Cernea, ed., PUTTING PEOPLE FIRST. Washington, DC: The World Bank [152].

Cernea, Michael M., 1991b. USING KNOWLEDGE FROM SOCIAL SCIENCE IN DEVELOPMENT PROJECTS. Washington, DC: World Bank [96].

Cernea, Michael M. 1992. THE BUILDING BLOCKS OF PARTICIPATION. Washington, DC: The World Bank [152].

Cernea, Michael M. 1993. "Culture and Organization: The Social Sustainability of Induced Development." SUSTAINABLE DEVELOPMENT. l (2): 13–29 [339].

Chandler, Clay. 1996. "World Bank Chief Chides Staff." THE WASHINGTON POST. March 30: C8 [18].

Chang, H. 1991. "Impressions of Mainland China Carried Back by Taiwan Visitors." In Ramon H. Myers, ed., TWO SOCIETIES IN OPPOSITION: THE REPUBLIC OF CHINA AND THE PEOPLE'S REPUBLIC OF CHINA AFTER FORTY YEARS. Stanford, CA: Hoover University Press [223].

Charlesworth, Julie and Alan Cochrane 1994. "Tales of the Suburbs: The Local Politics of Growth in the South-east of England." URBAN STUDIES. Vol. 31 (10): 1723–1738 [111].

Charlick, Robert B. 1984. ANIMATION RURALE REVISITED. Ithaca, NY: Cornell University Press [156].

Charlick, Robert B. 1993. "Corruption in Political Transition: A Governance Perspective." CORRUPTION AND REFORM 7(3): 177–187 [203].

Chazan, Naomi. 1991. "The Political Tranformation of Ghana Under the PNDC." In Donald Rothchild, ed., GHANA: THE POLITICAL ECONOMY OF RECOVERY. Boulder, CO: Lynne Rienner Publishers [212, 215, 278].

Chee, Chan H. 1986. "Singapore in 1986." ASIAN SURVEY 26(2): 159–163 [226].

Chege, Michael. 1994. "Swapping Development Strategies: Kenya and Tanzania after Their Founding Presidents." In David E. Apter and Carl G. Rosberg, eds., POLITICAL DEVELOPMENT AND THE NEW REALISM IN SUB-SAHARAN AFRICA. Charlottesville and London: University Press of Virginia [29, 31].

Chen, David W. 1994. "The Emergence of an Environmental Consciousness in Taiwan." In Murray A. Rubinstein, ed., THE OTHER TAIWAN: 1945 TO THE PRESENT. Armond, NY: M. E. Sharpe [236] Cheru, Fanu. 1992. "Structural Adjustment, Primary Resource Trade and Sustainable Development in Sub-Saharan Africa." WORLD DEVELOPMENT 21 (4): 497–509 [198].

Chetwynd, Eric and Mohamed M. Samaan. 1984. EGYPT, BASIC VILLAGE SERVICES. Washington, DC: USAID Internal Document [124].

Cheung, Paul P. L. 1990. "Micro-Consequences of Low Fertility in Singapore." ASIA-PACIFIC POPULATION JOURNAL 5(4): 35–46 [258] Chhibber, Ajay ET AL. 1993. GHANA 2000 AND BEYOND. Washington, DC: The World Bank Africa Regional Office [270, 286, 290, 291, 303].

Chira, Susan. 1995. "Care at Child Day Centers is Rated as Poor." NEW YORK TIMES. February 7: A12 [70].

Cho, Lee-Jay. 1994. "Culture, Insitutions, and Economic Development in East Asia." In Lee-Jay Cho and Yoon Hyung Kim, eds., KOREA'S POLITICAL ECONOMY: AN INSTITUTIONAL PERSPECTIVE. Boulder, CO: Westview Press [278, 294].

Cho, Lee-Jay and Kennon Breazeale. 1991. "The Educational System." In Lee-Jay Cho and Yoon Hyung Kim, eds., ECONOMIC DEVELOPMENT IN THE REPUBLIC OF KOREA: A POLICY PERSPECTIVE. Honolulu, HI: University of Hawaii Press [224].

Cho, Lee-Jay and Yoon Hyung Kim 1991. "Political and Economic Antecedents to the 1960s." In Lee-Jay Cho and Yoon Hyung Kim, eds., ECONOMIC DEVELOPMENT IN THE REPUBLIC OF KOREA: A POLICY PERSPECTIVE. Honolulu, HA: East-West Center [278].

Choguill, C. L. 1994. "Crisis, Chaos, Crunch? Planning for Urban Growth in the Developing World. URBAN STUDIES 31(6): 935–145 [142].

Choi, Kwang 1991. "Introduction of the Value-Added Tax." In Lee-Jay Cho and Yoon Hyung Kim, eds., ECONOMIC DEVELOPMENT IN THE REPUBLIC OF KOREA: A POLICY PERSPECTIVE. Honolulu, HA: East-West Center [302].

Chu, Yun-han. 1994. "Social Protests and Political Democratization in Taiwan." in Murray A. Rubinstein, ed., THE OTHER KOREA: 1945 TO THE PRESENT. Armond, NY: M.E. Sharpe [223, 234].

Chua, Beng-Huat. 1991. "Not Depoliticized but Ideologically Successful: The Public Housing Programme in Singapore." INTERNATIONAL JOURNAL OF URBAN AND REGIONAL RESEARCH 15(1): 24–40 [233].

Chung, Chen H., Jon M. Shepard, and Marc J. Dollinger. 1989. "Max Weber Revisited: Some Lessons from East Asian Capitalistic Development." ASIAN PACIFIC JOURNAL OF MANAGEMENT. Vol. 6(2): 307–321 [25].

Churchill, Anthony 1980. SHELTER. Washington, DC: The World Bank [132].

Clark, Ann. 1995. "India: Andra Pradesh Forestry." In Environment Department, ed., WORLD BANK PARTICIPATION SOURCEBOOK. Washington, DC: The World Bank [330].

Clark, John F. 1994. "Elections, Leadership & Democracy in Congo." AFRICA TODAY 41(3): 50–60 [209].

Clarke, Giles, Suhadi Hadiwinoto, and Josef Leitman, 1991. ENVIRONMENTAL PROFILE OF JAKARTA. Washington, DC: UNDP/World Bank Urban Management Program [65].

Cleaver, Kevin 1993. A STRATEGY TO DEVELOP AGRICULTURE IN SUB-SAHARAN AFRICA AND A FOCUS FOR THE WORLD BANK. Washington, DC: The World Bank [88, 91, 95, 98, 101].

Cleaver, Kevin M. and Gotz A. Schreiber 1994. REVERSING THE SPIRAL: THE POPULATION, AGRICULTURE, AND ENVIRONMENT NEXUS IN SUB-SAHARAN AFRICA. Washington, DC: The World Bank [92, 266].

Cleaver, Kevin M. and W. Graeme Donavan 1995. AGRICULTURE, POVERTY, AND POLICY REFORM IN SUB-SAHARAN AFRICA. Washington, DC: World Bank Discussion Paper 280 [90, 92, 93].

Clements, Paul 1993. "An Approach to Poverty Alleviation for Large International Development Agencies." WORLD DEVELOPMENT, 21 (10): 1633–46 [321].

Clifford, Mark L. 1994. TROUBLED TIGER; BUSINESSMEN, BUREAUCRATS, AND GENERALS IN SOUTH KOREA. Armonk, NY: M. E. Sharpe [223, 271, 278, 289, 295].

Clower, Robert W. ET AL. 1966. GROWTH WITHOUT DEVELOPMENT: AN ECONOMIC ANALYSIS. Evanston, IL: Northwestern University Press [21].

Cobbe, James. 1991. "The Political Economy of Education Reform in Ghana." In Donald Rothchild, ed., GHANA: THE POLITICAL ECONOMY OF RECOVERY. Boulder, CO: Lynne Rienner Publishers [274].

Cobbe, James and Boediono. 1993. "Education, Demographics, the Labor Market, and Development: Indonesia in the Process of Transition. JOURNAL OF ASIAN AND AFRICAN STUDIES 23(l-2):3–17 [260].

Cochrane, Glynn. 1983. POLICIES FOR STRENGTHENING LOCAL GOVERNMENT IN DEVELOPING COUNTRIES. Washington, DC: The World Bank [231].

Cohen, John M. 1993. "The Importance of Public Sector Reform: The Case of Kenya." THE JOURNAL OF MODERN AFRICAN STUDIES 31(3): 449–476 [190, 249].

Coll, Steve and Cindy Shiner 1994. "Military Rulers Drained Nigeria, Enriched Selves." THE WASHINGTON POST July 23: A1, A16 [55].

Cointreau-Levine, Sandra. 1992. PRIVATE SECTOR PARTICIPATION IN MUNICIPAL SOLID WASTE SERVICES IN DEVELOPING COUNTRIES. Washington, D.C.: World Bank Internal Document [35, 49].

Colletta, Nat J. and Gillian Perkins 1995. PARTICIPATION IN EDUCATION. Washington, DC: The World Bank [151, 334].

Cooperative Housing Foundation. 1992. PARTNERSHIP FOR A LIVABLE ENVIRONMENT. Silver Spring, MD: Cooperative Housing Foundation [121].

Cooper, John F. 1995. "Taiwan's Gubernatorial and Mayoral Elections." ASIAN AFFAIRS 22(2): 97–118 [235].

Corbo, Vittorio and San-Woo Nam. 1992. "Recent Evolution of the Macroeconomy." In Vittorio Corbo and Sang-Mok Suh, eds., STRUCTURAL ADJUSTMENT IN A NEWLY INDUSTRIALIZED COUNTRY: THE KOREAN EXPERIENCE. Washington, DC: The World Bank [279].

Costello, Mathew J. 1996. "Administrative Triumphs Over Politics: The Transformation of the Tanzanian State." AFRICAN STUDIES REVIEW 39(1): 123–148 [329].
Cothran, Dan A. 1994. STABILITY AND DEMOCRACY IN MEXICO: THE PERFECT DICTATORSHIP. Westport, CN: Praeger, 1994 [186, 196].
Coulter, Edwin M. 1987. PRINCIPLES OF POLITICS AND GOVERNMENT. Boston: Allyn and Bacon [39].
Country Operations Department 1995. GHANA: PRIVATE SECTOR ADJUSTMENT CREDIT. Washington, DC: World Bank Internal Report [296].
Cowell, Alan. 1993. "Broad Bribery Investigation Is Ensnaring the Elite of Italy." THE NEW YORK TIMES, March 3: A1, A8 [182].
Crane, George T. 1989. "The Adjustment Capacity of the State in Taiwan: State-Owned Enterprises and the Oil Shocks of the 1970s." In Hsin-Huang Michael Hsiao, Wei-Yuan Cheng, and Hou-Sheng Chan, eds, TAIWAN: A NEWLY INDUSTRIALIZED STATE. Taipei: National Taiwan University Press [2].
Crane, George T. 1995. "Wrong Choice for an Honorary Degree." THE WASHINGTON POST. August 30: A24 [223].
Crane, Randall. 1994. "Water, Markets, Market Reform and the Urban Poor." WORLD DEVELOPMENT 22(1): 71–83 [134].
Crewson, Philip E. and Bonnie S. Fisher 1997. "Growing Older and Wiser: The Changing Skill Requirements of City Administrators." PUBLIC ADMINISTRATION REVIEW 57 (5): 380–395 [63].
Crick, Bernard. 1960. THE AMERICAN SCIENCE OF POLITICS; ITS ORIGINS AND CONDITIONS. Berkeley, CA: University of California Press [116].
Crozier, Michael. 1964. THE BUREAUCRATIC PHENOMENON. Chicago: University of Chicago Press [131].
Crump, John. 1996. "Environmental Politics in Japan." ENVIRONMENTAL POLITICS. Vol. 5 (1): 115–121 [41].
Culhane, Dennis P., 1992. "The Quandaries of Shelter Reform: An Appraisal of Efforts to Manage Homelessness," SOCIAL SCIENCE REVIEW. Vol. 66 (3): 428–441 [65].
Currie, Elliott, 1985. CONFRONTING CRIME. New York: Pantheon Books [60].
Dahl, Robert A. 1971. POLYARCHY: PARTICIPATION AND OPPOSITION. New Haven: Yale University Press [202, 215].
Da Matta, Roberto. 1993. "Is Brazil Hopelessly Corrupt?" NEW YORK TIMES. Dec. 13: A17 [248].
Davey, Kenneth J. 1993. ELEMENTS OF URBAN MANAGEMENT. Washington, DC: The World Bank [113].
Davies, H.W.E. 1988. "The Control of Development in the Netherlands." TOWN PLANNING REVIEW 59: 207–220 [118].
Davis, Daniel, David Hulme, and Philip Woodhouse 1994. "Decentralization by Default: Local Governance and the View from the Village in The Gambia." PUBLIC ADMINISTRATION AND DEVELOPMENT 12: 253–267 [114].
Day, Patricia 1988. "The Public Regulation of Private Welfare—The Case of Residential and Nursing Homes for the Elderly." POLITICAL QUARTERLY 59: 44–54 [105].

de Franco, Silvio, Alberto Eguren and David Baughman. 1988. KOREA'S EXPERIENCE WITH THE DEVELOPMENT OF TRADE AND INDUSTRY. Washington, DC: The World Bank EDI [278].

de Juan, Aristobulo. 1991. "Does Bank Insolvency Matter? And What to do About It." In Philippe Callier, ed., FINANCIAL SYSTEMS AND DEVELOPMENT IN AFRICA. Washington, DC: World Bank EDI [29, 192].

DeLeon, Peter 1989. "Public Policy Implications of Systemic Political Corruption." CORRUPTION AND REFORM 2(3): 193–215 [169].

de Merode, Louis and Charles S. Thomas 1994. "Implementing Civil Service Pay and Employment Reform in Africa: The Experience of Ghana, the Gambia, and Guinea." In David L. Lindauer and Barbara Nunberg, eds., REHABILITATING GOVERNMENT: PAY AND EMPLOYMENT REFORM IN AFRICA. Washington, DC: The World Bank [210].

Deneke, Albert and Silva, Mauricio, 1982. "Housing Built by Mutual Help and Progressive Development: To What End?" In P. Ward, ed., SELF-HELP HOUSING: A CRITQUE. London: Alexandrine Press [77].

DePalma, Anthony, 1989. "Newark and New York: Two Cities, Two Results in Housing the Poor," THE NEW YORK TIMES (May 14): E23 [70].

DeParle, Jason 1996. "Slamming the Door." THE NEW YORK TIMES MAGAZINE. October 20: 52–57, 105 [175].

de Regt, Jacomina 1995. "Mozambique: Country Implementation Review." In Environment Department, ed., WORLD BANK PARTICIPATION SOURCEBOOK. Washington, DC: The World Bank [324].

de Soto, Hernando. 1989. THE OTHER PATH. New York: Harper & Row [142].

Devas, Nick 1989. "Financing Urban Services." In Nick Devas, ed., FINANCING LOCAL GOVERNMENT IN INDONESIA. Athens, OH: Ohio University Press [55].

Development Alternatives (DAI) 1996. "Export-led Development: The Kenya Experience." DAI Newsletter [102].

Devlin, John F. and Nonita T. Tap 1994. "Sustainable development and the NICs: Cautionary tales for the South in the New World (Dis) Order." THIRD WORLD QUARTERLY 15(1): 49–61 [236].

Dey, Harendra K. 1989. "The Genesis and Spread of Economic Corruption: A Microtheoretic Interpretation." WORLD DEVELOPMENT 17(4): 503–511 [187, 188, 195].

Dia, Mamadou. 1993. A GOVERNANCE APPROACH TO CIVIL SERVICE REFORM IN SUB-SAHARAN AFRICA. Washington, DC: The World Bank [248, 315].

Dia, Mamadou 1995, 1996. AFRICA'S MANAGEMENT IN THE 1990s AND BEYOND: FROM INSTITUTIONAL "TRANSPLANT" TO INSTITUTIONAL RECONCILIATION. Washington, DC: The World Bank [210, 328].

Diamond, Larry. 1990. "Three Paradoxes of Democracy." JOURNAL OF DEMOCRACY 1(3):49–59 [217].

Diamond, Larry 1994. "Promoting Democracy in the 1990s: Actors, Instruments, and Issues." American Political Science Association Annual Meeting, New York City [200].

Diamond, Larry, Juan J. Linz and Seymour Lipset 1989. "Preface." In Larry Diamond, Juan J. Linz and Seymour Lipset, eds, DEMOCRACY IN DEVELOPING COUNTRIES, VOL. 4: LATIN AMERICA. Boulder, CO: Lynne Rienner Publishers [215].
Dillinger, William. 1991. PROBLEMS OF COST RECOVERY. Washington, D.C.: World Bank Internal Document [186].
Dillinger, William 1991a. URBAN PROPERTY TAX REFORM. Washington, DC: The World Bank [46].
Dillinger, William 1993. DECENTRALIZATION AND ITS IMPLICATIONS FOR URBAN SERVICE DELIVERY. Washington, DC: The World Bank [113].
DiMaggio, Paul J. 1995. "Comments on What Theory Is Not." ADMINISTRATIVE SCIENCE QUARTERLY 40(3): 391–397 [61].
Doig, Alan. 1984. CORRUPTION AND MISCONDUCT IN CONTEMPORARY BRITISH POLITICS. Hammondsworth, Middlesex, England: Contemporary Books, 1984 [192].
Donavan, W. Graeme. 1994. MALAWI: ECONOMIC REFORM AND AGRICULTURAL STRATEGY. Washington, DC: The World Bank [90, 102].
Dove, Michael R. 1988. "Introduction: Traditional Culture and Development in Contemporary Indonesia." In THE REAL AND IMAGINED ROLE OF CULTURE IN DEVELOPMENT, ed. Michael R. Dove. Honolulu: U. of Hawaii Press [253].
Drew, Elizabeth. 1996. "Soft Money: The Reform That Corrupted the System." THE WASHINGTON POST. November 3: C7 [176].
Drohan, Madalaine. 1996. "London Traffic Trapped in Carraige Days." THE GLOBE AND MAIL. June 5: A8 [111].
Drucker, Peter F. 1974. MANAGEMENT. New York: Harper & Row [130].
Drum, Bernard ET AL. 1991. THE REPUBLIC OF GHANA: PUBLIC ENTERPRISE SECTOR REVIEW. Washington, DC: The World Bank Internal Document [292].
Dubnick, Melvin J. 1994. "A Coup Against King Bureaucracy." In John J. DiIulio, Jr., ed., DEREGULATING THE PUBLIC SECTOR. Washington, DC: The Brookings Institution [146].
Duke, Lynne 1995. "Disaffected in Zambia." THE WASHINGTON POST. September 12: A12 [211].
Earley, P. Christopher 1994. "Self or Group? Cultural Effects of Training on Self-Efficacy and Performance." ADMINISTRATIVE SCIENCE QUARTERLY 39 (1): 89–117 [63].
East Asia and Pacific Region 1995. PHILIPPINES: A STRATEGY TO FIGHT POVERTY. Washington, DC: World Bank Report No. 14933–PH [120].
East Asia and Pacific Region 1996. INDONESIA: DIMENSIONS OF GROWTH. Washington, DC: World Bank Report No. 15383–IND [53, 54].
Easterly, William and Stanley Fischer 1994. "What We Can Learn from the Soviet Collapse." FINANCE AND DEVELOPMENT. Dec: 2–5 [22].
Easterly, William and Ross Levine 1995. AFRICA'S GROWTH TRAGEDY: A RETROSPECTIVE, 1960–1989. Washington, DC: World Bank Research Working Paper 1503 [313].

Eastern African Department 1995. UGANDA: THE CHALLENGE OF GROWTH AND POVERTY REDUCTION. Washington DC: World Bank Report No. 14313-UG [237, 238, 239].

Eastern Africa Department 1996. TANZANIA: THE CHALLENGE OF REFORMS. Washington, DC: The World Bank Report No. 14982-TA [29, 310, 312, 316].

Eckstein, Harry. 1988. "A Culturalist Theory of Political Change." AMERICAN POLITICAL SCIENCE REVIEW 82:789-804 [243, 247].

Economic Commission for Europe 1996. STRATEGIES TO IMPLEMENT HUMAN SETTLEMENTS POLICIES ON URBAN RENEWAL AND HOUSING MOBILIZATION. New York and Geneva: United Nations [170].

Eigen, Peter 1992. "Focus on Corruption." HUMAN DEVELOPMENT REPORT (a TRANSPARENCY INTERNATIONAL Publication) [198].

Elazar, Daniel J. 1965. "The Shaping of Intergovernmental Relations in the Twentieth Century." ANNALS 359: 10-22 [109].

Emerson, Rupert. 1960. FROM EMPIRE TO NATION. Boston: Beacon [251].

Eng, Tew Siew 1996. "Character and Identity in Singapore New Towns: Planner and Resident Perspectives." HABITAT INTERNATIONAL 20 (2): 279-294 [234].

Environment Department 1995. WORLD BANK PARTICIPATION SOURCEBOOK. washington, DC: The World Bank [320].

Esman, Milton J. 1988. "The Maturing of Development Administration." PUBLIC ADMINISTRATION AND DEVELOPMENT 8(2): 125-139 [145].

Esman, Milton J. and Norman Uphoff 1984. LOCAL ORGANIZATIONS: INTERMEDIARIES IN RURAL DEVELOPMENT. Ithaca, NY: Cornell University Press [154].

Euben, J. Peter 1993. "Democracy Ancient and Modern." PS: POLITICAL SCIENCE AND POLITICS. 26(3): 478-480 [216].

Europe and Central Asia Department 1994. THE RUSSIAN FEDERATION: MANAGEMENT AND FINANCIAL TRAINING PROJECT. Washington, DC: The World Bank 12987-RU [334].

Europe and Central Asia Department 1995. RUSSIAN FEDERATION: URBAN TRANSPORT PROJECT. Washington, DC: World Bank [334].

Evans, Diana 1994. "Policy and Pork: The Use of Pork Barrel Projects to Build Policy Coalitions in the House of Representatives." AMERICAN JOURNAL OF POLITICAL SCIENCE 38(4): 894-917 [178].

Fatton, Robert Jr. 1992. PREDATORY RULE: STATE AND CIVIL SOCIETY IN AFRICA. Boulder, CO: Lynne Rienner Publishers [145].

Fayol, F. 1949. "General Principles of Management" In D. S. Pugh, ed., ORGANIZATIONAL THEORY: SELECTED READINGS, 2nd ed., 1984. Harmondsworth, Middlesex, England: Pelican Books [5, 64].

Fei, John C. H. 1991. "An Historical Perspective on Economic Modernization in the ROC." In Ramon H. Myers, ed, TWO SOCIETIES IN OPPOSITION: THE REPUBLIC OF CHINA AND THE PEOPLE'S REPUBLIC OF CHINA AFTER FORTY YEARS. Stanford, CA: Hoover University Press [223].

Feiler, Gil 1992. "Housing Policy in Egypt." MIDDLE EASTERN STUDIES 28(2): 295-312 [122].

Fernandes, Edesio. 1995. LAW AND URBAN CHANGE IN BRAZIL. Aldershot, Hants, England: Avebury [144].
Fesler, James. 1965. "Approaches to the Understanding of Decentralization." JOURNAL OF POLITICS 27: 530–545 [104].
Field, Brian. 1987. "Public Housing in Singapore." LAND USE POLICY. April: 147–156 [256].
Field, Brian and George Ofari. 1989. "Housing Stress and the Role of the State." HABITAT INTERNATIONAL. 13(3): 128–138 [232].
Fieldhouse, D. K. 1986. BLACK AFRICA 1945–1980: ECONOMIC DECOLONIZATION AND ARRESTED DEVELOPMENT. London: Allen & Unwin [272, 274].
Finin, Gerald, Norman Uphoff, and Suzanne Walen. 1984. STRATEGIES FOR SUPPORTING LOCAL INSTITUTIONAL DEVELOPMENT. Ithaca, NY: Cornell University Press [156].
Fisher, Julie. 1994. "Is the Iron Law of Oligarchy Rusting Away in the Third World?" WORLD DEVELOPMENT 22:129–143 [113].
Flynn, Robert 1986. "The Mediation of Bureaucratic-Professional Influence: Decentralization in Dutch Housing Policy." POLITICAL STUDIES 34:606–619 [119].
Fong, Pang Eng, Tan Chwee Huat, and Chen Soo May. 1989. "The Management of People." In Kerniel S. Sandhu and Paul Wheatley, eds., MANAGEMENT OF SUCCESS; THE MOULDING OF MODERN SINGAPORE. Singapore: Institute of Southeast Asian Studies [257].
Forrest, Tom 1993. POLITICS AND ECONOMIC DEVELOPMENT IN NIGERIA. Boulder, CO: Westview Press [38, 55].
Fox, Charles J. 1996. "Reinventing Government as Postmodern Symbolic Politics." PUBLIC ADMINISTRATION REVIEW 56 (3): 256–261 [307].
Fox, William F. 1994. STRATEGIC OPTIONS FOR URBAN INFRASTRUCTURE MANAGEMENT. Washington, DC: The World Bank [120].
Freeman, David M. and Max F. Lowdermilk 1991. "Middle-Level Farmer Organizations as Links between Farms and Central Irrigation Systems." In Michael M. Cernea, ed., PUTTING PEOPLE FIRST. Washington, DC: The World Bank [88, 91, 96].
French, Howard W. 1995. "Ivory Coast Vote Boycott Gains Favor At Election." THE NEW YORK TIMES. October 22: A9 [208].
Friedlander, Daniel and Gary Burtless. 1995. FIVE YEARS AFTER: THE LONG TERM EFFECTS OF WELFARE TO WORK PROGRAMS. New York: Russell Sage [68].
Frischtak, Leila L. 1994. GOVERNANCE CAPACITY AND ECONOMIC REFORM IN DEVELOPING COUNTRIES. Washington, DC: The World Bank [116].
Furlong, Paul. 1994. MODERN ITALY: REPRESENTATION AND REFORM. London and NY: Routledge [182, 184].
Gallagher, Mark G. 1991. RENT-SEEKING AND ECONOMIC GROWTH IN AFRICA. Boulder, CO: Westview Press [193].
Garn, Mike. 1995. DEMAND-BASED APPROACH: MAKING LARGE RURAL WATER SUPPLY AND SANITATION PROJECTS WORK. Washington, DC: UNDP/The World Bank [333].

Garnett, Harry, Sally Merrill, and John Miller 1988. URBANIZATION IN AFRICAN DEVELOPMENT: ISSUES AND OPPORTUNITIES. Washington, DC: USAID/Abt Associates [112, 300].

Garnier, Maurice, Atta Brou Noel, Christopher Schwabe, and James T. Thomson. 1992. THE EXPERIENCE IN IVORY COAST WITH DECENTRALIZED APPROACHES TO LOCAL DELIVERY OF PRIMARY EDUCATION AND PRIMARY HEALTH SERVICES. Burlington, VT: Associates for Rural Development [115].

Garvey, Brian 1991. "Patrimonial Economies and Informal Bureaucracies: Public Administration and Social Reality in the Least Developed Countries of the 1990s: A Review Article." PUBLIC ADMINISTRATION AND DEVELOPMENT ll(6): 591–600 [145].

Gboyega, Alex 1991. "Protecting Local Governments from Arbitrary State and Federal Interference: What Prospects for the 1990s?" PUBLIUS. Vol. 21(4): 45–60 [214].

Geilar, Samuel 1985. PUBLIC SECTOR REFORM AND PRIVATE SECTOR EXPANSION IN MALI: THE INSTITUTIONAL CONTEXT. Washington, DC: USAID [158].

Gibney, Frank. 1992. KOREA'S QUIET REVOLUTION: FROM GARRISON STATE TO DEMOCRACY. New York: Walker & Co. [278, 279, 281, 285].

Gilbert, Mark 1995. THE ITALIAN REVOLUTION: THE END OF POLITICS, ITALIAN STYLE?. Boulder, CO: Westview [175, 184].

Gillespie, Kate and Gwenn Okruhlik 1988. "Cleaning Up Corruption in the Middle East." THE MIDDLE EAST JOURNAL 42(1): 59–82 [187].

Gitonga, Afrifa K. 1988. "The Meaning and Foundation of Democracy." In Walter O. Oyugi, ET AL., eds., DEMOCRATIC THEORY AND PRACTICE IN AFRICA. Portsmouth, NH: Heinemann Educational Books [206].

Glaessner, Philip J. ET AL. 1994. POVERTY ALLEVIATION AND SOCIAL INVESTMENT FUNDS: THE LATIN AMERICAN EXPERIENCE. Washington, DC: World Bank Discussion Paper 261 [264].

Glazer, Myron P. and Penina Midgal Glazer 1989. THE WHISTLEBLOWERS. New York: Basic Books [178].

Gocking, Roger 1996. "Ghana's Public Tribunals: An Experiment in Revolutionary Justice." AFRICAN AFFAIRS 95: 197–223 [291].

Golden, Tim. 1993. "Where Politics and Poverty Intersect in Nicaragua, Signposts are Missing." NEW YORK TIMES. 31 August: A7 [342].

Goldman, Marshall I. 1994. "Do Business in Russia? For Now, No." THE NEW YORK TIMES. August 7: F9 [192] Goldsmith, Mike and Ken Norton 1983. "Central-Local Relations: The Irresistible Rise of Centralized Power." WEST EUROPEAN POLITICS 6 (4): 217–233 [111].

Gombay, Christie and Colleen O'Manique 1996. "Uganda." In Patricia L. McCarney, ed., THE CHANGING NATURE OF LOCAL GOVERNMENT IN DEVELOPING COUNTRIES. Toronto: U. of Toronto Press [187].

Good, Kenneth. 1992. "Interpreting the Exceptionality of Botswana." JOURNAL OF MODERN AFRICAN STUDIES 30(1): 69–91 [262].

Good, Kenneth. 1993. "At the Ends of the Ladder: Radical Inequalities in Botswana." JOURNAL OF MODERN AFRICAN STUDIES 31(2): 203–230 [262].

Goodman, Mary Ellen 1967. THE INDIVIDUAL AND CULTURE. Homewood, IL: Dorsey [247].
Gopal, Gita and Alexandra Marc. 1994. WORLD BANK FINANCED PROJECTS WITH COMMUNITY PARTICIPATION. Washington, DC: World Bank Discussion Paper 265 [318, 336].
Gordon, April A. 1996. TRANSFORMING CAPITALISM AND PATRIARCHY: GENDER AND DEVELOPMENT IN AFRICA. Boulder and London: Lynne Rienner [266, 267].
Gordon, David F. 1993. "Debt, Conditionality, and Reform." In Thomas M. Callaghy and John Ravenhill, eds., HEMMED IN. New York: Columbia University Press [308, 310, 315].
Gormley, William T. Jr. and B. Guy Peters 1992. "National Styles of Regulation: Child Care in Three Countries." POLICY SCIENCES 25: 381–399 [108].
Gould, David J. 1980. BUREAUCRATIC CORRUPTION AND UNDERDEVELOPMENT IN THE THIRD WORLD. New York: Pergamon Press [187].
Gould, David J. and Jose A. Amaro-Reyes 1983. THE EFFECTS OF CORRUPTION ON ADMINISTRATIVE PERFORMANCE: ILLUSTRATIONS FROM DEVELOPING COUNTRIES. Washington, DC: The World Bank [163].
Goulet, Dennis 1989. "Participation in Development: New Avenues." WORLD DEVELOPMENT 17(2): 164–175 [162].
Grabowski, Richard. 1994. "The Successful Developmental State: Where Does It Come From?" WORLD DEVELOPMENT 22(3): 413–421 [203].
Gran, Guy 1983. DEVELOPMENT BY PEOPLE: CITIZEN CONSTRUCTION OF A JUST WORLD. New York: Praeger Publications [146, 149].
Gray, Gwen. 1987. "Privatization: An Attempt That Failed." AUSTRAILIAN POLITICAL SCIENCE JOURNAL 22: 15–26 [105].
Green, Mark and Michael Waldman 1984. WHO RUNS CONGRESS? New York: Dell Publishing Company [175].
Grodzins, Morton 1966. THE AMERICAN SYSTEM: A NEW VIEW OF GOVERNMENT IN THE UNITED STATES. Chicago: Rand McNally [109].
Gueron, Judith M. and Edward Pauly, 1991. FROM WELFARE TO WORK. New York: Russell Sage Foundation [65, 66].
Guhan, S. 1995. THE WORLD BANK'S LENDING IN SOUTH ASIA. Washington, DC: The Brookings Institution [313, 320, 323, 324, 325, 331].
Gulhati, Ravi 1990. THE MAKING OF ECONOMIC POLICY IN AFRICA. Washington, DC: The World Bank [261].
Gulick, Luther 1937. "Notes on the Theory of Organization." In Luther Gulick and Lyndall Urwick, eds., PAPERS ON THE SCIENCE OF ADMINISTRATION. New York: Institute of Public Administration [5, 64].
Gunasekara, Charles 1995. "Philippines: Communal Irrigation." In Environment Department, ed., WORLD BANK PARTICIPATION SOURCEBOOK. Washington, DC: The World Bank [322].
Gunlicks, Arthur B. 1986. LOCAL GOVERNMENT IN THE GERMAN FEDERAL SYSTEM. Durham, NC: Duke University Press [107].
Gunlicks, Arthur B. 1993. "Introduction." In Arthur B. Gunlicks, ed., CAMPAIGN AND PARTY FINANCE IN NORTH AMERICA AND WESTERN EUROPE. Boulder, CO: Westview Press [176].

Gupta, Devendra B. 1985. URBAN HOUSING IN INDIA. Washington, DC: The World Bank [139].
Gustafson, D.J. 1991. "Institutional Sustainability Lessons from Cross-Case Analyses of Twenty Four Agricultural Extension Programs." Paper presented at the Annual Meeting of the American Scoiety of Public Administration, Washington, DC [85].
Gyimah-Boadi, E. 1991. "State Enterprises Divestiture: Recent Ghanaian Experiences." In Donald Rothschild, ed., GHANA: THE POLTICAL ECONOMY OF RECOVERY. Boulder, CO: Lynne Rienner Publishers [277].
Gyimah-Boadi, E. 1994. "Ghana's Uncertain Political Opening." JOURNAL OF DEMOCRACY 5(2): 75–86 [303–4].
Haas, Michael. 1990. "Third World Sub-Fascism and Corporate Dominance: The Case of Singapore." ASIAN PERSPECTIVE 14(1): 31–42 [223].
Hage, Jerald and Kurt Fisterbusch, 1987. ORGANIZATIONAL CHANGE AS A DEVELOPMENT STRATEGY. Boulder, CO: Lynne Rienner [84].
Haley, John O. 1991. AUTHORITY WITHOUT POWER: LAW AND THE JAPANESE PARADOX. New York: Oxford University Press [50].
Hambleton, Robin, 1993. "Reflections on Urban Government in the USA," POLITICS & POLICY, Vol. 21 (4): 245–257 [61].
Hamnett, Steve. 1985. "Political Framework and Developmental Objectives of Post-War Dutch Planning." In PUBLIC PLANNING IN THE NETHERLANDS, eds. Ashok K. Dutt and Frank J. Costa. Oxford: Oxford University Press [106, 118].
Hardoy, Jorge E. and David Satterthwaite 1989. SQUATTER CITIZEN: LIFE IN THE URBAN THIRD WORLD. London: Earthscan Publications [149, 161].
Hargrove, Edwin C. and John C. Glidewell, 1990. IMPOSSIBLE JOBS IN PUBLIC MANAGEMENT, Lawrence, KN: U. of Kansas [65].
Harmon, Michael M. and Richard T. Mayer. 1986. ORGANIZATIONAL THEORY FOR PUBLIC ADMINISTRATION. Boston: Little, Brown [39].
Harrigan, Jane 1991. "Malawi, Jamaica, and Guyana." In Paul Mosley, Jane Harrigan, and John Toye, eds., AID AND POWER. Volume 2: Case Studies. London and N.Y.: Routledge [322].
Harris, P. B. 1988. "Corruption and Responsibility in the People's Republic of China." INTERNATIONAL POLITICAL SCIENCE ASSOCIATION ANNUAL MEETING, Washington, DC [190].
Harris, Richard L. 1983. "Centralization and Decentralization in Latin America." In DECENTRALIZATION AND DEVELOPMENT, eds. G. Shabbir Cheema and Dennis A. Rondinelli. Beverly Hills, CA: Sage Publications [113].
Harrison, Paul 1987. THE GREENING OF AFRICA. London: Penguin Books [265].
Harriss, John 1995. "Japanization: Context and Culture in the Indonesian Automotive Industry." WORLD DEVELOPMENT 23(1): 117–128 [252].
Harrold, Peter and Associates 1995. THE BROAD SECTOR APPROACH TO INVESTMENT LENDING. Washington, DC: World Bank Discussion Paper 302 [322, 332, 337].
Harsch, Ernest 1993. "Accumulators and Democrats: Challenging State Corruption

in Africa." THE JOURNAL OF MODERN AFRICAN STUDIES 31(1): 31–48 [198, 199].

Harvey, Charles 1987. SUCCESSFUL MACROECONOMIC ADJUSTMENT IN THREE DEVELOPING COUNTRIES: BOTSWANA, MALAWI, AND PAPUA NEW GUINEA. Washington, DC: The World Bank [102].

Hasan, Abid and Owaise Saadat 1996. BANGLADESH: GOVERNMENT THAT WORKS. Washington, DC: The World Bank [308, 309, 311, 315, 345].

Hasan, Samiul 1992. "Upazila Development Planning in Bangladesh." ASIAN SURVEY 32: 802–814 [108, 113].

Hassan, Riaz. 1977. FAMILIES IN FLATS: A STUDY OF LOW INCOME FAMILIES IN PUBLIC HOUSING. Singapore: Singapore University Press [233].

Hauser, Philip M. ET AL. 1982. POPULATION AND THE URBAN FUTURE. Albany, NY: State U. of N.Y. Press [132].

Heady, Ferrel. 1979. PUBLIC ADMINISTRATION; A COMPARATIVE PERSPECTIVE. New York: Marcel Dekker [220].

Heady, Ferrel, 1991. PUBLIC ADMINISTRATION: A COMPARATIVE PERSPECTIVE. New York: Marcel Dekker [7].

Heaver, Richard and Arturo Israel 1986. COUNTRY COMMITMENT TO DEVELOPMENT PROJECTS. Washington, DC: The World Bank [326].

Heclo, Hugh and Henrik Madsen 1987. POLICY AND POLITICS IN SWEDEN: PRINCIPLED PRAGMATISM. Philadelphia, PA: Temple University Press [108, 123].

Hedlund, Stefan 1984. CRISIS IN SOVIET AGRICULTURE. New York: St. Martin's Press [221].

Heidenheimer, Arnold J. 1970. "The Context of Analysis." In Arnold J. Heidenheimer, ed., POLITICAL CORRUPTION: READINGS IN COMPARATIVE ANALYSIS. New York: Holt, Reinhart and Winston [165].

Heidenheimer, Arnold J. 1989. "Problems of Comparing American Political Corruption." In POLITICAL CORRUPTION: A HANDBOOK, eds., Arnold J. Heidenheimer, Michael Johnson, and Victor T. LeVine. New Brunswick, N.J.: Transaction Publishers [177].

Heidenheimer, Arnold J., Michael Johnston, and Victor T. LeVine 1989. "Terms, Concepts, and Definitions: An Introduction." In POLITICAL CORRUPTION: A HANDBOOK, eds., Arnold J. Heidenheimer, Michael Johnston, and Victor T. LeVine. New Brunswick, NJ: Transaction Publishers [167].

Heidenheimer, Arnold J., Hugh Heclo, and Carolyn Teich Adams 1990. COMPARATIVE PUBLIC POLICY: THE POLITICS OF PUBLIC CHOICE IN AMERICA, EUROPE, AND JAPAN. New York: St. Martin's Press [105].

Heirs, Ben and Gordon Pehrson 1982. THE MIND OF THE ORGANIZATION. New York: Harper & Row [130].

Held, David. 1992. "Democracy: From City States to a Cosmopolitan Order." In David Held, ed., PROSPECTS FOR DEMOCRACY. Oxford, England: Blackwell Publishers [216].

Herbst, Jeffrey. 1993. THE POLITICS OF REFORM IN GHANA, 1982–1991. Berkeley and Los Angeles: University of California Press 302].

Herbst, Jeffrey 1993a. "The Politics of Sustained Agricultural Reform in Africa." In

Thomas M. Callaghy and John Ravenhill, eds., HEMMED IN. New York: Columbia University Press [320].
Herbst, Jeffrey 1997. "Understanding Incomplete Liberalization in Africa." AMERICAN POLITICAL SCIENCE ASSOCIATION ANNUAL MEETING, Washington, D.C. [207].
Hersey, Paul and Kenneth Blanchard 1977. MANAGEMENT OF ORGANIZATIONAL BEHAVIOR. Englewood Cliffs, NJ: Prentice-Hall [129].
Hershkowitz, Allen and Eugene Salerni. 1987. GARBAGE MANAGEMENT IN JAPAN. New York: INFORM, Inc. [32, 36, 44].
Hill, Dillys M. 1987. "Mobilization and Participation: Singapore in the 1980s." PUBLIC ADMINISTRATION AND DEVELOPMENT 7(2): 333–349 [232].
Hill, Martin J. D. 1991. THE HARAMBEE MOVEMENT IN KENYA. London: The Athlone Press [150].
Himbara, David 1994. "Domestic Capitalists and the State in Kenya," in AFRICAN CAPITALISTS IN AFRICAN DEVELOPMENT, eds. Burce J. Berman and Colin Leys. Boulder and London: Lynne Rienner [250].
Hine., David. 1993. GOVERNING ITALY: THE POLITICS OF BARGAINED PLURALISM. Oxford: Clarendon Press [182, 183].
Hird, John A. 1991. "The Political Economy of Pork: Project Selection at the U.S. Army Corps of Engineers." AMERICAN POLITICAL SCIENCE REVIEW 85(2): 429–455 [177].
Hirschman, Albert 1970. EXIT, VOICE AND LOYALTY. Cambridge, MA: Harvard University Press [146].
Hobgood, Harlan 1992. SAHEL DECENTRALIZATION PROJECT REPORT, VOL II: FACILITATING TRANSITIONS FROM CENTRALIZED TO DECENTRALIZED POLITICS. Burlington, VT: Associates for Rural Development [124].
Hofheinz, Roy Jr. and Kent E. Calder 1982. THE EASTASIA EDGE. New York: Basic Books [222, 224, 283].
Holcombe, Susan H. 1993. "Managing Poverty Alleviation: Participation in Practice." AMERICAN SOCIETY FOR PUBLIC ADMINISTRATION NATIONAL TRAINING CONFERENCE, San Francisco: July 17–21 [80].
Holm, John D., Patrick P. Molutsi, Gloria Somolekae 1996. "The Development of a Civil Society in a Democratic State: the Botswana Model." AFRICAN STUDIES REVIEW 39(2): 43–69 [263].
Holmquist, Frank and Michael Ford 1994. "Kenya: State and Civil Society the First Year after the Election." AFRICA TODAY 41 (4): 5–25 [206, 208, 210].
Holmes, Malcolm 1996. THE BUDGET AND PUBLIC SECTOR PERFORMANCE IN DEVELOPING COUNTRY. Washington, DC: World Bank Unpublished Report [315].
Hood, Steven J. 1997. THE KUOMINTANG AND THE DEMOCRATIZATION OF TAIWAN. Boulder, CO: Westview Press [235].
Hopkins, Jack W. 1991. "Evolution and Revolution: Enduring Patterns and the Transformation of Latin American Bureaucracy." In Ali Farazmand, ed., HANDBOOK OF COMPARATIVE AND DEVELOPMENT PUBLIC ADMINISTRATION. New York: Marcel Dekker [94].

House, William J. and George Zimalirana 1992. "Rapid Population Growth and Poverty Generation in Malawi. JOURNAL OF MODERN AFRICAN STUDIES 30(1): 72–86 [247].
Hsiao, Hsin-Huang, Michael. 1994. "Political Liberalization and the Farmer' Movement in Taiwan." In Edward Friedman, editor, THE POLITICS OF DEMOCRATIZATION: GENERALIZING EAST ASIAN EXPERIENCES. Boulder, CO: Westview Press [228].
Huang, Sophia Wu. 1993. "Structural Changes in Taiwan's Agricultural Economy." ECONOMIC DEVELOPMENT AND CULTURAL CHANGE 42 (1): 45–65 [228].
Huat, Chua Beng. 1989. "The Business of Living in Singapore." In MANAGEMENT OF SUCCESS; THE MOULDING OF MODERN SINGAPORE., eds., Kerniel S. Sandhu and Paul Wheatley. Singapore: Institute of Southeast Asian Studies [256].
Hubbard, Joan Meyer 1994. "Grameen Bank." Brookings Institution Conference on Financial Services for the Poor. Washington, DC: September 28–30 [79].
Hummert, Vic. 1987. "How the Japanese Collect Garbage." THE NEW YORK TIMES. May 21: A26 [32].
Humphrey, John 1993. "Japanese Production Management and Labour Relations." JOURNAL OF DEVELOPMENT STUDIES 30(1):93–112 [252].
Huq., M. M. 1989. THE ECONOMY OF GHANA: THE FIRST 25 YEARS SINCE INDEPENDENCE. New York: St. Martin's Press [272, 274, 276, 277].
Huque, Ahmed S. 1986. "The Illusion of Decentralization: Local Administration in Bangladesh." INTERNATIONAL REVIEW OF ADMINISTRATIVE SCIENCES 52:79–85 [109, 113].
Huntington, Samuel P. 1971. "Political Development and Political Decay." In Claude E. Welch, Jr., ed., POLITICAL MODERNIZATION: A READER IN COMPARATIVE POLITICAL CHANGE. Belmont, CA: Wadsworth Publishing Company [214].
Huntington, Samuel P. and Joan M. Nelson 1976. NO EASY CHOICE: POLITICAL PARTICIPATION IN DEVELOPING COUNTRIES. Cambridge, MA: Harvard University Press [206, 215].
Husain, Ishrat. 1994. WHY DO SOME ECONOMIES ADJUST MORE SUCCESSFULLY THAN OTHERS? LESSONS FROM SEVEN AFRICAN COUNTRIES. Washington, DC: World Bank Policy Research Working Paper 1364 [213, 314].
Husain, S. Shahid 1994. "Civil Service Reform and Economic Development." In CIVIL SERVICE REFORM IN LATIN AMERICA AND THE CARIBBEAN; PROCEEDINTS OF A CONFERENCE, eds: Shahid Amjad Chaudry, James Reid, and Waleed Haider Malif. Washington, DC: The World Bank [264].
Hussi, Pekka ET AL. 1993. THE DEVELOPMENT OF COOPERATIVES AND OTHER RURAL ORGANIZATIONS: THE ROLE OF THE WORLD BANK. Washington, DC: The World Bank [238].
Hyden, Goran 1983. NO SHORTCUTS TO PROGRESS: AFRICAN DEVELOPMENT MANAGEMENT IN PERSPECTIVE. Berkeley and Los Angeles: University of California Press [190].

Hyden, Goran 1992. "Governance and the Study of Politics." In Goran Hyden and Michael Bratton, eds., GOVERNANCE AND POLITICS IN AFRICA. Boulder and London: Lynne Rienner Publishers [24].

Iacocca, Lee with William Novak 1984. IACOCCA: AN AUTOBIOGRAPHY. New York: Bantam Books [130].

Ibrahim, Youssef M. 1995. "Five Seek Presidency in Algeria; Election Violence Threatened." NEW YORK TIMES. October 3: A4 [209].

Ickis, John C. 1983. "Structural Responses to New Rural Development Strategies." In David C. Korten and Felipe B. Alfonso, eds., BUREAUCRACY AND THE POOR: CLOSING THE GAP. West Hartford, CN: Kumarian Press [127].

ICMA 1994. MAKING CITIES WORK: THE HONDURAN MUNICIPAL DEVELOPMENT PROJECT. Washington, DC: ICMA [123].

Iga, Mamoru and Morton Auerbach 1977. "Political Corruption and Social Structure in Japan. ASIA SURVEY 17(6): 556–561 [179].

Ilchman, Warren, 1968. "The Unproductive Study of Administration in Developing Countries." COMPARATIVE POLITICAL SCIENCE. Vol I (1): 218–238 [8].

Imam, Ayesha and Jibrin Ibrahim. 1992. "The Democratic Process: Problems and Prospects." DEVELOPMENT. No. 3: 17–19 [219].

Ingham, Barbara and A. K. M. Kalam 1992. "Decentralization and Development: Theory and Evidence from Bangladesh." PUBLIC ADMINISTRATION AND DEVELOPMENT 12: 373–385 [113].

Inglehart, Ronald. 1990. CULTURE SHIFT IN ADVANCED INDUSTRIAL SOCIETY. Princeton: Princeton University Press [263].

Islam, N. 1989. "Colonial Legacy, Administrative Reform and Politics: Pakistan 1947–1987." PUBLIC ADMINISTRATION AND DEVELOPMENT. 9(1): 271–285 [160].

Israel, Arturo 1987. INSTITUTIONAL DEVELOPMENT: INCENTIVES TO PERFORMANCE. Baltimore, MD: Johns Hopkins [84].

Israel, Arturo 1990. THE CHANGING ROLE OF THE STATE: INSTITUTIONAL DIMENSIONS. Washington, DC: The World Bank [146].

Israel, Arturo 1992. ISSUES FOR INFRASTRUCTURE MANAGEMENT IN THE 1990s. Washington, DC: World Bank Discussion Paper [138, 141, 147].

Jackson, Robert H. and Carl G. Rosberg. 1982. PERSONAL RULE IN BLACK AFRICA: PRINCE, AUTOCRAT, PROPHET, TYRANT. Berkeley and Los Angeles: The University of California Press [271, 272, 299].

Jackson, Robert H. and Carl G. Rosberg 1985. "The Marginality of African States." In Gwendolen M. Carter and Patrick O'Meara, eds., AFRICAN INDEPENDENCE: THE FIRST TWENTY FIVE YEARS. Bloomington, IN: Indiana University Press [190].

Jackson, Robert H. and Carl G. Rosberg. 1994. "The Political Economy of African Personal Rule." In David E. Apter and Carl G. Rosberg, eds., POLITICAL DEVELOPMENT AND THE NEW REALISM IN SUB-SAHARAN AFRICA. Charlottsville, VA: University Press of Virginia [205, 271, 272].

Jebuni, Charles D. 1994. GOVERNANCE & STRUCTURAL ADJUSTMENT IN GHANA. Washington, DC: The World Bank Private Sector Development Department [291, 232, 296, 299, 300].

Jeffries, Richard & Clare Thomas. 1993. "The Ghanaian Election of 1992." AFRICAN AFFAIRS. Vol. 92: 331-366 [271].
Jencks, Christopher 1994. THE HOMELESS. Cambridge, MA: Harvard University Press [305].
Johnson, Chalmers. 1987. "Political Institutions and Economic Performance: The Government-Business Relationship in Japan, South Korea, and Taiwan." In Frederic C. Deyo, ed., THE POLITICAL ECONOMY OF THE NEW ASIAN INDUSTRIALISM. Ithaca, NY: Cornell University Press [224, 225].
Johnson, Chalmers. 1994. "What is the Best System of National Economic Management for Korea?" In Lee-Jay Cho and Yoon Hyung Kim, eds., KOREA'S POLITICAL ECONOMY: AN INSTITUTIONAL PERSPECTIVE. Boulder, CO: Westview Press [270, 284, 294].
Johnson, Chalmers 1995. JAPAN: WHO GOVERNS? New York: Norton [170, 173, 175, 180, 181].
Johnson, Sonia R. 1996. EDUCATION AND TRAINING OF ACCOUNTANTS IN SUB-SAHARAN ANGLOPHONE AFRICA. Washington, DC: World Bank Technical Paper No. 305 [330].
Johnston, Michael 1982. POLITICAL CORRUPTION AND PUBLIC POLICY IN AMERICA. Monterey, CA: Brooks/Cole [171].
Joireman, Sandra Fullerton 1996. "The Minefield of Land Reform: Comments on the Eritrean Land Proclamation." AFRICAN AFFAIRS 95: 269-285 [267].
Jones, Jr., Augustus J. 1995. "Federal Responses to State and Local Claims of 'Undue Burden' in Complying with The Americans with Disabilities Act." PUBLIUS: THE JOURNAL OF FEDERALISM 25(3): 41-54 [118].
Jones, Bernard 1993. "Sweden." In LOCAL GOVERNMENT IN LIBERAL DEMOCRACIES, ed. J. A. Chandler. London and New York: Routledge [110].
Jones, Eric L. 1995. "Culture and its Relationship to Economic Change." JOURNAL OF INSTITUTIONAL AND THEORETICAL ECONOMICS 151 (2): 269-285 [244, 245, 253, 320].
Jones, Jerry and Ian Wiggle 1987. "The Concept and Politics of Integrated Community Development." COMMUNITY DEVELOPMENT JOURNAL 22(2): 107-117 [152].
Jones, William I. and Roberto Egli. 1984. FARMING SYSTEMS IN AFRICA. Washington, D.C.: The World Bank [265].
Joseph, Richard 1997. AFRICAN RENEWAL: REPORT OF A CONFERENCE ON STATE, CONFLICT AND DEMOCRACY IN AFRICA. Cambridge, MA: Massachusetts Institute of Technology [241].
Joseph, Richard 1997a. "The Reconfiguration of Power in Late-Twentieth Century Africa." AMERICAN POLITICAL SCIENCE ASSOCIATION ANNUAL MEETING, Washington, D.C. [207] Jowitt, Ken. 1992. "The Leninist Legacy." In EASTERN EUROPE IN TRANSITION., ed., Ivo Banac. Ithaca and London: Cornell U. [257].
Jreisat, Jamil E. 1991. "Bureaucratization of the Arab World: Incompatible Influences." In Ali Farazmand, ed., HANDBOOK OF COMPARATIVE AND DEVELOPMENT PUBLIC ADMINISTRATION. New York: Marcel Dekker [86].
Jreisat, Jamil E. 1991a. "The Organizational Perspective in Comparative and Devel-

opment Administration." In Ali Farazmand, ed., HANDBOOK OF COMPARATIVE AND DEVELOPMENT PUBLIC ADMINISTRATION. New York: Marcel Dekker [99].

Kahn, Alfred J. and Sheila B. Kamerman, 1975. NOT FOR THE POOR ALONE, Philadelphia, PA: Temple University Press [80].

Kalipeni, Ezekiel and Eliya M. Zulu. 1993. "Gender Differences in Knowledge and Attitudes Toward Modern and Traditional Methods of Child Spacing in Malawi." POLULATION RESEARCH AND POLICY REVIEW 4(1): 104–119 [247].

Kamerman, Sheila B. and Alfred J. Kahn 1989. "Child Care and Privatization under Reagan," in PRIVATIZATION AND THE WELFARE STATE, eds. Sheila B. Kamerman and Alfred J. Kahn. Princeton, NJ: Princeton University Press [148].

Kapoor, Kapil 1993. UGANDA: GROWING OUT OF POVERTY. Washington, DC: World Bank Internal Document [114].

Kardam, Nuket. 1993. "Development Approaches & The Role of Policy Advocacy: The Case of the World Bank." WORLD DEVELOPMENT 21(ll): 1173–1786 [319].

Keare, Douglas and Scott Paris 1983. EVALUATION OF SHELTER PROJECTS FOR THE URBAN POOR: PRINCIPAL FINDINGS. Washington, D.C.: The World Bank [133].

Keating, Michael 1991. COMPARATIVE URBAN POLITICS: POWER AND THE CITY IN THE UNITED STATES, CANADA, BRITAIN AND FRANCE. Brookfield, VT: Edward Elgar [110, 114].

Keehn, Edward B. 1990. "Managing Interests in the Japanese Bureaucracy." ASIAN SURVEY. Vol. 30(ll): 1022–1034 [50].

Kelly, Brian 1993. ADVENTURES IN PORKLAND. New York: Random House [168].

Kelm, Matthias. 1993. THE GAMBIA: LESSONS FROM SINGAPORE'S EXPERIENCE. Washington, DC: World Bank Unpublished Report [210].

Kenney, Martin and Richard Florida. 1993. BEYOND MASS PRODUCTION: THE JAPANESE SYSTEM AND ITS TRANSFER TO THE U.S. New York: Oxford University Press [37].

Kerr, Peter, 1993. "Prisoner 88A0802," NEW YORK TIMES MAGAZINE (June 27), pp. 23–27, 58–59 [60].

Kessides, Christine 1997. "World Bank Experience with the Provision of Infrastructure Services for the Urban Poor: Preliminary Identification and Review of Best Practices." Washington, DC: World Bank TWU-OR8 [132, 134, 135, 137, 140, 141, 142, 144].

Kettl, Donald F. 1990. "The Perils—and Prospects—of Public Administration," PUBLIC ADMINISTRATION REVIEW, Vol. 50 (July/August): 411-419 [59, 97].

Khashan, Hilal. 1992. "The Quagmire of Arab Democracy." ARAB STUDIES QUARTERLY 14(1): 18–31 [209].

Khuda, Barkat E., Sarah F. Harbison, and William C. Robinson. 1990. "Is Development Really the Best Contraceptive?: A 20-Year Trial in Comilla District, Bangladesh." ASIA-PACIFIC POPULATION JOURNAL 5(4): 10–14 [260].

Kierman, Matthew J. 1990. "Land-Use Planning." In URBAN POLICY ISSUES: CANADIAN PERSPECTIVES, eds. Richard A. Loreto and Trevor Price. Toronto: McClelland & Stewart [107].

Kim, Chung-yum. 1994. POLICYMAKING ON THE FRONTLINES: MEMOIRS OF A KOREAN PRACTITIONER, 1945-79. Washington, DC: World Bank Economic Development Institute [295].
Kim, Doug Hyun. 1991. "Alternative Social Development Strategies for Korea in the 1990s." In Gerald E. Caiden and Bun Woong Kim, editors, A DRAGON'S PROGRESS; DEVELOPMENT ADMINISTRATION IN KOREA. West Hartford, CN: Kumarian Press [229].
Kim, Kihwan and Danny M. Leipziger 1992. LESSONS OF EAST ASIA: A COUNTRY STUDIES APPROACH. Washington, DC: World Bank [301].
Kim, Pan S. 1992. "Who Serves the People? Educational Background of South Korean and Japanese Bureaucrats." AMERICAN REVIEW OF PUBLIC ADMINISTRATION. Vol. 22(4): 307-325 [282].
Kim, Sookon. 1994. "Korean Labor-Management Relations." In Lee-Jay Cho and Yoon Hyung Kim, editors, KOREA'S POLITICAL ECONOMY: AN INSTITUTIONAL PERSPECTIVE. Boulder, CO: Westview Press [226].
Kjellberg, Francesco 1981. "The Expansion of Local Finance in Norway." In THE LOCAL FISCAL CRISIS IN WESTERN EUROPE, ed. L. J. Sharpe. London and Beverly Hills, CA: SAGE Publications [110].
Klitgaard, Robert H. 1989. CORRUPTION AND THE WORLD BANK. Washington, DC: World Bank Internal Report [193].
Klitgaard, Robert H. 1989a. "Incentive Myopia." WORLD DEVELOPMENT 17(4): 447-460 [187].
Klitgaard, Robert H. 1990. TROPICAL GANGSTERS. New York: Basic Books [196-7].
Klitgaard, Robert H. 1991. ADJUSTING TO REALITY. San Francisco, CA: ICS Press [188].
Klitgaard, Robert. 1991a. IN SEARCH OF CULTURE. Washington, DC: World Bank Unpublished Document [253].
Knodel, John, Aphicat Chamratrithirong, and Nibhon Debayalya. 1987. THAILAND'S REPRODUCTIVE REVOLUTION: RAPID FERTILITY DECLINE IN A THIRD WORLD SETTING. Madison: U. of Wisconsin [247].
Koehn, Peter H. 1990. PUBLIC POLICY AND ADMINISTRATION IN AFRICA: LESSONS FROM NIGERIA. Boulder, CO: Westview Press [38, 55].
Koehn, Peter H. 1991. "Development Administration in Nigeria: Inclinations and Results." In Ali Farazmand, ed., HANDBOOK OF COMPARATIVE AND DEVELOPMENT PUBLIC ADMINISTRATION. New York: Marcel Dekker [89].
Koenig, Dolores 1986. "Research for Rural Development: Experiences of an Anthropologist in Rural Mali." In ANTHROPOLOGY AND RURAL DEVELOPMENT IN WEST AFRICA, eds. Michael M. Horowitz and Thomas M. Painter. Boulder and London: Westview [252].
Koh, B. C. 1989. JAPAN'S ADMINISTRATIVE ELITE. Berkeley and Los Angeles: University of California Press [37, 50, 180].
Kohli, Atul 1990. DEMOCRACY AND DISCONTENT: INDIA'S GROWING CRISIS OF GOVERNABILITY. Cambridge, MA: Harvard University Press [203, 222].
Kohli, Atul. 1993. "Democracy amid economic orthodoxy: trends in developing countries." THIRD WORLD QUARTERLY 14(4): 671-690 [209].

Korb, Lawrence J. 1995. "Peace Without Dividend: Why We Can't Seem To Cut the Defense Budget." THE WASHINGTON POST July 9: C1, C4 [177].

Korten, David C. (Ed.) 1986. COMMUNITY MANAGEMENT: ASIAN EXPERIENCE AND PERSPECTIVES. West Hartford, CT: Kumarian Press [127].

Korten, David C. 1986a. "Introduction: Community-Based Resource Management." In COMMUNITY MANAGEMENT, ed. David C. Korten. West Hartford, CT: Kumarian Press [128].

Korten, David C. 1986b. "Micro-Policy Reform—The Role of Private Voluntary Development Agencies." In COMMUNITY MANAGEMENT, ed. David C. Korten. West Hartford, CT: Kumarian Press [127].

Korten, David C. 1989. "The Community: Master or Client? A Reply." PUBLIC ADMINISTRATION AND DEVELOPMENT 9(5): 569–575 [145, 154, 156, 159].

Korten, David 1995. WHEN CORPORATIONS RULE THE WORLD. West Hartford, CN: Kumarian Press [306].

Korten, David C. and Philipe B. Alfonso (Eds.) 1983. BUREAUCRACY AND THE POOR: CLOSING THE GAP. West Hartford, CT: Kumarian Press [127].

Korten, David C. and Norman T. Uphoff 1981. BUREAUCRATIC ORIENTATION FOR PARTICIPATORY RURAL DEVELOPMENT. Washington, DC: NASPAA [158].

Kottack, Conrad Phillip 1991. "When People Don't Come First: Some Sociological Lessons from Completed Projects." In Michael M. Cernea, ed., PUTTING PEOPLE FIRST. Washington, DC: The World Bank [86].

Kpundeh, Sahr John 1993. "Prospects in Contemporary Sierra Leone." CORRUPTION AND REFORM 7(3): 237–247 [189, 190, 198].

Kraus, Jon. 1991. "The Political Economy of Stabilization and Structural Adjustment in Ghana." In Donald Rothchild, ed., GHANA: THE POLITICAL ECONOMY OF RECOVERY. Boulder & London: Lynne Rienner Publishers [274, 276].

Kristoff, Nicholas D. 1993 "The Riddle of China: Repression as Standard of Living Soars." NEW YORK TIMES. September 7: A1, A10 [202].

Kubr, Milan and John Wallace 1983. SUCCESS AND FAILURE IN MEETING THE MANAGEMENT CHALLENGE: STRATEGIES AND THEIR IMPLEMENTATION. Washington, DC: World Bank Staff Working Paper No. 585 [130].

Kulaba, Saitiel 1989. "Local Government and the Management of Urban Services in Tanzania." In AFRICAN CITIES IN CRISIS: MANAGING RAPID URBAN GROWTH, eds. Richard E. Stren and Rodney R. White. Boulder, CO: Westview Press [109].

Kwack, Sung Yeung. 1987. "The Economic Development of the Republic of Korea, 1965–1981." In Lawrence J. Lau, editor, MODELS OF DEVELOPMENT: A COMPARATIVE STUDY OF ECONOMIC GROWTH IN SOUTH KOREA AND TAIWAN. San Francisco, CA: ICS Press [224].

Lakoff, Sanford 1994. "Between Either/Or and More or Less: Sovereignty Versus Autonomy Under Federalism." PUBLIUS: THE JOURNAL OF FEDERALISM 24: 63–78 [107].

Laleye, Mouftau 1993. "Mechanics for Enhancing Ethics and Public Accountability in Francophone Africa." In Sadiq Rasheed and Dele Olowu, eds., ETHICS AND ACCOUNTABILITY IN AFRICAN PUBLIC SERVICES. New York: United Nations [189].

Lancaster, Carol. 1991-92. "Democracy in Africa." FOREIGN POLICY. 85 (Winter): 148-162 [205, 206].

Landell-Mills, Pierre. 1992. "Governance, Cultural Change, and Empowerment." THE JOURNAL OF MODERN AFRICAN STUDIES 30(4): 473-497 [249, 254].

Langseth, Petter 1994. CIVIL SERVICE REFORM IN UGANDA: OBJECTIVES AND STRATEGIC PLAN. Washington, DC: World Bank Discussion Paper [188].

Langseth, Petter 1995. CIVIL SERVICE REFORM IN UGANDA: LESSONS LEARNED. Washington, DC: World Bank EDI Working Paper No. 95-05 [329, 338, 340].

Langseth, Petter, Rick Stapenhurst and Jeremy Pope 1996. NATIONAL INTEGRITY: A PREREQUISITE FOR SUSTAINABLE DEVELOPMENT? Washington, DC: World Bank EDI Unpublished Report [329].

Langton, John 1984. "The Ecological Theory of Bureaucracy: The Case of Josiah Wedgwood and the British Pottery Industry." ADMINISTRATIVE SCIENCE QUARTERLY 29:330-354 [251].

La Noue, George R. and John C. Sullivan 1995. "Race Neutral Programs in Public Contracting." PUBLIC ADMINISTRATION REVIEW 55(4): 348-356 [178].

Larimer, Tim 1994. "Vietnamese Still Bank the Old-Fashioned Way." December 29: A21 [28].

LaSelva, Samuel 1993. "Federalism as a Way of Life: Reflections on the Canadian Experiment." CANADIAN JOURNAL OF POLITICAL SCIENCE 27: 220-234 [107].

Laski, Harold 1939. "The Obsolescence of Federalism." THE NEW REPUBLIC 98 (May 3): 367-369 [107].

Lauber, Daniel, 1991. "Racially Diverse Communities: A National Necessity." In Philip W. Nyden and Wim Wievel, eds., CHALLENGING UNEVEN DEVELOPMENT: AN URBAN AGENDA, New Brunswick, NJ: Rutgers U. Press [69].

Lauras-Lecoh, Therese 1990. "Family Trends and Demographic Transition in Africa." INTERNATIONAL SOCIAL SCIENCE JOURNAL 42(4): 475-492 [267].

Lederer, Gerder 1993. "Authoritarianism in German Adolescents: Trends and Cross-Cultural Comparisons." In STRENGTHS AND WEAKNESSES: THE AUTHORITARIAN PERSONALITY, eds. William F. Stone, Gerda Lederer and Richard Criste. New York: Stringer-Verlag [251].

Lee, Gary 1996. "In Food Safety Changes, Victories for Many." THE WASHINGTON POST. July 28: A4 [118].

Lee, Kyu Sik and Alex Anas. IMPACTS OF INFRASTRUCTURE DEFICIENCIES ON NIGERIAN MANUFACTURING: PRIVATE ALTERNATIVES AND POLICY OPTIONS. Washington, D.C.: World Bank Internal Document [42].

Lee, Sim Loo, Lim Lan Yuan and Tay Kah Poh. 1993. "Shelter for All: Singapore Strategy for Full Home Ownership by the Year 2000." HABITAT INTERNATIONAL 17(1): 85–103 [136].
Lee, Suk-Chae 1991. "The Heavy and Chemical Industries Promotion Plan (1973–79)." In Lee-Jay Cho and Yoon Hyung Kim, eds. ECONOMIC DEVELOPMENT IN THE REPUBLIC OF KOREA: A POLICY PERSPECTIVE. Honolulu, HA: East-West Center [295].
Leechor, Chad 1994. "Ghana: Frontrunner in Development." In Ishrat Husain and Rashid Faruqee, eds., ADJUSTMENT IN AFRICA: LESSONS FROM COUNTRY CASE STUDIES. Washington, DC: The World Bank [270, 291, 293, 297, 299].
Lee-Smith, Diana 1989. "Urban Management in Nairobi: A Case Study of the Matatu Mode of Public Transportation." In AFRICAN CITIES IN CRISIS, eds. Richard E. Stren and Rodney R. White. Boulder, CO: Westview Press [148].
Leete, Richard 1994. "The Continuing Flight From Marriage and Parenthood Among the Overseas Chinese in East and Southeast Asia." POPULATION AND DEVELOPMENT REVIEW 20(4): 811–829 [258].
Leftwich, Adrian. 1993. "Governance, democracy and development in the Third World." THIRD WORLD QUARTERLY 14(3): 605–624 [201, 204].
Leftwich, Adrian 1995. "Bringing Politics Back In: Towards a Model of the Developmental State." THE JOURNAL OF DEVELOPMENT STUDIES 31 (3): 400–427 [203].
Leipziger, Danny M. ET AL. 1992. THE DISTRIBUTION OF INCOME AND WEALTH IN KOREA. Washington, D.C.: The World Bank EDI [282, 283].
Leiserson, Avery. 1983. "Administration, Management, and Public Accountability." In Edwin C. Hargrove and Paul K. Conkin, eds., TVA: FIFTY YEARS OF GRASS ROOTS BUREAUCRACY. Urbana, Ill: University of Illinois Press [106].
Lemann, Nicholas, 1991. THE PROMISED LAND. New York: Vintage Books [69].
Lemann, Nicholas, 1994. "The Myth of Community Development," THE NEW YORK TIMES MAGAZINE (January 9): 28–31, 54–58 [70].
Lemarchand, Rene. 1992. "Africa's Troubled Transitions." JOURNAL OF DEMOCRACY 3(4): 99–102 [216].
Lemarchand, Rene. 1995. "Rwanda: The Rationality of Genocide." ISSUE: A JOURNAL OF OPINION 23(2): 8–11 [209].
Leonard, David K. 1987. "The Political Realities of African Management." WORLD DEVELOPMENT 15(7): 899–910 [249].
Leonard, David K. 1991. AFRICAN SUCCESSES: FOUR PUBLIC MANAGERS OF KENYAN RURAL DEVELOPMENT. Berkeley and Los Angeles: U. of California [249, 252].
LePoer, Barbara Leitch. 1991. SINGAPORE: A COUNTRY STUDY. Washington, DC: Library of Congress [256].
Levin, Martin A. and Barbara Ferman, 1985. THE POLITICAL HAND: POLICY IMPLEMENTATION AND YOUTH EMPLOYMENT PROGRAMS. New York: Pergamon Press [72].
LeVine, Victor T. 1975. POLITICAL CORRUPTION: THE GHANA CASE. Stanford, CA: Hoover University Press [163, 273].

Le Vine, Victor T. 1993. "Administrative Corruption and Democratization in Africa: Aspects of the Theoretic Agenda." CORRUPTION AND REFORM 7(3): 271–278 [210].
Levitan, Sar A., 1990. PROGRAMS IN AID OF THE POOR. Baltimore and London: The Johns Hopkins University Press [67].
Levitan, Sar A. and Benjamin H. Johnston. 1975. JOB CORPS: A SOCIAL EXPERIMENT THAT WORKS. Baltimore and London: The Johns Hopkins University Press [71].
Lewis, Oscar. 1968. A STUDY OF SLUM CULTURE. New York: Random House [250].
Lewis, Peter M. 1994. "State Structure, Elite Cohesion, and Economic Change: Nigeria and Indonesia Compared." AMERICAN POLITICAL SCIENCE ASSOCIATION ANNUAL MEETING, New York [52, 53, 54].
Lewis, Peter M. 1994a. "Endgame in Nigeria? The Politics of a Failed Democratic Transition." AFRICAN AFFAIRS 93: 323–340 [53, 55].
Lewis, Peter M and Howard Stein 1997. "Shifting Fortunes: The Political Economy of Financial Liberalization in Nigeria." WORLD DEVELOPMENT. Vol 25, No. 1: 5–22 [58].
Lewis, Stephen R. Jr. 1993. "Policymaking and Economic Performance: Botswana in Comparative Perspective." In BOTSWANA: THE POLITICAL ECONOMY OF DEMOCRATIC DEVELOPMENT, ed. Stephen John Stedman. Boulder & London: Lynne Rienner Publishers [262].
Liebenow, J. Gus 1987. LIBERIA: THE QUEST FOR DEMOCRACY. Bloomington and Indianapolis, IN: Indiana U. Press [260].
Liebenow, J. Gus 1987a. "Report on Tanzania." UNIVERSITIES FIELD STAFF INTERNATIONAL REPORTS, No. 3 [187].
Lieberson, Joseph S. 1985. A SYNTHESIS OF AID EXPERIENCE: SMALL FARMER CREDIT, 1973–1985. Washington, DC: USAID [30].
Lijphart, Arend 1968. THE POLITICS OF ACCOMMODATION: PLURALISM AND DEMOCRACY IN THE NETHERLANDS. Berkeley and Los Angeles, CA: U. of California Press [157].
Linden, Eugene. 1993. "Mega-Cities." TIME. January 11: 30–38 [33, 42].
Lindenberg, Marc M. 1993. THE HUMAN DEVELOPMENT RACE: IMPROVING THE QUALITY OF LIFE IN DEVELOPING COUNTRIES. San Franscisco, CA: ICS Press [22].
Liu, Alan P. 1987. PHOENIX AND THE LION: MODERNIZATION IN TAIWAN AND MAINLAND CHINA, 1950–1980. Stanford, CA: Hoover Institute [246].
Lofchie, Michael F. 1993. "Trading Places: Economic Policy in Kenya and Tanzania." In Thomas M. Callaghy and John Ravenhill, eds., HEMMED IN. New York: Columbia University Press [314].
Lofchie, Michael F. 1994. "The New Political Economy of Africa." in David E. Apter and Carl G. Rosberg, eds. POLITICAL DEVELOPMENT AND THE NEW REALISM IN SUB-SAHARAN AFRICA. Charlottesville and London: University Press of Virginia [23, 31].
Long, Millard. 1991. "Financial Systems and Development." In Philippe Callier,

ed., FINANCIAL SYSTEMS AND DEVELOPMENT IN AFRICA. Washington, DC: The World Bank [28].
Lopes, J. da Silva 1988. REFORM OF THE FINANCIAL SECTOR. Washington, DC: The World Bank [29].
Lorch, Donatella. 1994. "In Zambia, a Legacy of Graft and Drug Scandal Taints Democratic Reforms." NEW YORK TIMES. 30 January: A10 [331].
Lorch, Donatella. 1995. "Is Kenya Sliding Back Toward Repression?" THE NEW YORK TIMES. October 1: A3 [206].
Lovei, Laszlo and Dale Whittington. 1991. RENT-SEEKING IN WATER SUPPLY. Washington, DC: World Bank INU Report 85 [65].
Lovell, Catherine H. 1992. THE BRAC STRATEGY: BREAKING THE CYCLE OF POVERTY. West Hartford, CN: Kumarian Press [151, 162].
Lu, Hsiu-Lien Annette. 1994. "Women's Liberation: The Taiwanese Experience." In Murray A. Rubinstein, ed., THE OTHER TAIWAN: 1945 TO THE PRESENT. Armonk, NY: M. E. Sharpe [223].
Luckham, Robin. 1994. "The Military, Militarization and Democratization in Africa." AFRICA STUDIES REVIEW. 37(2): 13–75 [240].
Luger, Michael I. 1989. PRIVATE SECTOR OPTIONS FOR SOLID WASTE DISPOSAL: A BACKGROUND SURVEY FOR APPLICATIONS IN NIGERIA. Washington, D.C.: World Bank Internal Document [33].
Luna, Emmanuel M. Oscar P. Ferrer and Ulpiano Ignacio, Jr. 1994. PARTICIPATORY ACTION PLANNING FOR THE DEVELOPMENT OF TWO PSF PROJECTS. Manila, the Philippines: U. of the Philippines [135, 141, 143].
Macdonald, D. and P. Vopni 1994. "Policy Barriers to 50% Diversion of Municipal Solid Waste." WASTE MANAGEMENT & RESEARCH. 12:257–270 [32].
MacDougall, Terry 1988. "The Lockheed Scandal and the High Cost of Politics in Japan." In THE POLITICS OF SCANDAL, eds. Andrei S. Marvots and Mark Silverstein. New York: Holmes & Meier [181].
MacDougall, Terry E. 1989. "Democracy and Local Government in Postwar Japan." In Ishida Takeshi and Ellis S. Krauss, eds., DEMOCRACY IN JAPAN. Pittsburgh, PA: University of Pittsburgh Press [41, 43, 50].
Macintre, Andrew 1991. BUSINESS AND POLITICS IN INDONESIA. St. Leonards, Australia: Allen & Unwin [54].
Maier, Karl. 1992. "Nigeria: Biting the Bullet." AFRICA REPORT. Vol. 37(3): 44–47 [45, 56].
Maingot, Anthony P. 1994. "Confronting Corruption in the Hemisphere: A Sociological Perspective." JOURNAL OF INTERAMERICAN STUDIES AND WORLD AFFAIRS 36(3): 45–74 [189, 196].
Mansbridge, Jane. 1991. "Politics." In National Research Council, ed., THE TRANSITION TO DEMOCRACY: PROCEEDINGS OF A WORKSHOP. Washington, DC: U.S.A.I.D. [215].
Manski, Charles F. and Irwin Garfinkel. 1992. "Introduction." In Charles F. Manski and Irwin Garfinkel, eds., EVALUATING WELFARE AND TRAINING PROGRAMS. Cambridge, MA: Harvard University Press [66, 68].
Mao, Yu-Kang. 1991. "Institutional Organizations in Taiwan's Agricultural Development." in Peter Calkins, Wen S. Chern, and Francis C. Tuan, eds., RURAL

DEVELOPMENT IN TAIWAN AND MAINLAND CHINA. Boulder, CO: Westview Press [228].
Marc, Alexandre, Carol Graham, and Mark Schacter. 1993. SOCIAL ACTION PROGRAMS AND SOCIAL FUNDS. Washington, DC: World Bank [208].
Marcelino, Gileno Fernandez. 1994. "The National School for Public Administration." In Shahid Amjad Chaudhry, Gary James Reid and Waleed Haider Malik, eds., CIVIL SERVICE REFORM IN LATIN AMERICA AND THE CARIBBEAN. Washington, DC: World Bank Technical Paper No. 259 [329].
Marris, Peter and Anthony Somerset. 1973. AFRICAN BUSINESSMEN. Nairobi: East African Publishing House [249].
Martin, Curtis H. and Bruce Stronach 1992. POLITICS EAST AND WEST: A COMPARISON OF JAPANESE AND BRITISH POLITICAL CULTURE. Armonk, NY and London: M. E. Sharpe [179].
Mason, Andrew and Lee-Jay Cho 1991. "Population Policy." In Lee-Jay Cho and Yoon Hyung Kim, eds., ECONOMIC DEVELOPMENT IN THE REPUBLIC OF KOREA: A POLICY PERSPECTIVE. Honolulu, HA: East-West Center [278].
Massey, Douglas S. and Shawn M. Kanaiaupuni, 1993. "Public Housing and the Concentration of Poverty," SOCIAL SCIENCE QUARTERLY, Vol. 74 (March), pp. 109–121 [69].
Massolo, Alejandra 1996. "Mexico." In Patricia L. McCarney, ed., THE CHANGING NATURE OF LOCAL GOVERNMENT IN DEVELOPING COUNTRIES. Toronto: U. of Toronto Press [186].
Mathur, Hari M. 1986. ADMINISTRATIVE DEVELOPMENT IN THE THIRD WORLD. New Delhi: Sage Publications [162].
Mayo, Elton, 1933. THE HUMAN PROBLEMS OF INDUSTRIAL CIVILIZATION. Cambridge, MA: Harvard Business School [6, 84–85].
McGee, T. G. and Y. M Yeung 1977. HAWKERS IN SOUTHEAST ASIAN CITIES. Ottawa, Canada: International Development Research Centre [139, 151].
McGregor, Douglas, 1960. THE HUMAN SIDE OF ENTERPRISE. New York: McGraw-Hill [6, 104].
Mead, Lawrence M., 1997. "Opimizing JOBS: Evaluation Versus Administration." PUBLIC ADMINISTRATION REVIEW, Vol. 57, No. 2: 113–123 [68].
Mehmet, Ozay. 1993. "Rent-Seeking and Gate-Keeping in Indonesia: A Cultural and Empirical Analysis." Paper Prepared for the Institute of Southeast Asian Studies, Singapore [55].
MEIP (Metropolitan Environmental Improvement Program) 1994. JAPAN'S EXPERIENCE IN URBAN ENVIRONMENTAL MANAGEMENT. Washington, DC: The World Bank [33, 38, 41, 44, 47].
Mejia, Abel. 1994. "Brazil: Municipalities and Low Income Sanitation." In WORLD BANK SOURCEBOOK ON PARTICIPATION, ed. Environment Department. Washington, DC: The World Bank [136, 137, 142].
Melson, Robert and Howard Wolpe. 1971. "Modernization and the Politics of Communalism: A Theoretical Perspective." In NIGERIA: MODERNIZATION AND THE POLITICS OF COMMUNALISM, eds. Robert Melson and Howard Wolpe. East Lansing, MI: Michigan State University [253].

Metz, Helen C. 1992. NIGERIA: A COUNTRY STUDY. Washington, D.C.: Library of Congress [56].
Michels, Robert. 1958. POLITICAL PARTIES. New York: Collier Books [217].
Midgal, Joel S. 1987. "Strong States, Weak States: Power and Accommodation." In UNDERSTANDING POLITICAL DEVELOPMENT, eds. Myron Weiner and Samuel P. Huntington. Boston: Little, Brown, and Co. [146].
Miller, Norman and Rodger Yeager 1993. KENYA: THE QUEST FOR PROSPERITY. Boulder, CO: Westview Press [102, 249, 261].
Mills, Bradford ET AL. 1994. PUBLIC FINANCE AND PUBLIC EMPLOYMENT: AN ANALYSIS OF PUBLIC SECTOR RETRENCHMENT PROGRAMS IN GHANA AND GUINEA. Ithaca, NY: Cornell University CFNPP Publications Department [299].
Moe, Ronald C. 1991. "The HUD Scandal and the Case for an Office of Federal Management." PUBLIC ADMINISTRATION REVIEW 51(4): 298–307 [172].
Moeller, Philip W. 1990. HUMAN RESOURCES AND INSTITUTIONAL DEVELOPMENT IN THE ROAD SECTOR. Washington, DC: The World Bank [254].
Mommsen, Wolfgang J. 1989. THE POLITICAL AND SOCIAL THEORY OF MAX WEBER: COLLECTED ESSAYS. Chicago, IL: University of Chicago Press [220].
Montgomery, John D. 1988. BUREAUCRATS AND PEOPLE: GRASSROOTS PARTICIPATION IN THIRD WORLD DEVELOPMENT. Baltimore, MD: The Johns Hopkins University Press [152].
Montgomery, John D. 1991. "The Strategic Environment of Public Managers in Developing Countries." In Ali Farazmand, ed., HANDBOOK OF COMPARATIVE AND DEVELOPMENT PUBLIC ADMINISTRATION. New York: Marcel Dekker [99].
Moon, Pal Yong 1991. "A Positive Grain-Price Policy (1969) and Agricultural Development." In Lee-Jay Cho and Yoon Hyung Kim, eds., ECONOMOMIC DEVELOPMENT IN THE REPUBLIC OF KOREA: A POLICY PERSPECTIVE. Honolulu, HA: East-West Center [286].
Moon, Pal Yong. 1991a. "The Saemaul (New Community) Movement (1971)," in Lee-Jay Cho and Yoon Hyung Kim, eds., ECONOMIC DEVELOPMENT IN THE REPUBLIC OF KOREA: A POLICY PERSPECTIVE. Honolulu, HI: East-West Center [229, 230, 231].
Moore, Richard J. 1995. "Implementation and Sustainable Development: The Management of Policy Reform." In Daniel M. Schydlowsky, ed., STRUCTURAL ADJUSTMENT: RETROSPECT & PROSPECT. Westview, CN: Praeger [318, 320].
Morin, Pierre 1993. SENEGAL: TOWARDS THE NEXT STAGES OF PE REFORM AND PRIVATIZATION. Washington, DC: World Bank Sahel Department [193].
Morris, A. E. J. 1985. "Historical Roots of Dutch City Planning and Urban Form." In PUBLIC PLANNING IN THE NETHERLANDS, eds. Ashok K. Dutt and Frank J. Costa. Oxford: Oxford University Press [118].
Morris, Stephen D. 1991. CORRUPTION AND POLITICS IN CONTEMPORARY MEXICO. Tuscaloosa, AB: University of Alabama Press [185, 186, 191, 196].

Mosley, Paul. 1991. "The Philippines, Kenya, and Ecuador." In AID AND POWER, Vol. 2: CASE STUDIES. London: Routledge [323, 324].
Mosley, Paul, Jane Harrigan & John Toye. 1991. AID & POWER: THE WORLD BANK AND POLICY-BASED LENDING, VOL. I. London: Routledge [321, 323, 326].
Moss, Todd S. 1995. "U.S. Policy and Democratisation in Africa: The Limits of Liberal Universalism." JOURNAL OF MODERN AFRICAN STUDIES 32(2): 189–209 [237, 238].
Msolomba, E.H. 1991. "Malawi: Maintenance and Rehabilitation Management System." In THE ROAD MAINTENANCE INITIATIVE: BUILDING CAPACITY FOR POLICY REFORM. VOL. 2: READINGS AND CASE STUDIES. Washington, DC: The World Bank [254].
Muramatsu, Michi. 1986. "Central-Local Political Relations in Japan." JOURNAL OF JAPANESE STUDIES. 12(2): 304–327 [43, 44].
Myers, Ramon H. 1986. "The Economic Development of the Republic of China on Taiwan, 1965–1981." In Lawrence J. Lau, editor, MODELS OF DEVELOPMENT. San Francisco, CA: ICS Press [225, 227].
NAHRO, 1990. THE MANY FACES OF PUBLIC HOUSING. Washington, DC: NAHRO [70].
Nas, Tevtik R., Albert C. Price, and Charles T. Weber 1986. "A Policy-Oriented Theory of Corruption." AMERICAN POLITICAL SCIENCE REVIEW 80(1): 107–120 [191].
Nath, K. L. 1992. "Water, Sanitation and Solid Waste Management: The Calcutta Profile." in RESEARCH PAPERS, ed. USAID, Asia Regional Office. Calcutta: The Times Research Foundation [134].
Nchari, Anthony N. 1990. "Co-operatives as Decentralized Socio-Economic Institutions in Sub-Saharan Africa." In DECENTRALIZATION POLICIES AND SOCIO-ECONOMIC DEVELOPMENT IN SUB-SAHARAN AFRICA, eds. Ladipo Adamolekun, Robert Robert and Mouftaou Laleye. Washington, DC: The World Bank [149].
Ndegwa, Stephen N. 1997. "Citizenship and Ethnicity: An Examination of Two Transition Moments in Kenyan Politics." AMERICAN POLITICAL SCIENCE REVIEW 91(3): 599–616 [210].
Ndue, Paul Ntungwe. 1994. "Africa's Turn Toward Pluralism." JOURNAL OF DEMOCRACY 5(1): 45–55 [205, 209].
Nellis, John R. 1983. "Decentralization in North Africa: Problems of Policy Implementation." In DECENTRALIZATION AND DEVELOPMENT, eds. G. Shabbir Cheema and Dennis A. Rondinelli. London and Beverly Hill, CA: SAGE Publications [113].
Nellis, John R. 1989. CONTRACT PLANS AND PUBLIC ENTERPRISE PERFORMANCE. Washington, DC: The World Bank [158].
Nelson, Charles M. 1996. "PAT 101, Principles of Patronage." ISSUE: A JOURNAL OF OPINION. Vol. 24 (1): 45–51 [103].
Nelson, Joan M. 1992. ENCOURAGING DEMOCRACY: WHAT ROLE FOR CONDITIONED AID? Washington, DC: Overseas Development Council [202, 204, 239, 326].

Nenno, Mary 1989. "HUD After Reagan: A New Cycle of Policies and Partners." JOURNAL OF HOUSING. March/April: 75–81 [177].
Netherlands Scientific Council 1990. INSTITUTIONS AND CITIES: THE DUTCH EXPERIENCE. The Hague: Netherlands Scientific Council for Government Policy [118].
Newbury, Catharine 1995. "Background to Genocide in Rwanda." ISSUE: A JOURNAL OF OPINION 23(2): 12–17 [209].
Newfield, Jack and Paul Dubrul. 1977. THE ABUSE OF POWER: THE PERMANENT GOVERNMENT AND THE FALL OF NEW YORK. New York: Viking Press [170, 173].
Nicholson, Norman J. and Dilawar Ali Khan 1974. BASIC DEMOCRACIES AND RURAL DEVELOPMENT IN PAKISTAN. Ithaca, NY: Cornell University [160].
Nolan, Riall W. 1986. "Anthropology and the Peace Corps: Notes from a Training Program." In ANTHROPOLOGY AND RURAL DEVELOPMENT IN WEST AFRICA, eds. Michael M. Horowitz and Thomas M. Painter. Boulder, CO: Westview Press [245].
Norquest, David A. 1991. "A Unifying Conception of Politics." PS: POLITICAL SCIENCE & POLITICS. September: 504–505 [164].
Nugent, Paul. 1991. "Educating Rawlings: The Evolution of Government." In Donald Rothchild, ed. GHANA: THE POLITICAL ECONOMY OF RECOVERY. Boulder & London: Lynne Rienner Publishers 275].
Nunberg, Barbara 1992. MANAGING THE CIVIL SERVICE. Washington, DC: The World Bank [87, 94].
Nunberg, Barbara 1996. RE-THINKING CIVIL SERVICE REFORM; AN AGENDA FOR SMART GOVERNMENT. Washington, DC: World Bank Poverty and Social Policy Report [319, 328].
Nunberg, Barbara and John Nellis 1990. CIVIL SERVICE REFORM AND THE WORLD BANK. Washington, DC: World Bank Working Paper [187].
Nyang'oro, Julius E. 1994. "Reform Politics and the Democratization Process in Africa." AFRICAN STUDIES REVIEW 37(1): 133–149 [207].
Nye, Joseph S. 1967. "Corruption and Political Development: A Cost-Benefit Analysis." AMERICAN POLITICAL SCIENCE REVIEW 66(2): 417–427 [167, 191].
OECD 1987. ADMINISTRATION AS SERVICE; THE PUBLIC AS CLIENT. Paris: OECD [47, 61, 93, 147].
OECD 1987a. MANAGING AND FINANCING URBAN SERVICES. Paris: OECD [76].
OECD 1987b. REVITALIZING URBAN ECONOMIES. Paris: OECD [31].
OECD 1991. REGIONAL POLICIES AND PROBLEMS IN SWITZERLAND. Paris: OECD [160].
OED (Operations Evaluation Department) 1990. INDONESIA: THIRD AND FOURTH URBAN DEVELOPMENT PROJECTS. Washington, DC.: World Bank Internal Document [135].
OED (Operations Evaluation Department) 1990a; 1996 (A Third Evaluation). THE AGA KHAN RURAL SUPPORT PROGRAM IN PAKISTAN. Washington, DC: The World Bank [160–161].
OED (Operations Evaluation Department) 1994. TWENTY YEARS OF LEND-

ING FOR URBAN DEVELOPMENT 1972-1992. Washington, DC: World Bank Internal Document [133].
OED (Operations Evaluation Department) 1994a. URBAN PROJECTS—INDONESIA. Washington, DC: World Bank Internal Document [134].
OED 1996. "Improving Urban Services in Nairobi." OED PRECIS 115:l-4 [195].
Olayiwola, Peter. O. 1987. PETROLIUM AND STRUCTURAL CHANGE IN A DEVELOPING COUNTRY: THE CASE OF NIGERIA. New York: Praeger [52, 54].
Oliker, Stacey J. 1994. "Does Workfare Work?" SOCIAL PROBLEMS 41(2): 195–213 [66].
Oloka-Onyango, J. 1997. "Uganda's Benevolent Dictatorship." CURRENT HISTORY 96 (May): 212–215 [237, 240].
Olowu, Dele. 1990. "Achievements and Problems of Federal and State Transfers to Local Governments in Nigeria." In DECENTRALIZATION POLICIES AND SOCIO-ECONOMIC DEVELOPMENT IN SUB-SAHARAN AFRTCA, eds. Ladipo Adamoledun, Robert Robert, and Mouftaou Laleye. Washington, D.C.: World Bank EDI [45].
Olowu, Dele. 1992. "Urban Local Government Finance in Nigeria: The Case of Lagos Municipal Area." PUBLIC ADMINISTRATION AND DEVELOPMENT. Vol. 12(2): 19–32 [34].
Olson, Mancur 1982. THE RISE AND DECLINE OF NATIONS: ECONOMIC GROWTH, STAGFLATION & SOCIAL RIGIDITIES. New Haven & London: Yale University Press [22].
Olugbabe, Kola. 1989. "Sustaining Democratic Virtues in Nigeria: Expectations in the Third Republic." CORRUPTION AND REFORM 4(3): 245–281 [214].
Operations Policy Department 1993. HANDBOOK ON TECHNICAL ASSISTANCE. Washington, DC: The World Bank [317].
Operations Policy Department 1994. GOVERNANCE: THE WORLD BANK EXPERIENCE. Washington, DC: The World Bank [185, 342].
Osborne, David and Ted Gaebler. 1992. REINVENTING GOVERNMENT. Reading, MA: Addison-Wesley Publishing Co. [60, 72, 93, 147, 307].
Ostrom, Elinor, Larry Schroeder and Susan Wynne 1990. INSTITUTIONAL INCENTIVES AND RURAL INFRASTRUCTURE SUSTAINABILITY. Washington, DC: USAID [119, 150, 153].
Ouchi, William G. 1984. THE M-FORM SOCIETY. New York: Avon Books [180].
Ouma, Stephen O. A. 1991. "Corruption in Public Policy and Its Impact on Development: The Case of Uganda Since 1979. PUBLIC ADMINISTRATION AND DEVELOPMENT ll: 473–490 [185, 189, 195].
OXFAM International 1996. MULTILATERAL DEBT: THE HUMAN COSTS. Washington, DC: Oxfam International Position Paper [343].
Pae, Sung Moon. 1992. KOREA LEADING DEVELOPING NATIONS: ECONOMY, DEMOCRACY, AND WELFARE. Lanham, MD: University Press of America [269, 282, 289, 292].
Pae, Sung Moon. 1992a. "Korea: Leading the Third World Democratization." ASIAN AFFAIRS: AN AMERICAN REVIEW 19 (2): 81–98 [214].
Page, Edward C. and Michael J. Goldsmith 1987. "Centre and Locality: Functions,

Access, and Discretion." In CENTRAL AND LOCAL RELATIONS: A COMPARATIVE ANALYSIS OF WEST EUROPEAN UNITARY STATES. London: SAGE Publications [109].

Palmer, Monte, Ali Leila and El Sayed Yassin 1988. THE EGYPTIAN BUREAUCRACY. Syracuse, NY: Syracuse University Press [120–1].

Park, Chong Kee 1991. "The Health Insurance Scheme." In Lee-Jay Cho and Yoon Hyung Kim, eds, ECONOMIC DEVELOPMENT IN THE REPUBLIC OF KOREA: A POLICY PERSPECTIVE. Honolulu, HA: East-West Center [225].

Park, Chong Kee 1991a. "The 1966 Tax Administration Reform, Tax Law Reforms, and Government Savings." In Lee-Jay Cho and Yoon Hyung Kim, eds., ECONOMIC DEVELOPMENT IN THE REPUBLIC OF KOREA: A POLICY PERSPECTIVE. Honolulu, HA: East-West Center [281].

Park, Chong Kee 1994. "Tax Policies and Institutional Reform." In Lee-Jay Cho and Yoon Hyung Kim, eds, KOREA'S POLITICAL ECONOMY: AN INSTITUTIONAL PERSPECTIVE. Boulder, CO: Westview Press [301].

Park, Yung Chul 1991. "The Development of Financial Institutions and the Role of Government in Credit Allocation." In Lee-Jay Cho and Yoon Hyung Kim, eds., ECONOMIC DEVELOPMENT IN THE REPUBLIC OF KOREA: A POLICY PERSPECTIVE. Honolulu, HA: East-West Center [281].

Parkinson, Michael 1991. "Strategic Responses to Economic Change in European Cities." AMERICAN POLITICAL SCIENCE ASSOCIATION Annual Meeting, Washington, DC [31].

Parsons, Talcott. 1951. STRUCTURE AND PROCESS IN MODERN SOCIETIES. Glencoe, IL: The Free Press [245].

Paul, Samuel 1986. "The Strategic Management of Development Programs: Evidence from an International Study." In COMMUNITY PARTICIPATION IN DELIVERING URBAN SERVICES IN ASIA, eds. John C. Ickis, Edilberto de Jesus, and Rushikesh Maru. West Hartford, CT: Kumarian [254].

Paul, Samuel 1994. DOES VOICE MATTER? A STUDY OF THE IMPACT OF VOICE ON PUBLIC ACCOUNTABILITY. Washington, DC: The World Bank [146].

Pears, David, 1966. "Wittgenstein and Austin." In Bernard Williams and Alan Montefiore, eds., BRITISH ANALYTICAL PHILOSOPHY. London: Routledge & Kegan Paul [10].

Pei, Minxin. 1994. "The Puzzle of East Asian Exceptionalism." JOURNAL OF DEMOCRACY. 5(4): 90–103 [225, 227].

Peil, Margaret 1991. LAGOS: THE CITY IS THE PEOPLE. Boston, MA: G. H. Hall [33, 42].

Peil, Margaret 1996. "Ghana's Universities and Their Government: An Ambigouous Relationship." ISSUE: A JOURNAL OF OPINION 24(1): 52–56 [277, 288, 291, 298].

Pempel, T. J. 1982. POLICY & POLITICS IN JAPAN. Philadelphia: Temple University Press [37].

Pempel, T. J. and Micio Muramatsu 1993. THE JAPANESE BUREAUCRACY AND ECONOMIC DEVELOPMENT. Washington, DC: The World Bank EDI [181].

Perkins, Dwight H. and Michael Roemer 1993. "Differing Endowments and His-

torical Legacies." In David L. Lindauer and Michael Roemer, eds., ASIA AND AFRICA: LEGACIES AND OPPORTUNITIES IN DEVELOPMENT. Cambridge, MA: Harvard Institute for International Development [56].
Perlman, Bruce J. 1989. "Modernizing the Public Service in Latin America: Paradoxes of Latin American Public Administration." INTERNATIONAL JOURNAL OF PUBLIC ADMINISTRATION. Vol. 14(4): 671–704 [88].
Perlman, Janice E. 1990. "A Dual Strategy for Deliberate Social Change in Cities." CITIES 7: 3–15 [123].
Persaud, Thakoor and Waleed H. Malik 1994. "The Impact of Sociocultural and Governance Factors on Institutional Reform." In Shahid Amjad Chaudhry, Gary James Reid and Waleed Haider Malik, eds., CIVIL SERVICE REFORM IN LATIN AMERICA AND THE CARIBBEAN. Washington, DC: World Bank Technical Paper Number 259 [311, 315, 318, 324].
Peters, B. Guy. 1988. PUBLIC BUREAUCRACIES: PROBLEMS OF THEORY AND METHOD. Tuscaloosa: U. of Alabama Press [7, 36].
Peters, B. Guy 1991. "Government Reform and Reorganization in an Era of Retrenchment and Conviction Politics." In Ali Farazmand, ed., HANDBOOK OF COMPARATIVE AND DEVELOPMENT PUBLIC ADMINISTRATION. New York: Marcel Dekker [99].
Peters, B. Guy. 1994. "Managing the Hollow State." INTERNATIONAL JOURNAL OF PUBLIC ADMINISTRATION. 17(3&4): 739–756 [12].
Peters, John S. and Susan Welch 1978. "Political Corruption in America: A Search for Difinitions and a Theory." AMERICAN POLITICAL SCIENCE REVIEW 72(3): 974–984 [165].
Peters, Tom and Robert Waterman, Jr. 1982. IN SEARCH OF EXCELLENCE. New York: Harper & Row [104].
Peterson, Paul E., Barry G. Rabe, and Kenneth K. Wong 1986. WHEN FEDERALISM WORKS. Washington, DC: The Brookings Institution [117].
Phillips, Adedotun O. 1991. "Four Decades of Fiscal Federalism in Nigeria." PUBLIUS. Vol 21(4): 103–112 [45].
Phillips, A.O. 1991a. "Institutional Reform in Nigeria." PUBLIC ADMINISTRATION AND DEVELOPMENT. Vol. 11 (3): 229–232 [38].
Piccioto, Robert 1992. PARTICIPATORY DEVELOPMENT: MYTHS AND DILEMMAS. Washington, DC: World Bank Agricultural and Rural Development Series No. 8 [84].
Picciotto, Robert and Rachel Weaving. 1994. "A New Project Cycle for the World Bank." FINANCE AND DEVELOPMENT. December: 41–44 [325].
Pines, Marion. 1991. "Investing in Self-Sufficiency for Poor Families: Putting it All Together." In NAHRO & APWA, FAMILY SELF-SUFFICIENCY: LINKING HOUSING, PUBLIC WELFARE AND HUMAN SERVICES. Washington, DC: NAHRO [68].
Pinkney, Robert. 1994. DEMOCRACY IN THE THIRD WORLD. Boulder, CO: Lynne Rienner Publishers [200, 202, 204, 208, 210, 218].
Pinto, Rogerio and Angelous J. Mrope. 1994. PROJECTIZING THE GOVERNANCE APPROACH TO CIVIL SERVICE REFORM. Washington, DC: World Bank Discussion Paper 252 [211].

Poister, Theordore H. and Gregory Streib, 1995. "MBO in Municipal Government: Variations on a Traditional Management Tool." PUBLIC ADMINISTRATIVE REVIEW 55(1): 48–56 [77].
Polizatto, Vincent P. 1992. "Prudential Regulation and Banking Supervision." In Dimitri Vittas, ed., FINANCIAL REGULATION: CHANGING THE RULES OF THE GAME. Washington, DC: The World Bank [30].
Pollack, Andrew 1996. "South Korea's Ex-Strongman Denies Taking Bribes at Trial." NEW YORK TIMES. February 27: All [271].
Pollitt, Christopher. 1986. "Democracy and Bureaucracy." in David Held and Christopher Pollitt, eds., NEW FORMS OF DEMOCRACY. London: Sage Publications [220].
Popiel, Paul A. 1994. FINANCIAL SYSTEMS IN SUB-SAHARAN AFRICA: A COMPARATIVE STUDY. Washington, DC: The World Bank [26, 28, 29].
Porter, Michael E., 1990. THE COMPETITIVE ADVANTAGE OF NATIONS. New York: The Free Press [3, 182].
Porvali, H. 1993. "Ghana." In H. Porvali ET AL., THE DEVELOPMENT OF COOPERATIVES AND OTHER RURAL ORGANIZATIONS: SELECTED COUNTRY STUDIES. Washington, DC: World Bank Agricultural and Rural Development Series No. 8 [92].
Posthuma, Anne Caroline. 1995. "Japanese Techniques in Africa? Human Resources and Industrial Restructuring in Zimbabwe." WORLD DEVELOPMENT 23(1): 103–116 [251, 252].
Potts. Deborah 1994. "Urban Environmental Controls and Low-Income Housing in Southern Africa." In ENVIRONMENT AND HOUSING IN THIRD WORLD CITIES, eds. Hamish Main and Stephen Wyn Williams. West Sussex, England: John Wiley & Sons [141].
Power, Anne 1987. "The Crisis in Council Housing—Is Public Housing Manageable?" THE POLITICAL QUARTERLY 58: 284–295 [110].
Przeworski, Adam. 1992. "The Neoliberal Fallacy." JOURNAL OF DEMOCRACY. 3(3): 46–56 [202].
Pugh, Cedrick 1990. HOUSING AND URBANISATION. New Delhi: Sage Publications [131, 133, 136, 139].
Purcell, Dennis 1994. AGRICULTURAL EXTENSION: LESSONS FROM COMPLETED PROJECTS. Washington, DC: World Bank OED Report No. 13000 [87, 88, 89, 92, 93, 96, 98, 99, 101].
Pye, Lucian W. 1985. ASIAN POWER AND POLITICS: THE CULTURAL DIMENSIONS OF AUTHORITY. Cambridge: Harvard University Press [52, 246, 250].
Pye, Lucian W. 1988. "The New Asian Capitalism: A Political Portrait." In Peter L. Berger and Hsin-Huang Michael Hsiao, eds., IN SEARCH OF AN EAST ASIAN DEVELOMENT MODEL [284].
Quah, Jon S. T. 1994. "Cultural Change in the Singapore Civil Service." In CIVIL SERVICE REFORM IN LATIN AMERICA AND THE CARIBBEAN: PROCEEDINGS OF A CONFERENCE, eds., Shahid Amjad Chaudry, Gary James Reid, and Waleed Haider Malik. Washington, DC: The World Bank [257].
Quah, Jon S. T. 1995. "Sustaining Quality in the Singapore Civil Service." PUBLIC

ADMINISTRATION AND DEVELOPMENT 15 (2): 335–343. Operations Policy Department. 1994. GOVERNANCE: THE WORLD BANK'S EXPERIENCE. Washington, DC: The World Bank [225].
Quah, Jon S. and Stella R. Quah. 1989. "Government Intervention." In MANAGEMENT OF SUCCESS: THE MOULDING OF MODERN SIGNAPORE, eds. Kerniel S. Sandhu and Paul Wheatley. Singapore: Institute of Southeast Asian Studies [257].
Raab, Selwyn 1993. "Policy Flaws Tied to Cases of Extortion By Inspectors." THE NEW YORK TIMES. October 23: 23, 27 [141].
Rabasco, Lisa 1994. "State Recycling Rates." WASTE AGE 25(6): 48–55 [32].
Rabinovitch, Jonas with Josef Leitmann 1993. ENVIRONMENTAL INNOVATION AND MANAGEMENT IN CURITIBA, BRAZIL. Washington, DC: The World Bank [136].
Randall, Vicky and Robin Theobald. 1985. POLITICAL CHANGE AND UNDERDEVELOPMENT: A CRITICAL INTRODUCTION TO THIRD WORLD POLITICS. London: Macmillan [253].
Raphaeli, Nimrod, Jacques Roumani, and A. C. MacKellar. 1984. PUBLIC SECTOR MANAGEMENT IN BOTSWANA. Washington, DC: The World Bank [261].
Rapley, John 1994. "The Ivorien Bourgeoisie." In AFRICAN CAPITALISTS IN AFRICAN DEVELOPMENT, eds., Bruce J. Berman and Colin Leys. Boulder & London: Lynne Rienner [255].
Rapp, Brian W. and Frank M. Patitucci 1977. MANAGING LOCAL GOVERNMENT FOR IMPROVED PERFORMANCE: A PRACTICAL APPROACH. Boulder, CO: Westview Press [107].
Ravenhill, John. 1993. "A Second Decade of Adjustment: Greater Complexity; Greater Uncertainty." In Thomas M. Callaghy and John Ravenhill, eds., HEMMED IN. New York: Columbia University Press [309, 310, 323].
Ray, Edward John 1984. "Economic Distortions and Financial Reforms." In Dale W. Adams, Douglas H. Graham, and J. D. Von Pischke, eds., UNDERMINING RURAL DEVELOPMENT WITH CHEAP CREDIT. Boulder, CO: Westview Press [30].
Redding, S. G. 1988. "The Role of the Entrepreneur in the New Asian Capitalism." In IN SEARCH OF AN EAST ASIAN DEVELOPMENT MODEL, eds. Peter L. Berger and Hsin-huang Micahel Hsiao. New Brunswick, NJ: Transaction [246].
Reid, T. R. 1991. "Japan's Housing: Pricey, Chilly and Toilet-Poor." THE WASHINGTON POST March 4: A9 [175].
Rhodes, R. A. W., 1991. "Theory and Methods in British Public Administration: The View from Political Science." POLITICAL STUDIES, Vol. 33 (3): 533–554 [8, 61].
Rich, Bruce. 1994. MORTGAGING THE EARTH: THE WORLD BANK, ENVIRONMENTAL IMPOVERISHMENT, AND THE CRISIS OF DEVELOPMENT. Boston: Beacon Hill [317, 321, 322].
Rich, Spencer. 1992. "Job Training is Paying Off—For Some." THE WASHINGTON POST (May 23): A11 [67].
Richburg, Keith B. 1994. "African Press Endangered." THE WASHINGTON POST. June 14: A10 [190].

Richburg, Keith B. 1995. "Taiwan's Voters Narrow Ruling Party Majority." THE WASHINGTON POST December 3: A31 [235].

Riddell, Roger. 1993. "The Future of the Manufacturing Sector in Sub-Saharan Africa." In Thomas M. Callaghy and John Ravenhill, eds., HEMMED IN. New York: Columbia University Press [23, 312].

Rigg, Jonathan. 1988. "Singapore and the Recession of 1985." ASIAN SURVEY. 28(3): 340–352 [226].

Riggs, Fred W. 1964. ADMINISTRATION IN DEVELOPING COUNTRIES: THE THEORY OF PRISMATIC SOCIETY. Boston: Houghton Mifflin [85].

Rivera, Julius and Paul W. Goodman. 1981. "System-Environment Adaptation: Corporations in a U.S.-Mexico Border Metropolis." STUDIES IN COMPARATIVE INTERNATIONAL DEVELOPMENT 16:27–44 [251].

Roe, Alan 1991. "Financial Systems and Development in Africa." In Philippe Callier, ed., FINANCIAL SYSTEMS AND DEVELOPMENT IN AFRICA. Washington, DC: The World Bank [28].

Rogowski, Ronald. 1974. RATIONAL LEGITIMACY: A THEORY OF POLITICAL SUPPORT. Princeton: Princeton University Press [250].

Rohn, John A. 1991. "Ethical Issues in French Public Administration: A Comparative Study." PUBLIC ADMINISTRATION REVIEW 51(4): 283–296 [172].

Rondinelli, Dennis A. 1987. DEVELOPMENT ADMINISTRATION AND U.S. FOREIGN POLICY, Boulder, CO.: Lynne Rienner [59].

Rondinelli, Dennis A. and Henry P. Minis, Jr. 1990. "Administrative Restructuring for Economic Adjustment: Decentrlization Policy in Senegal." INTERNATIONAL REVIEW OF ADMINISTRATIVE SCIENCES. Vol 56: 447–466 [94].

Rose, Kalima 1992. WHERE WOMEN ARE LEADERS: THE SEWA MOVEMENT IN INDIA. London and New Jersey: ZED Books [155].

Rose-Ackerman, Susan 1978. CORRUPTION: A STUDY IN POLITICAL ECONOMY. New York: Academic Press [169].

Rose-Ackerman, Susan 1989. "Corruption and the Private Sector." in POLITICAL CORRUPTION: A HANDBOOK, eds. Arnold J. Heidenheimer, Michael Johnston, and Victor T. LeVine. New Brunswick, NJ: Transaction Books [171].

Roth, Gabriel and George Wynne 1982. FREE ENTERPRISE URBAN TRANSPORTATION. Washington, DC: Council for International Urban Liaison [148].

Rothchild, Donald. 1991. "Ghana and Structural Adjustment: An Overview." In Donald Rothchild, ed., GHANA: THE POLITICAL ECONOMY OF RECOVERY. Boulder & London: Lynne Rienner Publishers [286].

Ruffing-Hilliard, Karen 1991. "Merit Reforms in Latin America: A Comparative Perspective." In Ali Farazmand, ed., HANDBOOK OF COMPARATIVE AND DEVELOPMENT PUBLIC ADMINISTRATION. New York: Marcel Dekker [186].

Rufus Davis, S. 1978. THE FEDERAL PRINCIPLE: A JOURNEY THROUGH TIME IN QUEST OF A MEANING. Berkeley, CA: University of California Press [105].

Ruland, Jurgen 1992. URBAN DEVELOPMENT IN SOUTHEAST ASIA: RE-

GIONAL CITIES AND LOCAL GOVERNMENT. Boulder, CO: Westview Press [144].
Rupert, James 1996. "Ghanaians Vote as Nation Moves From Military Rule to Civilian Democracy." THE WASHINGTON POST December 8: A34 [271].
Russell-Robinson 1997. "African Female Circumcision and the Missionary Mentality." ISSUE: A JOURNAL OF OPINION 25(1): 54–57 [268].
Ruttan, Vernon W. 1991. "What Happened to Political Development?" ECONOMIC DEVELOPMENT AND CULTURAL CHANGE 39(3): 264–286 [24, 116, 255].
Saasa, Oliver S. 1994. STRUCTURAL ADJUSTMENT AND GOVERNANCE CAPACITY IN ZAMBIA: 1983–1994. Washington, DC: World Bank [211].
Sachs, Jeffrey. 1996. "Growth in Africa: It Can be Done." THE ECONOMIST, June 29: 19–21 [316, 323].
Sakong, Il. 1993. KOREA IN THE WORLD ECONOMY. Washington, DC: Institute for International Economics [283, 292].
Salmen, Larry F. 1987. LISTEN TO THE PEOPLE: PARTICIPANT-OBSERVER EVALUATION OF DEVELOPMENT PROJECTS. Washington, DC: The World Bank [319, 339].
Salmen, Larry. 1991. "Reducing Poverty." PUBLIC ADMINISTRATION AND DEVELOPMENT. Vol. ll(3): 295–302 [91, 92, 97].
Salmen, Larry F. 1995. BENEFICIARY ASSESSMENT: AN APPROACH DESCRIBED. Washington, DC: World Bank Environment Department Paper 023 [319, 340].
Sandbrook, Richard 1985. THE POLITICS OF AFRICA'S ECONOMIC STAGNATION. Cambridge: Cambridge University Press [23].
Sanger, David E. 1992. "North Korea's Isolation." THE NEW YORK TIMES MAGAZINE. November 15: 29–39 [223].
Sanger, David E. 1992a. "Power Failures Slow Philippine Vote Count and Feed Suspicions of Fraud." THE NEW YORK TIMES (May 24): 3 [64].
Sangmpam, S. N. 1992. "The Overpoliticized State and Democratization." COMPARATIVE POLITICS 24(4): 402–406 [219].
Sayre, Wallace S. and Herbert Kaufman 1965. GOVERNING NEW YORK CITY: POLITICS IN THE METROPOLIS. New York: Norton [170].
Schacter, Mark. 1995. "Recent Experience with Institutional Development: Lending in the Western Africa Department." In Petter Langseth, Sandile Nogxina, Daan Prinsoo, Roger Sullivan, eds., CIVIL SERVICE REFORM IN ANGLOPHONE AFRICA. Washington, DC: EDI/ODA [324, 328].
Schapiro, M. O. and S. Wainaina. 1991. "Kenya's Export of Horticultural Commodities." PUBLIC ADMINISTRATION AND DEVELOPMENT. Vol. ll(3): 257–262 [249].
Schmidt, Mary. 1993. FUNDASAL'S HOUSING FOR THE POOR, Washington, DC: World Bank Consultant Report [78].
Schmitter, Philippe C. 1994. "Dangers and Dilemmas of Democracy." JOURNAL OF DEMOCRACY 5(2): 57–74 [204, 216].
Schmitter, Philippe C. and Terry Lynn Karl. 1993. "What Democracy Is and Is Not." In Larry Diamond and Marc F. Plattner, eds., THE GLOBAL RESUR-

GENCE OF DEMOCRACY. Baltimore and London: The Johns Hopkins University Press [217].
Schneider, Mark ET AL. 1997. "Institutional Arrangements and the Creation of Social Capital: The Effects of Public School Choice." AMERICAN PUBLICAL SCIENCE REVIEW, Vol. 91, No. 1: 82–93 [81].
Schubeler, Peter 1996. PARTICIPATION AND PARTNERSHIP IN URBAN INFRASTRUCTURE MANAGEMENT. Washington, DC: The World Bank Urban Management Program [133].
Schwartz, Nathan H. 1991. "French Housing Policy in the Eighties: Complexity, Continuity, and Ideology." In John S. Ambler, ed., THE FRENCH WELFARE STATE, New York: New York U. Press [69, 80].
Searle, G. R. 1987. CORRUPTION IN BRITISH POLITICS: 1895–1930. Oxford: Clarendon Press [174].
Sebstad, Jennifer 1982. STRUGGLE AND DEVELOPMENT AMONG SELF-EMPLOYED WOMEN: A REPORT ON THE SELF-EMPLOYED WOMEN'S ASSOCIATION OF AHMEDABAD, INDIA. Washington, DC: USAID/S&T [154].
Segal, Aaron. 1995. "Can Democratic Transitions Tame Political Successions?" AFRICAN STUDIES ASSOCIATION ANNUAL MEETING, Orlando Florida [207, 240].
Server, O. B. 1996. "Corruption: A Major Problem for Urban Management." HABITAT INTERNATIONAL. Vol. 20, l: 23–41 [137, 138].
Shah, Anwar 1991. THE NEW FISCAL FEDERALISM IN BRAZIL. Washington, DC: The World Bank [159].
Sharpe, L. J. 1979. "Introduction." In DECENTRALIST TRENDS IN WESTERN DEMOCRACIES, ed. L. J. Sharpe. London and Beverly Hills, CA: SAGE Publishers [107, 110].
Sheng, Andrew. 1991. "The Art of Bank Restructuring: Issues and Techniques." In Philippe Callier, ed., FINANCIAL SYSTEMS AND DEVELOPMENT IN AFRICA. Washington, DC: The World Bank [26].
Sheppard, Marie. 1995. "Constraints to Private Enterprise in the FSU: Approach and Application to Russia." In Ira W. Liberman and John Nellis, eds., RUSSIA: CREATING PRIVATE ENTERPRISES AND EFFICIENT MARKETS. Washington, DC: The World Bank [203].
Sherif, Khaled F. 1993. REGIONAL STUDY ON PUBLIC ENTERPRISE REFORM AND PRIVATIZATION IN AFRICA. Washington, DC: World Bank Internal Document [292].
Shihata, Ibrihim F. I. 1991. THE WORLD BANK IN A CHANGING WORLD: SELECTED ESSAYS. Dordrecht, Netherlands: Martinus Nijhoff [317].
Shirley, Mary M. 1989. IMPROVING PUBLIC ENTERPRISE PERFORMANCE: LESSONS FROM SOUTH KOREA. Washington, DC: The World Bank [292].
Shirley, Mary ET AL. 1995. BUREAUCRATS IN BUSINESS: THE ECONOMICS AND POLITICS OF BUSINESS OWNERSHIP. Washington, DC: World Bank Policy Research Report [310, 312, 315, 317].
Siegelbaum, Paul J. 1996. REPORT OF THE CORRUPTION ACTION PLAN WORKING GROUP. Washington, DC: World Bank Public Sector Management Report [319, 326, 328, 341, 347].

Siffin, William J. 1991. "The Problem of Public Administration." In Ali Farazmand, ed., HANDBOOK OF COMPARATIVE AND DEVELOPMENT PUBLIC ADMINISTRATION. New York: Marcel Dekker [83, 86, 87].
Silverman, Jerry M. 1990. PUBLIC SECTOR DECENTRALIZATION. Washington, D.C.: The World Bank [153].
Silverman, Jerry M. 1992. PUBLIC SECTOR DECENTRALIZATION: ECONOMIC POLICY AND SECTOR INVESTMENT PROGRAMS. Washington, DC: The World Bank [108].
Silverman, Jerry M and Chang-Po Yang. 1991. REPUBLIC OF ZAMBIA: PUBLIC SECTOR MANAGEMENT REVIEW, VOL. I. Washington, DC: World Bank Internal Document [112].
Simeon, Richard 1986. "Considerations on Centralization and Decentralization." CANADIAN PUBLIC ADMINISTRATION 29: 445–461 [107, 116].
Sklar, Richard L. 1995. "The New Modernization." ISSUE: A JOURNAL OF OPINION. 23(1): 19–21 [200].
Smelser, Neil J. 1992. "Culture: Coherent or Incoherent." In THEORY OF CULTURE, eds. Richard Munch and Neil J. Smelser. Berkeley and Los Angeles: University of California Press [245].
Smillie, Ian. 1986. NO CONDITION PERMANENT: PUMP PRIMING GHANA'S INDUSTRIAL REVOLUTION. London: Intermediate Technology Publications [275, 276, 290].
Smith, B. C. 1985. DECENTRALIZATION: THE TERRITORIAL DIMENSION OF THE STATE. London: Allen & Unwin [109, 114].
Smith, B. C. 1996. UNDERSTANDING THIRD WORLD POLITICS. Bloomington and Indianapolis: Indiana University Press [2, 220].
Smith, Gerald H. 1997. "The Dichotomy of Politics and Corruption in a Neopatrimonial State: Evidence from Sierra Leone, 1968–1993," ISSUE: A JOURNAL OF OPINION. Vol. 25 (1): 58–62 [192].
Smith, Hedrick 1988. THE POWER GAME: HOW WASHINGTON WORKS. New York: Random House [175].
Smoke, Paul 1993. "Local Government Fiscal Reform in Developing Countries: Lessons from Kenya." WORLD DEVELOPMENT 21: 901–923 [112].
Snyder, Margaret C. and Mary Tadesse. 1995. AFRICAN WOMEN AND DEVELOPMENT: A HISTORY. London & New Jersey: Zed Books [268].
Soedjamoko 1986. "Social Energy as a Development Resource." in COMMUNITY MANAGEMENT, ed. David C. Korten. West Hartford, CT: Kumarian Press [128].
Soglo, Nicephore D. 1996. "An African Election: I Lost, but Democracy Won." THE WASHINGTON POST. August 21: A25 [331].
Song, Dae-Hee and Byung-Seo Ryu. 1992. "Agricultural Policies and Structural Adjustment." In Vittorio Corbo and Sang-Mok Suh, eds. STRUCTURAL ADJUSTMENT IN A NEWLY INDUSTRALIZED COUNTRY: THE KOREAN EXPERIENCE. Washington, DC: The World Bank [285].
Soon, Tech-Wong and C. Suan Tan. 1992. SINGAPORE: PUBLIC POLICY AND ECONOMIC DEVELOPMENT. Washington, DC: World Bank Unpublished Report [226].
Sorenson, Georg. 1993. DEMOCRACY AND DEMOCRATIZATION. Boulder, CO: Westview Press [201, 206, 217].

Southall, Aiden. 1973. CROSS-CULTURAL STUDIES OF URBANIZATION. New York: Oxford University Press [251].
Southern Africa Department 1993. OPPORTUNITIES FOR INDUSTRIAL DEVELOPMENT IN BOTSWANA: AN ECONOMY IN TRANSITION. Washington, DC: World Bank Internal Document [261].
Southern African Department. 1994. ZAMBIA POVERTY ASSESSMENT. Volume 2: RURAL POVERTY ASSESSMENT. Washington, DC: The World Bank Report No. 12985 ZA [212].
Spotts, Frederick and Theodore Wiser 1986. ITALY: A DIFFICULT DEMOCRACY. Cambridge: Cambridge University Press [174, 175, 182, 183].
Stackhouse, John. 1996. "A Train That Barely Left the Station." THE GLOBE AND MAIL. August 21: Bl [332].
Stavis, Benedict. 1982. "Rural Local Governance and Agricultural Development in Taiwan." In Norman T. Uphoff, ed., RURAL DEVELOPMENT AND LOCAL ORGANIZATION IN ASIA. New Delhi: MacMillen [228].
Steedman, David. 1994. CONFRONTING COUNTERPRODUCTIVE COUNTRIES: THE CHALLENGE OF FOREIGN AID. Washington, DC: World Bank Internal Report [328].
Steinberg, David I. 1984. "The Dynamics of Development in Rural Korea." In David Steinberg ET AL., eds. KOREAN AGRICULTURAL SERVICES: THE INVISIBLE HAND IN THE IRON GLOVE. Washington, DC: USAID [279, 285].
Stenberg, Carl W. 1984. "Beyond the Days of Wine and Roses: Intergovernmental Relations in a Cutback Environment." In FEDERALISM AND INTERGOVERNMENTAL RELATIONS, eds. Deil S. Wright and Harvey L. White. Washington, DC: ASPA [109].
Stewart, Frances, Sanjaya Lall, and Samuel Wangwe 1992. "Alternative Strategies: An Overview." In Frances Stewart, Sanjaya Lall and Samuel Wangwe, eds. ALTERNATIVE STRATEGIES IN SUB-SAHARAN AFRICA. New York: St. Martin's Press [276].
Stoker, Gerry 1995. "Intergovernmental Relations." PUBLIC ADMINISTRATION 73 (Spring): 101–122 [111].
Stone, Carl. 1986. CLASS, STATE & DEMOCRACY IN JAMAICA. New York: Praeger [203].
Stone, Andrew, Brian Levy, and Ricardo Paredes. 1992. PUBLIC INSTITUTIONS AND PRIVATE TRANSACTIONS: THE LEGAL AND REGULATORY ENVIRONMENT FOR BUSINESS TRANSACTIONS IN BRAZIL AND CHILE. Washington, DC: The World Bank [248].
Strassmann, W. Paul and Alistain Blunt 1994. "Land Prices and Housing in Manila." URBAN STUDIES 31(2): 267–285 [136].
Stren, Richard E. 1989. "Urban Government in Africa." In Richard E. Stren and Rodney R. White, eds., AFRICAN CITIES IN CRISIS: MANAGING RAPID URBAN GROWTH. Boulder, CO: Westview Press [195].
Stringer, William L. 1991. THE DEVELOPMENT OF CREDIT MARKETS IN KENYA FOR URBAN INFRASTRUCTURE AND HOUSING FINANCE. Washington, DC: USAID [29].
Struyk, Raymond J, Michael L. Hoffman, and Harold M. Katsura 1990. THE

MARKET FOR SHELTER IN INDONESIAN CITIES. Washington, DC: The Urban Institute Press [138].
Suh, Sang-Mok and Ha-Cheong Yeon. 1992. "Social Welfare During the Period of Structural Adjustment." In Vittorio Corbo and Sang-Mok Suh, eds. STRUCTURAL ADJUSTMENT IN A NEWLY INDUSTRIALIZED COUNTRY: THE KOREAN EXPERIENCE. Washington, DC: The World Bank [283].
Sullivan, Kevin 1997. "Japanese Incineration Fouls Navy Base's Air." THE WASHINGTON POST. November 24: A18 [33, 49].
Swee-Hock, Saw 1967. SINGAPORE POPULATION IN TRANSITION. Philadelphia, PA: University of Pennsylvania Press [258].
Tanaka, Masaru. 1992. "Reduction of and Resource Recovery from Municipal Solid Waste in Japan." WASTE MANAGEMENT & RESEARCH. Vol. 10: 453–459 [32, 44, 45, 48, 50].
Tanco, Arturo R. Jr. 1983. "Mobilizing National Commitment in a Multi-Agency Program." In David C. Korten and Felipe B. Alfonso, eds., BUREAUCRACY AND THE POOR. West Hartford, CT: Kumarian Press [128].
Tapales, Prosperpina Domingo 1996. "Philippines." In Patricia L. McCarney, ed., THE CHANGING NATURE OF LOCAL GOVERNMENT IN DEVELOPING COUNTRIES. Toronto: University of Toronto Press [119, 120].
Tendler, Judith and Sara Fredheim 1994. "Trust in a Rent-Seeking World: Health and Government Transformed in Northeast Brazil." WORLD DEVELOPMENT 22(12): 1771–1791 [264].
Theobald, Robin 1990. CORRUPTION, DEVELOPMENT AND UNDERDEVELOPMENT. Durham, NC: Duke University Press [174].
Thillairajah, Subapathy. 1993. DEVELOPMENT OF RURAL FINANCIAL MARKETS IN SUB-SAHARAN AFRICA, 2 Vols. Washington, DC: USAID [29, 30, 80].
Thomas, Frederick C. 1997. CALCUTTA POOR. Armonk, NY: M.E. Sharpe 134].
Thompson, Dennis F. 1993. "Mediated Corruption: The Case of the Keating Five." AMERICAN POLITICAL SCIENCE REVIEW 87(2): 369–381 [168].
Thompson, Victor A. 1961. MODERN ORGANIZATIONS. New York: Knoph [10].
Thomson, James T., E. Connerley, and James S. Wunsch 1986. DECENTRALIZED FINANCE AND MANAGEMENT FOR DEVELOPMENT. Washington, DC: USAID/RD/ST [122]. Thomson, James T. ET AL. 1989. OPTIONS FOR PROMOTING USER-BASED GOVERNANCE OF SAHELIAN RENEWABLE NATURAL RESORUCES. Washington, DC: Associates in Rural Development [265].
Thorbecke, Erik and Theordore van der Pluijm 1993. RURAL INDONESIA: SOCIO-ECONOMIC DEVELOPMENT IN A CHANGING ENVIRONMENT. New York: New York University Press [53].
Tien, Hung-mao. 1994. "Toward Peaceful Resolution of Mainland-Taiwan Conflicts: The Promise of Demcoratization." In Edward Friedman, ed., THE POLITICS OF DEMOCRATIZATION: GENERALIZING EAST ASIAN EXPERIENCES. Boulder, CO: Westview Press [235].
Toonen, Theo A. J. 1987. "The Netherlands: A Decentralised State in a Welfare Society." WEST EUROPEAN POLITICS 10: 108–127 [118].

Toonen, Theo A. J. 1996. "On the Administrative Condition of Politics: Administrative Transformation in the Netherlands." WEST EUROPEAN POLITICS 19(3): 609–632 [119].
Torrey, E. Fuller. 1986. WITCHDOCTORS AND PSYCHIATRY: THE COMMON ROOTS OF PSYCHOTHERAPY AND ITS FUTURE. New York: Harper & Row [250].
Townsend, James R. 1974. POLITICS IN CHINA. Boston: Little, Brown [246].
Toye, John. 1991. "Ghana." In Paul Mosley, Jane Harrigan, and John Toye, eds., AID AND POWER. Volume 2: CASE STUDIES. London: Routledge [331].
Tsurumi, E. Patricia 1990. FACTORY GIRLS: WOMEN IN THE THREAD MILLS OF MEIJI JAPAN. Princeton, NJ: Princeton University Press [252].
Tuchman, Barbara W., 1981. PRACTICING HISTORY: SELECTED ESSAYS. New York: Ballantine Books [7].
Tucker, Elizabeth and Anne Swardson 1988. "Buddy System Can Circumvent Laws." THE WASHINGTON POST. June 19: A12 [177].
Tummala, Krishna K. 1992. "India's Federalism Under Stress." ASIAN SURVEY 33: 539–553 [108, 113].
Turner, John E., Victor L. Hesli, Doug Suh Bark and Hoon Yu. 1993. VILLAGES ASTIR: COMMUNITY DEVELOPMENT, TRADITION AND CHANGE IN KOREA. Westport, CN: Praeger [229, 231].
Turner, John F. C. 1996. "Tools for Building Community: An Examination of 13 Hypotheses." HABITAT INTERNATIONAL. Vol. 20 (3): 339–347 [144].
Turner, John F. C. and R. Fichter (eds) 1972. FREEDOM TO BUILD. New York: McMillan [131].
Tutahirwa, Eldad M. and Peter G. Veit 1992. PUBLIC POLICY AND LEGISLATION IN ENVIRONMENTAL MANAGEMENT: TERRACING IN NYAREMBO, UGANDA. Washington, DC: World Resources Institute [96, 97].
Umali-Deininger, Dina. 1996. "New Approaches to an Old Problem: The Public and Private Sector in Extension." Washington, DC: World Bank Extension Workshop [84, 91, 92, 94, 95, 100].
Uphoff, Norman 1986. LOCAL INSTITUTIONAL DEVELOPMENT: AN ANALYTICAL SOURCEBOOK WITH CASES. West Hartford, CN: Kumarian Press [123].
Uphoff, Norman. 1991. "Fitting People to Projects." In Michael M. Cernea, ed., PUTTING PEOPLE FIRST. Washington, DC: The World Bank [149].
Van Arkadie, Brian. 1994. ECONOMIC STRATEGY AND STRUCTURAL ADJUSTMENT IN TANZANIA. Washington, DC: The World Bank [204, 213].
van de Walle, Nicolas. 1993. "The Politics of Nonreform in Cameroon." In Thomas M. Callaghy and John Ravenhill, eds., HEMMED IN. New York: Columbia University Press [309, 311, 313].
van der Linden, Jan. 1986. THE SITES AND SERVICES APPROACH REVIEWED. Hants, England: Gower Publishing Company [131, 142].
van der Linden, Jan. 1994. "Where Do We Go From Here?" THIRD WORLD PLANNING REVIEW 16(3): 226–240 [142].
Van Wart, Montgomery and N. Joseph Cayer 1990. "Comparative Public Administration: Defunct, Dispersed, or Redefined?" PUBLIC ADMINISTRATION REVIEW, Vol. 50 (March/April): 238–248 [62].

Van Wolferen, Karel. 1989. THE ENIGMA OF JAPANESE POWER: PEOPLE AND POWER IN A STATELESS SOCIETY. New York: Alfred A. Knoth [41, 179].
Vengroff, Richard and Hatem Ben Salen 1992. "Assessing The Impact of Decentralization on Governance: A Comparative Methodological Approach and Application to Tunisia." PUBLIC ADMINISTRATION AND DEVELOPMENT 12: 473–492 [114].
Verba, Sidney. "A Research Perspective." In National Research Council, ed., THE TRANSITION TO DEMOCRACY: PROCEEDINGS OF A WORKSHOP. Washington, DC: National Academy Press [216].
Verhelst, Thierry G. 1990. NO LIFE WITHOUT ROOTS: CULTURE AND DEVELOPMENT. London and N.J.: Ved Books [252].
Vieta, Kojo T. 1995. "Hard Times." WEST AFRICA 26 June-2 July: 999 [270].
Viloria, Julie 1991. "Indonesia's Community Infrastructure Programs." In Asian Development Bank, ed., THE URBAN POOR AND BASIC INFRASTRUCTURE SERVICES IN ASIA AND THE PACIFIC, VOL. III. Manila, The Philippines: Asian Development Bank [133, 138].
Vittas, Dimitri. 1992. "Introduction and Overview." In Dimitri Vittas, ed., FINANCIAL REGULATION: CHANGING THE RULES OF THE GAME. Washington, DC: The World Bank [27].
Vogel, David. 1986. NATIONAL STYLES OF REGULATION: ENVIRONMENTAL PROTECTION IN GREAT BRITAIN AND THE UNITED STATES. Ithaca and London: Cornell University Press [107].
Von Pischke, J. D. 1991. FINANCE AT THE FRONTIER: DEBT CAPACITY AND THE ROLE OF CREDIT IN THE PRIVATE ECONOMY. Washington, DC: The World Bank [79].
Wachman, Alan M. 1994. "Competing Identities in Taiwan." In Murray A. Rubinstein, ed., THE OTHER TAIWAN: 1945 TO THE PRESENT. Armonk, NY: M. E. Sharpe [223].
Wade, Robert. 1985. "The Market for Public Office: Why the Indian State Is Not Better at Development." WORLD DEVELOPMENT 13(4): 467–497 [185].
Wade, Robert. 1990. GOVERNING THE MARKET. Princeton, NJ: Princeton University Press [222, 225].
Wageman, Ruth. 1995. "Interdependence and Group Effectiveness." ADMINISTRATIVE SCIENCE QUARTERLY. 40(2): 145–180 [64].
Waldo, Dwight 1980. THE ENTERPRISE OF PUBLIC ADMINISTRATION. Novato, CA: Chandler & Sharp Publishers [6, 11, 128, 219].
Wallin, Gunnar 1991. "Towards the Integrated and Fragmented State: The Mixed Role of Local Government." WEST EUROPEAN POLITICS 14: 97–120 [107, 110].
Wamsley, Gary L. 1990. "Introduction." In Gary L. Wamsley ET AL., eds., REFOUNDING PUBLIC ADMINISTRATION. Newbury Park, CA: Sage Publications [60, 62].
Wapenhans, Willi A. 1993. OBTAINING RESULTS. Washington, DC: The World Bank [321].
Ware, Alan. 1992. "Liberal Democracy: One Form or Many?" In David Held, ed., PROSPECTS FOR DEMOCRACY. Oxford, England: Blackwell Publishers [217].

Warren, Michael D. 1991. USING INDIGENOUS KNOWLEDGE IN AGRICULTURAL DEVELOPMENT. Washington, DC: The World Bank [252].

Warwick, Daniel P. 1986. "The Indonesian Family Planning Program: Government Influence and Client Choice." POPULATION AND DEVELOPMENT REVIEW 12(3): 465–480 [260].

Watson, Gabrielle and N. Vijay Jagannathan. 1995. PARTICIPATION IN WATER AND SANITATION. Washington, DC: World Bank Participation Series 002 [139, 330, 335].

Weimer, David L. 1992. "Political Science, Practitioner Skill, and Public Management." PUBLIC ADMINISTRATION REVIEW, Vol 52 (May/June), pp. 240–245 [61].

Weldon, T. D. 1953. VOCABULARY OF POLITICS. Harmondsworth, England: Penguin [10, 63].

Werlin, Herbert H. 1972. "The Roots of Corruption: The Ghanaian Enquiry." THE JOURNAL OF MODERN AFRICAN STUDIES 10 (2): 247–266 [163, 245, 270].

Werlin, Herbert H. 1973. "The Consequences of Corruption: The Ghanaian Experience." POLITICAL SCIENCE QUARTERLY 88(1): 71–85 [163, 270].

Werlin, Herbert H. 1974. GOVERNING AN AFRICAN CITY: A STUDY OF NAIROBI, New York: Africana Publishing Company [7, 16, 132, 206].

Werlin, Herbert H. 1987. "Oh, Calcutta: The Challenge of Urban Misery." DEVELOPMENT INTERNATIONAL l(2): 17–21 [129].

Werlin, Herbert H. 1988. "The Theory of Political Elasticity." ADMINISTRATION AND SOCIETY 20(1): 46–70 [7, 129, 131].

Werlin, Herbert H. 1989. "Contingency Theory: The Wrong Door." INTERNATIONAL REVIEW OF ADMINISTRATIVE SCIENCES 55(1): 117–132 [8].

Werlin, Herbert H. 1989a. "The Community: Master or Client?" PUBLIC ADMINISTRATION AND DEVELOPMENT 9(4): 447–457 [127].

Werlin, Herbert H. 1990. "Decentralization and Culture: The Case of Monrovia, Liberia." PUBLIC ADMINISTRATION AND DEVELOPMENT 10 (3): 251–262 [186, 338, 342].

Werlin, Herbert H. 1991. "Ghana and South Korea: Lessons From World Bank Case Studies." PUBLIC ADMINISTRATION AND DEVELOPMENT. Vol. ll: 245–255 [270].

Werlin, Herbert H. 1992. "Linking Decentralization to Centralization." PUBLIC ADMINISTRATION AND DEVELOPMENT 12(3): 223–236 [145].

Werlin, Herbert H. 1994. "A Primary-Secondary Democracy Distinction." PS: POLITICAL SCIENCE & POLITICS. Vol 28 (3): 530–534 [9].

Werlin, Herbert H. 1994a. "Ghana and South Korea: Explaining Development Disparities—An Essay in Honor of Carl Rosberg." JOURNAL OF ASIAN AND AFRICAN STUDIES 29(3–4): 205–225 [271].

Werlin, Herbert H. 1994b. "Politics Versus Culture: Which is Stronger?" STUDIES IN COMPARATIVE INTERNATIONAL DEVELOPMENT 29(4): 3–24 [244].

Werlin, Herbert H. 1994c. "Revisiting Corruption: With a New Definition." INTERNATIONAL REVIEW OF ADMINISTRATIVE SCIENCES. Vol. 60 (4): 645–660 [9].

Werlin, Herbert H. and Harry Eckstein 1990. "Political Culture and Political Change." AMERICAN POLITICAL SCIENCE REVIEW 84(1): 249–258 [243].
Wescott, Clay 1994. "Civil Service Reform in Mexico." In CIVIL SERVICE REFORM IN LATIN AMERICA: PROCEEDINGS OF A CONFERENCE, eds., Shahid Amjad Chaudry, Gary James Reid, and Waleed Haider Malif [261].
Westebbe, Richard 1994. "Structural Adjustment, Rent Seeking, and Liberalization in Benin." In Jennifer A. Widner, ed., ECONOMIC CHANGE AND POLITICAL LIBERALIZATION IN SUB-SAHARAN AFRICA. Baltimore and London: The Johns Hopkins University Press [240].
West Central Africa Department 1995. GHANA: GROWTH, PRIVATE SECTOR, AND POVERTY REDUCTION. Washington, DC: World Bank Country Economic Memorandum [269, 270, 286, 297].
Western Africa Department 1994. PROJECT COMPLETION REPORT, NIGERIA: LAGOS SOLID WASTE AND STORM DRAINAGE PROJECT. Washington, DC: World Bank Internal Document [34, 36]. Whalley, John 1994. "Does Korea Need a Tax Reform in the 1990s?" In Lee-Jay Cho and Yoon Hyung Kim, eds., KOREA'S POLITICAL ECONOMY: AN INSTITUTIONAL PERSPECTIVE. Boulder, CO: Westview [301].
Whang, In-Joung. 1992. "Economic Management for Structural Adjustment in the 1980s." In Vittorio Corbo and Sang-Mok Suh, eds., STRUCTURAL ADJUSTMENT IN A NEWLY INDUSTRIALIZED COUNTRY: THE KOREAN EXPERIENCE. Washington, DC: The World Bank [280, 281].
Whicker, Marcia Lynn, Ruth Ann Strickland, and Dorothy Olshfski. 1993. "The Troublesome Cleft: Public Administration and Public Policy." PUBLIC ADMINISTRATION REVIEW. Vol 53 (November/December): 531–541 [62].
White, Leonard D., 1955. INTRODUCTION TO THE STUDY OF PUBLIC ADMINISTRATION. New York: Macmillan [5].
White, Louise G. 1987. CREATING OPPORTUNITIES FOR CHANGE: APPROACHES TO MANAGING DEVELOPMENT PROGRAMS. Boulder, CO: Lynne Rienner [85, 128].
White, Louise G. 1988. IMPLEMENTING ECONOMIC POLICY REFORMS: PROBLEMS AND OPPORTUNITIES FOR DONORS. Washington, DC: USAID [95].
White, Louise G. 1989. "Public Management in a Pluralistic Arena." PUBLIC ADMINISTRATION REVIEW 49(6): 522–531 [47].
Whittington, Dale ET AL. 1992. HOUSEHOLD DEMAND FOR IMPROVED SANITATION SERVICE: A CASE STUDY OF KUMASI, GHANA. Washington, DC: The World Bank [303].
Whyte, William F. 1991. SOCIAL THEORY FOR ACTION. Newbury Park, CA: SAGE Publications [63].
Widner, Jennifer A. 1993. "The Discovery of Politics: Smallholder Reactions to the Cocoa Crisis of 1988–90." In Thomas M. Callaghy and John Ravenhill, eds., HEMMED IN. New York: Columbia University Press [308].
Widner, Jennifer A. 1994. "Single Party States and Agricultural Policies: The Cases of Ivory Coast and Kenya." COMPARATIVE POLITICS 26(2): 127–148 [208].

Wilford, John Noble 1994. "Development Imperils Some Human Species." NEW YORK TIMES (January 2): D1 [253].
Wilkinson, Barry. 1988. "Social Engineering in Singapore." JOURNAL OF CONTEMPORARY ASIA 18 (2): 165–187 [226].
Williams, Donald G. 1992. "Accommodation in the Midst of Crisis? Assessing Governance in Nigeria." In Goran Hyden and Michael Bratton, eds., GOVERNANCE AND POLITICS IN AFRICA. Boulder and London: Lynne Rienner Publishers [38].
Williams, Harold W. 1986. "In Search of Bureaucratic Excellence." THE BUREAUCRAT 15: 15–19 [104].
Williams, Jack F. 1994. "Vernerability and Change in Taiwan's Agriculture." In Murray A. Rubinstein, ed., THE OTHER TAIWAN: 1945 TO THE PRESENT. Armonk, NY: M.E. Sharpe [227].
Williams, Jack F. and Ch'ang-yi Chang. 1994. "Paying the Price of Economic Development in Taiwan." In Murray A. Rubinstein, ed., THE OTHER TAIWAN: 1945 TO THE PRESENT. Armonk, NY: M.E. Sharpe [235].
Williams, Oliver P. and G. Van Colijn. 1980. "Territorial Politics and Resource Transfers in the Netherlands." In FINANCING URBAN GOVERNMENT IN THE WELFARE STATE, ed. Douglas E. Ashford. New York: St. Martin's Press [123].
Wilson, David C. 1996. "Stick or Carrot?: The Use of Policy Measures to Move Waste Management Up the Hierarchy." WASTE MANAGEMENT & RESEARCH. Vol. 14 (2): 385–398 [50].
Wilson, James Q. 1989. BUREAUCRACY: WHAT GOVERNMENT AGENCIES DO AND WHY THEY DO IT. New York: Basic Book [8, 36].
Wilson, James Q. 1994. "A New Approach to Welfare Reform: Humility." THE WALL STREET JOURNAL. December 29: A10 [60].
Wilson, William Julius. 1987. THE TRULY DISADVANTAGED: THE INNER CITY, THE UNDERCLASS, AND PUBLIC POLICY. Chicago, IL: U. of Chicago Press [250].
Wiser, William H. and Charlotte Viall Wiser 1971. BEHIND MUD WALLS: 1930–1960. Berkeley and Los Angeles: University of California Press [100].
Wolff, Michael 1992. "George Bush Won't Be Signing Any Autographs at the Summit." THE WASHINGTON POST. July 5: C4 [174].
Wolin, Sheldon S. 1960. POLITICS AND VISION: CONTINUITY AND INNOVATION IN WESTERN POLITICAL THOUGHT. Boston, MA: Little, Brown [4, 9, 11, 165, 215].
Wolin, Sheldon S. 1989. THE PRESENCE OF THE PAST: ESSAYS ON THE STATE AND THE CONSTITUTION. Baltimore and London: The Johns Hopkins University Press [116].
Wollheim, Richard. 1966. "On the Theory of Democracy." In Bernard Williams and Alan Montefiore, eds., BRITISH ANALYTICAL PHILOSOPHY. London: Routledge & Kegan Paul [10].
Woodall, Brian 1993. "The Logic of Collusive Action: The Political Roots of Japan's DANGO System." COMPARATIVE POLITICS 25(3): 297–312 [180].
World Bank 1989. SUB-SAHARAN AFRICA: FROM CRISIS TO SUSTAINABLE GROWTH. Washington, DC: The World Bank [89, 101, 195].

References and Citation Index 401

World Bank, 1991. INDONESIA: DEVELOPING PRIVATE ENTERPRISE. Washington, DC: World Bank Internal Report [55].
World Bank. 1992. GOVERNANCE AND DEVELOPMENT. Washington, DC: The World Bank [189, 335].
World Bank 1992a. POPULATION AND THE WORLD BANK: IMPLICATIONS FROM EIGHT CASE STUDIES. Washington, DC: World Bank Operations Evaluation Department [260].
World Bank 1993. SENEGAL PRIVATE SECTOR ASSESSMENT. Washington, DC: World Bank Internal Report [193].
World Bank 1993a. THE EAST ASIAN MIRACLE: ECONOMIC GROWTH AND PUBLIC POLICY. Washington, DC: The World Bank [222, 224, 225, 244, 258, 210].
World Bank. 1994. ADJUSTMENT IN AFRICA: REFORMS, RESULTS AND THE ROAD AHEAD. Washington, DC: The World Bank [195, 213].
World Bank, 1994a. INDONESIA: SUSTAINING DEVELOPMENT. Washington, DC: The World Bank [134].
World Bank, 1994b. NIGERIA: STRUCTURAL ADJUSTMENT PROGRAM: POLICIES, IMPLEMENTATION AND IMPACT. Washington, DC: World Bank Internal Report [45, 48, 49, 52, 55].
World Bank. 1994c. UKRAINE: THE AGRICULTURAL SECTOR IN TRANSITION. Washington, DC: The World Bank [221].
World Bank. 1995. THE WORLD BANK AND LEGAL TECHNICAL ASSISTANCE: INITIAL LESSONS. Washington, DC: The World Bank Legal Department [341].
World Bank. 1996. POVERTY REDUCTION AND THE WORLD BANK: PROGRESS AND CHALLENGES IN THE 1990s. Washington, DC: The World Bank [306, 316].
World Bank 1997. WORLD DEVELOPMENT REPORT 1997: THE STATE IN A CHANGING WORLD. Washington, DC: The World Bank [58, 289, 326].
World Bank LAC. 1994. PERU: PUBLIC EXPENDITURE REVIEW. Washington, DC: World Bank Report No. 13190–PE [327].
World Bank OED. 1991. OED STUDY OF BANK SUPPORT OF INDUSTRIALIZATION IN NEWLY INDUSTRIALIZING COUNTRIES. VOLUME II: CASE STUDY OF THE REPUBLIC OF KOREA. Washington, DC: World Bank Internal Document [279, 281].
World Bank OED 1994. GHANA: STRUCTURAL ADJUSTMENT INSTITUTIONAL SUPPORT PROJECT. Washington, DC: World Bank Internal Document [295, 296].
World Bank OED 1994a. GHANA: FIRST EDUCATION SECTOR ADJUSTMENT CREDIT. Washington, DC: World Bank Internal Document [274, 277, 301].
World Bank OED 1995. GHANA: COUNTRY ASSISTANCE REVIEW. Washington, DC: World Bank Internal Document [273, 288, 294, 296, 298, 302, 303].
World Bank OED 8573. 1990. FREE-STANDING TECHNICAL ASSISTANCE FOR INSTITUTIONAL DEVELOPMENT IN SUB-SAHARAN AFRICA. Washington, DC: The World Bank [328].

World Bank OED 9225. 1990. THE SUSTAINABILITY OF INVESTMENT PROJECTS IN EDUCATION. Washington, DC: The World Bank [328].

World Bank OED 12144. 1993. THE WORLD BANK'S ROLE IN HUMAN RESOURCE DEVELOPMENT IN SUB-SAHARAN AFRICA: EDUCATION, TRAINING AND TECHNICAL ASSISTANCE. Washington, DC: The World Bank [334].

World Bank OED 12922. 1994. INDUSTRIAL SECTOR REORIENTATION IN EAST AFRICA. Washington, DC: The World Bank [326].

World Bank OED 12923. 1994. OED STUDY OF BANK/MEXICO RELATIONS, 1948–1992. Washington, DC: The World Bank [321].

World Bank OED 13117. 1994. TWENTY YEARS OF LENDING FOR URBAN DEVELOPMENT 1972–92. Washington, DC: The World Bank [331].

World Bank OED 13273 1994. WORLD BANK ASSISTANCE FOR PRIVATIZATION IN DEVELOPING COUNTRIES. Washington, DC: The World Bank [314, 324].

World Bank OED 15222. 1995. MONITORING AND EVALUATION PLANS IN STAFF APPRAISAL REPORTS ISSUED IN FISCAL YEAR 1995. Washington, DC: The World Bank [319, 324, 338]. World Bank OED 16040. 1996. FISCAL MANAGEMENT IN ADJUSTMENT LENDING. Washington, DC: The World Bank [309].

Wraith, Ronald and Edgar Simpkins 1963. CORRUPTION IN DEVELOPING COUNTRIES. London: Allen & Unwin [174].

Wunsch, James S. 1991. "Sustaining Third World Infrastructure Investments." PUBLIC ADMINISTRATION AND DEVELOPMENT ll(1): 5–23 [155, 158].

Yahie, Abdullahi M. 1993. THE DESIGN AND MANAGEMENT OF POVERTY ALLEVIATION PROJECTS IN AFRICA: EVOLVING GUIDELINES BASED ON EXPERIENCE. Washington, DC: The World Bank Economic Development Institute [336].

Ya-li, Lu. 1991. "Political Modernization in the ROC: The Kuomintang and the Inhibited Political Center." In Mamon H. Myers, ed., TWO SOCIETIES IN TRANSITION: THE REPUBLIC OF CHINGA AND THE PEOPLE'S REPUBLIC OF CHINA AFTER FORTY YEARS. Stanford, CA: Hoover University Press [226].

Yeager, Rodger 1993. "The Ecological Price of Stability." In BOTSWANA: THE POLITICAL ECONOMY OF DEMOCRATIC DEVELOPMENT, ed., Stephen John Stedman. Boulder and London: Lynne Rienner [262].

Yeboah-Afari, Ajoa 1995. "VAT Rising Shakes Capital." WEST AFRICA 29 May–4 June: 840–841 [297].

Yong, Phang Sock. 1992. HOUSING MARKETS AND URBAN TRANSPORTATION: ECONOMIC THEORY, ECONOMETRICS AND POLICY ANALYSIS FOR SINGAPORE. Singapore: McGraw-Hill [233].

Young, Crawford. 1994. "Evolving Modes of Consciousness and Ideology: Nationalism and Ethnicity." In David E. Apter and Carl G. Rosberg, eds., POLITICAL DEVELOPMENT AND THE NEW REALISM IN SUB-SAHARAN AFRICA. Charlottesville and London: University Press of Virginia [55]. Young, Roland and Henry A. Fosbrooke. 1960. SMOKE IN THE HILLS: POLITICAL TEN-

SION IN THE MOROGORO DISTRICT IN TANGANYIKA. Evanston, IL: Northwestern U. Press [265].

Young, Timothy W. and Evans Clinchy 1992. CHOICE IN PUBLIC EDUCATION. New York: Teachers College Press [81].

Younger, Steven D. 1989. "Ghana: Economic Recovery Program—A Case Study of Stabilization and Structural Adjustment in Sub-Saharan Africa." In Earl L. McFarland, Jr., ed. SUCCESSFUL DEVELOPMENT IN AFRICA: CASE STUDIES OF PROJECTS, PROGRAMS, AND POLICIES. Washington, DC: The World Bank EDI [275].

Zigler, Edward, Sally J. Styfco and Elizabeth Gilman 1993. "The National Head Start Program for Disadvantaged Preschoolers." In Edward Zigler and Sally J. Styfco, eds., HEAD START AND BEYOND. New Haven, CN: Yale University Press [71].

Zimmerman, Robert F. 1993. DOLLARS, DIPLOMACY, AND DEPENDENCY: DILEMMAS OF U.S. ECONOMIC AID. Boulder, CO: Lynne Rienner [121].

Subject Index

While this book is not primarily intended as a textbook, I hope it will be so used for courses in development studies, comparative administration, and comparative politics because of my dissatisfaction with what is available in these fields. The index has been simplified for teaching purposes.

Africa: administrative weakness, 308–316; agricultural problems, 100–101; comparison with Asia, 55–56; culture, 265–268; debate over democracy, 208–214; universities, 103–104.

Administrative theory (see also political elasticity theory and public administration): confusion, 5–8, 83–86, 128–131; critique of behavioralism, 62–65; critique of the experimental design method, 65–72; critique of scientific management, 63–66; critique of systems theory, 85–86; danger of quantification, 63; decentralization, 116–117; defence of bureaucracy, 129–131; Management by Objectives, 77, 94–95; Total Quality Management, 77; Weberian theory, 131.

Agricultural extension (including the Training and Visit—T&V—approach): competitive practices, 92–94; conflict resolution procedures, 98–99; delegation of responsibility, 94; hiring qualified employees, 87–89; legitimacy, 96–98; management-by-objectives, 94–95; morale, 90–93; training, 88–89; two-way flows of communication, 97–98; women's needs, 98.

Corruption (see also political illness): cost-benefit analysis, 191–192; criticism of, 195–196; definition, 14, 163–173; intensifying factors, 185–192; Italy, 182–184; Japan, 179–182; offsetting factors, 173–184; primary and secondary corruption, 14, 164–167; rent-seeking, 192–195; United States, 175–180.

Credit programs (see also development as expanding financial power): Grameen bank, 79–81; njangi system, 149–150; Self Employed Women's Association (SEWA) of Ahmedabad, India, 154–155.

Decentralization (see also political elasticity theory): combining decentralization and centralization, 335–337; concept of federalism, 105–109; delegation of responsibility, 94–95; division of responsibility, 109–114; Egypt, 120–122; Holland, 118–119; Honduras, 123–124; measurement of, 114–115; Philippines, 119–120; promotion of, 122–125; public-private partnerships, 125; theory, 13, 115–117; to Non-Governmental Organizations, 111–112, 149–153; United States, 117–118; USAID efforts for, 122–125.

Democracy (see also political elasticity theory): Asian experience, 222–234; Benin, 240–241; definition (including the primary-secondary distinction), 9–10, 214–222; desirability in Africa, 205–214; foreign assistance for, 15, 200–205, 234–242; linkage to bureaucracy, 6, 219–222; linkage to development 14–15, 200–205; Singapore, 223–224, 231–234; South Korea, 223–225, 229–232; Taiwan, 223–225, 227–229; Uganda, 236–240.

Development (see also political elasticity theory): as environmental protection, 32–51; as expanding financial power, 25–32; as increasing motivation, 51–58, disparities (explanations for), 55–58, 269–304 (Ghana and S. Korea); importance of leadership, 253–263; importance of political software, 76–81; linkage to comparative politics, 4; meaning, 21–24; promotion of, 326–347; relationship to democracy, 200–205; requisites or underlying factors, 7–9, 154–157, 308.

Economics: criticism of, 2–3, 293–296; debt reduction, 199, 343–347; overreliance upon economists, 318–321; relationship to politics, 293–296.

Environmental protection (see also slum upgrading): Botswana, 262–263; comparison of Japan and Nigeria, 32–52; Niger, 265–266; Taiwan, 235–236.

Family planning: African and Asian comparison, 263–268; Indonesia, 259–261; Malawi, 247; Singapore, 256–260; Thailand, 247–248. Foreign aid (see also World Bank and decentralization): limitations of, 316–326; possibilities of a proactive approach, 326–347.

Ghana: administrative problems, 295–304; comparison with South Korea in regard to economic growth, 269–272; economic retrogression, 272–278; industrial failure, 289–292; problems of privatization and public enterprises, 292–293, 297–299; rural poverty, 286–288, 303–304; Value Added Tax, 302; urban sanitation, Kumasi, 303.

Indonesia (see also slum upgrading): comparison with Nigeria, 51–58; corruption, 55, 138; economic development, 52–55; governance, 55; standard of living, 42–43; Jakarta, 133, 134; standard of living, 52–53.

Japan (see also corruption and solid waste management): administration, 36–38, 50, 180–182; corporatism, 47–48; corruption, 179–182; decentralization, 43–45; organizational management, 36–38, 50, 251–252; Tokyo, 33.

Malawi: family planning, 247; road repair, 254; rural and female poverty, 101–102.

Motivation (see also development and political illness): explanations for, 55–58, 87; possibilities of intensification, 326–347; relationship to agricultural extension, 90–94; use in explaining economic disparities, 271, 294–295, 302–304.

Subject Index

Nigerea: barriers to political reform, 214; decentralization difficulties, 45–47; environmental problems of Lagos, 33–36; financial problems, 56–58; private sector problems, 48–49; public administration weaknesses, 38–39, 42–43, 45–47, 48–49, 56–57.

Political culture: acculturation and Westernization, 247–254; Botswana's cultural favoritism, 260–263; causes and manifestations of culture, 247–250; cultural change in Ceara, Brazil, 264–265 in Eritrea, 267–268, in Niger, 265–266; Indonesia's cultural guidance, 259–261; importance of leadership, 253–263, in regard to Ethiopian Airways, 255; linkage to political elasticity theory, 255–256; Malawi, 247, 254; meaning of culture, 245–247; rural African women, 266–268; Singapore's cultural engineering, 256–260.

Political elasticity theory (including the concepts of political hardware and political software): attainment of, 100; common sense approach, 86–100; examples of political elasticity, 117–119; examples of political inelasticity, 119–122; justification, 1–2, 18–19, 86, 157–162; limitations, 2–3, 25, 56–58, 264; linkage to bureaucracy and democracy, 219–222; meaning, 10–12; origins of, 5–11, 18–19; political hardware, 8–9, 23, 77–79; political implications, 60–61; political software, 8–9, 23, 59–81, 99–100; relationship to corruption, 185; relationship to decentralization, 115–118; relationship to democracy, 220–222; relationship to leadership capacity for cultural change, 255–256, 264–265; use of for a comparison of Ghana and South Korea, 284–293; use of for treating political illness, 305–308; use of, summarized, 12–17; used to criticize humanistic administrative theory, 129–131; used to criticize the New Development Administration, 11–12, 127–129, 145–162.

Political illness (also see secondary corruption under corruption): causation, 57–58; definition of, 14, 167, 305; intensifying factors, 184–192; linkage to secondary corruption, 167, 196–199; treatment of, 305–347.

Politics: definition of, 4–5, 11, 25, 61–64, 215–216; disdain for, 317–319; primary and secondary politics, 25, 61–62, 81; partisan, 168–169; relationship to administration, 61–65, 81, 171–174.

Poverty (see also development, economics, and credit programs): causes of, 308–316; meaning of, 21, 269–271, 305–307.

Public administration (see also political elasticity theory): concept of legitimacy, 96–97; definition, 81; experimental design methodology, 66–69; importance of, 4; linkage to political science, 4, 81; Management by Objectives, 77, 94; political software requisites, 86–99; popular participation, 149–153; promoting competition, 90–94, 333–335; reform of, 326–347; requiring prior reform, 327–330; supervision of, 95–96; systems theory, 85–86; theoretical weaknesses, 6–8, 59–61, 83, 99–100; Total Quality Management, 37, 77; two-way flows of communication, 97–98; use of benchmarks, 337–339; use of Non-Governmental Oranizations, 110–113, 149–152, 336–337; use of public-private partnerships, 125, 146–157, 308.

Public choice: in agricultural development, 92–94, 308; problems of, 146–149; theory of, 307–308,
Public enterprises (see also corruption, development, Ghana, and South Korea): contract plans, 158–159; crony statism, 309–311; privatization difficulties, 152–153, 213–214.

Rural development (also see agricultural extension, credit programs, decentralization, Ghana, and South Korea): African rural women, 266–268; Aga Khan Rural Support Program (AKSRP), 160–162; Former Soviet Union, 221–222; Taiwan's agricultural development, 227–229; Ukraine, 221–222.

Singapore: authoritarian rule, 223–224; consensus building, 226–223, 233–234, 256–257; cultural engineering, 256–260; economic development, 257–258; family planning, 258–259; governance, 225, 232–234; public communication, 226, 233–234; public housing, 231–234.
Sites and services: El Salvador's FUNDASAL project, 77–79; problems of, 72–77; theory, 131.
Slum upgrading: Calcutta's Bustee Improvement Program, 133, 134, 139; Jakarta's Kampung Improvement Program, 133–135; Manila, 133–136; theory, 131–144.
South Korea: administrative reform, 225; community development (the Saemaul Undong Movement), 229–232; corruption, 301; economic development, 224–225, 269–270; equalization of opportunity, 224–225, 282-283; industrial parks, 288–289; political repression, 223; public enterprises, 288–290; rural development, 284–286; Value Added Tax, 302.

Taiwan: agricultural development, 227–229; authoritanian rule, 223; democratization, 234–237; environmental degradation, 235–237; governance, 225; living conditions, 224–225.

Uganda: administrative reform, 328–329; political reform, 236–240.
United States (also see urban development): corruption, 175–179; decentralization, 117–118.
Urban development (see also credit programs, decentralization, sites and services, slum upgrading, and solid waste management): American urban studies, 65–72: community participation, 140–142; income-increasing programs, 138, 151–152; LDC urban studies, 72–76; rent control, 170–171; youth, 60.

Women (also see agricultural extension, credit programs, Malawi, political culture, and family planning): assisting African rural women, 90, 98, 266–268; comparison of Asian and African conditions, 266.
World Bank (see also foreign aid): counterproductive lending, 321–326; disdain for politics, 317–319; implementation problems, 324–326; publications, 16–18; reform proposals, 326–347; staff weaknesses, 318–321; slum upgrading projects, 143.

About the Author

Herb Werlin was born in Chicago in 1932 and grew up in Houston where his father (Joseph) was a professor of sociology and his mother (Rosella), a journalist and public relations specialist. His undergraduate degrees are from the University of Chicago and Oxford University (Exeter College); and his graduate degrees (in political science), from Yale and the University of California/Berkeley. His first book (on the Nairobi City Council, which emerged from his 1966 Ph.D. dissertation) was published in 1974.

Herb taught at many universities before retiring in 1993 from the University of Maryland's Urban Studies Department. From 1977 to 1984 he edited a newsletter (THE URBAN EDGE) for the World Bank. After that, in addition to teaching, he has done research, writing, and editing for a number of organizations. Since 1980, he has headed several workgroups (urban and development administration) for the D.C. Chapter of the Society for International Development.